ATTENTION AND AWARENESS IN FOREIGN LANGUAGE LEARNING

TECHNICAL REPORT #9

ATTENTION AND AWARENESS IN FOREIGN LANGUAGE LEARNING

edited by RICHARD SCHMIDT

SECOND LANGUAGE TEACHING & CURRICULUM CENTER
University of Hawai'i at Mānoa

02 01 00 99 98 6 5 4 3 2

Funds for the publication of this technical report were provided in part by a grant to the University of Hawai'i under the Language Resource Centers Program of the U. S. Department of Education.

ISBN 0–8248–1794–X

The paper used in this publication meets the minimum requirements of American National Standard for Information Sciences–Permanence of Paper for Printed Library Materials.

ANSI Z39.48–1984

Book design by Deborah Masterson

Distributed by
University of Hawai'i Press
Order Department
2840 Kolowalu Street
Honolulu, Hawai'i 96822

ABOUT THE NATIONAL FOREIGN LANGUAGE RESOURCE CENTER

THE SECOND LANGUAGE TEACHING AND CURRICULUM CENTER of the University of Hawai'i is a unit of the College of Languages, Linguistics, and Literature. Under a grant from the U.S. Department of Education, the Center has since 1990 served as a National Foreign Language Resource Center (NFLRC). The general direction of the Resource Center is set by a national advisory board. The Center conducts research, develops materials, and trains language professionals with the goal of improving foreign language instruction in the United States. The Center publishes research reports and teaching materials; it also sponsors a fellows program for senior scholars, an internship program, and a summer intensive teacher training institute. For additional information about Center programs, write:

Dr. Richard Schmidt, Director
National Foreign Language Resource Center
East-West Road, Bldg. 1, Rm. 6A
University of Hawai'i
Honolulu, HI 96822

NFLRC ADVISORY BOARD

CONTENTS

PREFACE

Issues related to the role of attention and awareness in learning lie at the heart of many theoretical and practical controversies in the foreign language field. Do learners have to attend to all aspects of language in order to learn or can some aspects of language be picked up without paying attention to them? If attention is necessary, what do learners attend to and notice in language classes and in more naturalistic settings, and what do they fail to notice? What can teachers do to make problematic aspects of the target language more salient to learners? If attention is necessary, is it sufficient? Do language learners also have to understand why the language works the way it does, or will unconscious acquisition processes operate to solve the learner's problems of analysis? If awareness is necessary or facilitative, how can teachers develop this? Should errors be corrected or left alone? Should grammar be explained? This collection of papers presents research into the learning of Spanish, Japanese, Finnish, Hawaiian, and English as a second language (with additional comments and examples from French, German, and miniature artificial languages) that bear on these crucial questions for foreign language pedagogy.

In the opening paper ("Consciousness and second language learning: A tutorial on the role of attention and awareness in learning," Richard Schmidt), these issues are discussed with reference to the importance of attention and awareness for all learning, with evidence drawn primarily from the field of experimental psychology. The first conclusion to be drawn is that not all learning is deliberate or intentional (one definition of "conscious" learning), since there is clear evidence for incidental, unintended learning, which can be very effective when the intended task focuses attention on what needs to be learned. For example, it is clearly possible to learn vocabulary through extensive reading, because the intended goal (reading for meaning) serves to focus attention on new and unfamiliar words. However, it is argued that if readers do not pay attention to new words when reading they will not learn them, i.e., that subliminal learning is impossible, no matter how much the idea of it may appeal to the popular imagination. Although it is logically impossible to ever prove this claim (it is not possible to prove that something is impossible), it should be quite possible to disprove it. One convincing demonstration of learning without attention would be enough, but so far there have not been any. Several studies purporting to demonstrate learning without attention are shown to really have demonstrated only a low level of learning associated with a low level of attention. Discussion of another important issue, the contrast between explicit learning (learning on the basis of conscious knowledge, insights, and hypotheses) and implicit learning (learning based on unconscious processes of generalization and abstraction) leads to a less clear-cut conclusion. It can be shown that many claims of unconscious learning in this sense follow either from an over-estimation of what has been learned (abstract rules are assumed to exist in the learner's mind when there is no evidence for them) or from under-estimation of what learners consciously know or think (often they are not even asked). Not all cases of this sort can be conclusively settled, however, so implicit learning remains a possibility with interesting theoretical and practical implications.

The next four chapters all deal with the question of what language learners notice when they encounter the target language, either in classroom settings or in more natural settings in which learning takes place through input and interaction with native speakers.

In Chapter 2 ("Intake from the speech stream: Speech elements that L2 learners attend to"), Hae Young Kim explores the linguistic context in which noticing takes place, specifically with reference to the prosodic characteristics of speech elements that affect perception. In a study comparing perception of the elements (words and phrases) of speech under normal and slowed conditions, Kim found qualitative and quantitative analysis of think-aloud protocols to be more informative than global measures of listening comprehension. Prosodic prominence, positional salience, and previous familiarity with a word are seen to be important factors contributing to what gets noticed. In this paper, Kim also tentatively identifies a series of developmental phases for processing the stream of speech in a foreign language, through which learners move as they progress from an initial phase, in which not even key words can be pick out of the speech stream, to an advanced phase in which listeners can not only encode almost all clauses in input but also the relationships among them.

In Chapter 3 ("Observer l'attention; Quelque résultats d'une étude de cas"), Diane Huot reports preliminary results from an ongoing case study of a seven year old girl with no previous exposure to English learning English during an extended stay in Hawaii. The primary data for this report consisted of journal entries recording the girl's metalinguistic comments and questions to her mother on a daily basis. Given that many theories of language acquisition assume that a metalinguistic stance towards language characterizes only the learning of older children and adults, what is most striking about this study is the picture that emerges of a seven year old as a very curious and acute observer of language. "Cyrie" clearly paid careful attention to what her friends and teachers said, compared the English she heard with her native French, translated, and formulated hypotheses to account for the regularities she observed in the English input. Her attention in all this was focused on meaning, but when attempts to derive meaning failed, her attention turned to form. A comparison of the language she produced with the journal entries supports the hypothesis that what she noticed (and commented upon) she subsequently produced. The study does not provide support for the common argument that children first acquire unconsciously and then later arrive at an explicit awareness of what they have already learned.

In Chapter 4 ("A study of uptake by learners of Hawaiian), W. Kahulu Palmeira investigates *uptake* (what learners report they have learned) in a third year university course in Hawaiian at the University of Hawai'i. This study is significant because previous investigations have reported that uptake is highly idiosyncratic, determined less by teachers' lesson plans than by whatever linguistic features incidentally happen to become the focus of discourse topicalization in classroom interaction, a process of social co-construction. Palmeira's research shows that in the particular classroom she investigated there was a close relationship between the instructor's intentions regarding the grammatical focus of a lesson and uptake as reported by the students in the class. There was also much less idiosyncratic reporting than found in other studies and a strong relationship between uptake reports and subsequent performance on a post test. In other words, students in this Hawaiian class generally did focus their attention on those structures that the teacher had planned for the day, reported that they learned those structures (instead of others that were not the teacher's target), and did appear to learn them. However, these conclusions apply primarily to the learning of grammatical structures and much less so for the learning of vocabulary, for which Palmeira reports a fair amount of incidental uptake.

Palmeira speculates that there might be several reasons for her findings, including the advanced level of the students in the course, their familiarity with the instructor and his classroom routines, and possible bias inherent in the methodology, which may induce students to report what they think they should have learned in a class rather than what they actually learned. However, the most likely explanation for Palmeira's findings probably lies in the nature of the class she observed and described. If a teacher has a grammatical structure of the day and most of a class is spent discussing, practicing and manipulating that structure, it is hardly surprising that most students would report at the end of the class that was what they learned that day. This is by itself not much of an argument for the use of such structural syllabuses, because it is possible that items uptaken in this way do not "stick" or become final intake. Nevertheless, Palmeira's findings are intriguing and call out for replication as well as further research in a variety of instructional settings.

Michael Roberts (Chapter 5: "Awareness and the efficacy of error correction") also reports an investigation of uptake, this time in a Japanese class, with quite different findings. Roberts' focus is on teacher corrections of learner errors in classes where the pedagogical approached (based on Jorden's influential Japanese texts) stresses such correction. Roberts argues that such corrections will not be of use to learners unless they realize that they are being corrected and understand the nature of the correction. In order to find out whether learners in these classes do notice and understand the corrections, he asked three students to view a videotape of their own class and indicate each time they were able to identify a teacher correction and to say why the student's utterance was incorrect. The results will be discouraging to those who subscribe to the "correct every error" principle, since the students in the class were able to identify less than half of the corrections made by the teacher and understood the nature of the error being corrected less than a quarter of the time, suggesting that teachers need to come up with better ways to provide learners with feedback that they will be able to both notice and understand.

The following three chapters address the question of what teachers can do to make problematic aspects of the target language more salient to learners so that they are able to notice crucial structural features of the language in the input to which they are exposed.

In Chapter 6, Renée Jourdenais, Mitsuhiko Ota, Stephanie Stauffer, Beverly Boyson and Catherine Doughty explore the effects of an attempt to make Spanish input more salient to learners by providing a group of subjects with texts in which all preterit and imperfect verb forms were highlighted. Think-aloud protocols were collected during a subsequent task in which subjects wrote a narrative. Analysis of the protocols and narratives of these subjects and of a control group exposed to the same text without visual highlighting showed that those who received the enhanced input both noticed more target features and produced more target features in their written output.

The next chapter, by Jennifer Leeman, Igone Arteagoitia, Boris Fridman, and Catherine Doughty, also reports an experiment with learners of Spanish, and again there is a comparison between a group receiving enhanced input with a control group not receiving such input. However, in this study, rather than using simple visual enhancement (as Jourdenais *et al.* did), the researchers used a variety of techniques that they call *focus-on-form* instruction, meaning that although the overall pedagogical approach was communicative and meaning was central to each lesson, attempts were also made to draw students' attention to specific formal aspects of the target language. A variety of techniques were employed to focus learners' attention on the target forms (once again the learning targets were the preterit and imperfect verb forms of Spanish), including visual enhancement and feedback related to the target structure, but excluding explicit metalinguistic discussion or presentation of rules. Analysis of several post-treatment measures showed that learners who received focus-on-form instruction significantly improved the accuracy and frequency with which they supplied the target forms, when compared to a control group of learners who received purely communicative instruction without any focus on form.

In Chapter 8 ("Input enhancement and rule presentation in second language acquisition"), Riikka Alanen used a visual enhancement technique (italics) in a study of the learning of beginning Finnish (participants in the study had no previous knowledge of Finnish) to see whether this would promote the learning of two aspects of Finnish structure: locative suffixes roughly comparable to English "in" and "on" (though not with a one to one relationship) and four types of consonant alternation. Alanen provided another group of participants with an explicit statement of the rules for these structures. A third group received both rule statements and visually enhanced input, and a control group was simply exposed to the unmodified linguistic input through a meaning-focused task. Results of a post-test on the target structures showed that the two groups given the rules (Rule and Rule & Enhance) outperformed the other groups. However, performance for these groups was far from perfect. Several learners showed clearly that they misunderstood the rules (their restatements of the rules they were given after the tests were inaccurate) and those misunderstandings were generally consistent with their productions. In other words, it is not what teachers explain and how they say it that matters, but what learners understand. Alanen does not argue that the explicitly provided rules were "internalized" in any direct sense. Her argument is that explicit rule statements merely served to focus the learners' attention more efficiently on the target language structures, leaving them free to formulate whatever specific hypotheses were most useful for them.

In Alanen's study, the effects of visual enhancement were not immediately clear, since the participants in the Enhance group did not outperform controls. It is possible that the particular technique used in this study (italicization) was simply ineffective, but Alanen draws a different conclusion based on an analysis of learner errors. She found that omission characterized the productions of subjects in the control group, while those who received visually enhanced input usually attempted a suffix and often came close, but did not recall the exact form of the target suffixes. Errors made by the two rule groups were different as well, showing evidence of both over-generalization and false hypotheses.

Like Jourdenais *et al.*, Alanen used a think-aloud procedure to identify what it was that learners noticed while engaging in the experimental task. The think-alouds revealed that learning outcomes were greatly influenced by the learners' focus of attention. Those learners who paid attention to the targets during the study phase also appeared to have acquired at least some aspects of them. This included some subjects in the control condition, revealing the importance of individual differences. Individual differences were much less apparent in the three treatment groups, suggesting that more explicit teaching approaches may have two benefits: they speed up acquisition of linguistic form and affect the acquisition process so that all learners (not just those with particular talent or motivation for structural analysis) show some evidence of acquisition.

The themes of individual differences in learning and manipulation of the conditions of learning are explored further in Peter Robinson's chapter (Chapter 9: "Aptitude, awareness and the fundamental similarity of implicit and explicit second language learning), which reports results from the most complex experimental design utilized in the various studies in this collection. In his dissertation research, Robinson compared the learning of two target structures of English (one "easy" rule and one "hard" rule) by Japanese learners under four conditions carefully controlled by computer presentation: an "implicit" condition, in which learners were told to try to memorize sentences they saw on the computer monitor; an "incidental" condition, in which learners were told to focus on the meaning of the sentences they saw; a "rule-search" condition, in which participants were told that the sentences exemplified structural rules that they should try to discover; and an "instructed" condition, in which participants were told the rules. In this chapter, Robinson investigates the claims of Reber and Krashen that learning in the instructed and rule-search conditions should be sensitive to individual differences in language aptitude, but learning in the implicit and incidental conditions should not. Using two measures of language aptitude (verbal memory and grammatical sensitivity), Robinson found that aptitude and learning were related in all conditions except the incidental condition. Even in the incidental condition, large numbers of subjects claimed to have looked for and noticed rules, however, so conscious processes seem to have been implicated in whatever incidental learning occurred.

Robinson also found that learners in the instructed condition had a strong advantage over all other subjects, at least for the easy rule. Since both of the studies reported in this collection that compared the effects of telling learners rules directly with less direct techniques such as telling them to look for rules or providing visual enhancement of target structures (Robinson's study of Japanese learners of English and Alanen's study of English learners of Finnish) found an advantage for explicit instruction, one might be tempted to conclude that the best way for foreign language learners to acquire grammar is to find teachers who will explicitly teach them the rules of the grammar. This would be a hasty conclusion, however, and one that most researchers would not agree with. The first thing to note is that both of these papers report short-term laboratory studies that say nothing about the durability of learning. As every experienced language teacher is aware, it is common to find that students who appear to have benefited from instruction on an immediate test of learning (instruction is good in the short run) often fail to show any knowledge of the same structures a semester later, whereas it is possible (though it has not yet been demonstrated) that less direct approaches may work better in the long run. The second point to be noted is that, as shown by Robinson's study, not all rules are equally amenable to direct instruction.

This point is developed further in the final paper in this collection ("Not all grammar rules are equal: Giving grammar instruction its proper place in foreign language teaching") by Jan Hulstijn. Many foreign language eschew grammar teaching almost completely, trusting in the ability of learners to acquire grammar through interaction, with a firm belief in the efficacy of unconscious acquisition processes. Taken as a whole, the papers in this collection do not support this approach; indeed, they provide good evidence that an exclusive focus on meaning in foreign language teaching results in weak control over the structural properties of language. The research reported here also fails to provide support for traditional views which emphasize the decontextualized teaching of grammar for its own sake. A middle ground needs to be found, but even that is not easy. One proposal, exemplified by the papers by Leeman *et al.* and Jourdenais *et al.*, is to embed a focus on form within an overall approach which is clearly communicative. In this approach, various techniques are used to draw the learners' attention to linguistic form encountered in input and interaction, but the focus is always still on meaning, with no explicit metalinguistic commentary and no decontextualized teaching of grammar. Others might argue that — because attention is a limited capacity resource and one cannot focus effectively on meaning and form at the same time — some decontextualization and explicit grammar instruction is necessary. If this approach is chosen, Hulstijn cautions that not all rules are equally teachable. In a discussion of both lexical rules (morphophonology) and non-lexical rules (syntax), Hulstijn proposes that at least the following criteria should be assessed before rules are taught: frequency, reliability, scope, whether learners need to have receptive or productive command, and ease of explanation.

There are no easy answers to the questions that most concern foreign language teachers. How can I make my classes both appealing to learners (fostering motivation) and effective in terms of helping them to gain control over the grammatical structure of the language? How can I ensure that they will do well on the tests that my department requires of all students and at the same time acquire real communicative ability in the language? Should I correct errors? How and when? The papers in this volume do not claim to provide conclusive answers to these questions; indeed it can be argued that research translated into a "best method" is not so much applied research as research mis-applied. However, it is the hope of both the authors and the editor of this volume that the research reported here will speak to the concerns of foreign language teachers and will provide some carefully gathered evidence that can guide teaching practice more effectively than either the perpetuation of traditional methods or the adoption of currently popular theories that rely more on rhetoric than on evidence for their appeal.

Richard Schmidt
University of Hawai'i at Mānoa

CONSCIOUSNESS AND FOREIGN LANGUAGE LEARNING: A TUTORIAL ON THE ROLE OF ATTENTION AND AWARENESS IN LEARNING

ABSTRACT

A number of issues concerning the role of consciousness in foreign language learning are identified, defined, and shown to be essentially the same as issues that have been much discussed and investigated in psychology. The psychological literature is reviewed (together with the available literature on foreign language learning) to find answers to the following questions: Is attention necessary for learning? Is awareness at the level of "noticing" required for learning? Is awareness at higher levels, such as awareness of abstract rules or principles, required for learning? The first conclusion to be drawn is that not all learning is deliberate or intentional (for example, it is clearly possible to learn vocabulary through extensive reading, without a clear intention to learn new words), but all learning does require attention (if readers do not pay attention to new words when they encounter them, they will not learn them). It is logically impossible to ever prove this claim, but it should be quite possible to falsify it. One convincing demonstration of learning without attention would be enough, but so far there have not been any. Several studies purporting to demonstrate learning without attention are shown to really have demonstrated only a low level of learning associated with a low level of attention. The question of whether subjective awareness is necessary (or even helpful) for learning is more controversial, and the evidence leads to less clear-cut conclusions. A low level of awareness, called here "noticing," is nearly isomorphic with attention, and seems to be associated with all learning. A higher level of awareness ("understanding") is involved in contrasts between explicit learning (learning on the basis of conscious knowledge, insights, and hypotheses) and implicit learning (learning based on unconscious processes of generalization and abstraction). It can be show that many claims of unconscious learning in this sense follow either from over-estimation of

Schmidt, Richard (1995). Consciousness and foreign language learning: A tutorial on the role of attention and awareness in learning. In Richard Schmidt (Ed.), *Attention and awareness in foreign language learning* (Technical Report #9) (pp. 1–63). Honolulu, Hawai'i: University of Hawai'i, Second Language Teaching & Curriculum Center.

what has been learned (abstract rules are claimed to exist unconsciously without adequate justification) or from under-estimation of what learners know consciously (often they are not even asked). Not all cases of this sort can be conclusively settled, however, so implicit learning remains a possibility with interesting theoretical and practical implications.

INTRODUCTION: THE PROBLEM OF CONSCIOUSNESS

Some questions that are important for foreign language pedagogy are not very interesting theoretically. Similarly, many teachers believe that theory and research in the field of foreign language learning or second language acquisition (SLA) are often irrelevant to their concerns (Pica, 1994). It seems to me that questions concerning the role of consciousness in learning, however difficult to answer, are important to all. These are issues that capture the attention of philosophers, psychologists, linguists, psycholinguists, and second and foreign language learning theorists. These issues are also of concern to language teachers, who have their own beliefs and positions with respect to these matters and for whom there are pedagogical consequences.

There are three major points of view represented in the foreign language teaching community. The first is the most traditional, and stresses the importance of conscious understanding and study for success in learning foreign languages. In this view, mistakes in a foreign language are the result of either not knowing the rules, forgetting them, or not paying attention. Generally speaking, the view is that knowledge comes first, followed by practice in applying what has been taught. For classroom practice, the traditional view leads to explicit discussion of the rules and regularities of the foreign language, comparisons with the native language, practice, and error correction. The value of communicative practice is seldom denied, but this sometimes takes second place to decontextualized explanation and drill. At the institutional level, there is likely to be lots of discussion about which structures should be included in the syllabus for the first semester, the second semester, and so on.

The second major point of view is that language learning (or "acquisition') is unconscious or subconscious (no one seems to make a distinction between the two terms). Language learning in natural settings (both L1 and L2) takes place through interaction and the processing of input. Successful language learning in schools also results from understanding and participating in social interaction with classmates and the teacher about topics that matter. Students can achieve a high level of proficiency, including a high level of grammatical accuracy, without any explicit focus on the language itself (Faltis and Hudelson, 1994, provide a recent clear expression of this view). If this view is correct, it follows that there should little or no concern with a structural syllabus for language learning (since learners learn at their own pace and according to a natural, built-in syllabus), pedagogy should be meaning-oriented rather than form-oriented, and there should be little or no direct explanation of grammar, focused practice, or error correction (Krashen, 1982, 1993; Krashen and Terrell, 1983; Prabhu, 1987). Many who hold this view consider themselves progressive or modern, although the tension between the focus-on-language school and the focus-on-meaning school might be better viewed as a series of a wide pendulum swings over the past century, rather than a straightforward progression. Those in the "communication" camp often view their more traditional colleagues as Neanderthals, and those who think language learning is hard work and requires considerable conscious effort may scoff at those who delude themselves into thinking that "chatting" is an effective way to learn a foreign language.

A third, intermediate view is clearly emerging in the foreign language profession. In this view, communicative, meaning-focused instruction is essential, but not all language features can be acquired when learners' attention is focused exclusively on meaning. A focus on form appears to be necessary and desirable, especially if provided within a communicative context (Lightbown and Spada, 1994). While input and interaction are important to establish a secure level of communicative proficiency, this is not because language learning is unconscious, but because input and interaction, attention, and awareness are all crucial for learning, and when understanding and application are poorly synchronized, there will be problems: fluency but premature stabilization in the case of completely meaning-focused learning, abstract knowledge but limited ability to perform in the case of overly conscious learners or those have been instructed with an excessive focus on form. In this view, explicit instruction does not lead directly to automatic, productive use, but direct instruction, consciousness-raising, and a focus on form are valuable to the extent that they help learners bring order to the input they encounter, facilitate understanding, and boost or support natural acquisition processes (DeKeyser, 1994; Doughty, 1991; N. Ellis, 1993, 1994a; R. Ellis, 1990, 1993; 1994; Fotos, 1993; Fotos and Ellis, 1991; Harley, 1994; Hulstijn, this volume; Hulstijn and de Graaff, 1994; Larsen-Freeman and Long, 1991; Lightbown and Pienemann, 1993; Long, 1988, 1991, in press; Loschky and Bley-Vroman, 1990; Rutherford, 1987; Skehan, 1992; VanPatten, 1993; White, Spada, Lightbown, and Ranta, 1991; Sharwood Smith, 1991, 1992; Terrell, 1991).

The purpose of this chapter is to examine the theoretical foundation for these views about pedagogy, through a review of the literature on consciousness and learning. It must be noted, however, that there are many in the scientific community who are skeptical of the possibility of integrating notions of consciousness into theory. Hardcastle (1993) provides a succinct summary of these objections:

- Theory cannot capture a first person perspective.
- Consciousness is causally inert with respect to explaining cognition.
- The notion "consciousness" is too vague to be a natural kind term.

The third objection, that "consciousness" is too vague to be a natural term, has been expressed in the foreign language field by McLaughlin (1990), who argues that the folk term is too ambiguous to be of any use. Sometimes when we say that we have done something consciously, we mean that we have done it deliberately, with intention and with effort, and when we say that we have done something unconsciously, we mean that we did it without meaning to or without effort. Other times, we might say that we learned something unconsciously, without paying attention to it or without noticing it. On other occasions, we talk of conscious knowledge, usually meaning knowledge (either deliberately sought or serendipitously found) that we are able to articulate, in contrast to knowledge that is intuitive and inexpressible. Such a range of partly distinct and partly overlapping meanings is not very helpful, so in this chapter I will deal separately with what I think are the main issues in the conscious/unconscious controversy in foreign language learning:

- Can there be learning without intention?
- Can there be learning without attention?
- Can there be learning without noticing?
- Can there be learning without understanding?

In response to Hardcastle's first objection to integrating consciousness into any theory, that theory cannot accommodate a first person perspective, I recognize the difficulties in this, but it should be tried. Consciousness is essentially a private, subjective phenomenon, perhaps inaccessible to precise measurement. Perhaps it would be better if we could leave it out of our theories, but it seems to me that if we require this we deny by fiat any role for the private, subjective experiences of learners as they grapple with language. In the 1970's, there was a movement to focus the emerging SLA field away from what teachers do and more towards what goes on inside the heads of language learners. Yet this orientation has seldom been realized, in the sense that learners are almost never asked about their learning or their accounts incorporated into theories of learning. This dismissal of what learners might have to say about their own learning is related to Hardcastle's third objection to incorporating consciousness into scientific description: it doesn't matter, because consciousness is epiphenomenal and plays no causal role in learning or any other aspect of life. In this chapter, I will argue against this epiphenomenalist position.

Even if the notion of consciousness is put aside to deal with more specific and precise aspects of what we mean by that term, there are many thorny methodological problem in trying to decide whether learning is intentional or incidental, attended or unattended, explicit or implicit. One solution to this problem is to adopt the "implicit stance" (Reber, 1993, p. 9). Assuming the primacy of the implicit, the role of unconscious processes is taken as axiomatic and the unconscious is assumed to be the default mode of learning. A second solution to the problem is to put the burden of proof on those who claim that particular processes are unconscious or that a particular knowledge base is tacit. In this paper I will adopt this second stance and will try to see the extent to which it is possible to defend the radical proposition that there is no such thing as unconscious learning. If there is no unconscious learning, it cannot be primary.

CAN THERE BE LEARNING WITHOUT INTENTION?

There is one sense in which much learning, including language learning, can be said to be unconscious and no one will argue. Both intentional and incidental (unintended) learning are common and easy to demonstrate experimentally. In many experimental tasks, it doesn't matter at all whether someone intends to learn or not or what part of the task they intend to master. What matters is how the task forces the material to be processed (Anderson, 1985; Eysenck, 1982). However, when a task does not focus attention on what needs to be learned, then intentional learning is superior if the motivation to learn leads to the exercise of effective cognitive and metacognitive strategies (Pintrich, 1989).

Elley (1991) summarized studies of the effects of book floods on students' acquisition of a second language in elementary schools, reporting that children who are exposed to high-interest story books are consistently found to learn the target language more quickly than students learning by means of structured (audio-lingual) programs. Krashen (1989) has reviewed the evidence that extensive reading is effective for spelling and vocabulary acquisition, incidental learning in the sense that in trying to do one thing (comprehend meaning in reading), something unintended (vocabulary acquisition) occurs.

Theories of SLA recognize that intentions do not cause learning by themselves. Gardner, whose well-known model of the role of motivation in second language learning in classroom settings stresses the importance of integrative motivation, argues that the desire to learn a second language is useless by itself and that motivated learners achieve more than unmotivated learners only because they are more active learners (Gardner, 1985, 1989). Crookes and Schmidt (1991) argue that motivation and intentions are important only when learners have choices. In foreign language learning, these choices often include whether to take classes or not, whether to pay attention in class or not, and so on. What is crucial to learning is attention, and the intention to learn may support this but it is not the only source.

Returning to the example of vocabulary learning, it seems reasonable to assume that one reason we learn words through reading is that when reading we pay attention to them. As N. Ellis (1994c) points out:

> ... people are strategic, active processors of information. Contra Krashen (1989), it does not follow that vocabulary has been subconsciously acquired from the fact that we have not been taught the vast majority of the words that we know. That we have not been taught vocabulary does not entail that we have not taught ourselves. An explicit vocabulary learning hypothesis would hold that there is some benefit to vocabulary acquisition from the learner noticing novel vocabulary, selectively attending to it, and using a variety of strategies to try to infer its meaning from the context. (p. 219)

One key issue in theories of incidental learning is whether or not the knowledge gained through incidental learning is represented mentally in a different fashion from knowledge gained through intentional approaches to learning. Following Lamendella (1977), who proposed that meaning oriented acquisition involves subcortical structures, in particular those parts of the limbic system responsible for drives and desires, Paradis (1994) argues that knowledge acquired incidentally leads to an implicit competence that is available for automatic use, while deliberate learning leads only to explicit knowledge, differently represented in the brain and not available for automatic use. However, evidence from psychological experiments generally does not support the idea that the incidental vs. intentional distinction results in different knowledge types (Dienes, Broadbent, and Berry, 1991; McLaughlin, 1990).

In summary, there can indeed be learning without intention, but this does not imply the existence of unconscious learning in any other sense.

CAN THERE BE LEARNING WITHOUT ATTENTION?

The orthodox position in psychology and cognitive science is that there is no learning without attention (Carlson and Dulany, 1985; Fisk and Schneider, 1984; Kihlstrom, 1984; Logan, 1988; Moray, 1959; Nissen and Bullemer, 1987; Posner, 1992; Shiffrin and Schneider, 1977; Velmans, 1991; Wolford and Morrison, 1980). This claim is often related to models of memory; it is argued that unattended stimuli persist in immediate short-term memory for only a few seconds at best, and attention is the necessary and sufficient condition for long-term memory storage to occur. In SLA as well, the claim has been made frequently that attention to input is necessary for input to become intake that is available for further mental processing (Carr and Curran, 1994; Scovel, 1991; Tomlin and Villa, 1994; van Lier, 1991, 1994). A number of researchers and theorists have further argued that there may be two types of learning (e.g., declarative and procedural, or explicit and implicit, or rule-based and instance-based) that differ in their reliance on awareness, but both depend on attention (Carr and Curran, 1994; Nissen and Bullemer, 1987; Tomlin and Villa, 1994).

Many experiments have provided support for the position that attention is necessary for encoding in long-term memory, predominantly using two experimental research paradigms: selective attention and divided attention. In selective attention studies, subjects are asked to pay attention to one source of information while ignoring another. There is plenty of evidence that adults are able to do this (though the ability develops slowly in children; for review and discussion, see Bialystok, 1990, 1993, 1994a, 1994b; Forest-Pressley, MacKinnon and Waller, 1985). An every-day example is the "cocktail party phenomenon," in which it is possible to eavesdrop on an intriguing conversation going on some feet away or even across a room while ignoring talk which is closer and louder. Well-known experimental variants of the selective attention paradigm are dichotic listening studies, in which different messages are presented to the left and right ears through headphones and subjects are told to listen to only one channel, and shadowing experiments, in which subjects hear two messages and try to say one of them right along with the speaker. Early results from such studies provided clear results in support of the need for attention for storage: recall and recognition tests administered after such experiments showed that only the information in the attended channel was remembered (Bowers, 1984; Cherry, 1953; Glucksberg and Cowan, 1970; Moray, 1959; Norman, 1969).

There are a few results from selective attention studies that show some later recognition of unattended information and suggest that selective attention may not be absolutely necessary for long-term storage (Allport, Antonis, and Reynolds, 1972), but interpreting these results runs afoul of a serious methodological difficulty: demonstrating that remembered stimuli are truly unattended (in spite of instructions) is very difficult to establish. For this reason, most researchers in the field prefer to work instead with the divided attention paradigm, in which subjects are told to carry out two tasks simultaneously, one of which is so demanding that it depletes all attentional resources, preventing subjects from attending to other stimuli.

Findings from divided attention studies also generally support the view that attention is essential for learning. For example, Nissen and Bullemer (1987) used a serial reaction time task in which on each trial a light appeared in one of four locations and subjects were instructed to press keys to indicate the presence of the light. In a single task learning experiment, one group of subjects was exposed to a repeating sequence of 10 positions, while another group was exposed to a random non-repeating sequence. Across eight blocks of trials, the group exposed to random sequencing improved their performance somewhat (indicating a practice effect), but not by much. Those exposed to the repeating sequence improved their reaction time significantly, indicating that they had learned the sequence and could anticipate where the next light would appear. Next, in a dual-task condition, some subjects were instructed to track the appearance of lights simultaneously with a tone counting task. A tone that was either high or low in pitch occurred at the beginning of each trial, and subjects were told to count the number of times the low tone occurred. The dual-task group revealed no convincing evidence of sequence learning, and the most impressive result from a series of experiments was that subjects who were trained under the dual-task condition were no better at responding to the position of lights in a subsequent single task situation than subjects who had no experience at all with any of the tasks (Nissen and Bullemer, 1987: 21).

Once again, however, a few studies using the divided attention paradigm have provided conflicting results. Kellogg (1980) showed that subjects who performed complex mental multiplication while faces were presented as secondary stimuli performed better than chance on a recognition test for the faces. In a widely cited recent study, Curran and Keele (1993) reported evidence for unattended learning using a variant of the Nissen and Bullemer serial reaction time task combined with tone-counting and comparing single-task with dual-task performance. Although few in number, these studies are worthy of careful scrutiny, because they purport to show at least the possibility of unattended learning.

Again the nagging question remains: was the learning in these experiments truly unattended? In the case of Kellogg's experiment, it seems very likely that it was not, because it is widely believed that although attentional capacity is limited, it is not completely fixed and is expanded when information is presented through different modalities such as the visual channel and the aural channel (Allport, Antonis, and Reynolds, 1972). Kellogg was aware of this problem and tried to control for it by asking subjects to visualize the aurally presented digits in the multiplication task in order to deplete both aural and visual attention, but it is not at all clear that subjects followed this instruction, and a moment's reflection should convince readers that visualizing arithmetic problems is not an easy task at all.

Curran and Keele's interpretation of their results is subject to a somewhat more complicated objection. In the Nissen and Bullemer version of the repeating sequence task (which showed no learning in the dual-task condition), each sequence presented to subjects was ambiguous, i.e., there was no event that was always followed by a predictable second event. Instead, a long sequence was used. Using letters to indicate screen positions, the sequence was: D-B-C-A-C-B-D-C-B-A. Note that D can be followed by either B or C; B can be followed by C or A; etc. In single-task learning, subjects exhibited slower responses for certain ambiguous serial positions (e.g., B or C appearing after D), which Nissen and Bullemer interpreted as evidence that subjects chunked the longer sequence into shorter sequences (e.g., D-B-C-A and D-C-B-A). The slow responses by subjects to the unpredictable element immediately following D in the two sets was interpreted as reflecting their uncertainty regarding which chunk was presented; there was no uncertainty as to what the last two elements of the chunk were (C-A in the D-B-C-A chunk and B-A in the D-C-B-A chunk) and their responses to those elements were faster.

Cohen, Ivry, and Keele (1990) found that if a repeating pattern had at least one unique stimulus position, subjects showed some learning in the dual task condition, and Curran and Keele (whose experiments showed some learning in the dual task position) also used patterns that had unique elements. Six different patterns were used, distributed randomly across subjects. Using numbers to indicate screen positions, the repeating sequences were:

Sequence 1: 1–2–3–2–4–3
Sequence 2: 1–2–3–1–3–4
Sequence 3: 1–4–3–1–3–2
Sequence 4: 1–4–2–3–1–2
Sequence 5: 1–3–2–4–1–2
Sequence 6: 4–2–3–2–1–3

In the six patterns above, there are numerous invariant relations. For example, in Sequence 1, an element in position 1 can only be followed by one in position 2, and an element in position 4 can only be followed by one in position 3. In Sequence 2, an element in position 2 can only be followed by one in position 3, and an element in position 4 can only be followed by one in position 1 (as the sequence repeats). Other sequences are not invariant but not all combinations are possible, and all of these sequences are different from randomly generated sequences in one simple but important respect: no element presented on the screen is ever followed by one in the same position.

The theory that attention is required for all learning (and that more complex learning requires more attention) predicts that there will be differences in learning depending on what kind of stimulus array is used. The type of stimulus array used by Nissen and Bullemer demands that subjects divide a longer sequence into parts and learn orders within parts. This requires a considerable allocation of attention to a long sequence and should be blocked easily by completing attentional demands, just what Nissen and Bullemer found. The type of stimulus array used by Curran and Keele should be partly learnable with much less attention, because some learning can be accomplished through simple item-item associations — and Curran and Keele did find some learning in the dual task condition.

Do Curran and Keele's experiments show *some* learning with *no* attention, however? Once again, this seems unlikely. In fact, Curran and Keele concede that "When we refer to one form of learning as nonattentional, we do not wish to imply that no attention whatsoever is used on the primary task ... [since] undoubtedly, subjects must in some sense attend to a visual stimulus to make a response" (1993:190). It is reasonable to assume, given Nissen and Bullemer's results, that attention to a six element sequence is indeed blocked by the competing tone-counting task, but not reasonable to assume that attention to simple two element sequences is similarly blocked. Curran and Keele argue that whether or not attention is completely blocked is not crucial to their concerns, but for the claim that learning without attention is possible, this distinction is crucial. The alternative explanation, that learning under the dual-task condition is not learning without attention but simple learning with a correspondingly small amount of attention (to small pieces of a longer sequence), seems entirely reasonable.

While the zero-point question (whether there can be learning with no attention) is theoretically interesting, the debate over this issue should not obscure a larger and much more secure finding, that the more one attends, the more one learns (Baars, 1988). Figure 1 shows a schematic representation of typical results from studies such as those reported by Curran and Keele, Nissen and Bullemer, and many others who have used dual-task learning with reaction time as the dependent variable. What is most striking about Figure 1 is the small (sometimes nonexistent) difference between performance on random sequences and performance on structured sequences under conditions of degraded attention, compared to the very large differences observed between both of those and the learning of structured sequences with focused attention. All seem to agree on the point that focal attention is essential for robust memory. Kellogg and Dare (1989), who argue that both attended and unattended encoding in memory are possible, emphasize that while their conclusion that attention is not necessary for very poor memory is of theoretical interest, this "does not imply that unattended encoding has any practical value ... [since] the degree of elaboration resulting from unattended encoding appears to be too limited to have any substantive influence on human cognition or behavior" (1989: 412).

Figure 1: Schematic representation of learning structured sequences under single task (focal attention) and dual task (degraded attention) conditions, compared to performance on random sequences

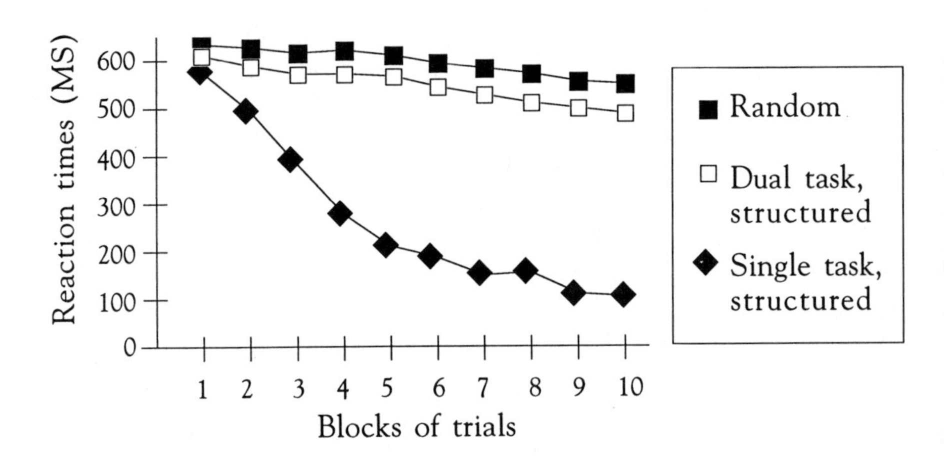

What does this mean for foreign language learning? Can we generalize from studies of reaction time on simple, controlled non-linguistic tasks to the much more complex (and far less controlled) domain of language learning, where accuracy rather than speed is the usual indicator of learning (except with respect to fluency concerns)? There are limits to the validity of such generalizations, but one possible implication from these studies is that while all aspects of language learning require some degree of focal attention, different aspects may require more or less of it. Following this line of thinking, the learning of individual words, collocations and short, fixed expressions (e.g., *pick*

it up, see you later in English; *c'est la vie* in French, *arigato gozaimasu* in Japanese) would require attention to be learned, but not nearly as much as longer, ambiguous sequences of language. Carr and Curran (1994) have observed that the complex sequences generated by syntax are highly ambiguous (almost every word can be preceded and followed by many different words, often from different syntactic classes), and are unlikely to be learned without focal attention. Because communicative interaction is always a divided attention task (requiring attention to literal, figurative, pragmatic, and interactional meaning in addition to linguistic form at all levels for full comprehension), this would predict that naturalistic, uninstructed language learners should be relatively better at acquiring vocabulary and formulaic expressions than at acquiring complex syntax, which seems to be generally the case. It also suggests that within instructional approaches that are primarily communicative, learning some aspects of language probably either requires or at least will benefit from some degree of decontextualization, whereas others may not.[1]

---

[1] Inflectional morphology falls somewhere in between lexicon and syntax with respect to attentional needs. In the case of bound morphemes, it could be argued that since these are short sequences, they can be learned associatively with minimal attention. However, the choice of which morpheme to produce in a particular context also requires attention to neighboring elements (e.g., to a nearby noun for gender and number agreement on adjectives) or not so neighboring elements (e.g., a more distant noun) or even to invisible aspects of the communicative context (e.g., to nouns that are understood from context but not overtly expressed, in the case of gender and number, or to speaker or hearer "perspective" in the case of article choice in English or aspectual choice in Romance languages). One would predict that more focal attention is required both to detect and to produce correctly inflected forms when the governing element is distant than when it is nearby and that getting things right when key elements are not overtly expressed will be most difficult. Zalewski (1993) has made a different prediction, arguing that inflectional morphology that is locally determined will be less likely to be attended to than more globally determined morphology, because the former is usually redundant and the latter more crucial for communication. Zalewski suggests that presenting morphology in global contexts will be more instructionally effective, because this will render them more cognitively salient, and the mental effort involved in processing them should also lead to better retention.

The best known attempts to apply models of attention and the divided attention paradigm to foreign language learning have been those of VanPatten (1990, 1993, 1994). Arguing that anyone can process input for meaning *or* for form, VanPatten suggests that the critical questions are whether learners can attend to form while simultaneously attending to meaning and, if so, what kind of form and under what conditions this is possible (VanPatten, 1994). VanPatten hypothesizes that when involved in communicative exchanges, learners process input for meaning before anything else, that they prefer processing lexical items to grammatical items, that they prefer processing "more meaningful" morphology before "less or non-meaningful" morphology (these concepts are not well-defined), and that before learners can process less meaningful morphology, they must be able to process communicative content at little or no cost to attention. This can be interpreted fatalistically (learners are not going to acquire less meaningful morphology until they are reasonably competent communicatively and then they will, so don't worry about it) or as a reason to include a focus on form within an instructional program. VanPatten argues for an interventionist approach to instruction, but argues strongly for structured, focused input processing activities, rather than traditional explanation plus output exercises. In one example of such input processing activities, learners of Spanish were instructed to focus attention on word order and clitic pronouns and practice correct form-meaning mappings when processing input strings. When compared to a group receiving more traditional (output oriented) instruction, both gained in production ability, but only those given the input processing treatment gained in both comprehension and production abilities (VanPatten and Cadierno, 1993).

A further extension of the hypothesis that attention is required for all learning is that what must be attended to is not just input from one channel as opposed to another or stimuli important to one task as opposed to another, but also different features of "the same" input (Schmidt, 1993b). This question has been less researched in psychology, but what evidence there is supports the idea. Hanson and Hirst (1988) point out that an event may be thought of as a cluster of attributes and report experiments supporting the hypothesis that attention to specific stimulus attributes is necessary in order to encode information about them. The only information for which there is evidence of automatic (unattended) encoding is the frequency of a stimulus event (Hasher and Zacks, 1979, 1984), but the frequency with which something occurs is not an attribute of an individual event itself. If true, the hypothesis that no learning of correlated stimulus attributes occurs without attention means that in order to acquire phonology, one must attend to phonology; in order to acquire pragmatics, one must attend to both linguistic forms and the relevant contextual features; and so forth. Nothing is free.

CAN THERE BE LEARNING WITHOUT NOTICING?

It is difficult to distinguish between paying attention to something and noticing or being aware of it. As Carr and Curran (1994) point out, these are often treated as synonyms: "If you are conscious of something, then you are attending to it ... and if you are attending to something, then you are conscious of it" (1994: 219). The view that attention and awareness at the level of noticing are flip sides of the same coin is also embodied in many classical definitions of attention, such as that of William James, who defined attention as "the taking possession by the mind, in clear and vivid form, of one out of what seem several simultaneously possible objects or trains of thought ... focalization, concentration, consciousness are of its essence ... it implies withdrawal from some things in order to deal more effectively with others" (1890: 403–404). Most modern psychologists make a distinction between attention and its correlated subjective experience, however, viewing attention as one of the basic mechanisms in an information processing system or "computational mind," while relating subjective experiences such as noticing what one attends to, remarking upon it, being aware of it, and so forth as features of "phenomenological mind" (Jackendoff, 1987). And here we run into several classical philosophical problems, generally referred to as the mind-body problem (Harnad, 1990, 1991; Nagle, 1974, 1993). How can the physical brain give rise to the non-physical experiences of consciousness? How could the subjective, non-material experiences of phenomenological mind ever affect the physical (neurologically grounded), computational mind? Could there be organisms (or machines) who were functionally exactly like us but felt or experienced nothing at all (the "absent qualia hypothesis"), and if so, would we be justified in calling them conscious?

Popular psychology tends to emphasize the influence of the mind on the body, but both mainstream psychology and many philosophers are firmly on the other side of the argument, giving the following responses to these questions: (1) no one knows quite how the physical brain and computational mind give rise to consciousness, but they do

(Gazzaniga, 1993; O'Keefe, 1985); (2) the direction of causality is one way: computational mind causes phenomenal mind but phenomenal mind has no causal efficacy (Jackendoff, 1987); and (3) if there were persons or machines who were functionally the same as us except that they experienced nothing, we might as well call them conscious, since internal mental events cannot be the data of science and the subjective side of things just does not matter (Dennett 1987, 1991). This is the essential epiphenomenalist argument.

To pursue these questions adequately would take us far beyond the scope of this chapter, but interested readers are referred to the work of Jackendoff (1987) in psychology and linguistics and Dennett (1987, 1991; Dennett and Kinsbourne, 1992) in philosophy, both of whose works are very interesting reading. The questions that need to be discussed here are more limited: can attention and noticing be independently defined in ways that are useful for understanding foreign language learning, and is there evidence for their dissociation, that is, learning with attention but without noticing?

Attention *can* be defined independently of its subjective correlates, and a very useful description of current theories of attention is provided by Tomlin and Villa (1994), which draws heavily on the work of Posner (1992; Posner and Petersen, 1990; Posner and Rothbart, 1991) and which can be summarized as follows:

- Attention is a limited capacity system.
- Automatic activities which require little or no attention do not interfere with each other.
- Controlled processes require attention and interfere with other control processes.
- Attention can be viewed as three separate but interrelated networks: alertness, orientation, and detection.
- Alertness represents a general readiness to deal with incoming stimuli.

- Orientation refers to a specific aligning of attention (e.g., to language form or to meaning).

- Detection is the cognitive registration of sensory stimuli.

- Detected information is available for other cognitive processing.

- Attention (specifically, detection) is not awareness.

The last of these points is the most relevant to this discussion. Tomlin and Villa argue, as have many others, that detection and further processing of stimuli can be dissociated from awareness of what is attended to, and that detection (not awareness) is what is important. Velmans (1991) has made this point most strongly, arguing that consciousness only *appears* to be necessary in a variety of tasks because they require focal-attentive processing. If consciousness is absent, focal-attentive processing is normally absent, but there are cases in which focal-attentive processing takes place and is effective without consciousness also being present. In a number of publications, I have argued the opposite point of view: that focal attention and awareness are essentially isomorphic, and that a causal role for subjective experience in learning cannot be ruled out (Schmidt, 1990, 1993a, 1993b, 1994a, 1994b). The "noticing hypothesis" states that what learners notice in input is what becomes intake for learning.

In several recent publications, claims that attention and awareness (at the level of noticing) are dissociated and that there is learning without awareness have been based on several of the same experiments dealing with reaction time in sequence learning referred to in the last section. For example, Carr and Curran (1994) refer to experiments by Nissen and Bullemer (1987), among others, as evidence for their assertion that there is little relationship between responses to a questionnaire assessing subject awareness and whether structural learning is shown in serial reaction time tasks. Tomlin and Villa (1994) cite Curran and Keele (1993) as evidence that "subjects can learn a repeating sequence but not be aware of that sequence" (1994: 193).

While both Carr and Curran (1994) and Tomlin and Villa (1994) are excellent review articles with much of great value for understanding the role of attention in foreign language learning, I find it surprising that these reviewers drew these conclusions based on the articles they cite. Since the Nissen and Bullemer and Curran and Keele articles have been discussed in some detail already in this paper, it seems appropriate to return to them to see the extent to which such claims are supported by the evidence. Considering the Nissen and Bullemer article, those authors did not say themselves that there was little relationship between awareness as assessed by a questionnaire and performance on the primary task. What they said was that in the single task repeating pattern (where learning was good) virtually all subjects reported noticing a sequence (1987: 9, 14) and that in the dual task condition (where no learning occurred) virtually no subjects reported noticing a repeating sequence (1997: 14, 29). One subject in the single task condition was not counted as aware because the experimenter forgot to elicit the information, and one subject in the dual task condition thought that there might have been a sequence in some trials but that it went away later. In other words, there was a *very* strong relationship between awareness and learning in these experiments. Nissen and Bullemer's claim that awareness of the existence of a pattern is not required for learning was based on other evidence, the fact that patients with Korsakoff's syndrome learned the sequence, to which I will turn momentarily.

Nissen and her colleagues have reported other experiments, however, in which they have presented evidence for learning patterns without awareness. Hartman, Knopman, and Nissen (1989) reported unaware learning of verbal associations in four experiments. The stimuli in these experiments were repeating 10-word sequences, such as MUSIC – RULER – LADY – OCEAN – LADY – RULER – MUSIC – LADY – RULER – OCEAN. (Once again, notice that some elements in the string are "ambiguous," but the pattern can be learned if the sequence is broken into chunks.) Learning was assessed by reaction time, and subjects were classified as "aware" or "unaware" on the basis on their ability to indicate any patterns they could report having noticed. In Experiment 1, there was a clear relationship between awareness and performance: aware subjects performed well, while unaware subjects showed no improvement beyond a practice effect shown by control subjects exposed to a completely random word sequence. In Experiments 2 and

3, aware subjects performed much better than the unaware group, but the latter nevertheless showed evidence of a significant, albeit small, amount of learning. In Experiment 4, both aware and unaware subjects gave clear evidence of learning across four blocks of trials. It would seem, therefore, that these experiments (especially Experiment 4) do provide evidence of sequence learning without awareness, were it not for one serious flaw. Not all of the subjects classified as "unaware" were truly unaware. For reasons that are hard to understand, Hartman et al. decided to classify all subjects who could not correctly report more than three consecutive words from the 10-word sequence as unaware. These subjects were, however, partly aware rather than unaware. (Unfortunately, Hartman et al. do not report the number of such partially aware subjects except for Experiment 1, in which 2 of 10 called unaware were partially aware.) Moreover, any three word sequence from the longer string should have had some effect on performance: a subject who has noticed the sequence MUSIC – RULER – LADY would respond rapidly to LADY; a subject who noticed the sequence RULER – LADY – OCEAN would respond rapidly to OCEAN; etc. The conclusion I draw, therefore, is that these experiments do not show learning without noticing, but rather more learning with more noticing and less learning with less noticing.

As for Curran and Keele (1993), those authors did not claim that unaware subjects learned a repeating sequence. What they reported was that subjects were classified as "more aware" and "less aware" (not "unaware") on the basis of questionnaire responses, and that all results from single task learning conditions clearly demonstrated that subjects who expressed less awareness showed less learning than those who expressed more awareness, who showed less learning in turn than subjects who had been explicitly instructed on the repeating sequence to which they were exposed (1994: 192). The dual task learning group was classified as "predominantly unaware" (1994: 194), and this group showed some learning, but not much. Curran and Keele reported that they were not really concerned with the problem of needing to establish complete absence of awareness and conceded that many subjects probably were partially aware. They made no claim that the small amount of learning observed under the dual task learning condition was learning without awareness. Their major claim instead was that "variations in single-task learning, caused by awareness differences, were not transferred to dual-task conditions" (1993: 192).

More and less aware subjects trained under the single task condition (on which their performance varied) did not vary when an attention demanding distracter task was added following the initial training. This is an important and interesting finding, suggesting that in foreign language learning the benefits of awareness in learning may not be of much immediate help in performance when many different tasks need to be attended to simultaneously. Asserting the irrelevance of awareness for automatic performance (Krashen 1985, 1994) is not the only theoretical solution to this dilemma, however, since there are models of controlled and automatic processing in which automatization is viewed as a gradual transition (with practice) through a number of stages from fully controlled processing (most demanding of attention and awareness) to controlled assist of mostly automatic processing to fully automatic processing (Schneider and Detweiler, 1988; Schmidt, 1992).

Four other sources of evidence have been cited in the literature as support for the claim that there is learning without awareness at the level of noticing: studies of subliminal perception, the phenomenon of blind-sight, studies of implicit memory, and sequence learning by amnesics. Each of these areas of research will be dealt with very briefly, to assess whether any of them show clear evidence of learning without awareness.

SUBLIMINAL PERCEPTION

Subliminal perception is, by definition, detection without awareness ("perception" means that stimuli are registered by the information processing system; "subliminal" means that this happens below the level of subjective awareness). There are two questions to be asked: does subliminal perception happen?, and does subliminal perception lead to learning? The answer to the first question is yes. Although the mere possibility of subliminal perception was controversial for a long time, there have been a large number of experiments in which subjects are presented with brief or low intensity stimuli which they do not detect (although they do fully attend). These experiments show subtle effects of such stimuli on behavior, and there is no doubt that subliminal perception exists as both a cognitive phenomenon (Schmidt, 1990, 1993a, 1993b) and as a social psychological phenomenon (Wyer and Srull, 1994). However, the power of such subliminal perception is nothing like the popular view of it, which is largely based on myth. For example, although many people "know" that in the 1950's clever advertisers used subliminal messages interspliced with cinematic frames to stimulate lobby sales of soft drinks, this is in fact a purely apocryphal story (Merikle, 1988; Moore, 1988). The answer to the second question, whether subliminal perception can lead to learning, seems to be no. Subliminal effects are shown only when very familiar stimuli are presented, activating already established mental structures. For example, Joordens and Merikle (1992) and many others have demonstrated effects for the subliminal presentation of English words, but none of these experiments have shown anything like the learning of new words. To date, psychologists have been unable to establish whether *any* of these effects constitute learning in the sense of establishing new concepts or mental structures. Reviewing the recent literature, Shanks and St. John (1994) conclude that although a few studies reporting subliminal learning have appeared, these are offset by a much more substantial body of negative evidence. Until it is shown that new mental concepts can be acquired in this way, subliminal perception is evidence for detection without awareness but not for learning without awareness. The practical consequence of this is that it would be foolish in the extreme to expect to learn any aspect at all of a foreign language through subliminal audio tapes (Greenwald, Spangeberg, Pratkanis, and Eskenazi, 1991). Sleep learning is equally unlikely to produce any detectable learning (Bootzin, Kihlstrom, and Schachter, 1990).

BLINDSIGHT

Blindsight (Dennett, 1991; Tye, 1993; Weiskrantz, 1986, 1990) is a condition in which certain patients have large blind areas in their visual fields due to brain damage to the occipital cortex. What is fascinating about such cases is that blindsighted people can, under some circumstances, accurately report what is in the "blind" visual field, without any experiential conscious going on. Blindsighted patients report that they cannot see anything; when they are asked to report what might be in the blind area, they are very reluctant to "guess" and typically do not believe what they are forced to say; and yet when they do guess, they are often accurate. Blindsightedness therefore constitutes a quite spectacular example of detection without awareness, of absent qualia. But we must ask the second question: does detection without awareness in blindsightedness constitute learning? The answer is no. The degree of detection in the "blind" area turns out, after all, to be very limited. Simple shapes (e.g., circles or triangles) can be recognized, together with familiar objects (e.g., a toothbrush), and even these not consistently. No attempts have been made to teach anything new to blindsighted patients by presenting new shapes (or words, for example) in the blind area, and no reason to think that this would be successful. As in the case of subliminal perception, a demonstration of detection without awareness does not stand up as a case for learning without both attention (detection) and awareness.

IMPLICIT MEMORY

Past learning experiences affect current behavior, even when we do not consciously recall the relevant prior events. This phenomenon is generally called *implicit memory*, in contrast to *explicit memory* (in which prior exposure is consciously recalled), and there is a huge literature on the differences between the two (for review, see N. Ellis, 1994b, 1994c; Robinson, this volume, in press; Schachter, 1987). Researchers have found that performance differs between direct memory tasks (e.g., recognition and recall tests) requiring conscious retrieval of material presented during the study phase of an experiment and indirect tests (e.g., lexical decision and word stem completion tests) that facilitate retrieval of the material without conscious attempts to recall (Robinson, in press). Many studies of implicit memory have involved word study, both with monolinguals and bilinguals (Ellis, 1994b), and implicit memory is clearly relevant to understanding foreign language learning. Suppose that a second year foreign language student is given a long list of words, some of which appeared in the first year instructional materials and some of which did not, and asked to say whether or not he or she had seen them before, and, if so, when. What we would expect is that such a student would be able to give quite specific details when and how some words were learned. This is called *episodic memory*. In other cases, the learner would be able to say that a word had been encountered before (there would be some incorrect reports as well), but not give details. Recognition memory of this kind is explicit memory but not episodic memory. There would be many other cases where the learner would not be able to recall whether or not a word had been encountered before, but if we asked learners to go through the list rapidly and indicate which of all the words on the list were real words in the foreign language, we should find that both accuracy and speed (response latency) are much better for the previously encountered words, that is, evidence for implicit memory. (This would be an interesting an useful classroom research study.)

The key question is whether evidence for implicit memory is evidence for learning without awareness and evidence against the noticing hypothesis. In my opinion, the whole area of implicit memory is simply irrelevant for the noticing hypothesis. The noticing hypothesis claims that learning requires awareness *at the time of learning*. It does not require that memory of that event be preserved, much less recalled each time the learned material is encountered.

LEARNING BY AMNESICS

In fiction, the most commonly represented form of amnesia is retrograde amnesia, when because of a blow to the head or psychological trauma people are unable to remember their past. In psychology, the most commonly studied form of amnesia is anterograde amnesia, in which (because of chronic alcoholism or brain damage) patients are unable to form new memories. An extreme case, that of "H. M." has been widely discussed in the literature (Ellis, 1994b). After surgery for treatment of epilepsy, H. M. had normal recall of events that occurred before his brain damage, but no memory for episodes that occurred after the operation. In these cases, however, there is a dissociation between implicit and explicit memory: "amnesics are severely impaired on the recall and recognition tests which involve a conscious recollection of the prior episode, but they show normal practice effects as a result of prior exposure" (Ellis, 1994b: 229). Numerous studies have shown that such amnesics can learn. Generally speaking, amnesics show zero acquisition of declarative knowledge, but fairly good (though subnormal) acquisition of procedural knowledge. They can acquire implicit knowledge of vocabulary form (the shape of words), but do not learn new words or form new word associations (Ellis, 1994b, 1994c). They demonstrate some learning of structural sequences generated by miniature artificial grammars, to be discussed in the next section (Knowlton, Ramus, and Squire, 1992). And in the Nissen and Bullemer (1987) experiment discussed in the previous section of this chapter, amnesics with Korsakoff's syndrome demonstrated sequence learning, even though they were completely unaware that they had practiced the task. Referring to anterograde amnesia as the "gold standard" of implicit learning, Carr and Curran (1994) conclude that these demonstrations of learning conclusively demonstrate the dissociation of attention and awareness in learning. Poldrack and Cohen (1994) similarly conclude that such learning is *prima facie* evidence of implicit learning.

I disagree. Demonstrations of implicit memory in anterograde amnesia are even less relevant for the question of implicit learning than are demonstrations of implicit memory in normal persons, for reasons that have been articulately expressed by Shanks and St. John (1994). The noticing hypothesis claims that awareness at the point of learning (Time 1) is required for all learning. Yet for various reasons, including the fact that concurrent reports of awareness during the process of learning are likely to bias the learning itself towards a more conscious mode, awareness must be assessed at some later time (Time 2). In all implicit learning studies, an inference must be made from no evidence of awareness at Time 2 to a lack of awareness at Time 1. For this inference to be valid at all, there must be high confidence that lack of awareness at Time 2 also reflects a lack of awareness at Time 1. In the case of normal subjects, this can perhaps be achieved. But in the case of anterograde amnesics, their essential problem is that they remember nothing of what they were aware of minutes before!

In summary, studies of subliminal perception and blindsight provide evidence for a dissociation between detection and awareness, but not between learning and awareness. Implicit memory studies and studies of learning by amnesics provide evidence for a dissociation between what one is aware of during on-line processing and what one is aware of later, but no evidence for learning without awareness at the point of learning. I conclude that there is no compelling evidence of any learning without awareness at the level of noticing. Subjective experience and information processing appear to be isomorphic.

This does not, I will admit, dispose of the epiphenomenalist position. I argued in the previous section that while it is in principle impossible to prove that attention is required for all learning, it should be possible to disprove that hypothesis (though no disproof has been found). I am not so sanguine that the noticing hypothesis can be either proved or disproved. It cannot be proved because subjective awareness is fleeting and cannot be completely recorded. It cannot be falsified for the same reason; reports of learning without awareness will always founder on the impossibility of demonstrating beyond doubt that a given test of awareness is exhaustive (Merikle, 1994).

Even if learning and awareness are perfectly correlated, this can probably be accounted for by a model of computational mind that does not mention subjective phenomena. Robinson (in press) suggests that the noticing hypothesis can be captured in a model of attention and learning that specifies a need not only for detection (which may be brief, with no permanent effect) but detection plus rehearsal in short-term memory. In such a model, detection plus rehearsal gives rise to awareness, but awareness is not needed as an explanatory concept. I would argue that the correlation between information processing and subjective experience is too high to be coincidental. Assuming that consciousness is a late evolutionary development, there must be some reason for its evolution, and all the evidence points to the fact that what consciousness is good for is learning. But those who maintain that the human brain is an information processing machine that does no more than other (insensate) machines will not be dissuaded from their position that conscious thoughts are irrelevant, or that we are any more than helpless spectators of our own existence. A hundred years of research in psychology and centuries of argumentation in philosophy have not resolved the issue, and I cannot resolve it here.

CAN THERE BE LEARNING WITHOUT UNDERSTANDING?

Throughout the previous section, I referred repeatedly to the notion of *awareness at the level of noticing*, without attempting to define the expression, which I must now do in order to deal with the question of whether there is learning without *understanding*, a higher level of awareness. I use "noticing" to mean conscious registration of the occurrence of some event, whereas "understanding," as I am using the term, implies recognition of a general principle, rule or pattern. Noticing refers to surface level phenomena and item learning, while understanding refers to deeper level of abstraction related to (semantic, syntactic, or communicative) meaning, system learning (Slobin, 1985). Since I restrict the usage of these terms for technical purposes and do not use them with their full range of meanings in everyday language, some examples of the intended distinction may be helpful.

- In forensics, noticing has to do with collecting the evidence, understanding with creating a theory of the crime.

- In sequence learning, experiments that require subjects to learn a fixed sequence of specific items or positions, such as ABBC or DCBA, are related to noticing only. But an experiment that requires subjects to generalize from a sequence such as ABBC to one that is related at a more abstract level (e.g., XYYZ) entails the higher level of awareness that I call understanding. I avoid all common usages such as "noticing" a principle or abstract pattern.

- In foreign language vocabulary learning, conscious registration of the form (phonological or orthographic) of a word is an example of noticing. Knowing the meaning of a word and knowing its syntactic privileges of occurrence (other than in collocations and fixed expressions) are matters of understanding.

- In morphology, awareness that a target language speaker says, on a particular occasion, "He goes to the beach a lot," is a matter of noticing. Being aware that *goes* is a form of *go* inflected for number agreement is understanding.

- In syntax, awareness that on some occasions speakers of Spanish omit subject pronouns is a matter of noticing. Being aware of that Spanish is a pro-drop language, which entails numerous syntactic consequences beyond such surface phenomena as the presence or absence of pronouns, is a matter of understanding.

- In pragmatics, awareness that on a particular occasion someone says to their interlocutor something like, "I'm terribly sorry to bother you, but if you have time could you look at this problem?" is a matter of noticing. Relating the various forms used to their strategic deployment in the service of politeness and recognizing their co-occurrence with elements of context such as social distance, power, level of imposition and so on, are all matters of understanding.

- In learning academic writing or other genres, remarking on the fact that journal articles are frequently subdivided into parts such as an introduction, method, results, discussion and conclusion is a matter of noticing. A learner of Japanese who comes to understand that the function of an initial section that might be called "introduction" is very different in English and Japanese is exercising the higher level of awareness I call understanding.

Since system learning clearly requires some process of generalization from individual instances, how does this happen? Because understanding can be either internally generated or externally provided, for those who are primarily concerned with foreign language teaching, the issue is often phrased as the question of whether or not explicit knowledge transmitted through instruction can become implicit knowledge (R. Ellis, 1993). For those who focus more on learning, especially learning through exposure to input, the question is whether system learning proceeds on the basis of conscious processes of induction such as hypothesis creation and testing or on the basis of more basic, unconscious mechanisms that may be encapsulated in a way that makes them unaffected by any conscious knowledge. Is there, or can there be, unconscious induction and abstraction? This is the heart of the acquisition versus learning distinction in the foreign language field and the heart of the controversy over implicit learning in psychology.

ARTIFICIAL GRAMMAR LEARNING AND NATURAL LANGUAGE

The battle in the foreign language field has been fought almost entirely in the realm of syntax, and in psychology also research using miniature artificial grammars (MAGs) has been the most discussed, so I will limit my report of research in psychology to studies using that particular paradigm. For nearly three decades, Arthur Reber has conducted experiments on the learning of miniature artificial grammars by adult subjects (Abrams and Reber, 1988; Reber 1967, 1969, 1976, 1989; Reber and Allen, 1978; Reber, Allen and Regan, 1985; Reber, Kassin, Lewis and Cantor, 1980; Reber and Lewis, 1977; Reber, Walkenfeld and Hernstadt, 1991). Many others have used the same experimental paradigm or variants of it (e.g., Brooks, 1978; Brooks and Vokey, 1991; Danks and Gans, 1975; Dienes, Broadbent, and Berry, 1991; Dulany, Carlson and Dewey, 1984; MacWhinney, 1983; Mathews, Buss, Stanley, Blanchard-Fields, Cho, and Druhan, 1989; Morgan, Meier, and Newport, 1987; Nation and McLaughlin, 1986; Perruchet and Pacteau, 1990; Vokey and Brooks, 1992). Reber (1989, 1992, 1993) has drawn upon the extensive results of such studies to formulate a general theory of implicit learning.

Although there have been numerous variations on the basic theme, the experimental paradigm developed by Reber involves exposing subjects to strings of letters (e.g., MXRMXT, VMTRRR) generated by an underlying "grammar" or rule system, usually a finite-state system that generate strings of symbols in a left-to-right, non hierarchical fashion, often referred to as a Markov grammar. In many experiments, groups of subjects are exposed to such input with either (a) instructions to try to figure out the rules for letter order or (b) instructions to memorize the examples for a memory test. The acquisition phase, typically a few hours but sometimes longer, is followed by a testing and transfer phase to assess what subjects have learned. The testing phase requires subjects to identify new letter strings as grammatical (i.e., generated by the rules of the underlying grammar) or ungrammatical (items that violate the grammar). In some experiments, the testing phase has also included probing subjects' awareness in order to find out whether they were able to discover and can verbalize the underlying rules of the system.

The basic findings from these experiments are as follows:

- Through exposure to examples, subjects become sensitive to underlying regularities in input, as shown by the fact that they can accurately characterize new strings which they have never seen before as grammatical or ungrammatical at above chance levels.

- Subjects are generally unable to verbalize the rules of the underlying grammar used by the experimenters to generate strings.

- The grammaticality judgments of subjects receiving rule-search or memorization instructions typically do not differ significantly.

Although there are major differences between MAG experiments and real language learning, the artificial grammars used in implicit learning studies are roughly analogous to natural languages, in the sense that sentences of the language are viewed in both cases as the product of a complex underlying system. Through exposure to input containing exemplars of the grammar, in second language learning as in artificial grammar experiments, learners do become sensitive to regularities in the input, suggesting that the underlying grammar is internalized in some sense. In both cases, grammaticality judgments are seen as an appropriate test of this internalized competence, and in both cases, real learning is only considered demonstrated through transfer to new examples.

Reber has interpreted the findings of MAG experiments as support for a detailed conception of the process by which one develops intuitive knowledge about the underlying structure of a complex stimulus environment, an account that may be relevant for theories of SLA. As used by Reber, implicit learning is characterized by a number of critical features, each of which is also claimed for foreign language learning:

- Learning MAGs is an unconscious *process*, in two senses. First, because whether or not subjects have the intention to discover rules (assumed to follow from the instructions and demands of the experimental task) does not make a difference in learning outcomes, artificial grammar learning is considered to be unintentional or incidental. Natural language acquisition is also most often considered to be unconscious in the sense that it is incidental or non intentional learning. Second, implicit learning is believed to involve induction without awareness, on the grounds that processes such as the formation and testing of conscious hypotheses (encouraged by rule-search instructions and blocked by the demands of the memorization condition) do not make a difference in the outcome of these experiments. The second of these interpretations of implicit learning as an unconscious process is considered basic. As Reber (1989) puts it, "the pickup of information takes place independently of consciousness or awareness of what is picked up" (p.231). Second language learning is also widely believed to involve induction without awareness. It is in this sense that Seliger's comment that "obviously, it is at the unconscious level that language learning takes place" (Seliger, 1983, p. 187) is most reasonably interpreted. Krashen is explicit on the matter. Conscious hypotheses about the underlying structure of language, whether obtained through rule teaching or through discovery by the learner, belong to *learning*, not *acquisition* in Krashen's theory (Krashen, 1985). Felix (1981, 1985, 1991) is another SLA theorist who stresses the irrelevance of conscious hypothesis formation and other conscious processes typical of problem solving behavior for successful acquisition. In Felix's view, such conscious processes are characteristic of adult second language learning, but they are ultimately detrimental to the process because general problem solving abilities are inferior to the innate, domain-specific language acquisition device with which they compete.

- The *product* of implicit learning is also largely unconscious. Once again, *unconscious* has several senses. The first of these is that the information acquired exceeds what can be verbally expressed. This represents a significant revision to Reber's earlier position that the knowledge acquired in artificial grammar learning studies is completely inaccessible to consciousness (Reber, 1965). Subsequent studies have shown that this extreme position is inaccurate, since subjects in such experiments show an increase in their ability to communicate their knowledge of underlying rule systems (Mathews et al., 1989; Reber and Lewis, 1977). However, Reber maintains that "the implicitly acquired epistemic contents of mind are always richer and more sophisticated than what can be explicated" (Reber, 1989, p. 229). With respect to foreign language learning, it is commonly argued that implicit knowledge sometimes can be brought to conscious awareness, but that such explicit knowledge is the end product of acquisition, not its cause (Bialystok and Bouchard Ryan, 1985). Chomsky's position on first language acquisition is somewhat different, since he has argued that the principles, conditions and rules of universal grammar that determine the course of first language acquisition are *in principle* inaccessible to conscious awareness (Chomsky, 1975, 1986, 1990). The second sense in which the knowledge resulting from implicit learning is said to be unconscious is that, whether or not such knowledge is potentially accessible to conscious awareness and is expressible, it is presumably not present in consciousness awareness and not used deductively as the basis for making grammaticality judgments in the testing phase (Reber, 1989, p. 230). Instead, such judgments are intuitive. With respect to this issue, most SLA theories are in agreement that consciously held rules can only be applied by language learners under limited circumstances and cannot serve directly as the basis for truly fluent language performance. There is less agreement concerning how fluent performance is achieved, however (for review, see Schmidt, 1992). Sharwood Smith (1981) theorized that it develops through practice from an earlier nonfluent stage in which rules are consciously applied. McLaughlin, Rossman and McLeod (1983) proposed a model based on Shiffrin and Schneider's (1977) information processing account of the development from controlled to automatic processing, avoiding discussion of conscious and unconscious processes. For others, there is no relationship at all between the application of consciously held rules and fluent production. Once again, Krashen's position is clearest by virtue of its categorical nature: only implicitly acquired knowledge can be the basis of fluent production.

- The product of implicit learning is abstract. The evidence for this derives from the fact that the knowledge acquired in such studies generalizes to strings that are not presented during the training phase, and even to different symbol sets as long as the same underlying rule structure is used to generate the strings (Reber, 1969, 1976; Mathews et al., 1989). Linguistic competence is similarly believed to be abstract.

In spite of a number of differences of interpretation and nuance, this comparison of theories based on artificial grammar experiments with theories of second language learning has identified a number of common issues. All of these issues are important for SLA theory, as well as for foreign language pedagogy, but the question of intentional vs. incidental learning, attended vs. unattended learning, the noticing hypothesis, and the issue of automatic performance are all separable from the most important issues involved in implicit learning studies, unconscious induction and abstractness of the knowledge that results from learning. It turns out that these two issues are intimately related.

UNCONSCIOUS ABSTRACTION AND ARTIFICIAL GRAMMAR LEARNING

The basic logic for establishing that implicit learning proceeds by unconscious induction in artificial grammar experiments is as follows:

- Establish that the system rests upon complex, abstract rules;

- Assess the performance of learners to establish that exposure has led to reasonably good performance in manipulating the outputs of the underlying grammar, including novel strings not encountered during training; and

- Assess learner awareness to establish lack of awareness of the underlying rules.

If all three conditions are met, the conclusion that some kind of unconscious abstraction is operative seems reasonable. To cast doubt on the reality of unconscious induction, one may attempt to show any of the following:

- The underlying knowledge is not as abstract as assumed;

- Learner performance is not as good as claimed; or

- Learners have more awareness than they have been given credit for.

In artificial grammar learning, the essence of the claim that implicit learning proceeds by an unconscious process of abstraction is that the experimenter's grammar has been internalized by learners without awareness. However, this claim has been challenged frequently, beginning with Dulany, Carlson, and Dewey (1984), who carried out an MAG experiment and then had subjects introspect their reasons for rejecting ungrammatical strings. Dulany et al. reported that their subjects reported personal sets of conscious rules (i.e., they had more awareness than they had been given credit for), and while these conscious rules were of much more limited scope than those built into the grammar by the experimenter, they predicted the judgments of grammaticality on novel test strings without significant residue (i.e., their performance wasn't so good to begin with), eliminating the need to posit any rules operating below the level of consciousness (i.e., the underlying knowledge was not as abstract as claimed). A number of recent MAG learning experiments have provided additional support for the claim that what is acquired is not abstract rules but more concrete knowledge, specifically knowledge of the likelihood of specific letter chunks appearing in grammatical strings (Brooks and

Vokey, 1991; Dienes, Broadbent, and Berry, 1991; Medin and Ross, 1990; Perruchet and Pacteau, 1990, 1991; Servan-Schrieber and Anderson, 1990).

The question of whether learning in MAG experiments and other implicit learning paradigms rests upon unconscious abstraction or much simpler forms of learning based on specific examples is currently the subject of lively debate (Shanks and St. John, 1994; Winter and Reber, 1994). However, there is a core of agreement concerning the mechanisms of implicit learning in MAG experiments. Reber's position is that the knowledge acquired in MAG experiments is abstract and that subjects can be said to have acquired knowledge of the underlying grammar "in some sense" (Reber, 1989, p. 221), but concedes that such knowledge is probably represented functionally in terms of sets of bigrams and trigrams, not as a formal system (p. 226). Abrams and Reber (1988), Hayes and Broadbent (1988) and Lewicki (1986) have all suggested that implicit learning should be viewed as a complex, covariational form of frequency counting. Mathews et al. (1989) hold the view that implicit learning is an automatic, memory-based process for detecting patterns of family resemblance among examples. Perruchet (Perruchet and Amorim, 1992; Perruchet, Gallego, and Savy, 1990; Perruchet and Pacteau 1991, 1992) rejects neither human abstraction ability nor the existence of unconscious processes. He accepts the existence of implicit learning, but argues that it rests upon the gradual accumulation of frequency information (Hasher and Zacks, 1979, 1984; Hintzman, 1976), rather than the ability to unconsciously abstract the complex rules used by the experimenter. Perruchet and Pacteau argue against the possibility of unconscious abstraction, on the grounds that abstraction is associated exclusively with explicit, conscious cognitive functions such as logical reasoning.

UNCONSCIOUS INDUCTION AND FOREIGN LANGUAGE LEARNING

Turning to implicit and explicit learning mechanisms in SLA, consider the following example of two learners apparently figuring out something about the target language through conscious analysis, including the formation and testing of hypotheses:

> While living in Spain, an English-speaking friend and I noticed that many times, after we had been talking at length with Spaniards, they would say *Pués nada*. At first, we felt a little insulted, since translated, it meant "Well, nothing," as if what we had been saying was worth nothing. Due primarily to our aggravation, which slowly turned into curiosity, we decided we were going to figure out what it meant. We therefore began taking mental notes of the times we heard it and reported back to each other our findings. We finally narrowed it down to the fact that it was used whenever there was a lengthy pause in a conversation. Having realized this, we decided that the next time we were out with Spaniards, we would say it whenever such a pause occurred. When we did, the mystery unraveled itself, for every time we used it, without fail, a new topic of conversation was begun. *Pués nada* was a way of closing one topic and moving on to another. (Hribar, personal communication cited in Hatch and Hawkins, 1989, p. 349)

Schmidt and Frota (1986) report numerous similar instances in which a learner's developing conscious understanding of the forms and functions of Brazilian Portuguese (recorded in a diary) matched the learner's performance in recorded interview data, including cases in which incorrect use could be traced to specific misanalyses of what was heard in input. However, many SLA theorists reject this "learner as linguist" view of acquisition, arguing that learners do not construct their internal grammars of the target language through analysis and hypothesis testing (Eubank, 1991; White, 1981), but assuming that learners do construct a theory of the language they are learning unconsciously (perhaps under the influence of an innate acquisition device) and that the learner's unconscious theory closely resembles the theory that the linguist constructs through conscious analysis of the distribution of possible and impossible sentences of the language, paraphrase relationships, and so forth. Parallel to assertions that MAG experiments demonstrate unconscious learning, claims for unconscious induction of an abstract underlying rule system in natural language also rest on the argument that there is a significant dissociation between what learners are aware of and the more abstract rules that linguistic theory holds govern the behavior of learners.

Krashen (1994) puts forth the "complexity argument": the system is too complex to be consciously learned. With particular reference to reading, Krashen argues that even the rules of spelling and phonics in English are exceedingly complex, far beyond the capacity of any student to consciously learn, and that vocabulary is an even clearer example, since there are too many words to learn one at a time. Citing

Smith (1988), Krashen points out that if estimates are correct that educated adults know about 156,000 words, this could not possibly be the result of 156,000 trips to the dictionary, 156,000 flash cards, or 156,000 fill-in-the-blank exercises. Of course this is true and this is an argument for incidental learning, but it is completely beside the point as far as implicit learning is concerned. The alternative explanation, which stresses conscious learning, is that we do learn base words one at a time (there is no other way, because they are arbitrary), whether we encounter them in reading or on word lists, and that derived words and compounds are learned through a combination of item learning and more generalized learning as we gradually become aware of regularities in form-meaning matching and extend our competence through analogy (e.g., from *racism* to *sexism* and *age-ism*) and other conscious processes.

Paradis (1994) provides a more compelling example of the complexity argument with respect to morphosyntax:

> Any native French speaker who taught French to speakers of another language had to refer to the grammar book the first time they were asked the inevitable question: "Why do you use the subjunctive in this sentence?" Before checking, the answer of course is "I don't know; it simply wouldn't sound right otherwise." "But why?" "Well, I don't have the faintest idea. I've been using the subjunctive in this context for 25 years, but I can't explain why." Whereupon the teacher quickly makes up a rule. Once you have looked it up, you teach that there are six expressions that are followed by the subjunctive, whether the subject of the verb that precedes is or is not co-referential with the subject of the verb that follows, and that another six expressions are followed by the subjunctive only if the subject of the first and of the second verb are not co-referential, for if they are, then the second verb must be in the infinitive. (p. 403)

VanPatten (1984, 1994) also refers to the subjunctive, this time in Spanish, as an illustration of the claim that attention (but not understanding) is required for learning:

> Bob Smith is a learner of Spanish, a language that actively distinguishes between subjunctive and indicative mood through verbal inflection in the present and past tenses. He begins to notice subjunctive forms in others' speech. He attends to it. Soon, he begins to use it in his own speech, perhaps in reduced contexts, but nonetheless he is beginning to use it. If you ask him for a rule, he might make one up. But in actuality, he doesn't

> have a rule. All he knows is that he has begun to attend to the subjunctive and the context in which it occurs and it has somehow begun to enter his linguistic system. He may or may not wind up with a native-like subjunctive rule system, but that is not the point. (p.p. 33–34)

Long (in press) provides a longer list of candidates for implicit learning:

> Any claim for the necessity of noticing for SLA in the higher level sense of understanding would be problematic. Some linguistic knowledge, such as several rules for English articles, and subtle aspects of the use of the T/V distinction to mark power and solidarity in Romance languages, is too abstract, complex or semantically opaque to be understood by linguistically naive learners. Some, such as gender-marking in French and English dative alternation, involve too many irregularities and fuzzy categories, and some, such as subject-auxiliary inversion after preposed negative adverbials ("Seldom have I seen ...") and uses of *whom* are too rare or perceptually non-salient. ... The fact that untutored, linguistically naive learners often are successful with such patterns suggests, therefore, that they usually learn them on the basis of the lower level conscious perception or implicitly.

In my opinion, none of these examples provides a very convincing case for implicit learning. Consider first the possibility that foreign language learners do not achieve a level of performance that is required to sustain the argument (VanPatten believes that this is not important, but as I have shown above, it is an essential link in the chain of argument). The subjunctive and T/V distinctions in both French and Spanish, gender marking in French, and the use of articles in English are all notorious problems in foreign language learning. This is true for both naturalistic, uninstructed learners and for classroom learners. Although the latter fact is an argument for the insufficiency of instruction, the typical failure of both instructed and uninstructed learners in these areas of grammar counts even more heavily against arguments for the success of implicit learning. Consider next the possibility that learners are aware of more than they are being given credit for. It seems to me that this might very well be the case with VanPatten's hypothetical learner Bob Smith, who may be forming partial rules on the basis of the examples of the Spanish to which he attends, but of course since this is a hypothetical case to begin with, we have no idea what Bob might or might not be aware of. My point is that it is misleading to assume ignorance when ignorance has not been demonstrated. Long's example of the English *who/whom* distinction is perhaps even a better example. This is not a core rule of English (it is disappearing from the language), but a rule of linguistic etiquette, subject to teaching in school and occasional corrections by parents who are concerned with such things. There is no reason to believe that it is acquired implicitly. Consider finally the possibility that the knowledge gained by learners is not as abstract as is being assumed. This very likely applies to Long's examples of inversion with negative adverbs (note that the example given to illustrate the "rule" is a formulaic chunk, *never have I* ...) and learning of the Spanish subjunctive (chunk learning is common in the early stages of foreign language learning), as well as to Paradis' description of the French subjunctive (assuming the description is correct), a collection of facts that certainly sound confusing when gathered together but which do not add up to an abstract rule.

As Brewer (1974), Dawson and Schell (1987), Ericsson and Simon (1984), and Shanks and St. John (1994) have pointed out, many illegitimate claims for implicit learning arise either when awareness is insufficiently assessed or when the linguist's concept of what has been learned is not required to produce the observed behavior. Nevertheless, I think that there is a case to be made for some implicit learning of foreign languages. My position is identical to that of Perruchet and Pacteau (1991), who emphasize both human abstraction abilities and the existence of unconscious processes, but reject the possibility of unconscious abstraction. For an example of how this solution can be applied to foreign language learning, we can return to one of the examples cited by Long, the acquisition of French gender. Gender acquisition in French seems a likely case of implicit learning (Schmidt, 1990), because no rules for distinguishing gender classes are taught to children, adult native speakers cannot formulate coherent or consistent rules, and the "rules" of gender assignment are more like fuzzy regularities than categorical rules. Sokolik and Smith (1992) proposed that connectionist networks are especially appropriate for modeling the learning of such fuzzy categories and described a computer-based connectionist network that learned to identify the gender of a set of French nouns based on the phonological shape of the noun and to generalize to new examples. MacWhinney, Leinbach, Taraban, and McDonald (1989) have provided an even more impressive connectionist model that successfully simulated the acquisition of the German definite article. There are six different forms of the article (*der*, *den*, *dem*, *des*, *die*, *das*), but since articles mark gender, number and case, there are sixteen different cells filled by the six forms. The result is that no form defines a unique combination of features, e.g., *der* marks the masculine nominative singular, the feminine genitive and dative singular, and the genitive plural. Gender assignment is so complex that some observers have concluded that there are no rules, but other have discovered 38 cues to gender, some phonological, some morphological and some syntactic, some absolute and some probabilistic. The dimension of plural maps directly onto nouns, but there are eight different ways to mark plural. Cues to case occur on the morphological, syntactic, and semantic level. MacWhinney et al. developed three computer simulations that successfully learned the article system. Two of these included various cues to gender. The third included only the raw phonological features of the noun stem. All three models learned the system and showed a good match to L1 developmental data, but the third — the most brute and blind of the three — outperformed the others in both training and generalization. What is important is that in the simulations of both Sokolik and Smith and of MacWhinney et al. it was demonstrated that implicit learning could take place (computers are not conscious), based on large collections of examples, but the mechanism of generalization was a complex form of frequency counting, not the abstraction of rules.

One account of implicit learning that, if it correct, cannot be reduced to simple associative learning is the universal grammar (UG) account, particularly versions of it in the second language field that argue for abstract parameters and parameter resetting. UG makes very interesting predictions concerning implicit learning:

- The assumption that UG is available to all language learners means that SLA learners already know a great deal about the target language before exposure and predicts that grammars of L2 learners will not violate UG principles, that interlanguages must be natural languages and not be describable as "rogue grammars." If UG is available in SLA, then L2 sentences that violate universal principles should also be judged ungrammatical without the need for any explicit knowledge of the principles involved or even any evidence from the L1 (Bley-Vroman, Felix, and Ioup, 1988; Finer, 1991). This is an interesting claim in itself, and one for which there is some evidence (Bley-Vroman, Felix, and Ioup, 1988), but since it concerns unmodified pre-existing knowledge it is not specifically relevant to the issue of implicit learning.

- If parameter setting or resetting is a part of L2 acquisition, then the theory predicts that where a cluster of structural properties represents a single parameter, all properties associated with that parameter setting should be acquired simultaneously (Finer, 1991). The parameter setting hypothesis is often presented as a claim about implicit learning: "Essentially, the [learner] 'notices' a triggering property in the input and then deduces that all the other correlated properties must also be present" (Bley-Vroman, 1989, p. 64).

In UG theory, parameters are abstract properties of grammar that cannot be directly equated with such surface-level phenomena as patterns or structures, and in the most interesting case a single parameter is held responsible at some deep level for seemingly unrelated surface properties. For example, by one account, the parameter of pro-drop includes the ability to omit subject pronouns, subject-verb inversion, and trace effects when subjects are extracted from clauses containing complementizers (White, 1985). If it could be shown that one aspect of a parameter language serves as the trigger for automatic adjustment of all other aspects of the parameter, this would constitute powerful evidence for implicit learning, because the proposed principles controlling generalization not just to different lexicalizations of a single structure but to completely different structures are so abstract that learners certainly never become consciously aware of them. If, on the other hand, each aspect of a parameter requires separate evidence, then no particular conclusions can be drawn concerning unconscious induction. White (1985, 1989, 1991, 1992) has attempted to show how such parameter resetting may work in second-language acquisition. Studies to date have not supported the abstract parameter re-setting hypothesis, but these have all involved short-term instruction, so it remains possible that implicit learning of this kind might emerge in future studies.

The issue of implicit learning remains open, with potentially interesting theoretical and pedagogic consequences. I close this section with two mysteries. The first is, why do we seem to know more than we can say? Consider the following examples of contraction in English:

1a. *When do you want to take the test?*

1b. *When do you wanna take the test?*

2a. *Who do you want to see?*

2b. *Who do you wanna see?*

3a. *Who do you want to take the test?*

3b. *Who do you wanna take the test?

For speakers who agree that 1b and 2b are acceptable and normal but 3b is not, the question is why is 3b unacceptable and how did you learn that? Is it plausible that you have heard 1b and 2b before (these exact sentences) and noticed the absence of 3b? This cannot be simply an example of chunk learning, because the chunk *who do you wanna* is normal enough in 2b but not in 3b. If you can see now what is wrong with 3b, is this something you were taught or thought about before? Assuming that there are foreign language learners of English who have the same intuitions (it is not clear to me whether they do, since several quite advanced ESL learners I have asked about these sentences have rejected both 3a and 3b), is this a case of implicit foreign language learning?

The second mystery is taken from DeKeyser (1994):

> There is a question I have asked many audiences over the last few years, and nobody has come up with a convincing example of what I, and *a fortiori* those who are eager to demonstrate the success of implicit second language learning, are looking for. I will leave it with the reader to ponder: How many people do you know personally (not from hearsay) who, as adults, have learned a language really different from their native language (not just a different dialect or a very closely related language), who have done this without any explicit teaching (or explicit learning from textbooks, linguistic fieldwork, or simply informal reflection ...) and who have attained a linguistic competence in that second language comparable to a native speaker? (p. 92)

IMPLICATIONS FOR FOREIGN LANGUAGE LEARNERS AND TEACHERS

In my interpretation, the literature reviewed here supports the hypothesis that attention is required for all learning. For those who would still maintain that some learning takes place without attention, it is important to stress that those psychologists who hold that view concede that whatever small amount of learning may take place unattended is interesting theoretically but of little practical value. I have also argued that detection (in the information processing sense), subjective awareness at the level of noticing, and learning all coincide. Learning at the higher level of understanding also seems crucial in most cases, and where generalization without awareness does seem to take place this is accomplished through simple associative learning applied to a rich memory base, rather than the unconscious induction of abstract rules.

The implications for language learners seem clear:

- Pay attention to input.

- Pay particular attention to whatever aspects of the input (phonology, morphology, pragmatics, discourse, etc.) that you are concerned to learn. Nothing comes free.

- Look for clues as to why target language speakers say what they say. Compare what you say with what target language speakers say in similar contexts. Build and test hypotheses when you can.

- If you cannot find a general principle to explain how something works, concentrate on noticing how specific instances are used in specific contexts.

It should be emphasized that only very modest implications for foreign language teaching can be drawn from the studies discussed in this paper, which have dealt with core theoretical issues, not the specifics of particular pedagogic techniques. As VanPatten (1994) points out, there is a great danger when talking about the role of consciousness in learning that this will be interpreted as a reactionary call for a return to the most traditional language teaching methods. It is not my intent to argue for abandonment of communicative language teaching or a return to traditional teaching methods, for the following reasons.

- The classic pedagogical question of how to communicate complex and richly structured information to learners resists any simple answer and is not resolved by recasting the discussion from one about conscious vs. unconscious learning to one that assesses the balance between lower-level associative learning and higher cognitive functions such as conscious hypothesis formation.

- An effective learning environment must cater to all aspects of language learning. Explicit skills are necessary for deep elaborative processing of semantic and conceptual representations, but naturalistic settings provide maximum opportunities for exposure and motivation (N. Ellis, 1994b, 1994c).

- Explicit instruction is more likely to facilitate L2 acquisition in the case of some features of language than in others (Hulstijn, this volume; VanPatten 1994).

- Instruction may work mainly indirectly rather than directly in L2 learning, through its role as a cognitive focusing device or advance organizer for learner attention (R. Ellis 1993; Reber, 1989; Schmidt and Frota, 1986; Seliger, 1979; Sharwood Smith, 1991; Terrell, 1991).

- Learning takes place within the learner's mind (brain) and cannot be completely engineered by teachers or syllabus designers. Students do not always attend to what teachers intend them to attend to (Slimani, 1992) and may prefer to achieve awareness at a higher or lower level that what is prepackaged by teachers.

- Even though many controlled studies show an overall advantage for explicit over implicit instructional approaches (Carroll and Swain, 1993; DeKeyser, 1994; Fotos, 1993; Lightbown and Pienemann, 1993; Master, 1994; Scott, 1990; VanPatten and Cadierno, 1993), classroom based studies that speak directly to the relative merits of experiential instructional approaches and awareness-oriented approaches remain inconclusive (Harley, 1994).

- The interesting question of whether instructional intervention should precede or follow exposure to input has been addressed in some experimental studies, but not resolved (Mathews et al., 1989; Reber, 1989)

- The results from single task and dual task learning experiments suggest that some level of decontextualization is probably valuable in foreign language teaching, but provide no clear basis for choosing among such instructional approaches as that of Loschky and Bley-Vroman (1990), who recommend the construction of closed communicative tasks that require attention to the target grammatical structures, that of R. Ellis (1993), who suggests that consciousness-raising considerations justify a return to a structural syllabus as long as it is understood that this cannot serve as a complete course, or that of Long (1991), who rejects any kind of structural syllabus as well as attention to linguistic forms except as these concerns arise incidentally during pedagogic tasks.

- Most pedagogical rules are wrong. Today's best linguistic descriptions will be revised next year (Paradis, 1994).

- Awareness alone (without input or interaction) is clearly inadequate. We all know people who know something *about* a language but can neither understand nor speak it.

Psychological studies of learning suggest that a pure meaning-focused approach to foreign language teaching is misguided, but there are many possible ways to combine exposure to input and communicative practice with a focus on form and consciousness raising (R. Ellis,

1994). Basic experimental research does not provide the answers to these detailed questions. I do not find this discouraging. It means that a great deal of theoretically interesting and practically important research lies ahead.

REFERENCES

Abrams, M., & Reber, A. W. (1988). Implicit learning: Robustness in the face of psychiatric disorders. *Journal of Psycholinguistic Research, 17*, 425–439.

Allport, D. A., Antonis, B., & Reynolds, P. (1972). On the division of attention: A disproof of the single channel hypothesis. *Quarterly Journal of Experimental Psychology, 24*, 225–235.

Anderson, J. R. (1985). *Cognitive psychology and its implications.* (2nd ed.) New York: Freeman.

Baars, B. J. (1988). *A cognitive theory of consciousness.* Cambridge: Cambridge University Press.

Berry, D. C. (1994). Implicit and explicit learning of complex tasks. In N. Ellis (Ed.), *Implicit and explicit learning of languages* (pp. 147–164). London: Academic Press.

Bialystok, E. (1990). The dangers of dichotomy: A reply to Hulstijn. *Applied Linguistics, 11*, 46–51.

Bialystok, E. (1993). Symbolic representation and attentional control in pragmatic competence. In G. Kasper & S. Blum-Kulka (Eds.), *Interlanguage pragmatics* (pp. 43–57). Oxford: Oxford University Press.

Bialystok, E. (1994a). Representation and ways of knowing: Three issues in second language acquisition. In N. Ellis (Ed.), *Implicit and explicit learning of languages* (pp. 549–569). London: Academic Press.

Bialystok, E. (1994b). Analysis and control in the development of second language proficiency. *Studies in Second Language Acquisition, 16*, 157–168.

Bialystok, E., & Bouchard Ryan, E. (1985). A metacognitive framework for the development of first and second language skills. In D. Forest-Pressley, G. MacKinnon, & T. Waller (Eds.), *Metacognition, cognition, and human performance* (pp. 207–252). Orlando, FL: Academic Press.

Bley-Vroman, R. (1989). What is the logical problem of foreign language learning? In S. Gass & J. Schachter (Eds.), *Linguistic perspectives on second language acquisition* (pp. 41–68). Cambridge: Cambridge University Press.

Bley-Vroman, R., Felix, S., & Ioup, G. (1988). The accessibility of universal grammar in adult language learning. *Second Language Research, 4*, 1–32.

Bootzin, R. R., Kihlstrom, J. K., & Schachter, D. L. (Eds.). (1990). *Sleep and cognition*. Washington, DC: American Psychological Association.

Bowers, K. (1984). On being unconsciously influenced and informed. In K. Bowers & D. Meichenbaum (Eds.), *The unconscious reconsidered* (pp. 227–272). New York: Wiley.

Brewer, W. F. (1974). There is no convincing evidence for operant or classical conditioning in adult humans. In W. B. Weimer & D. S. Palermo (Eds.), *Cognition and the symbolic processes* (pp. 1–42). Hillsdale, NJ: Erlbaum.

Brooks, L. R. (1978). Nonanalytic concept formation and memory for instances. In E. Rosch, & B. B. Lloyd (Eds.), *Cognition and categorization* (pp. 169–211). New York: Wiley

Brooks, L. R. & Vokey, J. R.. (1991). Abstract analogies and abstracted grammars: Comments on Reber (1989) and Mathews et al. (1989). *Journal of Experimental Psychology: General, 120*, 316–323.

Carlson, R. A., & Dulany, D. E. (1985). Conscious attention and abstraction in concept learning. *Journal of Experimental Psychology: Learning, Memory, and Cognition, 11*, 45–58.

Carr, T. H., & Curran, T. (1994). Cognitive factors in learning about structured sequences: Applications to syntax. *Studies in Second Language Acquisition, 16*, 205–230.

Carroll, S., & Swain, M. (1993). Explicit and implicit negative feedback: An empirical study of the learning of linguistic generalizations. *Studies in Second Language Learning, 15*, 357–386.

Cherry, E. (1953). Some experiments on the recognition of speech with one and with two ears. *Journal of the Acoustical Society of America, 25*, 975–979.

Chomsky, N. (1975). *Reflections on language*. New York: Pantheon.

Chomsky, N. (1986). *Knowledge of language: Its nature, origin and use*. New York: Praeger.

Chomsky, N. (1990). Accessibility "in principle." *Behavioral and Brain Sciences, 13*, 600–601.

Cohen, A., Ivry, R. I., & Keele, S. W. (1990). Attention and structure in sequence learning. *Journal of Experimental Psychology: Learning, Memory, and Cognition, 16*, 17–30.

Crookes, G. C., & Schmidt, R. (1991). Motivation: Reopening the research agenda. *Language Learning, 41*, 469–512.

Curran, T., & Keele, S. W. (1993). Attentional and nonattentional forms of sequence learning. *Journal of Experimental Psychology: Learning, Memory, and Cognition, 19*, 189–202.

Danks, P. L., & Gans, D. L. (1975). Acquisition and utilization of a rule structure. *Journal of Experimental Psychology: Human Learning and Memory, 1*, 201–8.

Dawson, M., & Schell, A. (1987). Human autonomic and skeletal classical conditioning: The role of conscious cognitive factors. In G. Davey (Ed.), *Cognitive processes and Pavlovian conditioning in humans* (pp. 27–55). Chichester: John Wiley and Sons.

DeKeyser, R. (1994). How implicit can adult second language learning be? *AILA Review, 11*, 83–96.

Dennett, D. (1987). *The intentional stance.* Cambridge, MA: MIT Press.

Dennett, D. (1991). *Consciousness explained.* Boston, MA: Little, Brown.

Dennett, D. C. & Kinsbourne, M.. (1992). Time and the observer: The where and when of consciousness in the brain. *Behavioral and Brain Sciences, 15*, 183–247.

Dienes, Z., Broadbent, D., & Berry, D. (1991). Implicit and explicit knowledge bases in artificial grammar learning. *Journal of Experimental Psychology: Learning, Memory, and Cognition, 17*, 875–887.

Doughty, C. (1991). Second language instruction does make a difference: Evidence from an empirical study of relativization. *Studies in Second Language Acquisition, 13*, 431–469.

Dulany, D. E., Carlson, R. A., & Dewey, G. I. (1984). A case of syntactical learning and judgment: How conscious and how abstract? *Journal of Experimental Psychology: General, 114*, 25–32.

Elley, W. B. (1991). Acquiring literacy in a second language: The effect of book-based programs. *Language Learning, 41*, 375–411.

Ellis, N. (1993). Rules and instances in foreign language learning: Interactions of explicit and implicit knowledge. *European Journal of Cognitive Psychology, 5*, 289–318.

Ellis, N. (1994a). Implicit and explicit language learning: an overview. In N. Ellis (Ed.), *Implicit and explicit learning of languages* (pp. 1–31). London: Academic Press.

Ellis, N. (1994b). Psychological perspectives on the role of conscious processes in vocabulary acquisition. *AILA Review, 11*, 37–56.

Ellis, N. (1994c). Vocabulary acquisition: The implicit ins and outs of explicit cognitive mediation. In N. Ellis (Ed.), *Implicit and explicit learning of languages* (pp. 211–282). London: Academic Press.

Ellis, R. (1990). *Instructed second language acquisition.* Oxford: Blackwell.

Ellis, R. (1993). The structural syllabus and second language acquisition. *TESOL Quarterly, 27*, 91–113.

Ellis, R. (1994). Metalinguistic knowledge and second language pedagogy. Paper presented at the American Association of Applied Linguistics, Colloquium on Awareness, Baltimore.

Ericsson, K., & Simon, H. (1984). *Protocol analysis: Verbal reports as data.* Cambridge, MA: MIT Press.

Eubank, L. (1991). Introduction. In L. Eubank (Ed.), *Point counterpoint: Universal grammar in the second language* (pp. 1–48). Amsterdam: John Benjamins.

Eysenck, M. W. (1982). Incidental learning and orienting tasks. In C. R. Puff (Ed.), *Handbook of research methods in human memory and cognition* (pp. 197–228). New York: Academic Press.

Faltis, C., & Hudelson, S. (1994). Learning English as an additional language in K–12 schools. *TESOL Quarterly*, 28, 457–468.

Felix, S. (1981). On the (in)applicability of Piagetian thought to language learning. *Studies in Second Language Acquisition*, 3, 201–220.

Felix, S. (1985). More evidence on competing cognitive systems. *Second Language Research, 1*, 47–72.

Felix. S. (1991). The accessibility of universal grammar in second language acquisition. In L. Eubank (Ed.), *Point counterpoint: Universal grammar in the second language* (pp. 89–103). Amsterdam: Benjamins.

Finer, D. L. (1991). Binding parameters in second language acquisition. In L. Eubank (Ed.), *Point counterpoint: Universal grammar in the second language* (pp. 351–374). Amsterdam: Benjamins.

Fisk, A. D., & Schneider, W. (1984). Memory as a function of attention, level of processing, and automatization. *Journal of Experimental Psychology: Learning, Memory, and Cognition, 10*, 181–197.

Forest-Pressley, D., MacKinnon, G., & Waller, T. (Eds.). (1985). *Metacognition, cognition, and human performance*. Orlando, FL: Academic Press.

Fotos, S. S. (1993). Consciousness-raising and noticing though focus on form: Grammar task performance versus formal instruction. *Applied Linguistics, 14*, 385–407.

Fotos, S, & Ellis, R. (1991). Communicating about grammar: A task-based approach. *TESOL Quarterly, 25*, 605–628.

Gardner, R. C. (1985). *Social psychology and language learning: The role of attitudes and motivation*. London: Edward Arnold.

Gardner, R. C. (1988). The socio-educational model of second-language learning: Assumptions, findings, and issues. *Language Learning, 38*, 101–126.

Gazzaniga, M. S. (1993). Brain mechanisms and conscious experience. In G. R. Bock & J. Marsh (Eds.), *Experimental and theoretical studies of consciousness* (pp. 247–257). New York: John Wiley.

Glucksberg, S., & Cowan, G. N. (1970). Memory for nonattended auditory material. *Cognitive Psychology, 1*, 149–156.

Greenwald, A. G., Spangeberg, E. R, Pratkanis, A. R., & Eskenazi, J. (1991). Double blind tests of subliminal self-help audiotapes. *Psychological Science, 2*, 119–122.

Hanson, C., & Hirst, W. (1988). Frequency encoding of token and type information. *Journal of Experimental Psychology: Learning, Memory, and Cognition, 14*, 289–297.

Hardcastle, V. G. (1993). The naturalists versus the skeptics: The debate over a scientific understanding of consciousness. *Journal of Mind and Behavior*, *14*, 27–50.

Harley, B. (1994). Appealing to consciousness in the L2 classroom. AILA Review, 11, 57–68.

Harnad, S. (1990). Lost in the hermeneutic hall of mirrors. *Journal of Theoretical and Experimental Artificial Intelligence*, 2, 321–327.

Harnad, S. (1991). Other bodies, other minds: A machine incarnation of an old philosophical problem. *Minds and Machines*, *1*, 43–54.

Hartman, M., Knopman, D. S., & Nissen, M. J. (1989). Implicit learning of new verbal associations. *Journal of Experimental Psychology: Learning, Memory, and Cognition*, *15*, 1070–1082.

Hasher, L., & Zacks, R. T. (1979). Automatic and effortful processes in memory. *Journal of Experimental Psychology: General*, *108*, 356–388.

Hasher, L., & Zacks, R. T. (1984). Automatic processing of fundamental information: The case of frequency of occurrence. *American Psychologist*, *39*, 1372–1388.

Hatch, E., & Hawkins, B. (1987). Second-language acquisition: An experiential approach. In S. Rosenberg (Ed.), *Advances in applied psycholinguistics*, Vol. 2, *Reading writing and language learning* (pp. 241–283). Cambridge: Cambridge University Press.

Hayes, N. A., & Broadbent, D. E. (1988). Two modes of learning for interactive tasks. *Cognition*, *28*, 249–276.

Hintzman, D. L. (1976). Repetition and memory. In G. H. Bower (Ed.), *The psychology of learning and motivation*, Vol. 10 (pp. 47–91). New York: Academic Press.

Hulstijn, J. H., & de Graaff, R. (1994). Under what conditions does explicit knowledge of a second language facilitate the acquisition of implicit knowledge? A research proposal. *AILA Review*, *11*, 97–113.

Jackendoff, R. (1987). *Consciousness and the computational mind*. New York: Academic Press.

James, W. (1890). *The principles of psychology*. New York: Holt.

Joordens, S., & Merikle, P. M. (1992). False recognition and perception without awareness. *Memory and Cognition*, *20*, 151–159.

Kellogg, R. (1980). Is conscious attention necessary for long-term storage? *Journal of Experimental Psychology: Human Learning and Memory*, 6, 379–390.

Kellogg, R. T., & Dare, R. S. (1989). Explicit memory for unattended information. *Bulletin of the Psychonomic Society*, *27*, 409–412.

Kihlstrom, J. (1984). Conscious, subconscious, unconscious: A cognitive perspective. In K. Bowers & D. Meichenbaum (Eds.), *The unconscious reconsidered* (pp. 149–211). New York: Wiley.

Knowlton, B. J., Ramus, S. J., & Squire, L. R. (1992). Intact artificial grammar learning in amnesia: Dissociation of classification learning and explicit memory for specific instances. *Psychological Science*, *3*, 172–179.

Krashen, S. D. (1982). *Principles and practice in second language acquisition*. New York: Pergamon.

Krashen, S. D. (1985). *The input hypothesis*. London: Longman.

Krashen, S. D. (1989). We acquire vocabulary and spelling by reading: Additional evidence for the input hypothesis. *Modern Language Journal*, *73*, 440–464.

Krashen, S. D. (1993). The effect of formal grammar teaching: Still peripheral. *TESOL Quarterly*, *26*, 722–725.

Krashen, S. D. (1994). The input hypothesis and its rivals. In N. Ellis (Ed.), *Implicit and explicit learning of languages* (pp. 45–77). London: Academic Press.

Krashen, S. D., & Terrell, T. (1983). *The natural approach: Language acquisition in the classroom*. New York: Pergamon.

Lamendella, J. (1977). General principles of neurofunctional organization and their manifestation in primary and second language acquisition. *Language Learning*, *27*, 155–196.

Larsen-Freeman, D., & Long, M H. (1991). *An introduction to second language acquisition research*. Essex, UK: Longman.

Lewicki, P. (1986). Processing information about covariations that cannot be articulated. *Journal of Experimental Psychology: Learning, Memory, and Cognition*, *12*, 135–146.

Lightbown, P. M., & Pienemann, M. (1993). Comments on Stephen D. Krashen's "Teaching issues: Formal grammar instruction." *TESOL Quarterly*, *26*, 717–722.

Lightbown, P. M., & N. Spada, N. (1994). An innovative program for primary ESL students in Quebec. *TESOL Quarterly*, *28*, 563–579.

Logan, G. D. (1988). Toward an instance theory of automatization. *Psychological Review*, *95*, 492–527.

Long, M. H. (1988). Instructed interlanguage development. In L. Beebe (Ed.), *Issues in second language acquisition* (pp. 114–141). New York: Newbury House.

Long, M. H. (1991). Focus on form: A design feature in language teaching. In K. deBot, R. B. Ginsberg, & C. Kramsch (Eds.), *Foreign language research in cross-cultural perspective* (pp. 39–52). Amsterdam: Benjamins.

Long, M. H. (In press). The role of the linguistic environment in second language acquisition. In W. Ritchie & T. Bhatia (Eds.) *Handbook of research on language acquisition*. (Vol. 2) *Second language acquisition*. New York: Academic Press.

Loschky, L., & Bley-Vroman, R. (1990). Creating structure based communication tasks for second language development. *University of Hawai'i Working Papers in ESL*, *9*, 161–212.

McLaughlin, B. (1990). "Conscious" versus "unconscious" learning. *TESOL Quarterly*, *24*, 617–634.

McLaughlin, B., Rossman, T., & McLeod, B. (1983). Second language learning: An information-processing perspective. *Language Learning*, *33*, 135–157.

MacWhinney, B. (1983). Miniature linguistic systems as tests of the use of universal operating principles in second-language learning by children and adults. *Journal of Psycholinguistic Research*, *12*, 467–478.

MacWhinney, B., Leinbach, J., Taraban, R., & McDonald, J. (1989). Language learning: Cues or rules? *Journal of Memory and Language*, *28*, 255–277.

Master, P. (1994). The effect of systematic instruction on learning the English article system. In T. Odlin (Ed.), *Perspectives on pedagogic grammar* (pp. 229–252). Cambridge: Cambridge University Press.

Mathews, R. C., Buss, R. R., Stanley, W. B., Blanchard-Fields, W. B., Cho, J. R., & Druhan, B. (1989). Role of implicit and explicit processes in learning from examples: A synergistic effect. *Journal of*

Experimental Psychology: Learning, Memory, and Cognition, 15, 1083–1100.

Medin, D. L., & Ross, B. H. (1990). The specific character of abstract thought: Categorization, problem solving, and induction. In R. J. Sternberg (Ed.) *Advances in the psychology of human intelligence*, (Vol. 5) (pp. 189–224). Hillsdale, NJ: Erlbaum.

Merikle, P. M. (1988). Subliminal auditory messages: An evaluation. *Psychology and Marketing, 5*, 355–372.

Merikle, P. M. (1994). On the futility of attempting to demonstrate null awareness. *Behavioral and Brain Sciences, 17*, 412.

Moore, T. E. (Ed.). (1988). Subliminal influences in marketing. *Psychology and Marketing, 5*, 291–372.

Moray, N. (1959). Attention in dichotic listening: Affective cues and the influence of instructions. *Quarterly Journal of Experimental Psychology, 11*, 56–60.

Morgan, J. L., Meier, R. P., & Newport, E. L. (1987). Structural packaging in the input to language learning: Contributions of prosodic and morphological marking of phrases to the acquisition of language. *Cognitive Psychology, 19*, 498–550.

Nagel, T. (1974). What is it like to be a bat? *Philosophical Review, 83*, 435–451.

Nagel, T. (1993). What is the mind-body problem? In G. R. Bock & J. Marsh (Eds.), *Experimental and theoretical studies of consciousness* (pp. 1–7). Chichester: John Wiley.

Nation, R., & McLaughlin, B. (1986). Novices and experts: An information processing approach to the "good language learner" problem. *Applied Psycholinguistics, 7*, 41–56.

Nissen, M., & Bullemer, P. (1987). Attentional requirements of learning: Evidence from performance measures. *Cognitive Psychology, 19*, 1–32.

Norman, D. A. (1969). Memory while shadowing. *Quarterly Journal of Experimental Psychology, 21*, 85–93.

O'Keefe, J. (1985). Is consciousness the gateway to the hippocampal cognitive map? A speculative essay on the neural basis of mind. In D. Oakley (Ed.), *Brain and mind* (pp. 59–98). London: Methuen.

Paradis, M. (1994). Neurolinguistic aspects of implicit and explicit memory: Implications for bilingualism. In N. Ellis (Ed.), *Implicit and explicit learning of languages* (pp. 393–419). London: Academic Press.

Perruchet, P., & Amorim, M-A. (1992). Conscious knowledge and changes in performance in sequence learning: Evidence against dissociation. *Journal of Experimental Psychology: Learning, Memory, and Cognition, 18*, 785–800.

Perruchet, P., Gallego, J., & Savy, I. (1990). A critical reappraisal of the evidence for unconscious abstraction of deterministic rules in complex experimental situations. *Cognitive Psychology, 22*, 493–516.

Perruchet, P., & Pacteau, C. (1990). Synthetic grammar learning: Implicit rule abstraction or explicit fragmentary knowledge. *Journal of Experimental Psychology: General, 119*, 264–275.

Perruchet, P., & Pacteau, C. (1991). Implicit acquisition of abstract knowledge about artificial grammar: Some methodological and conceptual issues. *Journal of Experimental Psychology: General, 120*, 112–116.

Pica, T. (1994). Questions from the language classroom: Research perspectives. *TESOL Quarterly, 28*, 49–79.

Pintrich, P. (1989). The dynamic interplay of student motivation and cognition in the college classroom. In M. Maehr & C. Ames (Eds.), *Advances in motivation and achievement*, (Vol. 6) *Motivation enhancing environments* (pp. 117–160). Orlando: Academic Press.

Poldrack, R. A., & Cohen, N. J. (1994). On the representational/computational properties of multiple memory systems. *Behavioral and Brain Sciences, 17*, 416–417.

Posner, M. I. (1992). Attention as a cognitive and neural system. *Current Directions in Psychological Science, 1*, 11–14.

Posner, M. I., & Petersen, S. E. (1990). The attention system of the human brain. *Annual Review of Neuroscience, 13*, 25–42.

Posner, M. I., & Rothbart, M. K. (1991). Attentional mechanisms and conscious experience. In D. Milner & M. Rugg (Eds.), *The neuropsychology of consciousness* (pp. 91–111). San Diego, CA: Academic Press.

Prabhu, N. S. (1987). *Second language pedagogy*. Oxford: Oxford University Press.

Reber, A. S. (1965). *Implicit learning of artificial grammars.* Unpublished MA. thesis. Brown University.

Reber, A. S. (1967). Implicit learning of artificial grammars. *Journal of Verbal Learning and Verbal Behavior, 77,* 317–327.

Reber, A. S. (1969). Transfer of syntactic structure in synthetic languages. *Journal of Experimental Psychology, 81,* 115–119.

Reber, A. S. (1976). Implicit learning of synthetic languages: The role of instructional set. *Journal of Experimental Psychology: Human Learning and Memory, 2,* 88–94.

Reber, A. (1989). Implicit learning and tacit knowledge. *Journal of Experimental Psychology: General, 118,* 219–235.

Reber, A. S. (1992). The cognitive unconscious: An evolutionary perspective. *Consciousness and Cognition, 1,* 93–133.

Reber, A. S. (1993). *Implicit learning and tacit knowledge: An essay on the cognitive unconscious.* Oxford: Oxford University Press.

Reber, A. S., & Allen, R. (1978). Analogy and abstraction strategies in synthetic grammar learning: A functionalist interpretation. *Cognition, 6,* 189–221.

Reber, A. S., Allen, R., & Regan, S. (1985). Syntactical learning and judgment, still unconscious and still abstract: Comment on Dulany, Carlson, and Dewey. *Journal of Experimental Psychology: General, 114,* 17–24.

Reber, A. S., Kassin, S. M., Lewis, S., & Cantor, G. W. (1980). On the relationship between implicit and explicit modes in the learning of a complex rule structure. *Journal of Experimental Psychology: Human Learning and Memory,* 6, 492–502.

Reber, A. S., & Lewis, S. (1977). Toward a theory of implicit learning: The analysis of the form and structure of a body of tacit knowledge. *Cognition, 5,* 333–561.

Reber, A. S., Walkenfeld, F. F., & Hernstadt, R. (1991). Implicit and explicit learning: Individual differences and IQ. *Journal of Experimental Psychology: Learning, Memory, and Cognition, 17,* 888–896.

Robinson, P. (in press). Attention, memory, and the "noticing" hypothesis. *Language Learning.*

Rutherford, W. (1987). *Second language grammar: Learning and teaching.* London: Longman.

Schachter, D. L. (1987). Implicit memory: History and current status. *Journal of Experimental Psychology: Learning, Memory, and Cognition, 13*, 501–518.

Schmidt, R. (1990). The role of consciousness in second language learning. *Applied Linguistics, 11*, 129–158.

Schmidt, R. (1992). Psychological mechanisms underlying second language fluency. *Studies in Second Language Acquisition, 14*, 357–385.

Schmidt, R. (1993a). Awareness and second language acquisition. *Annual Review of Applied Linguistics, 13*, 206–226.

Schmidt, R. (1993b). Consciousness, learning, and interlanguage pragmatics. In G. Kasper & S. Blum-Kulka (Eds.) *Interlanguage pragmatics* (pp. 21–42). Oxford: Oxford University Press.

Schmidt, R. (1994a). Implicit learning and the cognitive unconscious. In N. Ellis (Ed.), *Implicit and explicit learning of languages* (pp. 165–209). London: Academic Press.

Schmidt, R. (1994b). Deconstructing consciousness in search of useful definitions for applied linguistics. *AILA Review, 11*, 11–26.

Schmidt, R., & Frota, S. (1986). Developing basic conversational ability in a second language: A case study of an adult learner of Portuguese. In R. R. Day (Ed.), *Talking to learn: Conversation in second language acquisition* (pp. 237–322). Rowley, MA: Newbury House.

Schneider, W., & Detweiler, M. (1988). The role of practice in dual-task performance: Toward workload modeling in a connectionist /control architecture. *Human Factors*, 30, 539–566.

Scott, V. M. (1990). Explicit and implicit grammar teaching strategies: New empirical data. *The French Review*, 63, 779–788.

Scovel, T. (1991). *Attention, apperception, awareness, and acquisition.* Paper presented at the Thai TESOL Eleventh Annual Convention, Bangkok.

Seliger, H. (1979). On the nature and function of language rules in language teaching. *TESOL Quarterly, 13*, 359–369.

Seliger, H. (1983). The language learner as linguist: Of metaphors and realities. *Applied Linguistics*, 4, 179–191.

Servan-Schreiber, E., & Anderson, J. R. (1990). Learning artificial grammars with competitive chunking. *Journal of Experimental Psychology: Learning, Memory, and Cognition, 16*, 592–608.

Shanks, D. R., & St. John, M. F. (1994). Characteristics of dissociable human learning systems. *Behavioral and Brain Sciences, 17*, 367–447.

Sharwood Smith, M. (1981). Consciousness-raising and the second language learner. *Applied Linguistics, 7*, 239–256.

Sharwood Smith, M. (1991). Speaking to many minds: on the relevance of different types of language information for the L2 learner. *Second Language Research, 7*, 118–132.

Sharwood Smith, M. (1993). Input enhancement in instructed SLA: Theoretical bases. *Studies in Second Language Acquisition, 15*, 165–179.

Shiffrin, R. M., & Schneider, W. (1977). Controlled and automatic human information processing II: Perceptual learning, automatic attending, and a general theory. *Psychological Review, 84*, 127–190.

Skehan, P. (1992). Second language acquisition strategies and task-based learning. *Thames Valley University Working Papers in English Language Teaching, 1*, 178–208.

Slimani, A. (1992). Evaluation of classroom interaction. In J. C. Alderson & A. Beretta (Eds.), *Evaluating second language education* (pp. 197–220). Cambridge: Cambridge University Press.

Slobin, D. I. (1985). Crosslinguistic evidence for the language-making capacity. In D. Slobin (Ed.), *The crosslinguistic study of language acquisition*, (Vol. 2) *Theoretical issues* (pp. 1157–1256). Hillsdale, NJ: Erlbaum.

Smith, F. (1988). *Understanding reading.* (4th ed.). Hillsdale, NJ: Ablex.

Sokolik, M. E., & Smith, M. E. (1992). Assignment of gender to French nouns in primary and secondary language: A connectionist model. *Second Language Research*, 8, 39–58.

Terrell, T. D. (1991). The role of grammar instruction in a communicative approach. *Modern Language Journal, 75*, 52–63.

Tomlin, R., & Villa, V. (1994). Attention in cognitive science and second language acquisition. *Studies in Second Language Acquisition, 16*, 183–203.

Tye, M. (1993). Blindsight, the absent qualia hypothesis, and the mystery of consciousness. In C. Hookway & D. Peterson (Eds.), *Philosophy and cognitive science* (pp. 19–40). Cambridge: Cambridge University Press.

van Lier, L. (1991). Inside the classroom: Learning processes and teaching procedures. *Applied Language Learning, 2*, 29–68.

van Lier, L. (1994). Language awareness, contingency, and interaction. *AILA Review, 11*, 69–82.

VanPatten, B. (1990). Attending to content and form in the input: An experiment in consciousness. *Studies in Second Language Acquisition, 12*, 287–301.

VanPatten, B. (1993). Grammar teaching for the acquisition-rich classroom. *Foreign Language Annals, 26*, 435–450.

VanPatten, B. (1994). Evaluating the role of consciousness in second language acquisition: Terms, linguistic features & research methodology. *AILA Review, 11*, 27–36.

VanPatten, B., & Cadierno, C. (1993). Explicit instruction and input processing. *Studies in Second Language Acquisition, 15*, 225–241.

Velmans, M. (1991). Is human information processing conscious? *Behavioral and Brain Sciences, 14*, 651–669.

Vokey, J. R., & Brooks, L. R. (1992). Salience of item knowledge in learning artificial grammars. *Journal of Experimental Psychology: Learning, Memory and Cognition, 18*, 328–344.

Weiskrantz, L. (1986). *Blindsight: A case study and its implications.* New York: Oxford University Press.

Weiskrantz, L. (1990). Outlooks for blindsight: Explicit methodologies for implicit processes. *Proceedings of the Royal Society London, 239*, 247–278.

White, L. (1981). The responsibility of grammatical theory to acquisition data. In N. Hornstein & D. Lightfoot (Eds.), *Explanation in linguistics: The logical problem of language acquisition* (pp. 240–271). London: Longman.

White, L. (1985). The pro-drop parameter in adult second language acquisition. *Language Learning, 35*, 47–62.

White, L. (1989). *Universal grammar and second language acquisition.* Amsterdam: John Benjamins.

White, L. (1991). Adverb placement in second language acquisition: Some effects of positive and negative evidence in the classroom. *Second Language Research, 7*, 133–161.

White, L. (1992). On triggering data in L2 acquisition: A reply to Schwartz and Gubala-Ryzak. *Second Language Research*, 8, 120–137.

White, L., Spada, N., Lightbown, P. M., & Ranta, L. (1991). Input enhancement and L2 question formation. *Applied Linguistics, 12*, 416–432.

Winter, B., & Reber, A. S. (1994). Implicit learning and the acquisition of natural languages. In N. Ellis (Ed.), *Implicit and explicit learning of languages* (pp. 114–145). London: Academic Press.

Wolford, G. & Morrison, F. (1980). Processing of unattended visual information. *Memory & Cognition*, 8, 521–527.

Wyer, R., & Srull, T. (1994). *Handbook of social cognition* (Vol. 1). Hillsdale, NJ: Erlbaum.

Zalewski, J. P. (1993). Number/person errors in an information-processing perspective: Implications for form-focused instruction. *TESOL Quarterly, 27*, 691–703.

Hae-Young Kim
University of Hawai'i at Mānoa

INTAKE FROM THE SPEECH STREAM: SPEECH ELEMENTS THAT L2 LEARNERS ATTEND TO

ABSTRACT

To better understand the nature of the notorious problem of segmenting an acoustic string in second and foreign languages, this study looks at the relationship between the phonetic characteristics of speech input and speech comprehension, as well as developmental phases of speech perception as revealed by analyses of the retrospective reports of participants in a listening comprehension study. The effects of prosodic variations in input and developmental phases on speech perception highlight the significance of the phonological aspects of input and bear as well on questions of what factors determine or influence the noticing of forms that can lead to learning.

INTRODUCTION

Although there seems to be a general consensus that it is implicit knowledge, as opposed to explicit knowledge[1] that underlies proficient language use both for first language (L1) and a second or foreign language (L2), how this implicit knowledge is acquired is highly controversial (Hulstijn and de Graaff, 1994). While those holding interface positions argue that implicit knowledge can originate from explicit knowledge through automatization (the strong interface hypothesis), second language acquisition (SLA) research

1 Explicit knowledge is defined as "conscious awareness of the formal properties of target language, verbalizable on demand" while implicit knowledge is knowledge "which is intuitive and cannot be introspected or reported" (Schmidt, 1994: 5).

Kim, Hae-Young (1995). Intake from the speech stream: Speech elements that L2 learners attend to. In Richard Schmidt (Ed.), *Attention and awareness in foreign language learning* (Technical Report #9) (pp. 65–83). Honolulu, Hawai'i: University of Hawai'i, Second Language Teaching & Curriculum Center.

which has shown that acquisition of new knowledge is conditioned by current knowledge and that developmental sequences cannot be changed through instruction must be interpreted as evidence for either a non-interface position, that implicit knowledge develops and operates in and by itself without communication with explicit knowledge (Sharwood Smith, 1993) or a weak interface position, in which the influence of explicit knowledge is indirect, making its influence felt through guided processing of input (see Ellis, 1994; Larsen-Freeman and Long, 1991 for reviews). If implicit knowledge is not the result of explicit knowledge, then, does learning also take place implicitly, without the learner's awareness of what she is learning?

The role of the learner's awareness in learning has been seen in a new light by Schmidt (1993a; 1993b; 1994). While acknowledging the existence of implicit knowledge, he rules out the possibility that new forms which learners have not paid attention to can enter long-term memory. Noticing is a necessary and sufficient condition for converting input to intake. Given that noticing is not always a function of the learner's intention, however, what influences noticing of a form or form-function match other than the learner's readiness to learn the form, a "preexisting programming to make sense of language input" (Sharwood Smith, 1993: 170)? Another question that arises is how the end state of knowledge that is finally established can be related to the forms that were initially noticed and taken in. On the other hand, the extent of the learner's awareness of a form when it is encountered and noticed is likely to vary according to its "linguistic domain, complexity, scope and reliability, and semantic or formal redundancy" (Hulstijn and de Graaff, 1994).

In order to ground these questions in the actuality of the learner's experience with the language, it seems necessary to start with the perception of phonological input. While speech input is a major source of L2 acquisition, issues concerning the noticing of forms from a speech stream have not received their due attention in research.[2] In

[2] While diary study is a possible way to document noticing of forms in input as in Schmidt & Frota (1986), it is hard to come by a large amount of data this way because "making a record in a diary requires not only noticing but also a higher level of self-awareness" (Schmidt, 1993: 211).

child language development, however, descriptions of and experimentation on the primary task of segmenting speech into recognizable units are abundant. For example, it is reported that children at the ages between four and six have not acquired the processing ability to take advantage of sentence stress or focus, which is invariably used by adults (Cutler and Swinney, 1987). Various strategies that seem to be used by children to segment speech have been proposed: 1) breaking up the input into known and unknown, 2) relying on cues present in the prosody, and 3) using information about allophonic constraints (Jusczyk, 1993; Gow and Gordon, 1993; Slowiaszek, 1993). In comparison, L2 learners' approach to the task of segmenting speech has not been systematically investigated. To date, studies related to this have been mostly concerned with speech modification, with a focus on variables of speech rate and pauses (Call, 1985; Conrad, 1989; Derwing, 1990; Griffiths, 1990; cf. also Chaudron, 1988 and in press for a review of the studies on speech modification). Other than the effects of modification on comprehension and relationships between L2 processing ability and working memory capacity, little attention has been paid to the precise nature of the listener's accessing and processing of the speech input.

This paper reports what speech elements L2 learners are able to attend to in the stream of speech. Specifically, the study looked at prosodic characteristics of speech elements that affect perception and the developmental phases of speech perception. The prosody of input and its effect on perception bears on the question about factors that influence noticing of forms, which in this case is the linguistic (or phonological) characteristics of input. On the other hand, the developmental phases of aural processing appear to reflect the role of the learner's current knowledge of phonology and processing capacity in the noticing of forms.

METHOD

The study was an attempt to address the following questions

- What speech elements do L2 listeners perceive and attend to in connected speech?
- What are the phonological or prosodic characteristics of these elements?
- Can these characteristics be put into a pattern that is implicational and developmental?

PARTICIPANTS

Twenty-six Korean students from two Korean universities participated in the study on a voluntary basis. They were sophomores, juniors or seniors majoring in technology, engineering, physical education or English. Although no measure of their English proficiency was available, their reading knowledge was assumed to be high intermediate. They were randomly assigned to one of two different speech conditions (described in the next section). Based on the score of a short dictation test that was given prior to the main listening task, the students from each of the speech conditions were later matched in pairs for group comparisons. A t-test for differences in dictation between the two groups showed no difference with a two-tailed probability of .931.

SPEECH INPUT AND LISTENING TASK

Two different speech conditions were included in the design with a view to examining the effects of auditory and perceptual consequences of speech modification (slowing down). Avery, Ehrlich, and Yorio (1985) observed a major consequence of slowing down of speech to be elimination of sandhi effects (liaison, contraction and so forth), and this study pursued this line further to investigate the impact on perception of speech elements. Identical texts were read in two different ways by a female native speaker of American English. In one condition, the texts were read with normal phonological phrasing, which had pauses at the clause boundary most of the time and resulted in a speech rate of 189 words per minute. For the other condition, the reading was done with shorter phonological phrasing, with more frequent pauses at phrase boundaries, resulting in a speech rate of 126 words per minute. The recorded texts consisted of thirty passages which were three to six clauses long. The content of passages included discourse functions such as giving definitions, making requests, or explaining procedures. The listeners' task was to select a picture that matched each passage on hearing the passage once.

IMMEDIATE RETROSPECTION

The listening comprehension task was given individually in a quiet room by the investigator. After each item, as students selected pictures while listening to a passage, they were asked what they heard and why they chose the answer. They were encouraged to use either English or Korean as they preferred. The interviews were audio-recorded for later transcription and analysis.

Other possible methods of elicitation to answer the research questions that were considered but rejected were dictation and elicited imitation. Dictation was rejected not only because the amount of speech input that could be given at a time is very limited but also dictation engages the listener in a process that is distinct from ordinary speech processing[3] and it soon becomes too tedious for the listener. Likewise, elicited imitation was decided to be unsuitable not only because it is rather artificial as a comprehension task but also because subjects might develop test-specific strategies to remembering certain portions of the speech stream, probably the beginning of speech input (see Conrad, 1989 for discussion). In comparison, immediate retrospection after picture selection made it possible to engage the listener in processing extended pieces of speech, using ordinary comprehension process, viz. listening for meaning.

---

[3] Henrichsen (1984) used dictation which consisted of fifteen sentences which were about ten words long. His research focus was to examine the effects of the perceptual saliency of functional items, as determined by presence or absence of liaison or contraction, on "comprehension." Although use of dictation suited his purpose, to isolate one item from each sentence, it diverges from the interest of this study in attention to speech elements in on-line listening comprehension.

Although the subjects' self-reports may not be a complete or completely accurate representation of their processes, they still reflect part of what goes on inside and are a good source of investigation if we do not deny the relevance of subjective experience for understanding mental processes (Schmidt, 1994). Also, immediate retrospective interviews are deemed to be more reliable compared to on-line introspections or delayed retrospection, since they do not interfere with the processes of interest and are given before the onset of serious memory loss (Ericsson and Simon, 1980). Immediate retrospective interviews have been used in studies of listening comprehension, particularly to identify the use of learners' strategies (O'Malley, Chamot and Kupper, 1989) and to investigate interactions of top-down and bottom-up processes (Vandergritt, 1995). The method was recently used successfully to probe the processes of drawing inferences by Ross (in press), in a study that was designed to evaluate the validity of a listening comprehension measure. This study, though, is differentiated from those in that it was exclusively concerned with bottom-up processing.

ANALYSES

Scores on the comprehension task were compared between the two groups (normal and slowed condition) using paired t-tests. The self-report data from immediate retrospection were checked against transcripts of the input in order to identify all the speech elements attended to by the listeners. A template was prepared for each item, with the words of the passage in the top row and the subject IDs in the left-most column so that each row showed the speech elements that subjects reported they had heard. In this way, it was possible to identify the most to the least commonly perceived items, as well as to determine the scope of speech elements each individual was able to attend to. The scope of perception was quantified and then used for a group comparison. The following section reports results of both quantitative and qualitative analyses.

RESULTS AND DISCUSSION

COMPREHENSION SCORES

The comprehension scores of the picture identification task of the two groups are shown in Table 1. The difference in group means was not statistically significant (paired t-test: t=1.78, p<.10). The absence of difference appears to be due to the inappropriate difficulty level of the test (notice that correct response rates are almost 80%). In addition, thirty items of multiple-choice type may not be a fine enough measure. In contrast, analyses of the retrospective interview data that are reported below provided more insight into the speech comprehension and the effects of differing conditions.

Table 1: Picture identification task scores (k=30)

	Condition	Mean	S.D.
Group 1 (n=13)	Slow speech	24.92	3.29
Group 2 (n=13)	Normal speech	22.92	4.25

SPEECH ELEMENTS ATTENDED TO BY THE LISTENERS

The retrospection data showed some commonalties in those speech elements that were attended to by most subjects, especially prosodic prominence, positional salience and familiar phonological make-up.

The first research question was what speech elements are attended to by listeners. In this study, there seemed to be some core speech elements that were perceived by almost every subject. Certain elements in a passage were reported to be heard by almost every student, whereas other elements were reported by varying numbers. For example, for a passage, "It is coated with some black material called Teflon, so it cleans easily and cooks faster," almost every one reported *cooks* or *cooks faster*, some reported this plus *cleans easily*, a few others reported these plus *black* or *material*, and very few heard all of these and *it is coated with*. This seems to form a kind of implicational scale of intake. Another example is "Could I give you a ride?," where a scale of intake was also found, from *ride* to *you...ride*, to *could I give you a ride*. Those who only heard one word could not select the right picture, and those who only heard two words in this clause misinterpreted it as "Would you give me a ride?"

This observation leads to the second research question, why some speech elements were more likely to be heard than others, and whether this is related to phonological properties of the elements. One thing that a closer examination of the retrospective report data revealed was the phonetic prominence of noticed elements. They were the elements that contained a pre-tonic or a tonic; *tonic* being defined here as the primary stress (while *pre-tonic* refers to the secondary stress) in an intonational phrase that has one intonation contour and corresponds with a grammatical unit such as a clause or a phrase.[4] For example, when a passage, "Ann was very late this morning / she said she waited hours and hours / for the bus that never came," is spoken in three intonational phrases, tonics fall on *late*, *waited*, and *bus*. Not surprisingly, these three were the elements reported by most students if they heard anything at all. The next most reported elements in this example were *never came*, *hours and hours* and *this morning* (in the order of frequency of reports), which are in final position, a very salient position of the intonational phrase.

The salience of an element as a function of its position in the intonational phrase seemed to affect perception. In the case of "This is what you can have / when you feel like eating between meals," in which the tonic was on *eating* for the second intonational phrase, most students reported hearing *eating*. The next most reported elements were *when* and *meals*, which were again in the first or last position. Thus, positional salience of a speech element seems to determine its

[4] A "tonic" — a syllable that receives the most prominent phonological focus —, which was originally assigned to the right-most content word in a tone group by Halliday, can now be assigned to the new information in the right-most position excluding locatives (Tench, 1990). Although the model is faced with serious empirical problems when it is applied to spontaneous speech (Brown, Currie & Kenworthy, 1980), it was considered relevant for this study because the speech input was based on written scripts and its phonological phrasing was regular and clear. Tonics were identified by the investigator on an impressionistic basis.

auditory accessibility. However, without the hearer's lexical familiarity or familiarity with segmental sounds that compose an element, even the element with the tonic could not be accessed. For instance, "I can hold those parcels for you" has its tonic on *parcels*. But most students in this study failed to hear it, but only heard *I can* or *for you*. Without hearing the tonic, they of course failed to understand the meaning. Mis-hearing also revealed that certain phonemes in certain phonological environments caused problems. For example, some learners mis-recognized *ride* as *right*, *said* as *sat* (voiced stop /d/ in word-final position), *long* as *wrong* (the typical /l/ and /r/ problem for Korean learners), *a cup of* as *coffee* (/p/ and /f/ problem), *book shelf* as *book shop*, and *stairs* as *street* (liquids in consonant clusters in word-final position). Difficulties with particular segments were aggravated if they were not prosodically prominent.

THE EFFECTS OF SLOWING DOWN

Given that phonetic prominence contributes to perception of a speech element, it seems logical that different phonological phrasing, which affects the number of tonics, in turn will affect the accessibility of speech elements by hearers. Effects of different lengths of intonational phrases on perception were apparent in the number of speech elements heard by the subjects; more elements were heard in the slow speech condition (with short phrasing) than in normal speech condition (with long phrasing). For instance, with the following passage which was segmented differently as shown, all the subjects in both conditions reported hearing *CD's*, about half of each group heard *collect(ion)*, but only three (out of thirteen) in the normal condition heard *like* while ten (out of thirteen) in the slow condition heard it.

Normal: People have a collection of records or CD's if they like this

Slow: People have a collection / of records or CD's / if they like this

For the passage below, while ten subjects in the normal condition heard the tonic *pipe*, six subjects heard *fix*, and only two of them heard the first clause *the sink is leaking*. In comparison, eleven subjects in the slow condition heard *pipe*, nine of them heard *fix*, and eleven subjects heard the first clause.

Normal:	The sink is leaking/ would you have a look at the pipe and fix it?
Slow:	The sink / is leaking/ would you / have a look at the pipe / and fix it?

These are just two examples that show contrasts in the quantity of the intake that varied according to differing phrasing conditions. Not only did the number of tonics or prominent speech elements increase with shorter phonological phrasing, but the phonetic quality of the prominence elements seemed to be also affected. Tonics that were common to both of the conditions appeared to be rendered more prominent in the slow condition, which was probably due to longer duration in the articulation of the elements. For example, with the input "Could you tell me where the gas station is?," which formed one intonational phrase in the normal condition and was segmented into two (with a pause after *me*) in the other, although both had a tonic accent on *gas*, four subjects out of thirteen in the normal condition did not hear *gas station* at all whereas only two out of thirteen in the slow condition failed to do so. With another passage containing "there it is heated for pasteurization," which was read as a single phrase with the tonic on *pasteurization* in the normal condition while it was read as "there / it is heated / for pasteurization" in the slow condition, three subjects in the normal condition heard *pasteurization*, while six in the slow condition heard it.

To recapitulate, although the difference between the two speech conditions did not turn out to be significant by the measure of comprehension scores, it appeared to be so in the analysis of the subjects' self report data. The number of speech elements that subjects were able to attend to appeared to be affected by phonological phrasing, which determines the number and intensity of phonetically prominent elements.

PHASES OF AURAL PROCESSING

In previous sections we looked at the phonological characteristics of speech elements that were perceived by the subjects and also noted that speech elements formed a kind of scale in terms of accessibility. This section deals with the third research question of whether development patterns can be drawn from the observations of implicational relationships. The following implicational relationship among speech elements was identified from the phrase "It is put through a machine for canceling the stamps" by arranging elements heard by the least successful listeners through the most successful listeners.

machine	or	*stamps*
machine	and	*canceling stamps*
put through a machine	and	*canceling stamps*

As for the whole passage beyond the phrase level, "the mail goes through several steps (/) before it is delivered / the mail is collected (/) and taken to the post office / there (/) it is put through a machine (/) for canceling the stamps, speech elements perceived by the least to most successful listeners were ordered as follows: *mail, post office, machine, stamps* > *taken to the post office, put through a machine, canceling the stamps* > all five phrases. While the less successful listeners barely heard more than one word per phrase, the more successful ones heard more elements per phrase as well as more phrases.

Based on this possibility of inferring listening ability from the amount of speech elements that the learner can attend to, a scale of aural processing phases was devised. The scale is a modified version of one proposed by Ross (in press), which does not include consideration of the phonetic properties of speech input.[5] Five developmental phases in the reformulated scale are characterized as follows:

[5] Ross (in press) proposed eight aural processing stages based on how much of the input is correctly processed. The scale corresponds with a progression from smaller to larger phonological units, from syllables to lexical words to phrases. However, there is a big jump from Stage 7 to Stage 8.

Noise: Input is simply noise.

Phase 1 — Pre Key-Word Phase:
The listener cannot identify key words that bear phonetic prominence in speech, e.g., reporting *milk* or *meal* for *mail*.

Phase 2 — Key Words:
The listener identifies phonetically prominent words and forms associative relationship between them to understand, e.g., hearing *mail*, *machine* and *stamps*.

Phase 3 — Phrases:
The listener encodes not only key words but also less prominent surrounding elements that form a small grammatical unit such as a prepositional phrase or noun phrase, e.g., hearing *mail*, *(put) through a machine*, and *(canceling) stamps*.

Phase 4 — Clauses:
The listener encodes grammatical relationships between lexical words, identifying semantic relationships between arguments and predicate in a clause, e.g., hearing *the mail is collected, taken to the post office*, and *it is put through a machine...stamps*.

Phase 5 — Clause Plus:
The listener encodes not only almost all clauses in the input but also the relationships among them, e.g., hearing *the mail goes through several steps before it is delivered.*

Distraction: The listener's attention is diverted to other aspects of task than listening.
Syllable Restructuring: Association of a part of a key word to an unintended word.
Syllable Identification: Successful recognition of a monosyllabic key word.
Key Word Association: Identification of a single key word.
Linked Key Words: Hearing and linking more than one key words.
Phrases: Processing of grammatical items as well as lexical items.
Complete Images: Complete processing of the whole input.

The reason why the clause instead of the phonological or intonational phrase was chosen as a unit to determine the phonetic prominence is to accommodate the two different speech conditions set up for this experiment, in which the phonological phrase mapped into different grammatical units. The developmental scale thus defined does not claim that a given learner can be invariably assigned to one phase. Although we could hypothesize that other things being equal, a learner will probably function within a limited range of phases, the same learner will function at widely different phases as a result of different types of input which vary in content, genre, syntactic and lexical complexity, rate of speech and so on. Earlier in this paper, the observation was made that the prosodic characteristics of speech input affect the listener's perception. We might ask, then, whether manipulation of prosody as in the slow condition of this experiment influences the level of the learner's processing phases.

For a comparison of the two speech conditions in terms of their effects on processing stages, in other words, to see if slowing down and thereby enhancing the accessibility of speech element will boost up the learner's processing level, the subjects' retrospective report data were quantified by using the aural processing scale developed above. Points were assigned to each item: 1 point for Phase 1, 2 points for Phase 2, etc., and then the points for thirty items were added up for each subject. Although the scope of speech intake as defined in the scale was distinctly identifiable in most of the cases, a further criterion was needed for unclear cases. To be classified as belonging to a particular phase, more than two tokens of the phase within the item, if possible,[6] were required. However, there were harder cases. For example, some subjects reported hearing a full clause and a key word in a passage. This instance was assigned to Phase 3 on the assumption that the example is clearly beyond Phase 2 but does not demonstrate enough evidence for Phase 4. So, the scoring of the data based on the scale was sometimes inferential.

The results of this quantification of the retrospection data are shown below. As shown by the group means, the normal speech group operated at the level of Phase 3, while the slow speech group did very

6 More than half of the items contained more than two clauses in the passage.

slightly above Phase 3. This difference was not statistically significant, however (paired t-test: $t=1.54$, $p<.149$).

Table 2: Aural processing phases (k=5: mean per item)

	Condition	Mean	S.D.
Group 1 (n=13)	Slow speech	3.21	0.56
Group 2 (n=13)	Normal speech	3.04	0.40

The results seem to direct us to two different directions in interpretation. On the one hand, considering the small subject size, the group difference, although small and non-significant, still leaves room for the possibility that segmenting speech into smaller phrases pushes the learner to a higher aural processing level. To put it another way, by increasing the quantity and clarity of accessible speech elements, the listener might be encouraged to move from a more lexical mode, in which she relies on several key words for comprehension, to a more syntactic mode in which she encodes structural elements as well as more lexical elements in the speech. On the other hand, the results can be taken as non-existence of any effects of manipulating speech input on the listener's processing level. In other words, it is more a question of the learner's current ability than phonological characteristics of the input that determines the scope of speech elements she can attend to. Either interpretation, however, sounds too categorical, and in fact, many studies on input modification seem to point to the interaction between the learner system and input that triggers interlanguage development.

CONCLUSIONS

This study was an exploration into relationships between speech intake, specifically its phonetic characteristics, and developmental phases of aural processing. With more rigor and refinement in the research design and analyses, results about the effects of shorter phonological phrasing on upgrading of the level of aural processing could have been more clear. Also, given the fact that the validity of the proposed scale of phases of aural processing is in need of further testing, more questions have been raised than answered from this preliminary investigation. If there is a sequence of aural processing phases and if learner operate mostly at a certain phase of aural processing (other things being equal), how the transition from one phase to another occurs seems to be a pressing question, particularly in relation to the role of attention in language acquisition. If phonetically more accessible speech is conducive to a higher level of processing, will the induced upgraded level hold for processing fast speech in a due course of time? This refers us to the controversy over authentic versus modified materials in language learning. Which is more conducive to upgrading the learner's aural processing level, more exposure to more target-like fast speech with longer phrasing or listening to more careful, phonetically exaggerated speech with shorter phrasing? A pedagogical strategy of modulating careful and fast speeches needs to be developed and researched for its effect on the development of phonological knowledge.

Another question regarding the developmental sequence identified here is what makes one listener better than the other. In other words, what kind of phonological (or other types of) knowledge is involved in more successful listening? What enables the listener to encode not only more of prominent speech elements but also far less prominent structural elements? Syntactic knowledge may not be the only answer, considering that most subjects in this study had a good command of English syntax but still operated at low levels of aural processing. Is it simply a familiarity with instances of speech elements then? Or is it a higher level phonological knowledge such as knowledge of phonotactic and morphosyntactic rules that guide and facilitate lexical segmentation (Frazier, 1987)? These questions bring us back to the arena of debate over the place of rules in the knowledge of language and the role of drawing learners' attention to recurring linguistic patterns, a topic under heated debate (Schmidt 1993a, 1993b, 1994). More research into the development of phonological knowledge in the context of speech comprehension should make a valuable contribution to this debate.

ACKNOWLEDGEMENTS

An earlier version of this paper was written for a seminar at the University of Hawai'i. The study was started as part of a project at Center for Second Language Research, Social Science Research Institute, the University of Hawai'i, for which I was a research assistant. I thank Dr. Graham Crookes, the director at the time, for all his support and encouragement. Also, I'd like to thank Dr. Kyong-Jing Seok and Dr. Sang-Jun Jung at Seoul National University, Korea, for helping me with data collection, Dr. Eric Kellerman and Dr. Steve Ross for advice on research design and finally Dr. Craig Chaudron and Dr. Richard Schmidt for comments on an earlier draft. However, all the drawbacks are my responsibility.

REFERENCES

Avery, P., Ehrlich, S., & Yorio, C. (1985). Prosodic domains in foreigner talk discourse. In S. Gass, & C. Madden (Eds.), *Input in second language acquisition* (pp. 214–229). Newbury House: Rowley, Mass.

Brown, G., Currie, K. L., & Kenworthy, J. (1980). *Questions of intonation*. Baltimore: University Park Press.

Call, M. E. (1985). Auditory short-term memory, listening comprehension, and the input hypothesis. *TESOL Quarterly*, *19*, 765– 781.

Chaudron, C. (1988). *Second language classrooms: Research on teaching and learning*. New York: Cambridge University Press.

Chaudron, C. (In Press). Academic listening. In D. Mendelsohn, & J. Rubin (Eds.), *A Guide for teaching second language listening*. San Diego: Dominine Press.

Conrad, L. (1989). The effect of time-compressed speech on native and EFL listening comprehension. *Studies in Second Language Acquisition*, *11*, 1–16.

Cutler, A., & Swinney, G. (1987). Prosody and the development of comprehension. *Journal of Child Language*, *14*, 145–167.

Derwing, T. M. (1990). Speech rate is no simple matter. *Studies in Second Language Acquisition*, *12*, 303–313.

Ellis, R. (1994). *The study of second language acquisition*. Oxford: Oxford University Press.

Ericsson, K. A., & Simon, H. A. (1980). Verbal reports as data. *Psychological Review*, *87*, 215–251.

Frazier, L. (1987). Structure in auditory word recognition. *Cognition*, *25*, 157–187.

Gow, D. W., & Gordon, P. C. (1993). Coming to terms with stress: Effects of stress location in sentence processing. *Journal of Psycholinguistic Research*, *22*, 545–578.

Griffiths, R. (1990). Speech rate and NNS comprehension: A preliminary study in time-benefit analysis. *Language Learning*, *40*, 311–36.

Henrichsen, L. E. (1984). Sandhi-variation: A filter of input for learners of ESL. *Language Learning, 34*, 103–126.

Hulstijn, J. H., & de Graaff, R. (1994). Under what conditions does explicit knowledge of a second language facilitate the acquisition of implicit knowledge? A research proposal. *AILA Review, 11*, 97–112.

Jusczyk, P. W. (1993). From general to language-specific capacities: The WRAPSA model of how speech perception develops. *Journal of Phonetics, 21*, 3–28.

Larsen-Freeman, D. & Long, M. H. (1991). *An introduction to second language acquisition.* London: Longman.

O'Malley, J. M., Chamot, A. U., & Kupper, L. (1989). Listening comprehension strategies in second language acquisition. *Applied Linguistics, 10*, 418–437.

Ross, S. (In press). A retrospective approach to understanding inference in a second language listening task. In G. Kasper & E. Kellerman (Eds.), *Advances in communication strategy research.* Harlow, Essex: Longman.

Schmidt, R. (1993a). Awareness and second language acquisition. *Annual Review of Applied Linguistics, 13*, 206–226.

Schmidt, R. (1993b). Consciousness, learning and interlanguage pragmatics. In G. Kasper & S. Blum-Kulka (Eds.), *Interlanguage pragmatics* (pp. 21–42). New York: Oxford University Press.

Schmidt, R. (1994). Deconstructing consciousness in search of useful definitions for applied linguistics. *AILA Review, 11*, 11–26.

Schmidt, R., & Frota, S. (1986). Developing basic conversational ability in a second language: a case study of an adult learner of Portuguese. In R. Day (Ed.), *Talking to learn: Conversation in second language acquisition* (pp. 237–326). Rowley, Mass. : Newbury House.

Sharwood Smith, M. (1993). Input enhancement in instructed SLA: Theoretical bases. *Studies in Second Language Acquisition, 15*, 165–179.

Slowiaczek, L. M. (1993). Effect of lexical stress in auditory word recognition. *Language and Speech, 33*, 47–68.

Tench, P. (1990). *The roles of intonation in English discourse.* Frankfurt am Main: Peter Lang.

Vandergritt, L. (1995). Constructing meaning in L2 listening: Evidence from protocols. Paper presented at the American Association for Applied Linguistics, Long Beach, CA.

Diane Huot
Université Laval, Québec, Canada

OBSERVER L'ATTENTION: QUELQUES RÉSULTATS D'UNE ÉTUDE DE CAS

(OBSERVING ATTENTION: RESULTS OF A CASE STUDY)

ABSTRACT

This article presents results obtained from the first phase of a case study of a young francophone girl in a L2 language acquisition situation. Focused mainly on the metalinguistic reflection of a child acquiring an L2 and on the relationship between the child's observations and her actual L2 performance, the study is based on data from various sources, including a diary and weekly recordings of the child's oral production. The results presented here cover a four-month stay in Honolulu during which the girl attended public school and was looked after by a daycare service set up at the school after school hours. They are derived essentially from the diary kept by the mother, who systematically and daily recorded the child's spontaneous observations. The data are handled with a view to providing answers to the following questions: What does the child do when presented with new input, and what is she curious about? An analysis of the child's observations shows that the attention given to input involves a number of processes: 1) reporting what was observed; 2) making comparisons; 3) translation; 4) making rules, and 5) analysis. Although the child's attention is focused first and foremost on the meaning of the input, it turns to form whenever form interferes with meaning. This attention to form is particularly obvious when it comes to ruling making.

Ce texte présente une partie des résultats de la première phase d'une étude de cas menée auprès d'une fillette, unilingue francophone placée en situation d'acquisition de l'anglais L2. Axée principalement sur la réflexion métalinguistique de l'enfant qui acquiert une L2, et sur la relation entre les observations de l'enfant et ses réalisations effectives en L2, cette étude s'appuie sur des données issues de sources diverses dont un journal de bord et des enregistrements hebdomadaires des productions de l'enfant. Les résultats présentés ici correspondent à un séjour de 4 mois dans la ville de Honolulu où la fillette a évolué dans son nouveau milieu de vie en

Huot, Diane (1995). Observer l'attention: Quelques résultats d'une étude de cas [Observing attention: Results of a case study]. In Richard Schmidt (Ed.), *Attention and awareness in foreign language learning* (Technical Report #9) (pp. 85–126). Honolulu, Hawai'i: University of Hawai'i, Second Language Teaching & Curriculum Center.

fréquentant l'école publique et en ayant accès, après les heures de classe, au service de garderie mis sur pied sur les lieux de l'école. Ils proviennent essentiellement du journal de bord tenu par la mère qui a noté systématiquement et quotidiennement toutes les observations spontanées de l'enfant. Le corpus est traité en vue d'apporter des réponses aux questions suivantes: que fait l'enfant en présence du nouvel input? et qu'est-ce qui attire son attention? L'analyse des observations de l'enfant montre que l'attention portée à l'input comporte plusieurs opérations, dont celle 1) de rendre compte de ce qui a été observé, 2) d'effectuer des comparaisons, 3) de traduire, 4) de formuler des règles et 5) d'analyser. Bien que l'attention de l'enfant soit en priorité orientée vers l'aspect sémantique de l'input, elle est dirigée vers l'aspect formel dès que la forme nuit à la compréhension du sens. Cette attention portée à la forme est particulièrement évidente dans le cas de l'opération de formulation de règles.

INTRODUCTION

L'objet de ce texte est de présenter une partie des données d'une étude de cas menée auprès d'une fillette, unilingue francophone, placée en situation d'acquisition de l'anglais L2. L'ensemble de cette étude porte sur la mise en relation de la réflexion métalinguistique de l'enfant avec ses réalisations linguistiques effectives, afin reprendre dans un autre contexte l'étude de Schmidt and Frota (1986), et d'examiner l'hypothèse selon laquelle ce qui est appris aurait été au préalable observé par l'apprenant (Schmidt 1990, 1993a, 1993b).

Cette première partie des données correspond à un séjour de 4 mois dans la ville de Honolulu où la fillette a évolué dans son nouveau milieu de vie en fréquentant l'école publique et en ayant accès, après les heures de classe, au service de garderie mis sur pied sur les lieux de l'école. Bien que le corpus recueilli comporte une multitude de renseignements d'ordre linguistique et cognitif, nous nous limitons ici à ceux qui concernent des aspects liés à la question de l'attention et de la conscience dans l'acquisition de L2. L'examen des propos de l'enfant permet ainsi de voir ce qu'elle fait au moment où elle est placée en présence de la nouvelle L2 et de voir également ce qui attire son attention.

CONTEXTE DE L'ÉTUDE

Arrivée dans la ville de Honolulu avec sa mère en janvier 1994, l'enfant, Cyrie (désormais C.), n'avait guère été en contact avec l'anglais depuis sa naissance, survenue le 4 septembre 1986. Issue d'une famille francophone de la ville de Québec (ville à 99% francophone), elle était la cadette de trois filles. Elle fréquentait une école francophone, où elle n'avait pas encore entrepris, en 2e année du primaire, l'étude de l'anglais langue seconde. Avant son arrivée dans la ville d'accueil, elle n'avait été exposée qu'à sa langue maternelle, car le français constituait la langue de communication de la famille, celle du jeu dans la rue et dans la cour de l'école, et celle de ses émissions de télévision préférées. A l'exception de quelques visiteurs anglophones, qui avaient pu à l'occasion rendre visite à ses parents, elle n'avait à peu près pas entendu d'anglais avant son départ de Québec. Ses parents étant impliqués dans l'enseignement du français L2, elle avait cependant entendu, à quelques reprises, des accents d'étudiants non francophones en français. Le métier de ses parents et l'attitude favorable de ces derniers à l'égard des L2 avaient sans doute projeté à l'enfant une image positive de l'apprentissage des langues, mais la fillette n'avait pas encore manifesté un intérêt quelconque pour les L2.

PRÉSENTATION DE L'ENFANT

On peut présenter C. en disant que ses traits de personnalité dominants sont la gentillesse, la douceur et la facilité de contact avec autrui. Elle est d'une grande curiosité et s'intéresse à tout. Elle a également un grand sens de l'observation, est extrovertie, verbalise ses expériences et pose des questions à propos de tout. L'extrait suivant témoigne de son sens de l'observation que la fatigue ne semble pas arrêter:

Journal de bord, jour 1, entrée 1

> Après un voyage d'une quinzaine d'heures, nous arrivons fatiguées à l'aéroport de Honolulu où nous sommes accueillies par un collègue. A peine sortie de l'aérogare, C. observe immédiatement que des lanières de métal sont placées autour du tronc de chaque palmier. Elles veut savoir pourquoi on place de telles choses si haut dans les palmiers et supplie sa mère, qui n'avait rien remarqué de tout cela, de s'enquérir auprès de notre hôte.

Ayant eu le choix de rester à Québec avec son père ou d'accompagner sa mère à Honolulu, elle avait choisi d'aller avec sa mère parce qu'elle voulait, disait-elle, *rester avec maman*. Au moment de son départ, elle ignorait qu'elle serait exposée à une L2 car, a-t-elle indiqué ultérieurement, elle ne savait pas que l'on parlait anglais à Hawai'i et elle n'avait aucune idée de ce qu'était l'anglais. Pour elle, tout était français et sa représentation du monde l'était également.

Par ailleurs, elle avait déjà atteint une bonne maîtrise de sa L1. Elle s'exprimait correctement et avec nuances. Au plan scolaire, elle se situait dans la moyenne, car le fait d'avoir des amis et de bonnes relations avec eux lui semblait plus important que celui d'obtenir de bons résultats dans son bulletin scolaire.

Ayant subi le test *CEFT (The children's embedded figures test)* (Witkin et al., 1971) portant sur les styles cognitifs, elle a obtenu un score de 20 sur 25. On peut ainsi la qualifier d'indépendante du champ.

SES CONNAISSANCES ANTÉRIEURES DE L'ANGLAIS

Avant son départ de Québec, sa connaissance de l'anglais était nulle. Elle pouvait cependant dire *yes* et *no*, et compter en anglais de 1 jusqu'à 10. D'ailleurs, comme elle ne pouvait se représenter ce qu'était un milieu d'accueil qui ne parlait pas sa L1, ses premiers jours d'école ont été difficiles. Au plan linguistique, C. entrait en fait dans un monde qui pour elle était dépourvu de signification. Elle y remarquait bien des oiseaux qu'elle n'avait jamais vus, des arbres ou des fleurs dont elle ignorait le nom. Mais à chaque fois, elle communiquait dans sa L1 pour s'enquérir de leur nom auprès de sa mère qui lui répondait également en L1.

C'est au moment où elle a été placée dans la situation d'aller à l'école avec des enfants non francophones, qu'elle se rendit compte de la distance qui la séparait de ces derniers. Sa mère n'allait plus faire le lien entre elle et ce nouveau milieu. Pour la première fois, elle pleura. Elle avait peur, car elle ignorait si elle allait pouvoir mettre à profit ses connaissances antérieures pour interpréter les situations nouvelles qu'elle s'apprêtait à vivre. D'où son insécurité et son refus d'entrer dans ce monde.

Journal de bord, jour 2, entrée 1

> Le jour qui suit notre arrivée, nous nous rendons à l'école primaire du quartier, afin d'y inscrire C. Nous faisons une visite des lieux et parlons avec quelques enfants. La direction nous indique alors que C. commencera l'école, le lundi suivant. C'est à ce moment-là qu'elle se rend compte qu'elle devra évoluer dans un milieu dont elle ne connaît pas la langue. Elle se met à pleurer et me dit qu'elle ne veut pas aller à l'école: *C'est trop difficile*, dit-elle. *Pourquoi je dois apprendre l'anglais? Ils ne doivent pas apprendre le français eux?*

Journal de bord, jour 6, entrée 1

> Aujourd'hui, premier jour de classe, C. pleure et ne veut pas aller à l'école. La mère l'y accompagne, reviendra à midi pour manger avec elle à la cafétéria de l'école et la reprendra à 14h10.

A son arrivée à la porte de la classe, tous les enfants du groupe l'entourent et veulent savoir pourquoi elle pleure. La mère leur explique que C. ne comprend pas l'anglais et ne le parle pas non plus. Ces enfants, étonnés, ne peuvent concevoir que C. ne comprend rien. Un petit garçon du groupe s'approche d'elle et lui dit tout doucement:

it's easy
you say:
I   am
it means I am[1]

Mais cette explication ne semble pas convaincre C., qui n'a rien compris et qui, les larmes aux yeux, doit se séparer de sa mère et entrer dans la classe. Le premier jour de classe passé, il sera encore difficile de conduire C. à l'école pendant encore quelques jours.

EXPOSITION À LA L2

Pendant son séjour à Honolulu, l'enfant a fréquenté une classe de deuxième année dans une école unilingue anglophone, où elle recevait chaque matin 100 minutes d'anglais L2. Une journée normale d'école commençait à 8h00 et se terminait à 14h10, après quoi

1 Les espaces entre les mots correspondent à des silences entre chaque occurrence.

l'enfant demeurait sur les lieux de l'école où elle jouait avec ses petits camarades jusqu'à 17h30, dans le cadre du service d'après-classe.

D'autre part, elle regardait régulièrement la télévision en anglais, pendant au moins une ou deux heures chaque jour en semaine, et pendant quatre heures les samedis et les dimanches. En dépit des opinions négatives que peut susciter l'écoute de la télévision par un enfant, la mère, francophone, avait estimé que dans ce cas particulier un abonnement au *Disney Channel* constituait l'un des seuls moyens de prolonger le temps d'exposition à la L2, après les heures de classe et pendant les fins de semaine. Dans l'ensemble, l'enfant a ainsi été exposée à l'anglais pendant 15 semaines à raison d'une soixantaine d'heures par semaine, ce qui constitue 900 heures d'exposition à la L2 (60 h./sem x 15 sem= 900 heures). Le français est toutefois demeuré la langue de communication de la famille pendant toute la durée du séjour.

A la fin de son séjour, C. était capable d'interagir dans une conversation en L2 en face à face ou au téléphone. Elle semblait pouvoir évoluer aisément en L2 et, dans l'interaction, avait l'air bilingue. L'essentiel des renseignements est résumé au Tableau 1.

Tableau 1: Résumé des renseignements à propos de C.

Langue 1	français
Pays d'origine	Canada (Québec)
Âge	7 ans
Rang dans la famille	cadette d'une famille de 3 filles
Année scolaire	2e année du primaire
Motivation	non mesurée; semblait bonne
Connaissances antérieures de l'anglais	aucune
Connaissances d'une autre L2	aucune
Style cognitif (CEFT)	indépendant du champ
Nombre de jours d'exposition à la L2	107 jours
Cours ESL offerts par l'école	1h40 par jour
Total des heures d'exposition à la L2 dans la première tranche de l'étude	900 heures

CONDITIONS DE CUEILLETTE DES DONNÉES

Cette étude a été réalisée dans des conditions relativement uniques, dans le sens où la mère a vécu avec l'enfant pendant toute la durée du séjour et a été sa seule interlocutrice francophone. Une telle situation nous donne ainsi l'assurance que les observations spontanées de l'enfant sur la L2 n'ont pas pu lui être induites par un autre locuteur francophone.

A l'exception du temps passé à l'école et à l'après-classe, à l'exception également de deux ou trois heures où la fillette a pu être seule avec son père, venu rendre visite à la famille pendant une dizaine de jours, la mère a vécu constamment en présence de l'enfant pendant toute cette période. Il y a eu à certains moments un témoin, la soeur de douze ans de C., qui est venue passer 41 jours à Honolulu et qui est ensuite rentrée à Québec en compagnie du père. Mais sa présence n'a pas affecté le déroulement de l'observation, puisqu'elle aussi a fréquenté l'école et que, en dehors des heures de classe, la mère a été constamment présente pour recueillir les propos de C.

A titre d'observatrice, la mère a ainsi eu l'occasion d'entendre toutes les réflexions formulées spontanément par C., réflexions qu'elle a notées minutieusement et systématiquement, au fur et à mesure de leur avènement. Celles-ci étaient notées sur une feuille de papier immédiatement après avoir été entendues, et étaient entrées sur fichier informatique à la fin de chaque journée, lorsque la fillette dormait. La mère a ainsi été constamment à l'écoute de l'enfant, tous les jours, du lever jusqu'au coucher, et partout, dans l'auto, au restaurant, en marchant dans la rue, ou à la plage.

Ce mode d'observation a constitué en quelque sorte un mode vie. Il a du reste été rendu possible en raison des circonstances exceptionnelles qui ont étaient réunies: volubilité de l'enfant, disponibilité de la mère, éloignement de Québec, et exiguïté du lieu de vie à Honolulu. La fillette était, en effet, d'un naturel volubile; la distance qui sépare Honolulu de Québec avait entraîné une séparation d'avec la famille et les amis, une diminution des obligations quotidiennes, une faible fréquence des appels téléphoniques, d'où la grande disponibilité de l'observatrice et de son sujet. Et par ailleurs, celles-ci vivaient à Honolulu dans un appartement d'une pièce, ce qui signifiait que l'observatrice a constamment vécu en présence du sujet observé. Une telle promiscuité, bien que parfois difficile, a cependant permis une observation rigoureuse et constante de l'enfant et a constitué un moyen de s'assurer que les réflexions menées par l'enfant étaient bel et bien les siennes. Elle a permis également de suivre l'évolution de ces réflexions et de mieux percevoir les liens qui les unissaient.

Tout le temps passé avec l'enfant était consacré à la cueillette des données. Il n'y eut aucun répit dans la prise de notes. Si une observation était formulée dans l'auto pendant que la mère était au volant, cette dernière profitait d'un arrêt au feu rouge pour noter ce qu'elle venait d'entendre. L'observation suivante a été notée dans un restaurant japonais, sur l'emballage de papier qui recouvre les baguettes:

Journal de bord, jour 107

> Ce soir, comme nous arrivons à la fin du séjour et que le frigo est presque vide, nous allons manger au Sushi Bar près de chez nous. L'hôtesse nous place à une table qui est séparée de la table voisine par une petite cloison qui nous arrive à l'épaule. On peut donc voir et entendre les gens qui sont à cette table. Ils viennent d'arriver et lisent la carte pour faire leur choix. Tout à coup, C., qui entend tout et qui, l'air de rien, les écoute parler, me demande après avoir entendu l'un d'entre eux utiliser l'expression *let's go*: *let's go* ça veut dire *lâche* hein maman? (*lâche* dans le sens de *laisse-moi*).

La prise de note a été faite le plus discrètement possible. S'il arrivait que l'enfant demande à la mère pourquoi elle écrivait, cette dernière lui répondait qu'elle avait pensé à quelque chose pour ses cours et qu'elle voulait le noter immédiatement afin de ne pas l'oublier. S'il arrivait que la fillette voit que la mère prenait des notes à son sujet, la mère lui répondait qu'elle avait besoin de savoir comment sa fille procédait pour apprendre l'anglais, pour ensuite le dire à ses étudiants qui apprenaient une L2. La fillette acceptera cette justification et ne demandera plus rien à propos de la prise de notes.

MÉTHODE

CONSTITUTION DU CORPUS

Cette cueillette de données a donné lieu à un énorme corpus dont l'essentiel est présenté au Tableau 2. Il est constitué de cinq composantes correspondant à cinq sources d'information distinctes à savoir, 1) un journal de bord, 2) des enregistrement hebdomadaires de conversations, 3) des enregistrements au sujet des cours d'anglais (ESL), 4) des documents divers, et 5) des séances de rétrospection. Chacune des entrées de chaque source a été classée selon un ordre chronologique. Les analyses présentées dans cet article ne portent toutefois que sur les données consignées dans le journal de bord.

Journal de bord. Le journal de bord contient les observations du chercheur, la mère, et celles du sujet, la fillette. Les observations de la mère correspondent aux notes prises par cette dernière à propos de tout élément relatif à l'acquisition de L2 par C. Les observations de l'enfant correspondent aux propos spontanés de C. sur la L2 notés systématiquement par la mère. Ces observations spontanées sont parfois suivies d'observations dites ici "suscitées," dans le sens où une observation initiée par l'enfant donnait ensuite lieu à une question de la part de la mère. Chaque entrée dans le journal correspond soit à une remarque de la mère, soit à une observation de la fillette. Une intervention de C. est précédée et suivie d'un silence et porte sur un thème donné. Elle prend la forme d'une question, d'une assertion ou d'une exclamation. Toutes les interventions de C. ont été numérotées.

Enregistrements hebdomadaires de conversations. Un deuxième mode de cueillette des données a consisté en l'enregistrement hebdomadaire de l'enfant interagissant avec un autre enfant anglophone. Ces séances d'enregistrement d'une durée minimale de 60 minutes, ont permis d'observer au cours des semaines l'évolution de la compréhension et de l'expression de C. en anglais et d'étudier la correspondance entre les propos de l'enfant sur la L2 et les réalisations linguistiques effectives.

Cours d'anglais (ESL). Parallèlement à cette prise de notes quotidienne à propos des réflexions, observations et questions de l'enfant, un autre moyen de recueillir des données a été ce que l'on a dénommé ici ponctuellement *les cours d'anglais. (ESL)*. Si au début du séjour la prise de note était relativement facile en raison du petit nombre d'éléments que C. disait avoir appris, le recours à l'enregistrement s'est avéré nécessaire après un mois de séjour. Ainsi, à chaque soir, la mère procédait à une petite séance d'enregistrement à l'aide d'un magnétophone incorporé à la radio placée en permanence sur le comptoir de la cuisine. Elle demandait alors à l'enfant de parler de ce qu'elle avait appris au cours d'anglais, et de ce qu'elle avait appris de manière générale pendant sa journée. Des questions comme *Qu'est-ce que vous avez fait aujourd'hui au cours d'anglais*, ou *As-tu eu de la difficulté à te faire comprendre pas* Miss A. *aujourd'hui?* servaient généralement d'amorce à l'échange.

Documents divers. Un quatrième mode de cueillette des données regroupe tous les documents et bricolages produits par C. à l'école ou en dehors de l'école. Ces réalisations de l'enfant sont prise en compte dans la mesure où elles permettent d'observer l'emploi de certains éléments de la L2 par C.

Rétrospection. A la suite de la transcription et de l'analyse des enregistrements, une étape de mise en parallèle des données a consisté à voir si ce qui avait été produit dans les enregistrements figurait au préalable dans le journal de bord. A cette étape, nous avons tenu de courtes séances avec l'enfant pour les cas où des précisions complémentaires s'avéraient nécessaires. A ces occasions, nous avons été parfois étonnée de la mémoire de C. qui, pour un élément donné, avait gardé le souvenir du lieu et des circonstances d'apprentissage.

ANALYSE DU CORPUS

L'analyse du corpus correspond à l'analyse de chacune des composantes figurant au Tableau 2, à l'établissement de catégories, à la classification chronologique des catégories et à la mise en commun de tous les renseignements recueillis. Seules les données qui permettent de répondre à nos questions initiales sont prises en compte

Tableau 2: Cueillette des données (1e partie de l'étude)

Sources	Types de données	Fréquence de cueillette	Longueur
Journal de bord	spontanées[1]	quotidienne	107 jours 253 entrées
Enregistrement sur bandes magnétiques	spontanées	hebdomadaire	1 h./sem.
Cours d'anglais ESL	suscitées	quotidienne	5 minutes environ
Documents divers (bricolage, dessins)	spontanées	hebdomadaire	50 pages environ
Rétrospection	suscitées	occasionnelle	15 minutes par séance

[1] Parfois dites "suscitées"en réponse à une question initiée par C.

N.B: Les résultats présentés dans cet article proviennent de l'analyse des données obtenues au moyen de la source 1

dans le cadre de cet article. Elles proviennent principalement du journal de bord.

Les données du journal de bord sont nombreuses et variées et leur classement aurait pu être effectué de plusieurs façons. Ayant opté pour un classement relativement lâche au début, nous avons par la suite opéré des regroupements des propos de la fillette et, par ce biais, avons défini des catégories. Celles-ci s'articulent autour de 2 pôles, à savoir 1) ce que fait l'enfant face à la nouvelle information que constitue la L2, et face à certains éléments du milieu, et 2) ce sur quoi porte son attention.

QUE FAIT L'ENFANT? QU'EST-CE QUI ATTIRE SON ATTENTION?

Après avoir franchi l'étape des larmes et accepté la nécessité de se mettre à la tâche de l'acquisition de la L2, que fera la fillette? Comment s'y prendra-t-elle pour apprendre la L2? Bien qu'elle ne puisse de toute évidence répondre directement à ces questions, elle fournit toutefois des réponses indirectes, à travers ses propos notés dans le journal de bord et à travers quelques-unes de ses interventions faites lors des enregistrements.

Si nous avons dès le premier jour été frappée par son sens de l'observation, parce qu'à son arrivée elle remarque une composante du paysage qui n'avait pas attiré l'attention de la mère, il en sera toujours de même pendant toute la durée du séjour. Tout se passe comme si elle percevait, voyait ou captait des choses qui échappent à l'adulte. Ce sens de l'observation semble également jouer un rôle important dans la perception des éléments langagiers de la nouvelle langue à laquelle est exposée la fillette. Ceci nous conduit ainsi à nous interroger sur ce que l'enfant observe lorsqu'elle est placée en situation d'acquisition de la L2.

Les données recueillies montrent que C. a observé, remarqué ou noté de nombreux éléments. Mais, à l'exception de quelques cas où, en répondant à sa mère qui s'informe de sa journée, elle *rend compte* explicitement du fait qu'elle a appris un élément donné, ce n'est qu'indirectement qu'il est possible d'établir qu'un mot ou une phrase a retenu son attention ou suscité sa curiosité. Le fait d'avoir observé un élément de la L2 ne peut être en conséquence qu'étudié indirectement, à travers ses propos, qui traduisent une opération qu'elle réalise. Ainsi, on suppose que C. a observé un élément linguistique donné parce qu'elle le rapporte dans ses propos ou parce qu'elle accomplit, à propos de cet élément, une opération dont elle fait part, comme par exemple *effectuer des comparaisons entre deux éléments* ou *énoncer une règle*. Nous nous représentons ainsi sa démarche (illustrée à la Figure 1) en plusieurs points, entre lesquels il y aurait des relais.

Figure 1: Démarche d'observation de C.

ACCESSIBLE INDIRECTEMENT	ACCESSIBLE DIRECTEMENT	
Observe→	accomplit une opération→	à propos d'un élément ling. donné
Observe	en rendant compte	(substantif, formule, prononciation, etc.)
Observe	en comparant	(substantif, formule, prononciation, etc.)
Observe	en traduisant	(substantif, formule, prononciation, etc.)
Observe	en formulant des règles	(substantif, formule, prononciation, etc.)
Observe	en analysant	(substantif, formule, prononciation, etc.)

Le fait que la fillette ait observé un élément donné semble accessible indirectement à l'observateur externe, tandis que le fait qu'elle accomplisse une opération à propos d'un élément linguistique donné est directement accessible à ce même observateur. On peut voir que cinq opérations ont été identifiées. Elles représentent la manière selon laquelle C. aborde les éléments qui retiennent son attention et comment elle traite le nouvel input. Les observations formulées par C. ont ainsi été regroupées en catégorie de traitement, à savoir C. manifeste qu'elle observe un élément donné en 1) rendant compte de ce qu'elle a appris, 2) en effectuant des comparaisons entre deux éléments, 3) en traduisant, 4) en énonçant une règle, et 5) en analysant des éléments. Chaque opération porte sur un ou plusieurs éléments linguistiques.

C. REND COMPTE DE CE QU'ELLE A APPRIS

Régulièrement, en rentrant à pied de l'école, la fillette relatera sa journée à sa mère. Cette dernière profitera alors de l'occasion pour s'enquérir de ses progrès en L2. A la question *qu'est-ce que tu as appris aujourd'hui? ou qu'est-ce que vous avez fait aujourd'hui* la fillette répondra généralement très peu de choses, en donnant le nom d'une activité et en énumérant trois ou quatre mots de la L2 qu'elle a appris.

Journal de bord, jour 7, entrée 1

En revenant de l'école à pied, la mère et l'enfant parlent de choses et d'autres. La mère désire savoir comment est allée cette deuxième journée d'école. Elle lui demande notamment:

M.: qu'est-ce que tu as appris au cours d'anglais aujourd'hui?
C.: mouton
M.: comment on dit ça en anglais mouton?
C.: Je sais pas.

Journal de bord, jour 11, entrée 3

En revenant de l'école à pied, C. dit à sa mère:

C.: Maman, aujourd'hui, j'ai appris un mot qui veut dire *dehors*, je sais pas trop, mais quelque chose comme ça
M.: *outside?*
C.: non, quelque chose comme *recréation*
M.: *break?*
C.: non
M.: je sais pas ce que c'est *récréation* en anglais

Bien que les réponses obtenues à ce chapitre soient relativement peu nombreuses et qu'il faudrait, pour une vue d'ensemble, avoir analysé les données issues de la source 3 (*cours d'anglais ESL*), il est intéressant de signaler l'évolution de leur avènement. On constate en effet que C. rend compte de ce qu'elle appris en évoquant un élément linguistique donné de diverses façons, à savoir:

en L1 sans pouvoir traduire l'élément en L2 (dès le j. 7)
en L1 en pouvant traduire en L2 (dès le j. 43)
en L2 sans pouvoir traduire en L1 (dès le j. 29)
en L2 en pouvant traduire en L1 (dès le j. 34)
en L1/l2 en recourant aux deux langues dans une même phrase (dès le j. 107)

Elle rend compte de ce qu'elle a appris d'abord en L1. Elle pourra traduire vers la L2 à partir du jour 43, à l'exception des couleurs dont elle rend compte en français et qu'elle peut, dès le jour 16, traduire en L2. On observe une évolution dans le temps, à savoir que la traduction survient à la fin du premier mois du séjour. On remarque également que la curiosité de la fillette porte principalement sur des substantifs et des adjectifs de couleur, éléments dont elle traite essentiellement l'aspect sémantique, car elle ne s'intéresse qu'à leur sens.

C. EFFECTUE DES COMPARAISONS

A travers les réflexions que livre C. à propos de la nouvelle L2, on constate qu'elle effectue des comparaisons entre deux ou plusieurs éléments pour lesquels elle observe des ressemblances ou des différences. Elle compare tantôt un élément de L1 avec un élément de L2 (*comparaison L1/L2 ou intersystème*), et tantôt deux éléments de L2 entre eux (*comparaison L2/L2 ou intrasystème*).

COMPARAISON INTERSYSTÈME

La *comparaison L1/L2* occupe une place importante au début de son expérience d'apprentissage. Lors des premiers jours, son attention est attirée notamment par des *homophones L1/L2*, c'est-à-dire des éléments en L2 dont la prononciation est voisine de celle d'un élément de L1. Par exemple, les mots anglais *she* [ʃi] et *we* [wi] ont des correspondants en français au plan de la prononciation, *chie* [ʃi] et *oui* [wi] qui la font bien rire.

Journal de bord, jour 9, entrée 2

En revenant de l'école C. demande à sa mère, avec un petit sourire malin:

C.: Maman ça veut dire quoi *she*?
M.: *elle*
tu as: *I, you, he/she, we, you, they*
C.: ah! c'est drôle
chie pi *oui*!

Elle effectue aussi des liens entre la prononciation de deux mots, au moment où elle identifie des similitudes entre la prononciation du mot *coeur* français et celle de son correspondant anglais *heart*.

Journal de bord, jour 38, entrée 3

Le matin, dans l'auto, alors que nous nous rendons à l'école. Personne ne parle. C. dit tout à coup::

C.: Maman, en anglais on prononce pas le *c* hein?
M.: qu'est-ce que tu veux dire par ça?
C.: mais oui (impatiente)
coeur [kœR] ça fait *oeur* [3ɹ]

(Pour elle la prononciation de *coeur* s'apparentait à celle de *heart* avec la différence qu'elle n'avait pas entendu le *h aspiré* [h] de l'anglais et le *t* en final [t].)

Toujours au plan de la comparaison de L1 et de L2, elle remarque également, dès les premiers jours, qu'une différence syntaxique existe entre sa L1 et la L2, relativement à la place de l'adjectif. L'organisation syntaxique de L2 ne correspond pas sur ce plan à ses attentes qui elles dépendent de sa L1.

Journal de bord, jour 9, entrée 3

Ce soir, pour devoir, elle doit composer des phrases en français, les faire traduire par sa mère et copier cette traduction dans son cahier de *homework*. Son texte français se lit comme suit: *Mon jouet préféré est mon ourson en peluche brun. Je l'aime beaucoup. Il a le nez couleur de chocolat. Et il est très dou [sic].*

Ce texte a été traduit en anglais de la manière suivante: *My favorite toy is my brown teddy bear. I like him very much. He has a brown nose, brown as chocolate. He is very soft.*

En copiant ce texte, elle se met à pleurer et proteste en disant à sa mère sur un ton fâché:

C.: ben non! j'ai pas dit *mon favori jouet*, j'ai dit *mon jouet favori*.

(Elle refusera de copier cette traduction si elle doit maintenir une telle organisation syntaxique.)

Cette nouvelle organisation syntaxique de L2 représente à ses yeux une modification importante du sens, laquelle ne correspond pas tout à fait à son intention de communication, à ses attentes et à ses connaissances antérieures.

Son attention se portera aussi sur des congénères interlinguaux, notamment sur les *homographes L1-L2* comme *six/six* (j. 62), sur des *parographes* comme *caractère* (j. 30) ou *ingredient/ingrédient* (j. 88), sur des *faux amis*, comme *office/office* (j. 100) pour lesquels elle formule respectivement des observations. Les *homographes* désignent des mots qui ont un signifiant sonore différent et un signifiant graphique identique en anglais et en français et qui partagent au moins une signification. On appelle *parographe*, les mots qui s'apparentent par le signifiant graphique et qui demeurent reconnaissables à la lecture. (Tréville 1993, 38). Les *faux amis* sont les *mots anglais et français qui sont de même origine et dont on pourrait penser qu'ils veulent dire la même chose, alors qu'en fait leurs significations ne coïncident qu'en partie ou pas du tout* (Darbelnet 1969, 227).

Journal de bord, jour 29, entrée 3

Encore ce soir, elle doit composer des phrases en français, les faire traduire par sa mère et copier cette traduction dans son cahier de *homework*. Son texte français se lit comme suit: *Mon émission préférée s'appelle "l'île aux Blizars". C'est une émission d'aventure. C'est deux enfants qui cherchent un géant. Les autres personnages sont des marionnettes. Il y a le serpent, la libellule des sables, la sorcière et le chat.* La traduction anglaise est: *My favorite TV show is "l'île aux Blizars". It's an adventure show about two children who are looking for a giant. The other characters are puppets such as a snake, a dragon-fly, a witch and a cat.* Elle demande à sa mère:

C.: pourquoi tu mets le mot *caracter*? Il n'y en a pas? j'ai pas mis de mot qui était *caractère* là-dedans.

M.: c'est pour remplacer *personnage*

C.: mais *personnage*, c'est pas *caractère*. *caractère*, ça remplace pas *marionnette*, parce que *marionnette*, c'est *puppet*.

M.: j'ai dit *personnage*, minou.

C.: ah! bon.

Cette attention portée aux *congénères interlinguaux* l'amène même, vers la fin de son séjour, à s'interroger sur sa propre L1.

Journal de bord, jour 102, entrée 4

> Au restaurant, C. qui accompagne sa mère et qui ne veut pas manger, a la permission de lire son livre en attendant que celle-ci ait terminé son repas. Elle lit *Légendes de l'Amérique française*. Soudain, elle trouve la phrase suivante: *En revenant de l'office*...Elle dit alors:
>
> C.: regarde (puis elle ferme le livre et montre la page couverture). *Légendes d'Amérique française* et on dit *office*! Tu te rends compte!
> M.: oui, et alors?
> C.: mais *office* c'est bureau!
> M.: oui mais en français ça veut dire autre chose.
>
> (L'emploi du mot *office* lui apparaît ici incorrect. La mère lui explique alors que *office* peut signifier plusieurs choses en français, comme la "dépense" dans la maison de Louise et Pierre, ou une "cérémonie" quelconque. Dans le livre, il s'agit d'une cérémonie religieuse.)

Les comparaisons effectuées par C. concernent également le phénomène de *bifurcation* entre les deux langues. Ce terme, emprunté aux traducteurs, désigne les cas où un mot a un sens plus étendu que le mot de l'autre langue qui semble lui correspondre, ou inversement (Darbelnet 1969, 224). Il correspond plus ou moins aux termes *coalesced* et *split* de l'analyse contrastive évoqués par Larsen-Freeman et Long (1991, 56). Mais il ne s'agit pas ici de reprendre la voie de l'analyse contrastive dont les faiblesses ont été déjà signalées, mais plutôt d'emprunter leur terminologie. Un tel emprunt nous apparaît utile pour décrire l'un des types d'observations de C., où s'interrogeant sur l'aspect sémantique d'un élément de la L2, elle est arrêtée par l'aspect formel de celui-ci. C'est le cas du verbe anglais *to march* (j. 96) qui en plus d'être un homophone en anglais du mois de *March* (mars) ne semble pas avoir une étendue analogue à celle du verbe français *marcher* qui peut se traduire par *to march* ou *to walk*.

Les comparaisons L1-L2 rappellent encore ici la présence des connaissances antérieures de l'enfant dont la plus importante est sa L1. On connaît du reste l'importance de celle-ci dans la *structuration perceptive de l'input* et l'on sait que *la perception du nouveau à connaître se fait à partir de l'acquis* (Trévise 1994). Au plan phonétique C., qui entendait des groupements de sons qu'elle n'avait jamais entendus auparavant, rattachait ces nouveaux éléments à ceux de son expérience sonore. Au plan syntaxique, l'organisation de L2 ne correspondait pas à son expérience en L1.

Journal de bord, jour 63, entrée 2

En regardant un film à la télé, elle demande à sa mère qui est loin de l'appareil et qui ne voit pas l'écran:

C.: pourquoi ils mettent *la fin*? (en mettant un accent tonique sur le mot *la*)
M.: je ne comprends pas
C.: pourquoi, ils ne mettraient pas *fin*?

COMPARAISON INTRASYSTÈME

C. effectue également des comparaison entre deux éléments de la L2 (*comparaison L2/L2*). Dès les premiers jours, ayant observé deux prononciations différentes pour un même élément, elle s'interroge sur les différences entre *what is that?* et *what's that?*

Par ailleurs, après un mois de séjour, elle commence à porter attention à des *homophones* de L2, comme *why/y* (j.38), *two/too* (j.63), *flour/flower* (j.91) ou *but/butt* (j.97). La fin du premier mois correspond également au début de son intérêt pour la *synonymie* dans L2. Elle s'interrogera sur des différences de sens d'abord à propos de formules (*I'm sorry/excuse me*).

Enregistrement 1, 7, jour 34

Au début de l'enregistrement:

12 C.: *I'm sorry*, c'est *pardon*?
13 M.: oui
14 C.: excuse me
15
16 M.: dis-lui que tu changes le poisson d'eau
17 si tu veux qu'elle te regarde...
[elle avait été interrompue]

(un peu plus tard, pendant le même enregistrement)

196 C.: Maman, *I'm sorry*, là c'est *pardon*
197 M.: hm hm (dans le sens de *oui*)
198 C.: mais t'avais dit que *I'm sorry* c'était *excusez-moi*
199 M.: c'est les deux. L'un et l'autre
200 C.: mais... (elle s'impatiente)

et ensuite à propos de substantifs.

Journal de bord, jour 49, entrée 1

Dans l'auto, en allant à l'école:

C.: Maman, *photo* en anglais c'est *picture*? hein?
M.: comment tu sais ça?
C.: Ben R. l'a dit samedi quant tu as pris une photo de nous. pi je l'avais déjà vu avant.
M.: donc tu as déduit?
C.: oui.. *photographie* ça s'écrit comment en anglais?
M.: *p-h-o-t-o-g-r-a-p-h-y*
C.: c'est quoi la différence entre *photo* et *picture*?
M.: où est-ce que tu as vu *photo*?
C.: dans la vitrine d'un magasin. Il y a *photo* et *photography*.
M.: ah! là tu m'embêtes.

De plus, elle voudra connaître les nuances de sens entre des adjectifs, des adverbes (*there/here*), et des verbes.

Journal de bord, jour 62, entrée 3

C.: Maman, qu'est-ce que ça veut dire *small*?
M.: *petit*
C.: et *little*?
M.: *petit*
C.: donc, c'est quoi la différence?
M.: oh! là tu vas devoir regarder dans le dictionnaire!

Journal de bord, jour 89, entrée 1

En faisant un bricolage elle demande::

C.: Maman, c'est quoi la différence entre *like* et *love*?
M.: qu'est-ce que t'en pense?
C.: ben, je sais pas *like* c'est comme *aimer* et *love* c'est comme *aimer*.
M.: oui, mais tu n'as pas d'exemple? qu'est-ce que tu as entendu?
C.: ben euh. *I like the food* et *I love the food*
M.: ils disent les deux?
C.: oui
M.: un c'est *aimer un peu*, l'autre c'est *aimer beaucoup*
C.: *like* c'est *aimer un peu*, *love* c'est *aimer beaucoup*
M.: c'est ça

Toutes ces comparaisons entre L1-L2, et entre divers éléments de la L2 sont le reflet des efforts que C. déploie pour arriver à comprendre des nuances de sens. On trouve au Tableau 3 la présentation de l'ensemble des comparaisons, avec un exemple de chaque cas.

Tableau 3: Comparaison: Catégories et exemples

Catégories	Exemples
Comparaisons L1/l2	
1. Éléments lexicaux	
1.1 Homophones	we/oui [wi]
1.2 Homographes	six/six
1.3 Parographes	ingredient/ingrédient
1.4 Faux amis	office/office
1.5 Bifurcation (*coalesced* et *split*)	to march, to walk > marcher
2. Éléments syntaxiques	
2.1 Place de l'adjectif	my favorite toy/mon jouet préféré
2.2 Présence/absence du déterminant	the end/fin (dans un film)

Comparaisons L2/L2

1. Éléments lexicaux
    1.1 Synonymes — person/people
    1.2 Homonymes — two/to
2. Éléments grammaticaux — she/her
3. Éléments phonologiques — hear/ear

Au moment où C. effectue des comparaisons intersystème ou intrasystème, elle relève des différences ou des ressemblances entre des éléments. Une telle activité indique ainsi qu'elle observe des différences et/ou des distances entre L1/L2 et entre L2/L2.

C. TRADUIT

Plusieurs des propos de C. ont trait à la traduction, dans le sens où elle demande à sa mère la traduction d'un élément, ou encore traduit elle-même spontanément un élément. Les cas suivants se présentent dans nos données, à savoir:

C. demande une traduction de L1 vers L2
C. demande une traduction de L2 vers L1
C. traduit de L2 vers L1
C. traduit de L1 à L2
C. traduit de L2 à L1 (à partir de l'écrit)
C. traduit de L1 à L2 (à partir de l'écrit)
C. demande confirmation d'hypothèse de traduction de L2 à L1
C. demande confirmation d'hypothèse de traduction de L1 à L2

A l'exception du mot *yes* pour lequel elle demandera une traduction dès le jour 8, mais qu'en fait elle connaissait depuis Québec, l'essentiel des activités de traduction ne se déroule pas avant la fin du premier mois.

Journal de bord, jour 8, entrée 2

C.: Maman, ça veut dire quoi *yeah*?
M.: c'est *yes*
C.: pourquoi ils disent *yeah*?

M.: il y a les deux. comme nous on a *oui* et *ouais*. qu'est-ce que tu veux dire?

Journal de bord, jour 52, entrée 2

Nous nous arrêtons à un super marché devant lequel il y a un stand de *hot dogs*:

C.: Maman, c'est quoi que ça veut dire *hot*?
M.: *hot* ça veut dire *chaud*
C.: *dog* ça veut dire *chien*, donc *hot dog* ça fait *chien chaud*?

Son activité métalinguistique relative à la traduction est intense, si bien que la mère a parfois l'impression d'être en présence d'une machine à traduire. La traduction porte principalement sur le sens des éléments, tels que les substantifs (*friend/ami*), les adjectifs (*dernier/last*), les pronoms (*il/ils he/they*), les verbes (*veux/want*), les mots fonctionnels (*or/ou*), les connecteurs ou les mots liens dans le discours (*but/mais*), les formules et phrases (*quel est ton numéro de téléphone/what's your phone number?*). Elle veut connaître aussi la traduction d'éléments morphologiques.

Journal de bord, jour 102, entrée 1

Après une longue période de silence:

C.: maman c'est quoi que ça veut dire *quinze t h* ?
(elle prononce le *t* et le *h* séparément, comme si elle épellait)
M.: *ième*. donc quinzième

Les entrées qui concernent la traduction sont nombreuses dans le journal de bord, ce qui indique que cette opération occupe une place très importante dans l'activité métalinguistique de la fillette. Par ses activités de traduction, elle partage certains points avec les enfants des études de Malakoff et Hakuta (1991) dont les résultats montrent que les enfants traduisent abondamment. Mais elle s'en distingue aussi par l'âge (elle est au début du primaire et non à la fin) et par le nombre de langues connues, n'étant pas issue d'une famille bilingue.

Parmi les traductions que C. demande, il est intéressant de noter qu'au jour 100, elle demande la traduction des pronoms *il* et *ils* même après avoir reçu une explication et un certain enseignement de la part de sa mère. Car il faut signaler que dès le jour 9, au moment où elle s'interrogeait sur le sens de *she*, sa mère n'avait pu résister à la tentation de lui présenter tout le paradigme (*I*, *you*, *he/she we*, *you*, *they*). Elle lui avait du reste fait pratiquer ces pronoms en inventant une comptine qu'elle lui a récité au moins une fois par jour en rentrant de l'école entre les jours 10 et 15.

On remarque ainsi qu'à travers cette opération, l'attention de C. est tournée vers le sens des éléments, car elle cherche à traduire principalement des formules et des substantifs.

C. ÉNONCE DES RÈGLES

Les propos de C. recueillis dans le journal de bord et certaines de ses remarques lors des séances d'enregistrement indiquent qu'elle formule des règles à propos de la L2. Sur ce plan, elle ne se comporte pas de manière exceptionnelle, car nombreux sont les travaux sur l'acquisition des L2 qui font état de la présence de règles internes chez l'apprenant. Mais l'intérêt d'évoquer ici ces règles est qu'elle sont formulées explicitement par C., ce qui permet de voir ce qui attire son attention. Celles-ci concernent des règles de prononciation, de correspondance graphie-son, de traduction et d'emploi de la L2.

Il est intéressant de souligner que C. formule une règle dès le 12e jour après son arrivée. Celle-ci concerne la correspondance entre la prononciation et la graphie d'un son.

Journal de bord, jour 12, entrée 3

En s'amusant à copier des mots, elle dit:

C.: Maman, en anglais les mots en [e] one les écrit avec un *y*?
M.: hein?
C.: oui, comme dans *teddy*, comme dans *very*, comme dans *day*
M.: pas tout à fait

Elle formulera d'autres règles de correspondance graphie-son, dont la suivante qu'elle illustre d'exemples:

Journal de bord, jour 71, entrée 2

En roulant dans l'auto, elle dit tout à coup:

C.: Maman, tu sais, en anglais c'est facile. Quand c'est écrit *ee* on prononce en [i], quand c'est écrit juste un *e* on prononce [ə]
M.: qui t'a dit ça? Miss A.? (son enseignante)
C.: non, je l'ai trouvé toute seule
M.: as-tu des exemples?
C.: *reef, Jeneen*
M.: eh! bien, tu en sais des choses!

Parmi les règles de prononciation, mentionnons celle qui concerne le *r* [ɹ] anglais qu'elle avait de la difficulté à prononcer à son arrivée.

Journal de bord, jour 47, entrée 1

En route pour faire une randonnée pédestre avec R. et R., nous sommes assis dans le bus qui nous conduit du stationnement au début du sentier. C. dit tout à coup, après avoir vu une affiche:

C.: r en anglais, ça se prononce [aɹ]
(elle prononce ici le *r* parfaitement après avoir eu une certaine difficulté)
M.: euh...
C.: oui, comme dans *center*, *over*, *enter*

(Je remarque ici que C. est maintenant consciente de maîtriser la prononciation du *r* anglais, alors qu'au début, ce phonème lui avait causé des difficultés. Notre ami Craig s'appelait pour elle [kwɛg]. Elle avait du reste fait rire d'elle par sa soeur au jour 15, mais à ce moment-là, elle avait fait semblant de ne pas l'entendre.)

Elle formule également une règle de traduction, afin d'arriver à comprendre l'alternance entre les *she* et *her*, et entre *his* et son correspondant qu'elle n'a pas encore découvert. Ses difficultés s'expliquent ici par les différences entre le système du français et celui de l'anglais. Car le genre de *his* et *her* dépend en anglais du genre du *pôle de référence*, tandis qu'en français *son* et *sa* dépendent à la fois de la personne qui constitue le *pôle de référence* et du genre et du nombre de l'*élément dépendant* (Charaudeau 1992, 197).

Journal de bord, jour 88, entrée 3

En regardant la télévision elle demande:

C.: Maman, quand c'est *elle* c'est *she*?
quand c'est *lui* c'est *her*?
M.: *son*
C.: *his*?
M.: *son*
C.: *his name* c'est *lui*
he
ah! je comprends pas!

Au plan de la pragmatique, C. porte un intérêt à une règle d'emploi de la L2 qui concerne la prise de contact. C'est avec une très grande assurance, qu'elle corrigera sa mère au moment où cette dernière emploiera *how are you*?

Journal de bord, jour 38, entrée 1

Le matin, dans l'auto, en allant conduire la soeur aînée de C. à l'école, la mère s'adresse à cette dernière en anglais pour plaisanter::

M.: *how are you*?
C.: c'est pas poli de dire *How are you*, il faut dire *hi*
soeur: non, *hi* c'est *allo* et *how are you*, c'est *comment ça va*

Ce feed-back fourni par la soeur aînée ne convainc pas C. qui plus tard formulera une règle à peu près analogue à celle-ci, au moment où elle présentera à sa mère le *French dictionry [sic]* qu'elle a préparé pour sa meilleure amie R.

Journal de bord, jour 83, entrée 3

C. prépare une surprise pour son amie C. Elle fabrique un dictionnaire français-anglais qu'elle lui remettra en cadeau. Elle écrit un mot et en donne la traduction française, qu'elle accompagne aussi de dessins. Elle y travaillera toute la semaine, en ajoutant quotidiennement quelques mots. Il sera terminé au jour 87. Elle l'emballera dans une enveloppe. Sur la page couverture elle a écrit:

French dictionry [sic]
gril [sic] = fille
(accompagné d'un dessin d'une fille)
sur la première page on lit:
hi = bonjour or salut (accompagné du dessin d'une main)
mon = my *I = je*
fleur = flowers (suivi d'un dessin)
livre = book (+ dessin)
poisson = fish (+ dessin)
petit(e) = small or little
gros(e) = big
hier = yesterday
soleil = sun (plus dessin d'un soleil avec lunettes fumées)

En le présentant à sa mère elle le commente en disant:

C.: le premier mot c'est toujours *hi*
M.: ensuite qu'est-ce que tu mets?
C.: comment on écrit ça *my*?
M.: *m - y*
C.: comment on écrit ça *flowers*? (elle prononce le *s* de *flowers*)
M.: *f- l-o* (elle épelle)
C.: t'es sûre que c'est pas *f-l-a*?
M.: oui
C.: ça fait [fla]
M.: ensuite?
C.: *w-e-r-s*
C.: j'ai fait *hi bonjour* ou *salut*
mon *my*
I *je*
fleurs *flower*
livre *book*

Dans l'ensemble, on constate ainsi que la formulation de règles faite par C. concerne surtout des éléments formels du langage.

C. ISOLE DES PARTIES D'UN ENSEMBLE ET LES ANALYSE

En plus de l'opération *traduction* qui implique une forme d'analyse, on compte un certain nombre d'observations du journal de bord qui indiquent que C. effectue un découpage et analyse les éléments de la L2. En effet, à partir du jour 38, elle manifeste la capacité d'extraire un mot, une formule ou une expression de la chaîne parlée en vue d'en faire un découpage et une certaine analyse. Cette extraction lui permet d'isoler une partie d'un élément donné, afin d'arriver à en comprendre le sens. Les éléments que C. isole et analyse sont généralement issus d'énoncés entendus antérieurement. Elle s'interroge sur une partie de mot (le *o* de *o'clock* ou le *fly* de *dragon-fly*), ou d'expressions (*teddy* dans *teddy bear*) et sur une composante de phrase (*got* dans *I got new shoe [sic]*).

Journal de bord, jour 91, entrée 5

C.: ça veut dire quoi *o*?
M.: quoi?
C.: oui *one o'clock*
M.: mais tu le sais pas?
C.: ben
M.: *one?*
C.: *un*
M.: *clock?*
C.: *horloge*
M.: le *o* c'est pour l'heure

Les observations de C. laissent voir qu'elle analyse des formules et des phrases de la L2, afin de mieux en comprendre le sens. Elle a porté attention notamment aux éléments présentés au Tableau 4.

Mais cette forme d'analyse observée à travers les propos de la fillette n'exclut pas qu'elle puisse d'autre part utiliser dans son discours en L2 de telles formules ou phrases. Une telle utilisation pourrait alors conduire un observateur à déduire que ces formules ou phrases sont utilisées comme des touts non analysés. Mais un examen attentif des propos de C. montrent que les formules ou phrases entendues comme un tout dans l'interaction, peuvent être ensuite analysées avant d'être utilisées. Il y aurait ainsi dans son cas un relais (celui de l'analyse) entre le fait d'entendre l'élément globalement et celui de l'utiliser comme un tout. Le comportement de C. semble différent à cet égard de celui des enfants observés par Wong Fillmore (1979, 211). Celle-ci écrit en effet que ses sujets (recourant à la stratégie C–2) relevaient des expressions de type *formule* et commençaient à parler en utilisant

Tableau 4: Attention portée à des composantes d'une formule ou d'une phrase

Formules ou phrases	Porte attention à:
Hurry up (j. 81)	*up* (et à un autre moment à *hurry*)
Jack in the box (j. 77)	tous les mots
Yesterday, I got new shoe [sic] (j. 90)	*got* (elle connaît déjà les autres mots)
Are you my friend? (j.53)	*are* (elle avait entendu *I* au lieu de *are*) (elle connaît déjà les autres mots)
Where is the car? (j. 75)	tous les mots
I do not say this (j. 76)	*not* (elle connaît déjà les autres mots)
We will help you (j.42)	tous les mots
Could you move, please? (j.103)	*could* (elle connaît déjà les autres mots)

ces expressions qui avaient été *acquises et utilisées comme un tout non analysé* (notre traduction) (*the children in this study applied strategy* C–2 *by picking up formulaic expressions -expressions which were acquired and used as unanalyzed wholes*). Mais ces différences peuvent être aussi imputables à des différences dans les conditions d'observation. Car C. communiquait ses réflexions sur une base longitudinale à sa mère et ses propos n'auraient peut-être pas été aussi abondants ou explicites, si elle avait dû s'adresser de façon ponctuelle à un expérimentateur qu'elle connaissait à peine.

OBSERVATIONS SUR LES OBSERVATIONS: QU'EST-CE QUI ATTIRE NOTRE ATTENTION?

Les observations de la fillette ont permis de dégager des opérations et de voir comment elle réagissait en présence du nouvel input. Un examen de la distribution temporelle de ces opérations et de leur importance relative peut également nous permettre de mieux cerner ce sur quoi elle focalise son attention au moment où elle aborde la nouvelle L2.

DISTRIBUTION TEMPORELLE DES OPÉRATIONS

La distribution des opérations de C., dont les données sont présentée au Tableau 5, est ensuite illustrée dans le Graphique 1.

Tableau 5: Distribution temporelle des opérations

Opérations	Nombre	Moyenne	Écart- type	Médiane	25e percentile	75e percentile
1	41	42.7	27.7	34	16	66
2	36	68	28	80	44	91
3	151	71.1	24.4	80	53	91
4	12	70	29.7	85	42.5	91
5	13	74	25.1	77	53	91

Dans le graphique, l'abscisse représente les jours (107) et l'ordonnée, les opérations (1. rendre compte, 2. comparer, 3. traduire, 4. formuler des règles et 5. analyser). L'intérieur du graphique contient des boîtes. L'intérieur du graphique contient des boîtes de forme rectangulaire. La paroi latérale gauche de chaque boîte représente le 25e percentile, la paroi latérale droite, le 75e percentile, et la ligne à l'intérieur de chaque boîte, la médiane. L'intervalle délimité entre les extrémités droite et gauche de chaque boîte (c'est-à-dire les parties de la boîte qui ont l'allure de lignes épaisses) devrait contenir 99% des observations, si les données sont distribuées normalement. On peut voir ainsi par ce graphique que les opérations ne s'échelonnent pas également dans le temps. L'opération 1 se retrouve davantage en début d'apprentissage, entre les 20e et 60e jours, au moment où l'enfant, moins autonome, raconte toute son expérience nouvelle à sa mère. L'essentiel des opérations 2 et 4 commence à apparaître après le 40e jour, tandis que les opérations de traduction et d'analyse semblent, par rapport aux autres, survenir un peu plus tard dans le temps.

Graphique 1: Opérations réparties dans le temps

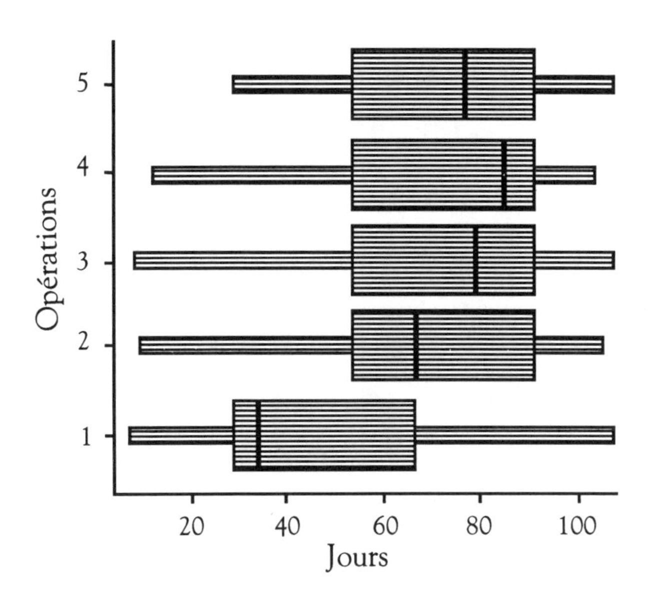

IMPORTANCE RELATIVE DES OPÉRATIONS

On peut voir ensuite au Tableau 6, l'importance proportionnelle de chacune de ces opérations et vers quel type d'élément linguistique C. tourne son attention. Parmi les 253 entrées relevées dans le journal de bord, on constate que la traduction a occupé la plus grande place. On voit également que dans le cas de toutes les opérations, les

Tableau 6: Opérations et leur objet

Attention portée à:	Rend compte	Compare	Traduit	Formule règles	Analyse
Adjectif	8 20% (8/41)	5 14% (5/36)	9 6% (9/151)	0 0%	0 0%
Adverbe	0 0%	2 6% (2/36)	12 8% (12/151)	1 8% (1/12)	3 23% (3/13)
Connecteur	0 0%	1 3% (1/36)	4 3% (4/151)	0 0%	0 0%
Formule	0 0%	5 14% (5/36)	29 19% (29/151)	2 17% (2/12)	0 0%
M.f fonctionnel	0 0%	1 3% (1/36)	6 4% (6/151)	0 0%	0 0%
Élément morphologique	0 0%	0 0%	1 0,6% (1/151)	0 0%	0 0%
Partie de phrase	0 0%	0 0%	2 1,3% (2/151)	0 0%	0 0%
Phrase	6 15% (6/41)	0 0%	14 9% (14/151)	0 0%	4 31% (4/13)
Phonème	0 0%	0 0%	0 0%	1 8% (1/12)	0 0%
Pronom	0 0%	2 0,79% (2/36)	10 7% (10/151)	1 8% (1/12)	0 0%
Substantif	26 63% (26/41)	18 50% (18/36)	50 33% (50/151)	7 58% (7/12)	5 38% (5/13)
Verbe	1 2% (1/41)	2 6% (2/36)	14 9% (14/151)	0 0%	1 8% (1/13)
Total	41 16,21% (41/253)	36 14,23% (36/253)	151 59,68% (151/253)	12 4,74% (12/253)	13 5,14% (13/253)

observations de la fillette portent pour une bonne part sur des substantifs. Le Tableau 7 contient ces mêmes données regroupées en catégories plus larges, à savoir 3 catégories pour la nature des éléments qui retiennent l'attention de C., et 3 catégories pour les périodes de temps. Les catégories relatives à la nature des mots sont les mots pleins (adverbes, adjectifs, pronoms, substantifs, verbes), les phrases (formules, parties de phrases et phrases) et 3) les autres (morphologie, mots fonctionnels, connecteurs, phonèmes). Le regroupement des jours représente la période 1 (du jour 1 au jour 30), la période 2 (du jour 31 au jour 60) et la période 3 (du jour 61 au jour 107). On constate ainsi que dans l'ensemble, la période 3 semble plus active et que l'attention de l'enfant est avec le temps attirée par un nombre croissant d'éléments. Les mots pleins font l'objet de commentaires dans une proportion de 70% et les phrases dans une proportion de 25%. On remarque aussi le faible pourcentage d'éléments morphologiques.

Tableau 7: Regroupement des objets de l'attention par catégories et regroupement des jours par période de temps

Attention portée aux:	Période 1 (du jour 1 au jour 30)	Période 2 (du jour 31 au jour 60)	Période 3(du jour 61 au jour 107)	Total
Mots pleins	24 13%(24/181)	46 25% (46/181)	107 59%(107/181)	177 70%(177/ 253)
Phrases	5 8% (5/62)	24 39% (24/62)	33 53%(33/62)	62 25% (62/253)
Autres	0 0%	7 50% (7/14)	7 50% (7/14)	14 5% (14/253)
Total	29 11% (29/253)	77 30% (77/253)	147 58% (147/253)	253 100%

ATTENTION PORTÉE AU SENS OU À LA FORME?

La partie qui précède montre que l'attention de C. est axée principalement sur l'aspect sémantique de l'input, car en essayant de décoder le sens des messages qu'elle reçoit, la fillette rend compte d'éléments qu'elle a appris, effectue des comparaisons, des traductions, des formulations de règles et analyse des parties de mots ou de phrases.

On observe cependant que dans certains cas, surtout au moment où elle formule des règles, son attention est tournée vers des aspects formels de l'input. Le Tableau 8 présente les données regroupées en opérations en regard de l'attention orientée vers le sens ou la forme.

Tableau 8: Attention portée à la forme ou au sens

Opérations	Forme	Sens	Forme/ sens	Total
Rend compte	0 0%	41 100%	0 0%	41 100%
Compare	9 25%	19 53%	8 23%	36 100%
Traduit	0 0%	148 99%	3 1%	151 100%
Formule des règles	10 84%	1 9%	1 9%	12 100%
Analyse	0 0%	10 77%	3 23%	13 100%
Total	19	219	15	253

On constate ainsi que lorsque C. rend compte d'éléments et les traduit, son attention est portée entièrement sur leur sens (100% pour l'opération *rendre compte* et 99% pour la *traduction*). Seules, les formulations de règles portent davantage (84%) sur des éléments formels de l'input. La Figure 2 permet de visualiser encore davantage l'importance du sens sur celle de la forme et, l'importance de l'opération de traduction.

A travers les observations de la fillette, on peut voir ainsi qu'elle est intéressée en priorité à l'aspect sémantique de l'input. A cet égard, son comportement donne raison à VanPatten 1992 (1994, 32) dans l'une de ses hypothèses relatives au fait que les apprenants traiteraient d'abord le sens des éléments de l'input en L2 avant leur forme. Par ailleurs, en examinant la nature des éléments qui font l'objet de

Figure 2: Histogramme des opérations en regard de l'intérêt portée l'aspect sémantique ou formel des éléments

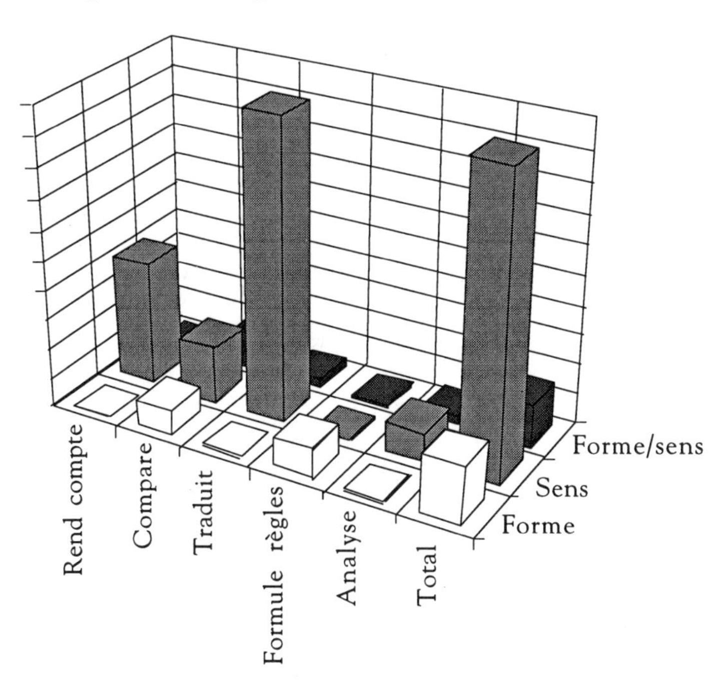

ses observations, nous remarquons une forte prédominance des éléments lexicaux sur les éléments grammaticaux, ce qui semble indiquer qu'en début d'apprentissage les mots pleins, porteurs de concepts, attirent plus l'attention que les mots fonctionnels, porteurs de relations. L'importance des éléments lexicaux pour le débutant était du reste signalée par Hatch (1983, 74), au moment où celle-ci indiquait que le fait de connaître des éléments lexicaux peut rendre la communication possible pour celui qui ne possède que les rudiments de la L2 et dont le but est de communiquer en L2. Le comportement de C. semble encore ici aller dans le sens d'une autre des hypothèses formulées par VanPatten (1994, 32), selon laquelle l'apprenant aurait tendance à traiter les éléments lexicaux de préférence aux elements grammaticaux en vue d'avoir accès à l'information d'ordre sémantique (notre traduction) (Learners prefer processing lexical items to grammatical items (e.g., morphological markings) for semantic information). Dans l'ensemble, C. laisse voir que la quête du sens est sa préoccupation dominante. Elle ne semble s'intéresser à la forme des éléments et focaliser son attention sur celle-ci qu'au moment où la forme nuit à la compréhension du sens. C'est du moins ce qui se passe pour C. en début d'apprentissage.

PRINCIPE DE LA "PERCEPTION DE LA DIFFÉRENCE OU DE LA DISTANCE" (*NOTICE THE GAP PRINCIPLE*)

Schmidt and Frota (1986) ont énoncé un principe qu'ils ont appelé "principe de la perception de la différence ou de la distance" (notre traduction) (*notice the gap principle*), selon lequel un apprenant commencera à acquérir une forme de la L2 sans se distinguer du locuteur natif, si et seulement si, cette forme est présente dans un input compris et s'il observe cette forme de manière consciente (notre traduction) ("*a second language learner will begin to acquire the targetlike form if and only if it is present in comprehended input and "noticed" in the normal sense of the word, that is consciously*") (p.311). Selon ce principe, l'apprenant effectuerait une comparaison entre ce qu'il perçoit dans l'input et ce qu'il produit lui-même dans la L2.

Or, les observations de C., bien qu'il s'agisse ici de sa réflexion métalinguistique et non de son interaction dans la L2, comportent, d'une certaine manière, des manifestations de ce principe, dans le cadre de l'opération dénommée *comparaison*. Car au moment où la fillette effectue des comparaisons intersystème ou intrasystème, elle relève des différences ou des ressemblances entre éléments de la L1 et de la L2, et entre divers éléments de la L2. Cette opération indique ainsi, que la fillette applique ce principe de la "perception de la différence ou de la distance," non seulement en comparant ce qu'elle dit à ce qu'elle a observé, mais aussi en comparant entre eux des éléments observés dans l'input (comparaison intrasystème), ou en comparant des éléments observés dans l'input à des éléments observés dans sa L1. Est-il juste alors de parler d'une extension de ce principe? Celui-ci semble du reste effectif très tôt dans l'acquisition, du moins chez C., puisque l'une des premières questions de la fillette provenait de l'observation d'une différence entre deux éléments de la L2, à savoir *yes* et *yeah* (j. 8).

Les observations de C. comportent certaines entrées qui contiennent des énoncés comme *je l'ai deviné* ou *à force de l'entendre, j'ai fini par comprendre*.

Journal de bord, jour 85, entrée 2

C.: *now* ça veut dire *maintenant* hein?
M.: comment tu fais pour le savoir?
C.: je l'ai deviné
je commence à deviner
à force de l'entendre dire par tout le monde je finis par deviner!

On trouve également des cas où C. induit le sens d'un élément parce que le contexte situationnel ou le contexte linguistique est suffisamment clair.

Journal de bord, jour 100, entrée 1

Aujourd'hui, la mère a transcrit l'enregistrement fait au jour 34. Il s'agit d'un enregistrement de 60 minutes pendant lequel C. jouait avec son amie. La mère remarque que C. a utilisé *come*, alors que cet élément n'a pas fait au préalable l'objet d'observations de la part de la fillette. La mère lui demande alors::

M.: *come* tu le sais?
C.: oui
M.: comment tu as appris ça?
C.: ben euh.. ils le disaient et ça avait l'air que c'était *viens* donc je l'ai appris!

Elle comprend ainsi le sens de certains éléments par induction, l'induction impliquant une part d'incertitude, ou dans les termes de Pinker (1994, 378) un nombre infini d'hypothèses. Mais à en juger par le contenu et le nombre des observations notées dans le journal de bord, cette pratique de l'induction ne signifie pas que C. apprend de manière inconsciente. Au contraire, son apprentissage semble constituer une activité qui nécessite un haut niveau de conscience et une perception fine de ce qu'elle est en train d'accomplir.

Les limites de ce texte ne nous permettent pas ici de soulever d'autres questions qui pourraient être abordées à la lumière de nos données, notamment celle du rôle de la rétroaction, de la part de l'enseignement ou de l'importance de la littéracité. Mais les propos de la fillette abordent de nombreux sujets qui touchent des questions à l'ordre du jour en linguistique appliquée. Ils nous ont amenée notamment sur les chemins de sa mémoire et fait circuler à travers les réseaux de ses associations. Elle a déduit, dira-t-elle, le sens du mot *airplane* en voyant l'avion sur un timbre au bureau de poste. Elle a compris le sens des mots *open* et *closed* qu'elles a vus à la porte de magasins à Honolulu, parce qu'elle s'est rappelée les avoir déjà vus sur un panneau de signalisation, à l'entrée de la côte Gilmour sur les Plaines d'Abraham à Québec, côte qui doit être fermée à la circulation en hiver. L'histoire de ces mots, amorcée à Québec, s'est dénouée à Honolulu, grâce à une association successive de situations. Ils suivent en fait un cheminement temporel en relais qui, décrits dans les termes de Schmidt (1990), donne ce qui suit:

relais 1: perception des éléments faite de façon plus ou moins consciente à Québec, à l'entrée de la Côte Gilmour, sur les Plaines d'Abraham;

relais 2: observation (*noticing*) des éléments, faite de façon consciente; elle rapporte verbalement ce qu'elle a observé; l'observation a eu lieu dans des magasins de Honolulu;

relais 3: compréhension (*understanding*) des éléments, ce qui implique une analyse consciente, car ses propos dénotent qu'elle compare ce qu'elle a vu à Québec avec ce qu'elle a vu à Honolulu.

CONCLUSION

Nous avons présenté ici une partie des résultats de la première phase de notre étude menée auprès d'une fillette de 7 ans, unilingue francophone, placée en situation d'acquisition de l'anglais L2. Les données ont été recueillies dans des conditions relativement exceptionnelles, une mère notant de façon systématique, sur une base longitudinale, toutes les observations spontanées de sa fille relatives à cette expérience d'acquisition de la L2. Cet article correspond à la partie de nos données recueillies dans le journal de bord, que nous avons analysées du point de vue de l'attention portée à l'input. Nous savons maintenant que C. aborde la nouvelle information en rendant compte de certains éléments, en comparant certains d'entre eux, en les traduisant, en formulant des règles et en analysant. Nous savons également que ses observations concernent principalement des éléments lexicaux et que la découverte de l'aspect sémantique de l'input a préséance sur l'aspect formel de celui-ci. Il faut attendre cependant le dépouillement des étapes ultérieures de nos données pour savoir si l'enfant va continuer de traiter le nouvel input de la même façon.

Comme adulte, nous nous étonnons de l'abondance et de la richesses des observations que l'enfant unilingue a pu faire à propos de la L2, d'autant plus qu'il s'agissait de données spontanées qui n'ont pu lui être induites par un autre francophone. Il ressort de ces observations spontanées que l'apprentissage d'une L2 correspond pour C. à une activité hautement consciente, dont elle fait part, dont elle discute et pour laquelle elle requiert des rétroactions. De telles observations correspondent ici à l'idée de Baars (1988) selon laquelle la conscience semble essentielle à l'apprentissage. Il ressort aussi des observations spontanées de C. que l'apprentissage d'une L2 nécessite une attention soutenue, ce qui semble donner raison à Schmidt (1990, 1993a, 1993b).

Nous savons cependant qu'une étude de cas est aussi une étude de caractéristiques individuelles au sens de Skehan (1989), et qu'aucune généralisation ne peut en être tirée. Mais comme apprenant adulte nous en tirons une leçon pour une étude ultérieure de L2. Nous retenons ce sens aigu de l'observation, cet état d'alerte constant, cette entière disponibilité à la L2, cette capacité de faire des liens et des associations avec des expériences antérieures.

Son haut niveau de conscience et l'acuité de ses sens tranchent sur le comportement d'un adulte, tantôt intéressé, tantôt absent, tantôt attentif, tantôt indolent. L'attention de l'enfant travaille en permanence, celle de l'adulte en intermittence. Y a-t-il là matière à expliquer tant de différences?

ACKNOWLEDGEMENTS

Je remercie le professeur Richard Schmidt de son appui dans la mise sur pied de cette étude. Je suis reconnaissante également envers le professeur Craig Chaudron, alors directeur du *Department of ESL*, et envers tous les professeurs et étudiants que j'ai côtoyés pendant mon stage au sein de ce département, pour le climat de travail remarquable qu'ils créent par leur compétence et leur enthousiasme pour la linguistique appliquée. Je remercie enfin le personnel de la Kuhio Elementary School.

REFERENCES

Baars, B. J. (1988). A *Cognitive theory of consciousness*. Cambridge: Cambridge University Press.

Charaudeau, P. (1992). *Grammaire du sens et de l'expression*. Paris: Hachette Éducation.

Darbelnet, J. (1969). *Pensée et structure*. New York: Charles Scribner's Sons.

Hatch, E. (1983). *Psycholinguistics: A second language perspective*. Rowley, MA: Newbury House Publishers.

Larsen-Freeman, D., & Long, M. H. (1991). *An introduction to second language acquisition research*. London: Longman.

Malakoff, M., & Hakuta, K. (1991). Translation skill and metalinguistic awareness in bilinguals. In E. Bialystok (Ed.), *Language processing in bilingual children*. Cambridge: Cambridge University Press.

Pinker, S. (1994). How could a child use verb syntax to learn verb semantics? *Lingua*, 92, 377–410.

Schmidt, R., & Frota, S. (1986). Developing basic conversational ability in a second language: A case study of an adult learner of Portuguese. In R. R. Day (Ed.), *Talking to learn: Conversation in second language acquisition* (pp. 237–322). Rowley, MA: Newbury House.

Schmidt, R. (1990). The role of consciousness in second language learning, *Applied Linguistics*, *11*, 129–158.

Schmidt, R. (1993a). Awareness and second language acquisition. *Annual Review of Applied Linguistics*, *13*, 206–226.

Schmidt, R. (1993b). Consciousness, learning, and interlanguage pragmatics. In G. Kasper & S. Blum-Kulka (Eds.), *Interlanguage pragmatics* (pp. 21–42). Oxford: Oxford University press.

Skehan, P. (1989). *Individual differences in second-language learning*. London: Edward Arnold.

Tréville, M. C. (1993). *Rôle des congénères interlinguaux dans le développement du vocabulaire réceptif: Application au français langue seconde*. Québec: CIRAL, Publication B–188.

Trévise, A. (1994). Représentations métalinguistiques des apprenants, des enseignants et des linguistes: Un défi pour la didactique. In B. Py (Éd.), *L'acquisition d'une langue seconde, VALS ASLA Bulletin Suisse de Linguistique Appliquée*, 59, 171–190.

VanPatten, B. (1994). Evaluating the role of consciousness in second language acquisition: Terms, lingusitic features, and research methodology. *AILA Review*, *11*, 27–36.

Wong Fillmore, L. (1979). Individual Differences in Second Language Acquisition. In C. J. Fillmore, D. Kempler, & W. S-Y, Wang (Eds.), *Individual differences in language ability and language behavior* (pp. 203–228). New York: Academic Press, 203–228.

Witkin, H. A., Oltman, P., K., Raskin, E., & Karp, S. A. (1971). *Manual: Embedded figures test, Children's embedded figures test, Group embedded figures test.* Palo Alto: Consulting Psychologists Press, Inc.

W. Kahulu Palmeira
University of Hawai'i at Mānoa

A STUDY OF UPTAKE BY LEARNERS OF HAWAIIAN

ABSTRACT

In previous studies, *uptake* or what learners claim to learn has been shown to reflect language topicalized not only by teachers but also that topicalized by learners in classroom discourse. Uptake has also been shown to be highly idiosyncratic, reflecting differential attention to discourse by individual learners. These characteristics of uptake suggest that actual language learning or "syllabus as reality" often differs from that which is planned by teachers or "syllabus as plan." The present study investigated the uptake of high to advanced learners of Hawaiian in a university course based on a structural syllabus. It was found that uptake can be a predictable indicator of learning, based on post measures on both structural and vocabulary items. Results also found uptake to be less idiosyncratic than previously suggested. The present study suggests that the characteristics of uptake may vary according to the type of syllabus and language levels of learners.

INTRODUCTION

Studies of *uptake* — what learners claim to have learned from a particular lesson — have focused on relationships between discourse features in classroom interaction and learners' perceptions of learning. Allwright's (1984) notion of uptake concerns the idea that language learning is a constructive process, in which contributions from participants in interactions lead to learning opportunities. One of the aims of studies of uptake is to distinguish between learning opportunities created by the teacher and those which may instead be attributed to student initiative and attention to discourse. Rather than expecting that learning outcomes are the products only of a well executed lesson plan, thus enabling teachers or researchers to predict

Palmeira, W. Kahulu (1995). A study of uptake by learners of Hawaiian. In Richard Schmidt (Ed.), *Attention and awareness in foreign language learning* (Technical Report #9) (pp. 127–161). Honolulu, Hawai'i: University of Hawai'i, Second Language Teaching & Curriculum Center.

which linguistic items will be uptaken by learners, it has been argued that individual learners will perceive what is important in different ways. Thus, uptake is concerned with relating learning outcomes to their immediate and potentially determining environment, through focusing on discoursal and interactive processes in the classroom.

Slimani has examined discourse in classroom interaction through evaluating the "quality of interaction which leads to learners' claims of uptake" (1992:197). Following Allwright, Slimani focused on learning which was the result of input that is jointly constructed, or what actually happened in an instructional setting, as opposed to (but not excluding) input which was planned beforehand and largely produced by the teacher. Uptake, according to Slimani, reflects both what teachers intend for students to learn, as well as aspects not previously anticipated by learners or teachers. In this view, learner autonomy, in terms of how students vary in attending to input in the classroom environment, plays an important role in determining how learning takes place.

These studies have been able to relate claims by learners to the sources of input, suggestive of what has actually attracted the learners' attention in discourse. However, they have been less successful in identifying awareness, in terms of what actually directed students' attention to particular sources. Similarly, it is not clear as to what extent learners are aware of their own learning during instruction, but uptake may provide some evidence of the circumstances in which the input was noticed or attended to.

SLIMANI'S STUDIES OF UPTAKE

Slimani (1989, 1992) has reported on her study of uptake by thirteen Algerian students, low-intermediate to advanced beginners of English, enrolled in a six-month intensive ESL program. Students in this program met for a total of 24 hours a week; the classes were observed for two hours a week for six weeks. Learners were given uptake charts at the end of each of six observed classroom sessions and directed to provide as many details as possible on all points that they were able to recall from the day's lesson. Additional "uptake identification probes" were given to students approximately three hours after the first "uptake recall" charts, in order for them to distinguish items they listed which were learned in that particular lesson from those already partly known previously and from those which were available in the lesson but remained unclear to students. Both of the latter items were not further treated in the study, as the goal was to isolate the newly uptaken items and uncover sources in the interactive classroom work to explain the claims regarding learning, or uptake. Claims of either previous partial knowledge or unclear knowledge from the immediate lesson alone were not considered relevant to the instances of learning claimed for the particular lesson.

The major findings by Slimani focused on the relationship between discourse features and the learners' uptaken items, in which it was found that uptaken items were those that were made topical and focused upon, overtly and largely by the teacher with an explicit use of metalanguage. However, only 44% of what was explicitly focused upon in the classroom discourse was claimed by learners to have been learned, and 36% was not mentioned or noticed (another 20% of topicalized items were claimed to be previously known). Slimani suggests that this indicates a picture of "syllabus as reality" as opposed to the "syllabus as plan" (Slimani 1992: 209). In addition, while teacher talk made up the bulk of those linguistic items which were topicalized (158 items or 77.5% in classroom discourse, compared to 46 items or 22.5% by learners), learner topicalization produced proportionally more uptake. More precisely, only 49.4% of teacher topicalization was reported as uptake, while 79.9% of learner topicalization was reported as uptake. However, on the questionnaire eliciting learners' perceptions of their allocation of attention during the lessons, students ranked the input supplied by the teacher as most important, reflecting perhaps the sheer quantity of teacher topicalized items of uptake. Slimani suggests that based on the discourse features examined, however, "learners do, unknowingly, profit from their classmates' contributions" (Slimani 1989: 229).

Slimani also found that students' claims indicated that uptake was highly idiosyncratic, in that typically only a few learners at any one time "happened to take the information in" (1992: 213). For example, nearly 75% of the total number of claims was reported by no more than three learners at a time, and 37% was reported by only one person at any one time. A much smaller number of claims (3.2%) was simultaneously made by nine to eleven subjects. Thus, uptake in this study does not appear to reflect learning which is consistent with a prescribed syllabus. As Slimani notes, "many of the claimed items were not intended to be taught by the teacher, but arose incidentally and became topics in discourse terms" (Slimani 1992, p. 207).

It is not clear what type of syllabus was used by the teacher in Slimani's study, although it appears that language objectives were utilized as the focus of instruction and practice. Slimani's observations indicated that the instructional situation was highly teacher-fronted and devoid of group activities. It is likely that the type of syllabus used in classroom studies on uptake strongly influences how uptake is reported. Since the syllabus type often guides or limits the types of interactions and learning processes in second or foreign language classes, it is likely that these influence differential outcomes in different learning situations. It may also be the case that uptake varies according to the levels of the second language learners, as well as other individual differences.

The present study is a variation of Slimani's study of uptake, motivated to explore further the nature of uptake, and to investigate whether any differences found might be predictable based on the syllabus type. The major differences between this investigation and Slimani's concern (1) the focus on advanced learners of Hawaiian in a university language classroom context, as opposed to beginning level learners; (2) instruction based on a primarily structural syllabus; and (3) the inclusion of an external measure of intake regarding the linguistic items which were the focus of instruction. Additionally, the present study does not attempt to exhaustively locate the actual instances of all topicalized discourse in the classroom, but instead is limited to the prevalent discourse features of the teacher which relate specifically to the target items. The main purposes of the study are to investigate the relationship between instruction and uptake and to see whether claims of uptake also reflect learning as evidenced by external measures of the target items of instruction.

Three research questions addressed in this study were:

- To what degree does uptake reflect instructional procedures and intended learning outcomes (i.e., target linguistic structures and vocabulary)?
- What are some relationships between uptake and subsequent performance?
- Can uptake, in this situation, be considered idiosyncratic?

The first question investigates relationships between uptake and instructional goals. Slimani's study did not focus on the relationship between the uptake of targeted items and the teacher's intended focus, but rather located the uptake as being topicalized by either the teacher or students. This may reflect the research interest of identifying uptake which is a result of student interaction rather than teacher directed language, distinguishing between "syllabus as reality" vs. "syllabus as plan." The present study differs in investigating the relationship between perceived learning outcomes (i.e., uptake) and the intended learning of linguistic structures within a structural syllabus language course. The second question addresses relationships between uptaken items and subsequent performance of these items on posttest measures. More specifically, within a structural syllabus, pre- and posttest measures should indicate whether positive outcomes are achieved within the study period. Possible relationships between uptake and student performance on posttest measures may indicate whether uptake can predict subsequent performance. The third general question addresses differences among learners in terms of how uptake is reported. This more specifically investigates Slimani's finding of the highly idiosyncratic nature of uptake.

BACKGROUND TO THE STUDY

Because of the small number of native speakers and second language speakers of Hawaiian and the limited use of Hawaiian in the community, many learners of Hawaiian in university or other community settings (high schools, night courses and Hawaiian immersion) depend largely on the classroom for sources of linguistic input, particularly the language abilities of and input provided by the teacher. However, because the majority of those learning Hawaiian are ethnically Hawaiian and influenced by recent attempts to revitalize the mother tongue of this indigenous culture of Hawai'i, many students have high levels of motivation to learn Hawaiian. Students studying to become Hawaiian immersion teachers, for example, are likely to be highly motivated. Thus, learning a second language in this study differs from that of learning English in Slimani's study in the sense that the majority of students are learning the language of their cultural heritage, which has undergone dramatic language shift and loss.

Another difference between the present study and Slimani's research is that the teacher in this study participated in the investigation, by providing the objectives and target language items to be used instructionally for the short unit that took place over the five class sessions of this study. In addition, the instructor provided in-depth information regarding his instructional procedures, based on a structural syllabus centered on a select reading for the unit. This enabled the planning of pre- and posttests based on the target items which were the focus of instructional procedures for the time period of the study. The instructor also devised the posttest measures, which were similar to the types of examinations students were familiar with in the course.

METHOD

PARTICIPANTS AND SETTING

Eighteen adult students enrolled in a third-year Hawaiian language class at the University of Hawa'i at Mānoa participated in this study. However, five of these students missed the second pretest and were not included in some of the analyses. For the majority of the study, 13 students are included, while the additional five students are included in the results concerning vocabulary only. The students were nearing the completion of the second semester of third year Hawaiian and were considered by the instructor to be at advanced levels in Hawaiian. The class met three times per week for 50 minutes. The teacher was an experienced third- and fourth-year instructor in Hawaiian, highly proficient in Hawaiian as a second language.

INSTRUCTIONAL METHODS

Classroom instruction and interaction was conducted almost entirely through the medium of Hawaiian. The teacher used a structural syllabus, incorporating teacher fronted and directed interactions with students focusing primarily on the target structures. This portion of instruction took up approximately 40 percent of the class period. Students worked in small groups (20 percent of class time) on tasks designed to elicit the target structures in discourse among peers. A teacher-fronted review and discussion session towards the end of the period (20 percent of class time) also focused primarily on the target grammatical structures. Thus, teacher directed interaction was largely used and the primary discourse topics, in both large and small group discussions, were structures that were the primary instructional goals for the class period. Thus, the structural nature of instruction provided repeated opportunities for direct focus on the target structures throughout the class sessions.

For this short unit, the instructional materials included only a short reading, although other handouts (on grammatical structures or vocabulary) are sometimes used by this instructor. The students were expected to read the material on their own and to become familiar with new vocabulary items in the reading. New vocabulary used instructionally during class sessions were related to the reading, but were not necessarily target items. Other new vocabulary items used in large group interactions, largely non target items, were used to facilitate the uptake of target structures.

LINGUISTIC TARGET ITEMS

The Hawaiian structures and vocabulary targeted by the instructor in this study are displayed below. There were eight target structures (with additional variations) and ten target vocabulary items, which made up the linguistic focus of this unit (three days of instruction). For a fuller outline of target structures and vocabulary, see Appendix A.

Target Structures

- *Inā ua VERB, ua VERB*, 'if...then'
- *Inā i VERB, inā ua VERB*, 'if...then' (subjunctive)
- *ka'a*, 'to have changed possession' (stative verb):
- *lilo*, 'to be taken by' (stative verb)
- *eo*, 'to lose' (stative verb)
- *I hewa*, 'fault' (stative verb)
- *no PRONOUN iho*, (benefactive reflexive pronoun)

PRE- AND POSTTEST MEASURES

Pretests and posttests were administered similar to the types of quizzes or examinations familiar to students in this class. These included target structures and vocabulary items that were the intended instructional foci during the time of the study. The test consisted of twenty sentences for nine different structures students were to construct and ten vocabulary items. There were 20 possible total points for correct responses on structures, and 10 points for correct responses for vocabulary items. The post test also elicited learner background information, including information on previous years of language learning in high school or college, age of first exposure to a second language, goals for continued study or degrees and careers involving Hawaiian language. These data were for exploratory purposes and are not further considered in this paper.

UPTAKE CHARTS

The uptake charts (shown in Appendix B) referred students to respond to the question, "He aha nā mea āu i a'o mai ai ma ka ha'awina i kēia lā?" ("What have you learned from today's lesson?). The charts varied slightly on the three days. However, the main categories in which students were to provide uptake were of the following types of items:

- *nā analula* (grammatical patterns/structures)
- *nā hua'ōlelo* (lexical items/vocabulary)
- *nā kumuhana a me nā mana'o hou aku paha* (content or other remarks)

After completing the charts, the students indicated how well they thought they learned each item reported, as well as specifying whether they recalled having learned this through the teacher or peers previous to that day. These data, however, were not included in further analyses for this study.

PROCEDURES

The study took place over a period of five class sessions, nearly a two-week period, three sessions of which involved observation and audio-recording of large-group classroom interaction. Small-group work and interaction was not audio-recorded systematically. Prior to the start of instruction in the first two sessions, pretests were administered, followed by the regular instruction for approximately 30 minutes. At the end of each of the first three sessions, students were given the uptake charts and directions to complete them. The third session differed in that there was no pretest given on that day, but the class session also included a discussion of the reading from which some of the grammatical structures were drawn. The fourth session consisted of a review of target items for the previous three sessions, largely comprised of translation of sentences from English to Hawaiian, in addition to review of unrelated items in preparation for the semester final examination. The posttest was given during the fifth session, and the instructor used the additional time in the last session for regular instruction and review.

ANALYSES

Both qualitative and quantitative analyses were performed on the corpus of data on the uptaken linguistic items. These included frequency counts for both target and non-target grammatical structures and vocabulary. A repeated measures ANOVA was performed on the pre- and posttests, done separately for 20 items for target structures and 10 target vocabulary items.

RESULTS

The results are presented in three general sections. General relationships between the nature of uptake and instructional goals are displayed and discussed in the first section, with initial descriptive analyses on frequencies and distribution of uptake across and within the three instructional sessions. The second section examines relationships between uptaken items and the performance of students on these items on pre- and posttest measures. The analyses in the final section concern questions regarding the idiosyncratic nature of uptake.

UPTAKE AND INSTRUCTION

Uptake in this study is defined as items which students claimed to have learned during a specific class session. The total number of uptake claims for the three-day period and the number and percentage of these which were structural or vocabulary items are presented below in Table 1.

Overall, of the 204 claims of uptake for three days, there was a slightly higher percentage for vocabulary (52.5%) than for grammatical structures (47.5%). The uptake for lexical items was largely reported in Session 2, while the remaining claims for structures were reported over the three instructional sessions.

Table 1: Number and percentage of uptake claims (grammatical structures and vocabulary)

	Uptake by linguistic type	Percentage of total uptake
Grammatical Structures	97	47.5%
Vocabulary	107	52.5%
Total Number of Claims	204	100%

The quantity and types of uptaken items for the three days varied. The number of uptaken claims are shown below in Table 2 with respect to each of the three instructional sessions. Also displayed is the number of items uptaken for structures and lexical items from each session's total uptaken claims.

Table 2: Student claims of uptake (structures and vocabulary) by class session

Session	Total Claims Per Day	Structures	Vocabulary
1	29	25	4
2	148	56	92
3	27	16	11

As shown above, by far the most claims were made on Session 2, with the majority of uptake being lexical items. However, there was also more uptake of structures for Session 2 than the other two days combined. Session 1 and Session 3 have comparable amounts of uptake, with a slightly larger number of structures for Session 1 and a slightly larger number of vocabulary items for Session 3.

This next section considers the nature of the uptaken items for each of the three sessions. This addresses the relationship between the uptaken items and the target instructional items for each day, which may partially account for the wide differences in the amount of reported uptake per day.

SESSION 1

Two target structures were the focus of instruction in Session 1, for which 12 of 13 students (85%) reported each of the two target structures as uptake. The remaining student used a general term for these related structures and thus was counted only once. This indicates that both target structures were focused upon instructionally and were attended to by students. The fact that only four lexical items were reported also supports the relationship between uptake and targeted items, since vocabulary was not an instructional focus. However, this may also be an artifact of the method whereby students were asked to report "learned" items as opposed to reporting anything that they could recall. Also, because the class was obviously structured and the students were very familiar with this instructor, students may have reported what they thought the instructor wanted them to learn. In either case, the data suggest that in this instructional setting, there appears to be a strong relationship between instructional goals and the reporting of uptake following instruction.

Although not included in the uptake counts, a few students under the category of "other content" included place names in Hawaiian, which appeared to have been learned when used in the large group interactions, though these were not target items. Place names were used to facilitate discussions in large teacher-centered, and small learner-centered groups, as well as to practice the two target structures. Overall, it appears that uptake was clearly related to the items targeted through instruction, although there was also some uptake of incidentally encountered vocabulary.

SESSION 2

In the second session, learners reported many more uptaken items. There was also a larger number of target items as the focus of instruction in this session than on the other two days. Claims concerning the uptake of structures accounted for a total of 56 or 38% of the total 148 claims for Session 2. Table 3 displays the number of uptake claims for each of five target structures and the percentage of students reporting uptake on each target structure. Appendix C displays the same type of information but with respect to the number of claims for different variations of each target structure.

As shown in Table 3, there was more variation in the number of claims made by different students (n=16) than with claims of structures for Session 1 target items, since there were only two structures for Session 1. However, the three major structures which received the largest claims of uptake, items 1, 2 and 4, were within a comparable range with between 69 and 88 percent of students claiming these as uptake. These three target items may have been considered new to a larger number of students. The third structure, although also a target item, was a more common variation of the structure. This was due to the more common term *lanakila* ('victory' or 'victorious') being used there. Students likely had prior exposure to this term and may not have considered it new. If students were aware of their previous knowledge of this structure, it is less likely that they would claim this as uptake of new knowledge.

Table 3: Number of items and percentage of students claiming uptake of grammatical structures for Session 2

Grammatical structure	Total claims	Percentage of students making claims
1. stative verb sentence (*ua ka'a*)	11	69%
2. agentive stative verb sentence (*ua eo*)	13	81%
3. intransitive verb sentence (*ua lanakila*)	2	13%
4. agentive stative verb sentence (*ua lilo*)	14	88%
5. review structures from session	10*	31%
6. non-target structures claimed	6	38%

n=16
*represents two claims each for five students

Claims regarding item 5 were made by five students (two claims each) for the two structures which were the focus of instruction in Session 1 and reviewed in Session 2. The five students who reported these again as uptake in Session 2, unlike the majority of students, were students who had more difficulties with these structures (as indicated by uptake charts and posttest results following Session 2). Thus, the review appeared to have a positive effect on the learning of these structures by students who initially found them difficult.

The remaining six claims were for structures that were discussed briefly in class and not targeted for instruction. Non-targeted items were minimally reported, but provide some indication of uptake of language in the classroom which was not necessarily targeted instructionally (i.e., incidental learning).

VOCABULARY

Unlike the other two sessions, Session 2 included an instructional focus on target vocabulary items (k=10). Of a total of 92 claims of uptake of vocabulary items, 36 claims (39%) were made with respect to the target vocabulary while a larger number (56 claims or 61%) was made for vocabulary items which were topicalized in some way but were not targeted items. Appendix D displays the number of claims of uptake for both target and non-target vocabulary items.

In this study, topicalized (and non-topicalized) target items were identified by the instructor and confirmed by observation of these in classroom discourse by the investigator. Since the instructor used a structural syllabus, with more specific and limited intended outcomes, these items were pervasive and more easily identifiable in retrospective analysis. That is, it was clear that the target items specified by the teacher for instruction were of primary focus and were topicalized repeatedly. For vocabulary, some items were not topicalized. Students were expected to have independently located the meanings of these vocabulary items through their reading selection. Unfortunately a discourse analysis which could increase the validity of these observations was not performed. A discourse analysis would also have provided more information on the degree to which they were topicalized, in which contexts (large or small groups; teacher or students) and other possible conversation which arose more incidentally through the discussions and interactions.

Two of the targeted items, *inoa moho* ('championship' or 'title') and *kiwi* ('horn, of a bull'), received the largest number of claims, ten and eleven respectively. Only three other target items were uptaken, with between four and six claims each. However, one-half of the target items were not uptaken, which directly reflects the fact that these items were not topicalized in classroom interaction, by either the teacher or students that day. That is, these target items were found in the reading, but were not used or present in the oral input during the session.

There were 15 additional vocabulary items claimed as uptake, with a total of 56 claims. While not being target items, these were used to facilitate instruction of target structures. Thus, this vocabulary focus appeared to arise incidentally in the discourse focusing on target structures. The 15 non-target items received at least one claim of uptake each. However, the majority of these received between two and four claims each. Three items received between seven (*hainakā*, 'handkerchief'; *kīpuka'ili* 'lasso') and eleven (*maku'u* 'saddle') claims each. (Appendix D also displays these non-target vocabulary items and the frequencies of claims per item.) This finding supports the claim that learning does not necessarily occur based on what is planned or targeted but can be facilitated through interaction and classroom discourse. In this case, target structures which were at least minimally topicalized within the classroom interactions were more likely perceived as uptake by students than target vocabulary structures, which received less attention instructionally. Thus, in general, it seems that the match between instructor intentions and uptake is closer for structures than for vocabulary. This may reflect the repetitive nature of the instructional focus on target structures.

SESSION 3

Session 3 was similar to the first session in having a smaller number of target structures, with one major structure in which two main variations were focused on. There were a total of 27 claims of uptake, 16 were structures (59%), and 11 were vocabulary items (41%).

Table 4: Number of items and percentage of students claiming uptake of grammatical structures for Session 3

Structure	Total claims	Percent of students
1. *I PAINU PIKO i/iā ʻĀKENA ʻAʻANO*. (*I* + stative verb + subject (exp) + agent marker + agent)	11	100%
2. *I hewa ke keiki i ka makua.*	3	27%
3. *I hewa iā ʻoe.*	0	—
4. non target structures	2	18%

n=11

All eleven students for this session reported uptake of the main structure, in terms of its constituent parts with Hawaiian terminology, as shown in number one above. This reflects the nature of the structure, in which the following markers, highlighted, are critical for correct usage of this type of stative-agentive structure:

> ***I*** *painu piko* ***i*** *kikino*. (***I*** verb subject ***i*** noun)
>
> ***I*** *hewa ke keiki* ***i*** *ka makua.*

With regards to stative verb usage, the structural components rather than the particular phrases were uptaken, which may reflect a strategy for learning this structure.

There was a total of 11 uptaken vocabulary items, three target and eight non-target. The small number of uptaken vocabulary items appears related to the minimal use of these lexical units to facilitate the focus on structures and discussion of the story. Eight of the items were from the story, although only three were target lexical items.

UPTAKE AND SUBSEQUENT PERFORMANCE

This section addresses how uptake, as a self-report of learning, compares with other measures of learning. In general, there appeared to be a positive relationship between reported uptake of target items and performance on the posttest. All students showed improvement between pre- and posttests, shown on an ANOVA done for the entire group. In the repeated measures of the entire group's pre- and posttest performances on grammatical structures, there were 13 subjects and 20 items total. The pretest mean was 5.0, with a mean of 15.9 for the posttest. This indicates that there was a substantial gain made during the instructional period, and most of the items were not previously known.

The following analyses were done to examine how likely items that were uptaken were also found to be correct on the posttest measure. Table 5 displays the number of students claiming each structure as uptake and the number and percentage of students with the correct response for that structure on the posttest.

Table 5 indicates a very strong relationship between uptake and subsequent performance. Indeed, for one of the structures, *no'u iho* (benefactive reflexive pronoun), there was no uptake reported, and only one student was found to have this correct on the posttest, which is likely due to previous knowledge of the structure. Besides being found in the reading, *no'u iho* is related to the *ia'u iho* (object reflexive pronoun) structure normally taught in second year Hawaiian. However, the brevity of instructional focus likely influenced the lack of uptake of this structure.

Nearly all students used the former, *ia'u iho* structure in sentences requiring the new structure (*no'u iho*). This may support the direct effect that instructional focus and time on task (more as opposed to less emphasis) has on intake. Had more time been spent on the distinctions between the two, perhaps both the number of uptake claims and accuracy on the posttest would have increased.

Table 5: Number of students claiming uptake by structure and number and percentage of students who were 100% by structure on posttest

Structure	Number of students with uptake claim per structure	Students with 100% accuracy on posttest for each structure	Percent of students with 100% accuracy on posttest
inā i	14	14	93.3%
inā ua	15	12	80.0%
i hewa	14	8	57.1%
*no'u iho**	0	1	7.1%
eo	11	9	69.3%
ka'a	8	4	30.8%
lilo	9	5	38.4%

*not taught; found in reading

Similarly, certain vocabulary items appear predictably problematic in terms of instructional focus, uptaken items and posttest results. This refers to the five items which were not focused on instructionally, i.e., were not even present in the input and were not uptaken at all on the day of instruction (Session 2).

An item analysis done on the posttest for vocabulary showed that the following items receiving the most incorrect answers were also those items not uptaken, as shown in Table 6.

Table 6: Frequency of incorrect vocabulary responses on posttest

Vocab. item number	1	2	3	4	5	6	7	8	9	10
Students incorrect	7	10	9	4	16	12	18	6	17	16

(n=18)

Table 7: Number of student claims of uptake claims by lexical items and number of students correctly supplying lexical item on posttest

Target lexical items	Translation	Claimed as uptake	Number of students correct on posttest
1. *inoa moho*	('championship', 'title')	9	11
2. *ho'ohei pipi*	('to rope cattle')	4	8
3. *ahona iki*	('to be a little better, of a condition')	0	9
4. *eo*	('victory–*kikino*'/noun)	5	14
5. *kōko'olua*	('companion of two', 'sidekick')	0	2
6. *'āha'i*	('to carry off, as in victory')	0	6
7. *hia'ai*	('to be delighted')	0	0
8. *kiwi*	('horn, of a bull')	10	12
9. *ho'i nele*	('to return empty handed')	0	1
10. *kōwaliwali*	('to twirl–*hehele*'/ transitive verb)	5	2

A majority of students had responded incorrectly to items 5, 6, 7, 9, and 10. Except for item 10 which received some uptake claims, none of those items which were incorrect by the majority of students received any uptake claims.

Table 7 also shows a strong relationship between the number of claims per vocabulary item and the number of correct answers on the posttest. Interestingly, the item receiving the most correct responses on the posttest, *eo*, was only reported as uptake by five students. However, this term is also part of a major structure taught, in which this term was of primary focus. Students reported the term, *eo*, within the structure, as uptake, but the majority did not report this term by itself as a new vocabulary item. The items which were not reported as uptake by a single student, received correct responses by 11–50% of the students. These items were not present in the oral input, but were expected to be attended to through the reading. However, this appears less successful than the oral input provided instructionally on the uptaken items.

LEARNER DIFFERENCES IN UPTAKE

Some apparent differences in the reporting of uptake are briefly discussed here. For the most part, all students appeared to report uptake of structures focused on in respective sessions. As shown in Table 8 below, in Session 1 (n=13), 12 students reported the two structures focused on instructionally. However, in Session 2, there was a larger range of number of items reported by each student (n=16). For Session 3, the majority or seven of the students (n=11) reported the main target structure, while four students claimed between two and three.

This tends to show that in this study the findings of uptake are not as highly idiosyncratic as in Slimani's study. The data above for Sessions 1 and 3, especially, indicate that the majority of students reported the same number of structures. It is possible that because these are more advanced learners, they are able to focus on and benefit from this type of instruction, within the medium of the target language. Perhaps there is a more restricted range of what they would consider "new" in the language than would more beginning learners. However, this non-idiosyncratic outcome may also reflect the highly structured nature of instruction and the students familiarity with the instructor and learning processes in this class. Finally, these findings might also be a function of the uptake chart instructions, which asked them to list what they thought they learned, rather than anything they attended to and recalled.

Table 8: Range of uptake frequency of total structures claimed per session/student

Number of students claiming structures	1 structure	2 structures	3 structures	4 structures	5 structures
Session 1 (n=13)	1	12	–	–	–
Session 2 (n=16)	–	2	7	3	4
Session 3 (n=11)	7	3	1	–	–

In Sessions 1 and 3, the majority of students reported no uptake of vocabulary. Vocabulary was not a focus for these sessions, although between four and six students on each of these days reported between one and three items each, which shows that non-target items were also uptaken incidentally.

Table 9: Range of uptake frequency of total vocabulary claimed per session by students

No. of vocabulary claims	0	1	2	3	4
Session 1 (n=13)	9	4	–	–	–
Session 3 (n=13)	7	3	1	2	–

For the second session, however, there was a wider range of claims of uptake, between two to eleven items. This shows more individual variation than all other reporting.

Table 10: Range of uptake frequency of total vocabulary claimed for Session 2 by students

No. of claims per student	2–3	4–5	6–7	8–9	10–11
No. claiming this range	3	7	1	3	2

Asking students to report their uptake in this study also revealed differences in the level of explicitness of reporting on certain target structures. For example, for Session 1, some students included information by which the two related target structures are distinguished. One of the target structures is a conditional (past event actually occurred or true statement), while the other is a subjunctive (something not completed or true.) The following are samples of comments made to distinguish the two, reported as uptake (translated into English from Hawaiian):

Inā ua verb, *ua* verb ('if...then': conditional)

1. If you went, then...
2. Use when it is clear that an action has truly been done
3. A true statement
4. If (you) did it before, (use) *inā ua*
5. If I worked at the *Pūnana Leo* (used correctly)

Inā i verb, *inā ua* verb ('if...then': subjunctive)

1. If you <u>had</u> gone, then...
2. Use when it is known that an action was not done
3. An untrue statement
4. If (you)* didn't do it before, (use) *inā i*
5. If I worked at the bank (used incorrectly)
   **items/comments in parenthesis are author's*

A few students were less explicit in reporting uptake, and would merely indicate the structure, for example, by the following:

inā ua (if <u>marker</u>)
inā i (if <u>marker</u>)

However, these differences in reporting in terms of more or less explicitness do not appear to predict whether students learned the structures well or not, as some students who were less explicit were among those who did well on the posttests and students who rarely have difficulties in acquiring new structures according to the instructor.

DISCUSSION

One primary research question of this study involved examining the relationship between uptake and instructional goals or objectives. Since Slimani found that a larger percentage of uptake was topicalized by the learners rather than the teacher, and because uptake was found to be largely idiosyncratic (i.e., varying for individuals), this suggested that learners may not actually benefit as greatly as generally assumed, based on the teacher's objectives. However, in the present study, findings on this relationship indicate a rather strong association between the language reported as uptake by the learners and that of target structures. That is, the majority of students reported uptake which directly reflected the instructional objectives. This is likely due, at least in part, to the structural syllabus used in this course, where much of the teacher directed interactions and small group work was focused on the target structures repeatedly throughout the session.

There was a stronger match between grammatical structures and instructional goals than that found for vocabulary. Target vocabulary were not reported as uptake as consistently as structures. Uptaken vocabulary items were reported for both target and non-target vocabulary. This may have been due to a number of reasons. Non-target vocabulary was used to facilitate interactions focused on the grammatical structures, thus, this uptake may be considered incidental to the intended learning outcomes. These data share some resemblance to Slimani's study in that learners exhibited more variation with these claims than any other, in terms of specific items and number of items claimed. In addition, while these claims did not reflect the teacher's plan, they were evidently noticed and attended to by some learners. The rather high levels of uptake of non-target vocabulary does support the notion of uptake reflecting the "syllabus as reality" rather than reflecting only that which is planned by the instructor. Target vocabulary items that were not uptaken were those that were not present in the classroom discourse, as the teacher expected students to acquire these through the reading selection.

The second research question addressed the relationship between uptake and subsequent performance on target linguistic items. The findings showed that the reporting of uptake is strongly related to the percentage of correct usage on a posttest. In general, structures with a larger number of uptake reports were produced accurately more often than structures which were not uptaken as often.

This study found little idiosyncratic reporting of uptake with respect to structures, with a wider range of individual differences for vocabulary uptake. One possible explanation for the non-idiosyncratic nature of uptake for structures in this study concerns the more advanced levels of the students in the language, where the focus of instruction may be more specific and there is less new input available in general than for beginners. Also advanced learners may make use of other strategies and background knowledge, as appeared in some cases here. This was found in the types of reporting for specific structures (explicit explanation, explicit pattern of constituent parts displayed), in the use of related structures in providing contrast for distinguishing structures, and using previous knowledge to aid intake of structures at a higher level in the language.

Thus, in this study, uptake appeared to be a fairly consistent consequence of instructional focus and predictor of posttest results. Although it cannot be claimed that uptake implies long-term intake and retention, as might be claimed had additional posttests been done at longer intervals from initial instruction, uptake at least relates to initial intake. Slimani posits that it may be misleading to predict which linguistic items will be uptaken by learners, and as such, evaluations of student learning may not actually capture the fuller range of uptake. From the perspective of learning as co-productions which are socially constructed events, it is clear from Slimani's study of topicalization and uptake that learners can pick up items which differ from that planned by the teacher. However, perhaps uptake also varies according to the type of syllabus and instructional procedures used in particular classes, which may account for some of the differences found in the present study. At least some of the findings of this study, for structures especially, suggest that evaluations based on teachers' plans may be an appropriate means for assessing student learning.

One of the limitations of this study regards the way in which students were instructed to report uptake, in terms of what they thought they had learned in the lesson. The fact that more target than non-target structures were reported as uptake may be an artifact of the collection procedures, in which students focused more on structures perceived as the main focus of the lesson, rather than attempting to recall other language used. They may have also reported what they thought the instructor expected. Another limitation is that careful discourse analyses were not performed in order to provide more confirming evidence for the amount of topicalization of each target structure, in addition to language not planned to be focused on by the instructor.

The fairly strong relationships found between uptake and instruction and uptake and subsequent performance, may reflect the specific methods used and questions asked, which differed from previous studies. Uptake, or how learners attend to language in the classroom, may directly reflect both the type of syllabus used and the levels of learners, and may vary accordingly. Further research on uptake should consider a focus on interaction in various types of language courses, with more refined methods for considering the relationship between uptake and classroom discourse, instructional methods and performance. Additionally, posttests given over a longer period of time could also give more accurate confirmation of learning.

REFERENCES

Allwright, R. L. (1984). The importance of interaction in classroom language learning. *Applied Linguistics* 5, 156–171.

Slimani, A. (1992). Evaluation of classroom interaction. In J.C. Alderson & A. Beretta (Eds.), *Evaluating Second Language* Education (pp. 197–221). Cambridge: Cambridge University Press.

Slimani, A. (1989). The role of topicalisation in classroom language learning. *System*, *17*, 223–234.

APPENDIX A: TARGET HAWAIIAN STRUCTURES

Note the following abbreviations:

SM	subject marker	
OM	object marker	
AGM	agent marker	
VM	verb marker	
VMP	verb marker	(completed/perfective)
DET	determiner	

1. ***Inā ua VERB, ua VERB*** ('if...then')

Inā	*ua*	*hele*	*'oe*	*i*	*ka*	*Merry Monarch,*	*ua*	*'ike*	*'oe*
If	VMP	go	you	to	DET	Merry Monarch,	VM	see	you

i	*ka*	*hula.*
OM	DET	hula

'If you went to the Merry Monarch, (then) you saw the hula'

'If you went to the Merry Monarch, (then) you had to have seen the hula'

2. ***Inā i VERB, inā ua VERB*** ('if...then': subjunctive)

Inā	*i*	*hele*	*'o*	*Lei*	*i*	*ka*	*Merry Monarch,*	*inā*	*ua*
If	VM	go	SM	Lei	to	DET	Merry Monarch,	then	VM

'ike	*'o*	*ia*	*i*	*ka*	*hula.*
see	SM	she	OM	DET	hula

'If Lei had gone to the Merry Monarch, (then) she would have seen the hula'

3. ***ka'a*** ('to have changed possession', 'passed to'): ka'a + subject (experiencer) + destination

a.

Ua	*ka'a*	*ka*	*inoa moho*	*o*	*ka*	*pōpeku*	*iā*	*Kanalui.*
VMP	pass	DET	title	of	DET	football	to	St. Louis

'The football championship passed to (the possession of) St. Louis' (St. Louis took the football championship)

b.

Ua	*ka'a*	*ka*	*lanakila*	*iā*	*ia.*
VMP	pass	DET	victory	to	him

'The victory passed to (the possession of) him' (He was victorious)

4. ***lilo*** ('to be taken by'): lilo + subject (experiencer) + agent marker+ agent

a.

Ua	*lilo*	*ka*	*inoa moho*	*o*	*ka*	*pōpeku*	*iā*
VMP	taken by	DET	title	of	DET	football	AGM

Kanalui.
St. Louis

'The football championship was taken by St. Louis' (St. Louis took the football championship)

b.

Ua	*lilo*	*ka*	*lanakila*	*iā*	*ia.*
VMP	taken by	DET	victory	AGM	him

'The victory taken by to him' (He was victorious)

5. ***eo*** ('to lose'): eo + subject (experiencer) + agent

Ua	*eo*	*'o*	*Keoua*	*iā*	*Kamehameha.*
VMP	lose	SM	Keoua	AGM	Kamehameha

'Keoua lost to Kamehameha' (Kamehameha defeated Keoua)

6. ***I hewa*** ('fault'): I + stative verb + subject (exp) + agent marker + agent

a.

I	*hewa*	*ke*	*keiki*	*i*	*ka*	*makua.*
VM	error	DET	child	AGM	DET	parent

'The error of the child is caused by the parent' (The mistakes of the child are the fault of the parents)

b.

I	*hewa*	*iā*	*'oe*
VM	error	AGM	you

'(someone's) error is caused by you' (You are at fault)

7. ***iā* PRONOUN *iho*** (object reflexive pronoun)

Ua	*nānā*	*'o*	*ia*	*iā*	*ia*	*iho.*
VMP	look	SM	he	OM	he	reflexive

'He looked at himself'

8. ***no* PRONOUN *iho*** (benefactive reflexive pronoun)

Ua	*hana*	*lākou*	*no*	*lākou*	*iho.*
VMP	do	they	for	they	reflexive

'They worked for themselves' (They worked on their own, i.e., without assistance)

TARGET VOCABULARY

1. *inoa moho* — 'championship', 'title'
2. *ho'ohei pipi* — 'to rope cattle'
3. *ahona iki* — 'to be a little better, improved, of a condition'
4. *eo* — 'victory–*kikino*' (noun)

5. *kōko'olua* 'companion of two', 'sidekick'
6. *'āha'i* 'to carry off, as in victory'
7. *hia'ai* 'to be delighted'
8. *kiwi* 'horn, of a bull'
9. *hoka* 'to return empty handed'
10. *kōwaliwali* 'to twirl–*hehele*' (transitive verb)

APPENDIX B: UPTAKE CHARTS

ʻO ____________________

He aha nā mea āu i aʻo mai ai ma ka haʻawina i kēia lā?

(What are things you have learned from today's lesson?)

- Nā analula:

- Nā huaʻōlelo:

- Nā kumuhana a me nā manaʻo hou aku paha: (content and other comments)

- He aha nā mea huikau a i ʻole mō ʻakāka ʻole iā ʻoe? (things that are confusing or not clear to you?)

APPENDIX C: SESSION 2 CLAIMS OF UPTAKE FOR TARGET AND NON-TARGET ITEMS

	Total	Percent of Total
1. stative verb sentence	11	(20%)
ua ka'a ka ___ *iā* ___. (9)		
ua ka'a ka ___ *o* ___ *iā* ___. (1)		
**ua ka'a ka* ___ *o* ___ *ma luna o* ___. (1)		
2. agentive stative verb sentence	13	(23%)
ua eo 'o ___ *iā* ___. (10)		
ua eo 'o ___ *ia'u.* (1)		
ua eo (general) (2)		
3. intransitive verb sentence	2	(4%)
ua lanakila 'o ___ *ma luna o* ___. (1)		
ua lanakila (general) (1)		
4. agentive stative verb sentence	14	(25%)
ua lilo ka lanakila iā ___. (8)		
**ua lilo ka inoa moho iā* ___. (6)		
5. review structures from Session 1	10	(18%)
Inā ua, ua (5)		
Inā i, ua (5)		
6. non-target structures	6	(11%)
Iā wai i ka'a ai...(3)		
Hā'ule iā mākou (3)		

APPENDIX D: TARGET VOCABULARY CLAIMS

TARGET VOCABULARY ITEMS CLAIMED
(10 items: 33 total claims)

1.	*inoa moho*	‘championship’, ‘title’	9
2.	*ho‘ohei pipi*	‘to rope cattle’	4
3.	*ahona iki*	‘to be a little better, of a condition’	0
4.	*eo*	‘victory’	5
5.	*kōko‘olua*	‘companion of two’, ‘sidekick’	0
6.	*‘āha‘i*	‘to carry off, as in victory’	0
7.	*hia‘ai*	‘to be delighted’	0
8.	*kiwi*	‘horn, of a bull’	10
9.	*ho‘i nele*	‘to return empty handed’	0
10.	*kōwaliwali*	‘to twirl’	5

NON-TARGET VOCABULARY ITEMS CLAIMED
(15 items: 56 total claims)

1.	*ho‘ohei*	var. of ho‘ohei pipi (target item 8)	2
2.	*wili, wiliwili*	‘to wind, wrap, as legs of cattle’	3
3.	*poholo*	‘to slip over, as rope over head of calf’	2
4.	*kaula‘ili*	‘leather rope’	2
5.	*maku‘u/kamakū*	*‘saddle horn’	11
6.	*hainakā*	‘hankerchief’, ‘neckerchief’	7
7.	*kīpuka‘ili*	‘lasso’	7
8.	*kaula*	‘rope’	2
9.	*ho‘ohina*	‘to tackle, as a calf’ (+ var. ho‘ohā‘ule-to drop)	4
10.	*noho lio*	‘saddle’	1
11.	*pōhina*‘i	‘basketball’	4

12.	*pōhili*	‘baseball’	4
13.	*pōwāwae*	‘soccer’	3
14.	*pōpeku*	‘football’	1
15.	*ka‘a*	‘to transfer’ (part of structure)	3

Michael A. Roberts
University of Waikato, New Zealand

AWARENESS AND THE EFFICACY OF ERROR CORRECTION

ABSTRACT

Much attention has been paid to the treatment of learner errors in foreign/second language learning. The findings suggest limitations on the effectiveness of error correction practices. This study attempts to further clarify the conditions necessary for error correction to result in student learning. First the literature on error correction is reviewed. Work on the role of consciousness in second language learning is then examined. The study takes as its focus an examination of the classroom interaction between the teacher and class members in a teacher-fronted class in Japanese as a foreign language at the University of Hawai'i, and looks at the extent to which learners are able to correlate teacher feedback with errors in their L2 utterances. Although the size of the subject sample is too small to generate a generalizable conclusion, the evidence suggests that not only must L2 learners recognize that they are being corrected, but also that they must understand the nature of the error.

INTRODUCTION

The treatment of L2 learners' errors has been the subject of much debate and investigation among both SLA researchers and teaching practitioners. This paper is an attempt to relate recent work on the role of consciousness in second language learning to the efficacy of error correction. The study takes as its focus an examination of the classroom interaction between the teacher and class members in a teacher-fronted class in Japanese as a foreign language, and attempts to examine the extent to which learners are able to correlate teacher feedback with the errors in their L2 utterances.

Roberts, Michael A. (1995). Awareness and the efficacy of error correction. In Richard Schmidt (Ed.), *Attention and awareness in foreign language learning* (Technical Report #9) (pp. 163–182). Honolulu, Hawai'i: University of Hawai'i, Second Language Teaching & Curriculum Center.

ERROR CORRECTION

Perspectives on the efficacy of error-correction are distributed along a continuum which exhibits a range of positions from interventionist to non-interventionist. The Audiolingual Method, which saw language learning as a process of habit formation based on extensive practice, typifies the interventionist position. Practitioners believed that student errors were harmful because they led to the formation of bad habits. If errors occurred they were to be corrected immediately. The non-interventionist position is typified by Krashen and Terrell (1983) in their Natural Approach, in which error correction is proscribed. Illustrative of an intermediate position, which does not proscribe, but questions the efficacy of error-correction, is that taken by Long (1977) who suggests that much of the corrective feedback supplied to L2 learners is erratic, ambiguous, ill-timed, and ineffective in the short term.

There is an interesting study by Tomasello and Herron (1989) in which they took a group of sentences for which an L1 (English) transfer strategy would produce incorrect sentences in the L2 (French). Students' inevitable transfer errors were then corrected immediately by the teacher. They called this the "Garden Path Technique." When compared with a control group in which students were just taught the French form and told it differed from English, the Garden Path group performed significantly better on a post-test.

A study by Day, Chenowith, Chun and Luppescu (1983) suggests that classroom teachers should look to the type of native speaker feedback given to non-native speakers outside the classroom as a model for corrective feedback in the classroom. In contrast with Long's claim about the nature of corrective feedback by classroom teachers, they conclude that NS feedback outside the classroom was both clear and consistent. It typically came in the turn immediately following the incorrect NNS utterance and was most often direct ("on-record" in Brown and Levinson's (1978) terminology) and focused (specifically related to error). They also noted that the type of errors which attracted corrective feedback were those which inhibited conversation, *viz.* factual errors, discourse errors, and vocabulary items. Interestingly, syntactic errors, which comprise the bulk of classroom error correction were corrected only 7% of the time as opposed to 89.5% for factual errors, 35% for discourse errors and 15% for word choice errors. They quote Judd (1978) as claiming that "since many of the errors in syntax will only disappear in time, classroom exercises might be better devoted to vocabulary enrichment" (p. 75).

Vigil and Oller (1976) outline a model of rule fossilization. They define fossilization as a process whereby certain linguistic items, rules and sub-systems become relatively permanently incorporated into the "grammatical system of a second language learner" (p. 281). They include both target-like and non-target-like forms in this process. For them, feedback comes via two channels: cognitive and affective. They also make a distinction between expected and unexpected feedback. Predominantly negative feedback in the affective channel is predicted to result in abortion of further attempts at communication. Positive affective feedback coupled with a predominant expectation of positive cognitive feedback predicts a tendency toward fossilization. However, the combination of positive affective feedback with a predominant expectation of negative cognitive feedback provides a strong destabilizing influence in the development of learner grammars, a desirable state when the interlanguage grammar is short of the L2 target. The implication for classroom teachers of this model is that in order to benefit from the destabilizing influence of corrective feedback in the cognitive domain, it is necessary for them to engender the expectation of positive feedback in the affective domain.

Finally, Chaudron (1988) provides an extensive review of the literature on error correction both at the theoretical and empirical levels. He characterizes studies as attempting to address five questions, and summarizes their findings as follows:

1. Should errors be corrected? This should ultimately be determined by evidence of the efficacy of correction ("a difficult phenomenon to demonstrate")

2. When should learner errors be corrected? The consensus seems to be:

    - when they pertain to the pedagogical focus of the lesson, and
    - when they significantly inhibit communication.

3. Which errors should be corrected? Hendrickson (1978) suggests as prime candidates for treatment:

   - errors that impair communication,
   - errors that have highly stigmatizing effects on the listener, and
   - errors that occur frequently.

4. How should errors be corrected? Chaudron gives an adaptation of Day, et al.'s (1984) turn taking framework, Allwright's (1975) taxonomy of feedback functions and his own (1977) taxonomy of feedback types and features.

5. Who should correct errors? As an alternative to teacher correction of errors, Chaudron cites studies such as those by Wren (1982) on the incidence of student self-correction and Long and Porter (1985) on student peer correction.

ROLE OF CONSCIOUSNESS

In his classic article on the significance of learners' errors, Corder (1967) makes an important distinction between input and intake. Input is "what is available for going in," whereas intake is "what goes in." He notes that the presentation of a particular linguistic form to a class by a teacher does not constitute intake. Krashen (1983) seems to believe that input becomes intake by mere virtue of the fact that it is comprehensible and occurs with a certain minimal frequency in the input. This seems to assume that communication of meaning, in some way translates to the acquisition of syntactic form. Chaudron (1985) draws on work by Faerch and Kasper (1980) suggesting that there are two types of intake: that which is "simply reduced and decoded as communication," and that "relating to learning (i.e., input on the basis of which the learner forms her hypotheses about the L2 rules and tests them out subsequently." Building on this Chaudron characterizes the phenomenon of speech processing as a continuum ranging from preliminary intake (focusing on speech processing as perception and comprehension) to final intake (focusing on the processes used to organize stored data into linguistic systems).

Schmidt (1990) discusses the role of consciousness in second language learning. Referring to Chaudron's concept of preliminary intake, he proposes the hypothesis that intake is that part of the input that the learner notices. Noting the lack of empirical evidence in this area, he cites his own diary study with Frota (Schmidt and Frota 1986) in which they analyze his acquisition of Brazilian Portuguese. Among other things they note that the teaching of forms did not guarantee their appearance in his output; that forms that never appeared in the input did not appear in his speech; that high frequency in input correlated positively with appearance in output; and that the emergence of new forms in speech matched up with journal comments relating to noticing something in the input. They also discuss the principle of "noticing the gap," becoming aware that what the learner produces is not what target language speakers say, and conclude that as a minimum, the learner must realize that he or she is being corrected. Based on this, Schmidt (1990) suggests conscious noticing as the necessary and sufficient condition for converting input to intake. In an analogous manner, it is the hypothesis of this study that the efficacy of error correction is directly related to the condition that the L2 learner not only recognize that he/she is being corrected, but understands the nature of the correction.

METHOD

In order to test the hypothesis, it was decided to examine how much error correction students actually noticed and understood in a class in which error correction played a significant part in the teacher's approach. Further, it was decided to sort the results according to error types and error correction types to see if these had a significant bearing on results.

PARTICIPANTS

The study is an analysis of the interaction between teacher and student in a teacher-fronted classroom in Japanese as a foreign language at the University of Hawai'i at Mānoa. The students were all native speakers of American English. The class was for beginners and used as its text *Japanese: the Spoken Language* (Jorden and Noda 1987). The format of the class was such that the students memorized short core conversations and the teacher created contexts in which the students could perform their memorized roles. By altering the stimulus, the teacher created variations allowing the students to generalize their knowledge to a wider variety of situations. It is a feature of the methodology associated with this text that teachers are encouraged to actively correct student errors.

DATA COLLECTION

The study draws on Slimani's (1992) assertion that teacher and student agendas often differ in the classroom and in fact what stands out in students' minds at the end of a class is quite different from what stands out on the teacher's agenda. Slimani studied ESL learners in Algeria and had students fill out uptake reports at the end of each of six classes. She counted 256 instances of topicalization (items that became however briefly the topic of conversation rather than simply being part of the classroom discourse). Fifty two (20.31%) of these were claimed as already known. Ninety two (35.93%) were topicalized but not claimed as learned. One hundred and twelve (43.75%) were claimed by students as uptake. An interesting point is that although

77.45% of the topicalization was effected by the teacher and only 22.54% by the students, the *rate* of uptake of student initiated topicalization was higher than that of teacher initiated topicalization.

Whereas Slimani relied on students' memory at the end of the class to fill out her uptake sheet, this was deemed to be impractical in the present study. It was felt that a more precise measure could be obtained by having students view a video of the class and report on their notice of error correction. An entire fifty minute class was videotaped and transcribed by the writer. Several days after the class, three student volunteers from the class were asked to watch the video right through and note down the meter reading every time they thought the teacher was correcting someone. They were also asked to identify the nature of the error. Each of the three students performed this exercise in isolation and were instructed to try and go straight through without stopping, but were told that they could stop and go back if they needed to clarify anything. The writer remained unobtrusively in the room and observed that none of the three students exercised the option of stopping the tape. The students did not have access to the written transcript of the lesson. The writer also analyzed the transcript and compared his analysis with those of the students.

ANALYSIS

The writer analyzed teacher correction types into the following categories:

Request	Teacher requests repeat of student utterance
Repeat	Teacher repeats question
Recast[1]	Teacher models correctly recast form of student's incorrect utterance

[1] I originally used the term "model" here, but in research currently being undertaken by Long (in press), he makes a distinction between "models" (teacher provides target-like input before the learner has attempted to produce at all) and "recasts" (teacher adds or changes morphosyntactic information to a learner's utterance without changing its essential meaning). As none of the tokens in this

Partial recast	Similar to the preceding, but teacher only models the segment of the utterance in which the error occurs
Confirmation check	Teacher reacts to an utterance which is out of step with discourse flow using a confirmation check
Cue	Teacher cues student to repeat utterance
Other	Other categories with only one or two tokens, e.g., pattern modeling, rephrasing of a question, gestures, or returning to the start of discourse topic sequence

For the purposes of illustration the following segments are included from the transcription (underlined text is incorrect; bold text indicates the category token):

Request

Student: *Mae ni koosyuu denwa yo… koosyuu denwa arimasu yo… arimasu ne*

'In front a public phone... there is a phone... there is, isn't there?'

Teacher: ***Moo ichido itte kudasai*** (Request)

'Please say it again'

Student: *Mae ni koosyuu denwa ni… mae ni koosyuu denwa arimasu ne*

'In front in the public phone... there's a phone in front, right?'

Repeat

Teacher: *Ikutsu kaimasu ka*

'How many will you buy?'

Student: *Anoo… ikutsu…* (slow to digest meaning of question)

'Uhm... how many ...'

---

study fit the former category, I have decided to follow Long and use the term recast.

Teacher: ***Ikutsu kaimasu ka*** (Repeat)
'How many will you buy?'
Student: *Hitotsu o kaimasu*
'I'll buy one'
Teacher: **Hitotsu kaimasu** (Repeat)
'I'll buy one'
Student: *Hitotsu kaimasu*
'I'll buy one'

Partial recast

Student: *Ueno eki no mae ni mo Tookyoo eki no...ni mo arimasu yo*
'Both in front of the Ueno Station and of the Tokyo Station... there are'
Teacher: ***Tookyoo eki no mae ni mo*** (Partial recast)
'In front of the Tokyo Station'
Student: *Tookyoo eki no mae ni mo arimasu yo*
'There is also one in front of the Tokyo Station'

Confirmation check

Teacher: *Sumimasen ga, koosyuu denwa wa dochira ni arimasu ka*
'Excuse me, where is the public phone?'
Student: *Biru ni arimasu*
'It's in the building'
Teacher: ***Biru ni arimasu ka*** (Confirmation check)
'In the building?'
Student: *Biru no mae ni arimasu*
'It's in front of the building'

Cue

Student 1: *Chotto chiisai desu ga, ookii no wa arimasu ka*
'It's a little small; do you have a big one?'
Student 2: *Sumimasen, ookikunai desu*
'I'm sorry, it isn't big'

Teacher: ***Ookii no wa...*** (Cue)
'A big one ...'
Student 2: *Ooki no wa gozaimasen*
'We don't have a big one'

The errors themselves were analyzed into the following types:

- Particles
- Vocabulary
- Phonology
- Word order
- Pragmalinguistic errors (correct utterances that do not achieve the function that the speaker intends)
- Information errors
- Understanding errors

RESULTS

STUDENT RECOGNITION OF ERROR CORRECTION

The data were examined for their distribution across error types and error correction categories. Table 1 shows the number of error corrections recognized and understood by the student participants. As can be seen, Slimani's finding that what teachers think students are learning and what students are actually perceiving are often two different scenarios seems to have its parallel in the area of error correction.

Table 1. Student perception of errors and error correction

	Researcher	Subject 1	Subject 2	Subject 3
Number of teacher error corrections noted	92	22 [23.9%]	42 [45.7%]	34 [37.0%]
Number of instances where subject understood nature of error		15 [16.3%]	18 [19.6%]	23 [25.0%]

ERROR CORRECTION TYPES

Table 2 shows the distribution of student judgments across the different categories of error correction.

The first column lists the error correction categories. The second gives the number of tokens in each category — for example, the researcher identified 27 instances of recast in the lesson — multiplied by 3 participants to give the total number of 81 opportunities for noticing the correction behavior. The third column is subdivided into two

Table 2. Student perception of errors and error correction

Error correction categories	# of opportunities for noticing	Instances of noticing		Instances of understanding	
	[# of tokens x 3 subjects]	Number	% of total	Number	% of total
Recast	[27 x 3]= 81	27	33.3	15	18.5
Partial recast	[38 x 3] = 114	49	42.9	32	28.2
Cue	[10 x 3] = 30	9	30	3	10
Request	[6 x 3] = 18	5	21.7	2	11.7
Repeat	[4 x 3] = 12	5	42.5	2	17.5
Confirmation check	[3 x 3] = 9	0	0	0	0
Other	[4 x 3] = 12	3	25	2	17.5

columns. The one on the left, labeled "Number," gives the total number of instances (among the three student participants) that the correction behavior by the teacher was noticed. The one on the right column expresses this figure as a percentage of the total number of opportunities for noticing. If all 3 students had noticed all 27 instances of recast there was a potential for 81 instances of noticing. The fourth column is similarly subdivided and gives the number of instances of understanding the nature of the error as a percentage of the total number of opportunities for noticing. Although percentages cannot be taken to suggest much when the number of tokens is small, the figures for the recast category in general and the partial recast category in particular do seem to indicate a greater level of noticing error correction and understanding the nature of the error. This is perhaps to be expected, because the partial recast focuses the learner's attention more narrowly on the segment containing the error.

Table 3 shows the distribution of the student judgments across the different error types.

Table 3. Student perception of errors and error correction distributed across error types

Error types [# of tokens]	# of opportunities for noticing [# of tokens x 3 subjects]	Instances of noticing		Instances of understanding	
		Number	% of total	Number	% of total
Particles	[47 x 3] = 141	49	34.7	32	22.8
Vocabulary	[16 x 3] = 48	22	45.6	12	25
Phonology	[6 x 3] = 18	9	50	7	38.3
Order	[5 x 3] = 15	2	14	1	6
Understanding	[5 x 3] = 15	8	54	1	6
Sociopragmatic	[5 x 3] = 15	6	40	3	20
Pragmalinguistic	[4 x 3] = 12	2	17.5	0	0
Information	[4 x 3] = 12	0	0	0	0

With the small number of tokens in the lower types it is difficult to make any generalizations, and in the larger categories, there do not appear to be any striking differences.

DISCUSSION

Moving away from the quantitative side of the analysis, there are quite a few instances of errors being made consistently even after specific error correction. This would seem to suggest that the learners' interlanguages are at least in part systematic, though still short of the L2 target. Excerpts 1 and 2 illustrate this phenomenon. Once again, underlined text indicates the error and bold text indicates the teacher's correction.

Excerpt 1 (in first three minutes of lesson)

Student 1: *Ee mae ni… mae nimo (1) ushiro…<u>ushiroe</u> ni mo arimasu yo* (vocabulary error)
'Yes, in front...both in front and in back...in back'

Teacher: ***Un…ushiro ni mo arimasu yo*** (Partial recast)
'...in the back'

Student 1: *Ushiro ni mo arimasu yo*
'In the back'

Excerpt 2 (in last five minutes of lesson)

Student 1: *Anoo (3) paakingu wa <u>ushiroe</u> ni arimasu* (vocabulary error)
'Uhm...parking's around the back'

Teacher: ***Ushiro ni arimasu*** (Partial recast)
'It's around the back'

Student 1: *Ushiro ni arimasu*
'It's around the back'

Not only was there evidence of learners returning to their *own* mistakes, but also of them making mistakes identical to those of *other learners* quite soon after the other learner had been corrected. This is illustrated in Excerpts 3 and 4.

Excerpt 3 (meter reading 1159)

Student 2: *Keeki no... Ueno eki no keeki mise* (particle error)
'Cake... the Cake shop at Ueno Station'

Teacher: ***Ueno eki no ...*** (Cue)
'The Ueno station'

Student 2: ... *mae keeki mise* (particle error)
'... front cake shop'

Teacher: ***Mae no...*** (Cue)
'front...'

Student 2: ... *mae no keeki no mise ni mo..*
'... both in the cake shop'

Excerpt 4 (meter reading 1213)

Student 3: *Mae no keeki mise..*(particle error)
'The cake shop in front..'

Teacher: ***Keeki no mise*** (Partial recast)
'Cake shop'

Student 3: *Keeki no mise dake..*
'Just the cake shop..'

These observations seem to indicate that the students have either not noticed the earlier corrections or perhaps noticed the correction activity on the part of the teacher but not understood the nature of the error. A third possibility is that they have both noticed and understood briefly, but only in a brief episode in short term memory which served to facilitate preliminary intake but did not have sufficient impact to become final intake. Of particular interest is the fact that student 3 in Excerpt 4 was one of the student evaluators and did not note the error correction when he reviewed the tape.

It would be one-sided not to point out that there were also instances of corrections sticking. Excerpt 5 (meter reading 995) shows how student 4 was having difficulty with the placement of *ni mo* (locative particle + 'also') in the double *mo* construction. (Place A *ni mo* place

B *ni mo arimasu* = 'There are some both in Place A and in place B'). Excerpt 6 which follows about five minutes later (meter reading 1085) shows that he has worked it out. This is also of special significance because student 4 was also one of the student judges and not only noted the error correction, but also gave an accurate description of the error.

Excerpt 5 (meter reading 995)

Teacher: *Dochira desu ka*
'Where is it?'

Student 4: *Uh (3) Ueno eki no mae ni... ni mo (2) kooshuu... kooshoo denwa.*(vocabulary error)
'Uh (3) in front of Ueno station (2) public... public telephone..'

Teacher: *Kooshuu denwa* (Partial recast)
'Public telephone'

Student 4: *Kooshuu denwa <u>ni mo (2) ni (3) to</u>...* (information error)
'At public phone also (2) in (3) and...'

Teacher: *Un kooshuu denwa to* (Partial recast)
'Yes, public phone and...'

Student 4: *Kooshuu denwa <u>ni mo arimasu</u>* (information error)
'It's also in the public phone'

Teacher: *Arimasu ka* (Confirm)
'Is it?'

Student 4: (laughs)

Teacher: *Kooshuu denwa to kooban no* (Cue)
'Public phone and police box'

Student 4: *... aida <u>desu</u>* (vocabulary error)
'..between them'

Teacher: *Aida...* (Cue)
'Between'

Student 4: *<u>... arimasu</u>* (particle error)
'... it is'

Teacher: *Aida* ... (Cue)
'Between'
Student 4: ... *ni mo*
'also'

Excerpt 6 (meter reading 1085)

Teacher: *Doko ni... doko desu ka. Dochira desu ka*
'Where... where are they? Where are they?'
Student 4: *Ueno eki no mae ni mo kooshuu denwa to kooban no aida ni mo arimasu*
'Both in front of the station and between the public phone and the police box'

Given the length of the response being sought by the teacher, it is quite remarkable that student 4 managed to get it right in Excerpt 6, when he had experienced such difficulty just five minutes previously in Excerpt 5.

It was suspected that L2 proficiency might be a significant contributing factor in determining whether or not students noticed error corrections and understood the nature of errors so noticed. The class teacher was requested to rank the three student judges in order of proficiency. As the class was team-taught we were able to get the concurrence of both teachers that the order of proficiency on oral Japanese was subject 1 > subject 2 > subject 3. This was actually the reverse of the order of success in identifying the nature of the error. Even when looking just at performance in metalinguistic tasks, subject 3 was considered by both teachers to be ranked after the other two. The possibility of an effect for proficiency seems not to be realized, however. It is possible that there may even be an inverse relationship between proficiency and noticing error correction. Although it is not testable with the data in this study, it may be that the less proficient students experience more correction than those who are more proficient and thus are more finely tuned to the teacher's error correction signals.

CONCLUSION

In summary, this study has looked at the efficacy of error correction in a teacher-fronted class. The findings suggest that students are only aware of corrective activity in the classroom a fraction of the time and even when they are, it is not likely that they understand the nature of the error in many instances. In fact, the student evaluators used in this study would have been more aware of the error correction process than in a normal class because it was the focus of the task they were asked to perform. In light of Schmidt's conclusion that noticing is the necessary and sufficient condition for input to become intake, we must reassess the value of error correction in the learning place. Although it is not within the purview of this limited study, it seems that the challenge to teachers is to come up with ways that will provide learners with feedback that they will be able to both notice and understand.

ACKNOWLEDGMENTS

This chapter is a revision of a paper originally presented at the Eighth Biennial Conference of the Japanese Studies Association of Australia, held at the University of Newcastle, Australia, July 6–10, 1993. I am indebted to Richard Schmidt for comments and suggestions.

REFERENCES

Allwright, R. (1975). Problems in the study of the language teacher's treatment of learner error. In M. Burt & H. Dulay (Eds.), *On TESOL '75: New directions in second language learning, teaching and bilingual education*. (pp. 96–109). Washington, DC: TESOL.

Brown, P., & Levinson, S. (1978). Universals in language usage: Politeness phenomena. In E. Goody (Ed.), *Questions and politeness: Strategies in social interaction*. (pp. 56–289). Cambridge: Cambridge University Press.

Chaudron, C. (1977). A descriptive model of discourse in the corrective treatment of learners' errors. *Language Learning*, *27*, 29–46.

Chaudron, C. (1985). Intake: On models and methods for discovering learners' processing of input. *Studies in Second Language Acquisition*, *7*, 1–14.

Chaudron, C. (1988). *Second language classrooms: Research on teaching and learning*. Cambridge: Cambridge University Press.

Corder, S. (1967). The significance of learners' errors. *International Review of Applied Linguistics*, *5*, 161–170.

Day, R., Chenowith, N., Chun, A., & Luppescu, S. (1983). Foreign language learning and the treatment of spoken errors. *Language Learning and Communication*, *2*, 215–224.

Day, R., Chenowith, N., Chun, A., & Luppescu, S. (1984). Corrective feedback in native-nonnative discourse. *Language Learning*, *34*, 19–45.

Faerch, C., & Kasper, G. (1980). Processes and strategies in foreign language learning and communication. *The Interlanguage Studies Bulletin — Utrecht*, *5*, 47–118.

Hendrickson, J. (1978). Error correction in foreign language teaching: Recent research and practice. *Modern Language Journal*, *62*, 387–398.

Jorden, E., & Noda, M. (1987). *Japanese: The spoken language*. New Haven, CT: Yale University Press.

Judd, E. (1978). Vocabulary teaching and TESOL: A need for reevaluation of existing assumptions. *TESOL Quarterly, 12*, 71–76.

Krashen, S. (1983). Newmark's 'ignorance hypothesis' and current second language acquisition theory. In S. Gass & L. Selinker, (Eds.), *Language transfer in language learning.*(pp. 135–153). Rowley, MA: Newbury House.

Krashen, S., & Terrell, T. (1983). *The natural approach*. New York: Pergamon.

Long, M. (1977). Teacher feedback on learner error: Mapping cognitions. In H. Brown, C. Yorio, & R. Crymes, (Eds.), *On TESOL '77*, (pp. 278–93). Washington, DC: TESOL.

Long, M. (in press). The role of the linguistic environment in second language acquisition. In W. Ritchie & T. Bhatia, (Eds.), *Handbook of language acquisition, vol. 2: Second language acquisition*. New York: Academic Press.

Long, M., & Porter, P. (1985) Group work, interlanguage talk, and second language acquisition. *TESOL Quarterly, 19*, 207–228.

Schmidt, R. (1990). The role of consciousness in second language learning. *Applied Linguistics, 11*, 129–158.

Schmidt, R., & Frota, S. (1986). Developing basic conversational ability in a second language: A case study of an adult learner of Portuguese. In R. R. Day (Ed.), *Talking to learn: Conversation in second language acquisition* (pp. 237–326). Rowley, MA: Newbury House.

Slimani, A. (1992). Evaluation of classroom interaction. In J. Alderson & A. Beretta (Eds.), *Evaluating second language education* (pp. 197–221). Cambridge: Cambridge University Press.

Tomasello, M., & Herron, C. (1989). Feedback for language transfer errors: The garden path technique. *Studies in Second Language Learning, 11*, 385–395.

Vigil, N., & Oller, J. (1976). Rule fossilization: A tentative model. *Language Learning, 26*, 281–295.

Wren, D. (1982). A case study in the treatment of oral errors. *Selected Papers in TESOL, 1*, 90–103. Monterey, CA: Monterey Institute of International Studies.

Renée Jourdenais, Mitsuhiko Ota, Stephanie Stauffer,
Beverly Boyson & Catherine Doughty
Georgetown University

DOES TEXTUAL ENHANCEMENT PROMOTE NOTICING? A THINK-ALOUD PROTOCOL ANALYSIS

ABSTRACT

One of the theoretical rationales for *focus on form* is the notion that second language (L2) learning requires noticing of what is to be learned. Various techniques of input enhancement have been developed with the hope that they promote noticing of target forms. While their effectiveness has been evaluated in terms of subsequent acquisition of the target forms, few attempts have been made to investigate whether enhanced input is processed differently by learners. The purpose of this study was to determine whether one input enhancement technique — textual modification — can make L2 forms more noticeable and affect learner on-line processing of forms.

In this study, native speakers of English in a second semester Spanish class at Georgetown University were assigned to enhancement and comparison groups. Participants in the enhancement group received a sample text in Spanish with all preterit and imperfect verb forms highlighted; participants in the comparison group received the same text with no typographical modification. Think-aloud protocols were collected during a subsequent task in which participants wrote a picture-based narrative similar to that presented in the sample text. Analysis of the data revealed that enhancement participants' protocols contained more episodes related to selection and conjugation of preterit and imperfect verbs than did those of the comparison participants. Enhancement participants also produced more target features in their written production. The results indicate that textual enhancement promotes noticing of target L2 form and has an effect on learners' subsequent output.

Jourdenais, R., Ota, M., Stauffer, S., Boyson, B., & Doughty, C. (1995). Does textual enhancement promote noticing? A think-aloud protocol analysis. In Richard Schmidt (Ed.), *Attention and awareness in foreign language learning* (Technical Report #9) (pp. 183–216). Honolulu, Hawai'i: University of Hawai'i, Second Language Teaching & Curriculum Center.

INTRODUCTION

Research demonstrating the insufficiency of second language (L2) learning from positive evidence alone (Pavesi, 1986; Schmidt, 1983; Swain, 1991; White, 1991) and the claim that L2 acquisition requires noticing (Schmidt, 1990, 1993; Tomlin and Villa, 1994) are the empirical and theoretical bases of recent claims for the need of L2 instruction that will lead learners to identify the differences between their interlanguage and the target language ('consciousness-raising,' Sharwood Smith, 1981; 'input enhancement,' Sharwood Smith, 1991; 'focus on form,' Long, 1991). However, the bulk of the research in instructed L2 acquisition focuses mainly on the effect of instructional modification as measured by the relationship between the input learners receive and their subsequent linguistic performance. Lacking in this line of research is the investigation of the learners' processing of input. This is undoubtedly due to the difficulty in observing the internal processing of learners and the unpredictability of cognitive reaction to external stimuli. In an effort to contribute to an understanding of internal input processing, the purpose of this study was to observe the differences in such processing of enhanced and unenhanced input through the use of think-aloud protocol analysis.

FOCUS ON FORM

Studies have shown that neither the structuralist approaches of the 1950's and 60's, in which communicative contexts were mostly lacking, nor the more naturalistic and communicative approaches of the 1970's and 80's, which de-emphasized any systematic treatment of the structure (e.g., syntax and morphology) of the L2, have adequately addressed the full complement of second language learners' needs (see e.g., Lightbown, 1985; Lightbown and Spada, 1990). Striking a balance between emphasizing accurate production of L2 forms and promoting meaningful communication in real contexts has been a recent concern in the field of second language teaching and acquisition.

A well-known case which illustrates this point is that of the immersion programs in progress in Canada since the 1970's (see, e.g., Hammerly, 1987; Swain, 1985; Swain and Lapkin, 1989, 1994).

Children and adolescents in these programs attend classes from kindergarten through high school in which all of the instruction during the initial years and much of the instruction in the later years is delivered in the target language. According to Krashen's theory of comprehensible input (1985), these students should achieve high fluency and comprehension of the target language, as they have received large "doses" of native-language input in a communicative setting over an extended period of time. However, studies of these programs have shown that the communicative approach used in such settings is not sufficient to give learners the necessary competence they need to produce target-like forms in the L2 by the time they have completed many years of study (see, e.g., Day and Shapson, 1991; Hammerly, 1987; Harley, 1993; Swain and Lapkin, 1989). Hammerly (1987, p. 397) has pointed out that the students in this setting seem to settle for functional communication and, consequently, to stabilize in their L2 production. Such observations have led language teachers and researchers to inquire about how to incorporate a systematic treatment of the formal properties of language within a communicative approach to language teaching.

Long (1991) has introduced the term *focus on form* as a means of describing phenomena that induce a learner to attend to linguistic form within a meaningful context. Long specifically contrasts this idea with traditional grammar instruction, which he calls *focus on forms*, and which involves teaching forms exclusively or in isolation. The purpose of focus on form research is to investigate the effects of explicit and/or implicit focus on a language form — usually, but not limited to, an aspect of syntax or morphology — within a communicative setting which requires interaction and negotiation of meaning in real language contexts. A key distinction is that it is the learner who focuses on the form; the teacher, materials designer, or researcher can hope only to set up the conditions for such a focus.

Encouraging learners to focus on form may be accomplished through various methods; manipulating the input is one. Sharwood Smith (1993) mentions several types of enhanced input which may focus learners on form: explicit discussion of the form, metalinguistic description of the form, and provision of implicit error correction through the use of special patterns of stress or intonation, or through the use of gestures or facial expressions. Another type of implicit priming for focus on form — textual enhancement (Lorch, 1989; Sharwood Smith, 1993) — is the method employed in this study (discussed below).

Studies have also demonstrated that focus on form in meaningful contexts can affect the accuracy of L2 output (e.g., Day and Shapson, 1991; Doughty, 1991; Kowal and Swain, 1994; Swain and Lapkin, 1994). In fact, it has been argued that opportunities for comprehensible output are essential for developing target-like production skills in a second language (Swain, 1985). The think-aloud protocol employed by this study has been chosen as a way of observing the learners' noticing of input and processing of linguistic form.

NOTICING AND ATTENTION IN SLA

A major component of focus on form can be seen as one of focusing learners' attention on features of the L2. While many SLA researchers agree that some kind of attentional process is required for input to become intake, opinions vary as to amount and type of attention necessary for SLA (Gass, 1986; Gass and Selinker, 1994; Hulstijn, 1989; Rutherford and Sharwood Smith, 1985; Sharwood Smith, 1991, 1993; Schmidt, 1990, 1993, 1994; Tomlin and Villa, 1994). Schmidt, for example, argues that "noticing is the necessary and sufficient condition for the conversion of input to intake for learning" (1994, p. 17), where noticing is operationalized as "availability for self report" (1990, p. 132) at or immediately after the experience. Noticing, therefore, entails conscious registration of the contents of focal attention. Tomlin and Villa (1994), however, hold that conscious registration is not a necessary component of attentional process in second language learning. Instead, detection is proposed as the minimally necessary process of acquisition, and is the process "by which particular exemplars are registered in memory" (Tomlin and Villa 1994, p. 193). Detected information is available for further cognitive processing, such as hypothesis formation and testing. But detection does not require awareness. Information can be detected without the learner being aware of this having occurred.

Although it is still debatable whether or not conversion of input to intake requires conscious registration in addition to focal attention, there is no disagreement that noticing (i.e., being aware of certain forms) requires focal-attentive processing. At this stage of SLA research, as suggested by Schmidt (1994), it would be wiser to test the hypothesis that more noticing leads to more learning, rather than to pinpoint the zero-point (or threshold; Baars, 1988) for acquisition.

INPUT ENHANCEMENT OF WRITTEN TEXT

Focus on the formal properties of language can be initiated not only by providing negative feedback on ill-formed forms in the learner output, but also by making more salient certain well-formed forms in the input (Sharwood Smith, 1993). Techniques employed to enhance input in written text include manipulation of typography (i.e., larger type sizes, different typefaces) and use of typographic cues (i.e., *italic*, **bold face**, CAPITAL LETTERS, underlining, color coding, etc.).

Although there is a fair amount of L1 research showing the effectiveness of underlining as measured by recall of cued words in text (Fowler and Barker, 1974; Hartley, Bartlett, and Branthwaite, 1980; Lorch 1989), few studies have been carried out to investigate the direct effects of textual input enhancement in second language learning. One study that did use typographic manipulation to look at the effect of written input is Shook (1990). In this study, 48 learners of Spanish received one of three different exposure conditions to the written input which included the target form (Spanish present perfect). The first enhancement group received a text with the target structures in bolded uppercase letters along with instructions to focus on those structures; the second group received the same text but no specific instructions; and the comparison group received the text without highlighting and no specific instructions to focus on any forms. No significant differences were found among the three groups in a post-treatment multiple-choice translation task, a multiple-choice sentence completion task, and a free written recall of the passage. A second study also found no significant effects for textual input enhancement through the use of uppercase letters (White, 1994).

White's study is among the few that address the role of noticing in the processing of written input. She reports that when participants who had received the enhanced input were asked about their reactions, they replied that they hadn't noticed the uppercase letters. A number of explanations could be proposed to explain the lack of noticing: perhaps input enhancement is intrinsically ineffectual; perhaps the participants were accustomed to such variations in typeface; perhaps the participants were not ready to attend to the enhanced feature; or perhaps the participants already had comparison over the feature that was enhanced, and so the feature wasn't salient.

In order to investigate the direct relation of input and noticing, on-line processing of linguistic input must be observed without external manipulation or intervention on the part of the researcher. As Harley points out, what is needed in this area of research is more emphasis on "the 'inside' perspective of the learners involved and what they report themselves to be aware of" (1994, p. 66).

THINK-ALOUD PROTOCOL

Protocol analysis, or the use of verbal reports, can provide researchers with a means of observing the cognitive processes of language learners. Ericsson and Simon (1993) cite studies from a variety of fields, including cognitive science, psychology, and education, which demonstrate that participants will report information which is 'heeded,' or attended to, during the performance of a task. The assumption that underlies protocol analysis is that information in focal attention is available for verbalized report. Verbalizations such as those obtained during think-aloud protocols allow researchers to observe the cognitive processes of participants, without influencing the sequencing of thoughts (Ericsson and Simon, 1993).[1]

Research that requires such verbalizations may make use of concurrent, retrospective, or intervention protocols, depending on whether the researcher wishes to collect the reports during the entire time that the task is being performed, after the task has been completed, or at specific points during the performance of the task. During a concurrent think-aloud protocol, participants are asked to

---

1 Some studies do suggest that protocols "frequently slow down subjects' progress, relative to subjects' progress under normal task conditions" (Stratman & Hamp-Lyons, 1994, p. 89). This effect, were it to be demonstrated, would not confound the purpose of our study.

verbalize their thoughts as they complete a task. These verbalizations are recorded, and then transcribed and encoded for later analysis. Categories for analysis are usually derived in a bottom-up fashion (Ericsson and Simon, 1993).

Concurrent think-aloud protocols have been used by researchers in the field of applied linguistics to observe the cognitive processes of both native and non-native speakers as they perform many types of tasks. Hosenfeld (1976), for example, proposed that protocols be used to collect data about what language learners really process as they complete tasks that are supposed to require processing of L2 forms. She reported the results of a study in which college Spanish students demonstrated that it was usual for them to complete their Spanish homework without processing the language of the exercises for meaning. Other types of learner strategies have been studied through the use of protocol analysis by Vann and Abraham (1990), who contrasted the protocols of successful and unsuccessful language learners as they completed various tasks, and by Raimes (1987), who contrasted the strategies of remedial and advanced ESL writers as they composed essays in the L2.

The collection of think-aloud protocols has also become a widely-used method of studying not only writing strategies, but also the process of writing for both first and second language learners (Hayes and Flower, 1980; Smagorinsky, 1994; Swain and Lapkin, 1994; Swarts, Flower, and Hayes, 1984). In an investigation of the composition processes of L2 writers in French in which they made use of a concurrent think-aloud protocol, Swain and Lapkin (1994) found that production in the learner's second language can lead learners to notice gaps in their linguistic knowledge. Through the use of such protocols, therefore, researchers are able to observe, at some level, the cognitive processes of L2 learners as they produce and analyze their second language.

The participants in this study, native speakers of English, performed concurrent think-aloud protocols as they wrote in Spanish, their second language. Categories for analysis and evidence of participants' focus on linguistic form were derived from the data.

FORMS FOR ANALYSIS: SPANISH PRETERIT AND IMPERFECT

The Spanish preterit and imperfect forms were chosen for this study for two reasons. First, these are forms that had been taught uniformly (albeit perhaps traditionally) to the participants of the study. Furthermore, these forms commonly present difficulties for native speakers of English who are learning Spanish (Stokes, 1985).

The Spanish preterit and imperfect forms incorporate different aspects of the past tense. The preterit is used for actions, events, or conditions of definite duration which were completed in the past. The imperfect is used to emphasize an indefinite duration of time, and is also used to report patterns of habitual action, mental and emotional states, and background conditions, including the way things looked or sounded, or the time of day (Allen, Méndez-Faith, and Gill, 1986, pp. 203–207):

> ***Perdí*** *las joyas que* ***tenía*** *en mi malleta.*
>
> (preterit) (imperfect)
>
> 'I lost the jewelry that I had in my suitcase.'

The most prominent difficulty encountered by native speakers of English in using these forms is in distinguishing which form is appropriate in a given context. Stokes says that "in Spanish the most obvious and pervasive aspect error lies within the choice between the two nonperiphrastic past tenses, the preterit and the imperfect" (1985, p. 377). Stokes also points out that even students who have mastered individual sets of verbs and their semantic functions have difficulty using them appropriately when faced simultaneously with all possible inflectional variables of tense, aspect, mode, person, and number. The need for students to integrate these variables if successful communication and accurate production are to take place has been recognized by Spanish language educators, although they may advocate different approaches for instruction (e.g., Delgado-Jenkins, 1990; Ozete, 1988; Reckart, 1978; and Stokes, 1985).

The present study does not take up this question of instruction, but rather tests the ability of tutored L2 students to notice the need for these forms and to produce them within a communicative context. Should the study find that enhanced input does lead to more noticing, then language teachers could find this technique useful for increasing the salience of the preterit and imperfect forms in Spanish. (See Leeman et al., this volume, for a study of the effect of instruction on these forms.)

THE STUDY

RESEARCH QUESTIONS

The purpose of this study was to observe the direct relation between input enhancement and noticing, as well as the effects on subsequent L2 production. Two research questions were posed:

i) Does positive input enhancement of target forms promote L2 learners' noticing of the forms?

ii) Does positive input enhancement of target forms affect subsequent L2 production?

We expected that input enhancement would both promote noticing and influence production of preterit and imperfect Spanish verbs.

PARTICIPANTS

The participants were 14 native speakers of English (12 male, 2 female) enrolled in second semester Spanish classes (Introductory Level II) at Georgetown University. All participants were volunteers. All participants reported Spanish instruction at the high school level: the average length of instruction was 4.2 years. None of the participants had lived in a Spanish-speaking country. Participants had been introduced formally to Spanish preterit and imperfect verbs during the six weeks prior to the study.

PRETEST

As the purpose of the study was to investigate differences in processing, it was necessary to minimize any priming effect due to association of the target forms with the experiment. To ensure this, administration of a pretest by the researchers was avoided. Participants' prior knowledge of the target features was determined by scores received on the preterit/imperfect section of a mid-term examination which had been developed and administered by the

Spanish department 4 weeks prior to the study. In this section of the test, students were asked to use preterit or imperfect verbs to fill in 10 blanks in a short passage. Participants' scores ranged from 2 to 10 points out of a possible 10, with a mean of 8.14.

SAMPLE TEXT

Participants received a sample text as a stimulus for a writing task which was developed as follows. The text was a written narration of the story of Little Red Riding Hood. Three native speakers of Spanish were asked to narrate the story in writing. The written narrations were then merged and edited by the researchers into a final version called the sample text, which was checked by another Spanish speaker for accuracy and readability. The sample text was written in the past tense throughout and contained 18 preterit and 10 imperfect verbs. English translations were provided for six vocabulary items which did not appear in the textbook used in Introductory II classes. This sample text was then printed out in two versions on an Apple StyleWriter using TrueType fonts. In one version, the entire text was printed in one font type (Times) and size (12 point). In another version, however, all preterit and imperfect verbs were underlined and printed in a different font (New York). In addition to this, the preterit verbs were shadowed, and the imperfect verbs were bolded, making them appear slightly larger and ostensibly more salient:.

Unenhanced version:

> Un cazador que pasaba cerca escuchó los gritos de Caperucita. El cazador disparó al lobo y salvó a la niña y a la abuela que seguía viva en el estómago del lobo.

Enhanced version:

> Un cazador que **pasaba** cerca escuchó los gritos de Caperucita. El cazador disparó al lobo y salvó a la niña y a la abuela que **seguía** viva en el estómago del lobo.

The sample text also included pictures to accompany the story. (See the Appendix for samples of the task materials).

WRITING TASK MATERIALS

Instructions for the writing task were printed on the same sheet as the sample text. English directions ("Narrate the sequence of pictures that you have been given, describing what happened to María and José last Christmas") and a Spanish cue (*Era diciembre del año pasado...*) were provided in order to evoke past tense narration. Participants also received a sequence of pictures on which to base their narration. The picture sequence consisted of 13 frames; three were split frames depicting concurrent events to elicit imperfect verbs. A list of vocabulary items with English translations accompanied the pictures.

PROCEDURE

The participants were matched according to their scores on the preterit/imperfect section of the midterm, and members of each pair were randomly assigned to comparison or enhancement groups.

Data were collected from each subject individually. First each subject was asked to complete a participant agreement form and a brief demographic questionnaire. The enhancement procedure was then introduced by means of the following script (adapted from Ericsson and Simon, 1993), which was read aloud by the researcher:

> In this experiment we are interested in what you think about when you write in Spanish. In order to find out, I am going to ask you to THINK ALOUD as you write. What I mean by "think aloud" is that I want you to tell me EVERYTHING you are thinking, from the time you finish reading the sample text I'll be giving you, until you complete the writing task. I would like you to talk CONSTANTLY from the time you finish the sample until you finish writing. I don't want you to try to plan out what you say or try to explain to me what you're saying. Just act as if you are alone in the room speaking to yourself. What's most important is that you keep talking, and talk clearly and loudly enough to be heard. If you are silent for any period of time I will remind you to talk by saying "What are you thinking?" Similarly, if you begin to speak softly, I may ask you to speak a little more loudly. I will not be able to help you in any way — and you will not be allowed to use a dictionary or any other writing aid. You will be video and

> audio-taped while you work on the task. Do you understand what I want you to do?

The protocol technique was then modeled as the researcher solved a mathematical problem on paper ("Multiply 24 x 26"). The subject was then asked to practice the technique with a similar mathematical problem ("Multiply 14 x 34").

Next, the writing task was described to the subject. Again, a script was followed:

> For your writing task, you'll be asked to narrate this series of pictures (Show task pictures). You must write the task in Spanish, but you can Think Aloud in either Spanish or English. Also, I'll be asking you to write in pen, so that you do not erase any changes you make in your text. Just draw a single line through any changes or errors and continue writing. There are a few vocabulary words provided at the end of both the sample text and the task pictures to assist you.
>
> OK, so you have an idea of what I'd like, I'll give you this sample (Give sample text with sample pictures). In this sample text, a native speaker of Spanish told the story of Little Red Riding Hood, as based on the pictures. I'd like you to do the same with your set of pictures. Please begin THINKING ALOUD as soon as you finish reading the text. And remember, I'll remind you to keep talking. You'll have 30 minutes to write. Now, please read the sample text, and begin your task.

The researcher sat quietly to the side of the subject in order to follow the progress of the subject. Whenever a 3-second pause occurred, the researcher prompted the subject with "What are you thinking?" Upon completion of the task, the researcher asked the subject if he or she would like to review and/or revise the written text. The subject continued to think aloud during the revision process. The entire session was video and audio-taped.

DISCARDED DATA

The data from four participants, two from each group, were discarded. Three participants failed to complete the task as described to them: one did not read the sample text or the prompt and therefore did not receive the input; another began narrating directly onto the pictures, instead of the response sheet, not having seen the prompt; and a third subject described the pictures, rather than narrating them. The fourth subject's data were discarded due to researcher error in task administration. The researcher failed to prompt the subject during his pauses. As a result, the pauses were quite long and the think-aloud report was incomplete.

CODING OF THINK-ALOUD PROTOCOL TRANSCRIPTS

Transcripts of the remaining think-aloud protocols were examined for the presence of language episodes, defined as "any segment of the protocol in which a learner either spoke about a language problem s/he encountered while writing and solved it either correctly or incorrectly; or simply solved it without having identified it as a problem" (following Swain and Lapkin's definition of language episodes, 1994, p.13). Researchers individually reviewed the data in order to propose possible coding subcategories and then met as a group to agree upon a coding system to apply to the data. Language episodes were subcategorized and coded as either V-episodes ('verb-related episodes') or Non-V-episodes ('non-verb-related episodes'). These subcategories were defined as follows:

V-episodes	Language episodes related to processing of the morphology of the verb and its aspectual functions, but excluding lexical search for verbs.
Non-V-episodes	All other language episodes. Most of these consisted of lexical search, deliberations over spelling, and so forth.

Because this study is concerned with participants' non-lexical processing of verb forms, the category of Non-V-episodes was not further subdivided. Each V-episode was coded according to whether the episode involved (a) an explicit mention of non-lexical, verb-related processing, or (b) an implicit treatment of the verb, operationalized as successive utterance of two different verb forms (but not coded as such in cases where one of these forms could have been interpreted as a truncated version of the other). The 'explicit mention' category was further divided into explicit mention of aspect,

E(a) (e.g., imperfect or preterit[2]), and explicit mention of other verb-related features, E(other). See Table 1 for examples of coded language episodes.

Table 1: Language episodes

Classification	Example	Code
Non-Verb-Related	"...fall is um *c- caer.*"	Non-V
Verb-Related	"...*y explice, explica...*"	I
Implicit treatment	but NOT "..*vol, volvi, volvían...*"	—
Explicit mention of aspect	"*Entonces la policia,* u, *corre,* nn now we're back in the present."	E(other)
	"I think it's supposed to be in preterit. *Chocó.*"	E(a)
	"*Volvar* is *-ar.*"	E(other)
	"I'm going to have to make this preterit or imperfect...we'll make it uh *iban.*"	E(a)

Language episodes were coded as E(a), explicit mention of aspect, only when participants actually mentioned the word "preterit" or "imperfect" in their protocol. Some cases strongly indicated that the subject was processing verbal aspect. For example,

4. "So that was the action going on. Meanwhile. The guy escaped. So that's the definite happening, action."
5. "*Estan, estas, estuvieron, estaban.*"
6. "*Estuvimos?* God, it's the past, um, *estar, esta:mos, esta:ba:mos*?

However, these were not coded as E(a), in order to avoid over-interpretation. (4 and 6 were coded as E(other), and 5, as I.)

[2] It should be noted that all explicit mentions of aspect involved mention of either preterite or imperfect or both.

All of the above coding was accomplished in the first instance by two of the researchers after a norming session with the other researchers. The only mismatches that were found involved episodes that were coded by one researcher but missed by the other or were coded as one episode by one researcher and as two by the other. In the case of missing episodes, the researcher who had missed the episode coded on the spot and then compared. In the case of segments of the protocol that had been coded as differing numbers of episodes, these were easily resolved through discussion of what should constitute the boundary between episodes. It was decided that a single episode could contain repetitions, but that it needed to retain one focus and have no interruptions. Where the focus changed or where one focus was interrupted by another focus (even if the first focus was resumed), then separate episodes were coded. The following are examples of such decisions:

7. A focus interrupted by another episode (coded as three total episodes):

   Episode 1: "What is the plural of the preterit? *Encontro- encontre- encon-*"

   Interrupting Episode 2: "We will say (scribbling noise as the student rewrites a verb on another part of the composition paper) *acostan.*"

   Episode 3: "*encontro encontro encontre encontreís encontron* and 'found' that'd be preterit"

8. Two distinct episodes which are adjacent to one another (coded as two episodes):

   Episode 1: "... uh *preterit* and *les miró mirar*"

   Episode 2: "It's a regular verb"

In the end, the comparisons of 530 episodes showed very high agreement on assignment to categories of E(a), E(other) or I. During the interrater discussion, however, six of these episodes could not be agreed upon and were brought to the attention of the other researchers and were resolved by consensus. Finally, in reviewing the data, one researcher noticed four episodes that had been missed by everyone. These, too, were brought to the attention of the others and agreed upon without dissent. Thus, a total of 534 language episodes were coded.

CODING THE WRITTEN PRODUCT

Written products were analyzed for accurate use of preterit and imperfect verbs. A native speaker of Spanish was asked to evaluate verb use in the written products, supplying the appropriate verb form where necessary and offering alternative verb forms if more than one form was possible in a given context. Obligatory contexts for preterit and imperfect forms were defined as contexts in which only a preterit or imperfect verb was appropriate. For several instances where the native speaker judged that either an imperfect or a preterit verb was appropriate in the context, suppliance of either form was coded as Accurate. Where the preterit was appropriate and the subject supplied the preterit form, the use was coded as Accurate. Likewise, where the imperfect was required and the subject gave an imperfect form, the verb was also coded as Accurate. Verbs were not analyzed for spelling or agreement errors. In cases where a subject supplied an imperfect verb where the native speaker judged that a preterit verb was appropriate, that instance was coded as I→P. Similarly, when the subject used a preterit verb where an imperfect was needed, the use was coded P→I. If either the preterit or imperfect was obligatory, and the subject provided some other form of the verb, such as the present tense, the verb use was coded as Other.

There were two instances where, due to spelling, it was difficult to determine whether the subject was using a preterit tense spelled incorrectly, or a present tense spelled incorrectly. One of these instances was in the comparison group where a subject used *entre*, which should have been either *entró* in the preterit or *entra* in the present. The other instance was in the enhancement group where one subject wrote *pusen*, which should have been either *pusieron* in the preterit or *ponen* in the present. As there was no evidence to the contrary in the protocols, in order to maintain our conservative coding style, these two instances were discarded.

RESULTS

HYPOTHESES

The particular hypotheses tested during the analysis of the think aloud protocols were:

1. There will be more language-episodes involving the use of preterit and imperfect verbs in the protocols of participants receiving textually-enhanced input than in those of participants receiving unenhanced input.

2. The use of preterit and imperfect verbs in the written production of the enhancement group participants will be more target-like than that of the comparison group participants.

DIFFERENCES IN PROTOCOLS

Because the participants had been carefully matched on their preterit/imperfect scores on the Spanish department midterm and then randomly assigned to enhancement and comparison groups, it could be safely assumed that the two groups were equal in ability and that any differences that obtained would be due to the enhancement procedure. Hypothesis 1 predicted that there would be more Language-episodes (L-episodes) involving the use of preterit and imperfect verbs in the protocols of enhancement participants than in those of comparison participants. We will first look at those L-episodes related to any kind of verb usage, i.e., V-episodes.

Table 2 displays V-episodes as a proportion of total L-episodes produced by each subject. A Wilcoxon rank sums test comparing the percentages of V-episodes indicates that there is no significant difference between the comparison and enhancement groups in the proportion of V-episodes in total L-episodes ($z = 0.731$, n.s.). (Figure 1 shows the breakdown of V-episodes in both groups.)

Table 2: Number of V- and non-V-episodes, and percentage of V-episodes in total L-episodes.

Subject	V-episodes	Non V-episodes	Total L-episodes	V-episodes as % of L-episodes*
Comparison				
ME	12	5	17	70.59
TD	12	18	30	40.00
BR	6	12	18	33.33
BF	17	33	50	34.00
ED	54	75	129	41.86
Enhancement				
JS	11	25	36	30.56
BM	37	30	67	55.22
CA	48	63	111	43.24
JE	30	19	49	61.22
BC	13	14	27	48.15

Note: * Comparison between groups

	n	z	p
Comparison	5	.731	.465 (n.s.)
Enhancement	5		

Figure 1: Frequency data: V-episodes

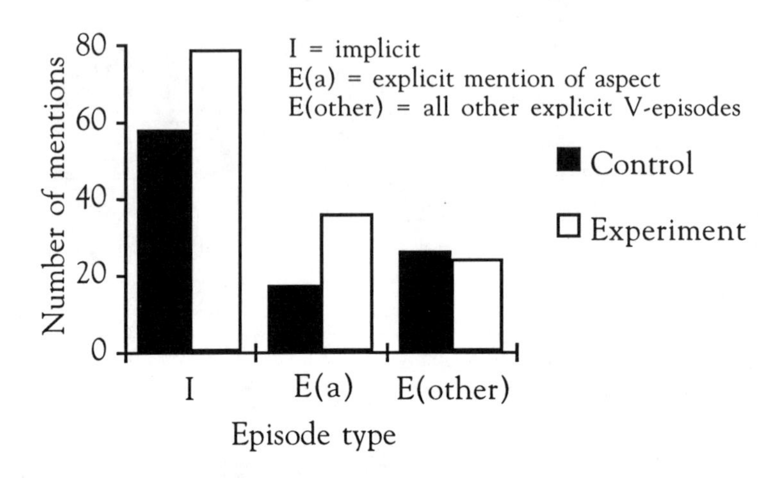

Table 3 displays the explicit mentions of aspect (E(a)) as a proportion of all V-episodes coded as explicit mentions (E(all). As for the explicit V-episodes, there is a significant difference between the enhancement and comparison groups in regard to explicit mention of aspect as shown by a Wilcoxon rank sums test ($z = -2.20$, $p < 0.05$). The strength of association ($\eta^2=0.605$) indicates that more than 60% of the variance in the ranks of explicit mention of aspect as a percentage of all explicit V-episodes is indeed attributable to the enhancement.

Table 3: Explicit mention of aspect as a proportion of all explicit V-episodes: A comparison of means

Subject	E(a)	E(all)	E(a) as % of E(all)
Comparison			
ED	13	26	50.0
BF	2	8	25.0
BR	0	5	0.0
TO	0	1	0.0
ME	0	3	0.0

Enhancement			
CA	8	19	42.1
JS	4	4	100.0
BC	0	0	N/A
JE	12	16	75.0
BM	12	21	57.1

Note: * Comparison between groups

	n	z	p	η^2
Comparison	5	–2.20	.0278 (<.05)	.605
Enhancement	4*			

(As can be seen in the results shown in Tables 2 and 3, although Hypothesis 1 is not supported in terms of the overall amount of V-episodes, a finer analysis shows that when verb decisions were explicit, the enhancement group mentioned their deliberations about verb *aspect* more often than did the comparison group.

DIFFERENCES IN WRITTEN PRODUCTION

The second research question of this study sought to investigate the immediate effect of textual input enhancement on the learner's subsequent production. Hypothesis 2 predicted that the use of preterit and imperfect verbs in the written production of the enhancement group participants would be more target-like than that of the comparison group participants. The differences in the use of preterit and imperfect verbs between the two groups are shown in various ways in Table 4. The difference in the percentages of correct verb aspect supplied in obligatory contexts (see column labeled "Accurate Suppliance") is found to be significant in a Wilcoxon rank sums test ($z = 2.19$, $p < 0.05$, $\eta^2 = 0.533$). Thus, Hypothesis 2 is supported.

Table 4 also shows not only that the enhancement participants demonstrated more target-like usage of the preterit and imperfect verb forms, but that their scores fell within a narrow range. Percentages of correct suppliance ranged from 64–84% in the enhancement group

Table 4 : Verbs supplied in obligatory contexts in written production

Subject	Oblig. contexts	Accurate suppliance		Wrong aspect P → I		Wrong aspect I → P		Other		Past attempts	
	#	#	%*	#	%	#	%	#	%	#	%
Comparison											
ME	19	3	(15.8)	0	(0.0)	0	(0.0)	16	(84.2)	3	(15.8)
TD	29	3	(10.3)	2	(6.9)	0	(0.0)	24	(82.8)	5	(17.2)
BR	20	12	(60.0)	0	(0.0)	0	(0.0)	8	(40.0)	12	(60.0)
BF	18	13	(72.2)	1	(5.6)	0	(0.0)	4	(22.2)	14	(77.8)
ED	31	23	(74.2)	3	(9.7)	4	(12.9)	1	(3.2)	30	(96.8)
Enhancement											
JS	25	21	(84.0)	2	(8.0)	0	(0.0)	2	(8.0)	23	(92.0)
BM	26	21	(81.8)	4	(15.4)	0	(0.0)	1	(3.9)	25	(96.2)
CA	42	34	(81.0)	5	(11.9)	0	(0.0)	3	(7.1)	39	(92.9)
JE	25	16	(64.0)	2	(8.0)	5	(20.0)	2	(8.0)	23	(92.0)
BC	28	22	(78.6)	3	(10.7)	2	(7.1)	1	(3.6)	27	(96.4)

Note: P → I indicates suppliance of preterite form where the appropriate form is the imperfect. I → P indicates suppliance of imperfect form instead of an preterite verb. Suppliance was marked 'other' when either the preterite or imperfect verb was required and no past tense verb was supplied.

Note: Past attempts refers to any attempts at past time reference, whether accurate or not.

Note: Comparison between groups on Accurate suppliance

	n	z	p	η^2
Comparison	5	2.19	.0286 (<.05)	.533
Enhancement	5			

Note: Comparison between groups on Past attempts

	n	z	p
Comparison	5	-1.57	.116 (n.s.)
Enhancement	5		

(See Figure 2). The scores of comparison group members, on the other hand, were more spread out. Their accuracy of suppliance ranged from 10 to 74%.

Figure 2: Percentage of correct forms supplied in obligatory context (individual scores)

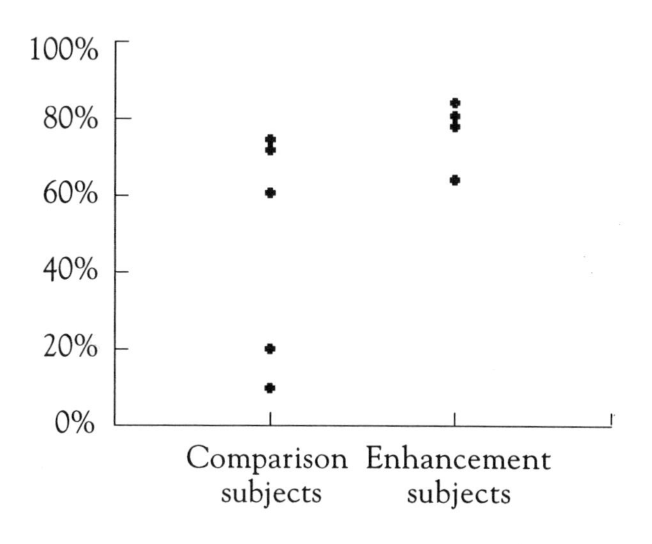

DISCUSSION

Although the data were not collected concurrently with the provision of input, the results suggest that the input modification created a difference between the two groups in the immediate processing of input. Enhancement and comparison groups in this study differed significantly in their percentage of explicit mentions of preterit and imperfect forms. This supports the first hypothesis, which stated that there would be more L-episodes involving the use of preterit and imperfect verbs in the enhancement participants' protocols. The difference in the frequency of mention of the target forms indicates that the enhancement participants had been primed for processing of the target forms. This may have been caused by increased registration of the input stimulus due to the textual modification. Whether most participants were aware of the enhancement, however, cannot be determined by this study, as only one enhancement subject remarked on the appearance of the sample text. It can be said, however, that enhancement participants detected the forms, as detection does not require awareness (Tomlin and Villa, 1994). It is also worth noting that the explicit mentions of the comparison group were largely the product of one subject. His protocol accounts for more than half of the explicit V-episodes of the comparison group. Most participants in the comparison made few explicit mentions at all.

Analysis of the written production also demonstrates a striking difference between the two groups in their overall use of the past tense. The enhancement group simply provided more target forms (preterit and imperfect) in obligatory contexts in their written production. However, it is doubtful that the difference in production is due to change in the knowledge of the target features or to increased control over them. As a matter of fact, it seems that the difference is due to the fact that the enhancement group attempted more past tense verbs. While the enhancement group supplied past tense verbs in (median =) 93% of obligatory contexts, only (median =) 60% of the comparison group's verbs were in the past tense. (See "Past Attempts" column of Table 4: though the difference between groups is not significant, this appears to be due to the aberrant contribution of one subject). Thus, the enhancement participants seemed to have been primed for the use of past tense verbs as an effect of the input enhancement. In fact, as shown in Table 5, where past tense verbs were supplied in the written production of both the experimental and control groups, the proportion of accurately-supplied aspect does not differ significantly. A Wilcoxon rank sums test of the difference between groups with respect to accurate suppliance of aspect as a proportion suppliance of past tense verbs yields $z = -0.73$, a result that is not significant.

Table 5: Percentage of accurate verb aspect within total attempts at past

Comparison		Enhancement	
Subject	%	Subject	%
ME	100.0	JS	91.3
TD	60.0	BM	84.0
BR	92.9	CA	87.2
BF	100.0	JE	70.0
ED	76	BC	81.5

Note: Comparison between groups on Accurate aspect/Past attempts

	n	z	p
Comparison	5	–0.73	.46 (n.s.)
Enhancement	5		

Further research is necessary to test whether the frequency differences observed in the post-treatment production can have a lasting effect on use of the target forms. Investigation is also needed to examine the effect of input enhancement on the internalization of forms to which learners have not yet been exposed. The forms used in this study were already familiar to the participants, as demonstrated by their scores on a pre-enhancement test.

CONCLUSION

The purpose of this study was to investigate the internal effects of input enhancement through textual manipulation. The results indicate that processing of input is affected by the textual enhancement of target forms. This provides evidence that input enhancement can be an effective means of drawing learners' attention to target features of the L2. Also, the participants in our study who received the enhanced text used the target form more frequently in obligatory contexts. This seems to suggest that textual enhancement may lead to better subsequent L2 production of the forms. The pedagogical implications of these findings are that typographical modification can be used as an effective technique for enhancing salience of language features that may prove difficult for L2 learners.

Although the results of this study are promising, they should be interpreted with caution. It has been noted that expert participants may be expected to perform differently from novices on think-aloud protocols (Smagorinsky, 1994; Stratman and Hamp-Lyons, 1994), though research to demonstrate this is not available. The participants of our study have been controlled as systematically as possible, given situational constraints, for expertise in writing skills and in comparison of the L2 forms. Because fine comparison has not been exercised, however, there is a possibility that individual differences in expertise may be influential.

In addition to this point, Stratman and Hamp-Lyons (1994) raise the question of whether the think-aloud task itself causes participants to perform differently from participants under normal task conditions. This "reactivity" is the subject of their study. Their findings indicate that the protocol itself did have an effect, but that it is possible that it affected only the amount, but not the nature, of "certain kinds of verbal processing" (p. 108). They, however, reject this weak interpretation, and caution that further study is needed to determine whether concurrent think-aloud protocols may change the nature of processing — thereby lessening their validity as research tools for studies like this one.

The individual differences observed in our data suggest that various factors, such as writing skills and proficiency level, may interact with the way in which learners process input. Furthermore, we cannot predict the effect that interaction between writing skills and Spanish language proficiency may have on the cognitive processing involved in a task such as the one in this study. Studies that tease apart these variables are, therefore, recommended.

REFERENCES

Allen, E. D., Méndez-Faith, T., & Gill, M. M. (1986). *¿Habla español? Essentials*. New York: Holt, Rinehart and Winston.

Baars, B. J. (1988). *A cognitive theory of consciousness*. Cambridge: Cambridge University Press.

Day, E., & Shapson, S. (1991). Integrating formal and functional approaches in language teaching in French immersion: An enhancement study. *Language Learning, 41*, 25–58.

Delgado-Jenkins, H. (1990). Imperfect vs. preterit: A new approach. *Hispania, 73*, 1145–1146.

Doughty, C. (1991). Second language instruction does make a difference: Evidence from an empirical study of relativization. *Studies in Second Language Acquisition, 13*, 431–469.

Ericsson, K. A., & Simon, H. A. (1993). *Protocol analysis: Verbal reports as data* (2nd ed.). Boston: MIT Press.

Fowler, R. L., & Barker, A. S. (1974). Effectiveness of highlighting for retention of text material. *Journal of Applied Psychology, 59*, 358–364.

Gass, S. (1986). An interactionist approach to L2 sentence interpretation. *Studies in Second Language Acquisition, 8*, 19–37.

Gass, S., & Selinker, L. (1994). *Second language acquisition*. Hillsdale, NJ: Lawrence Erlbaum.

Hammerly, H. (1987). The immersion approach: Litmus test of second language acquisition through classroom communication. *Modern Language Journal, 71*, 395–401.

Harley, B. (1993). Instructional strategies and SLA in early French immersion. *Studies in Second Language Acquisition, 15*, 245–260.

Harley, B. (1994). Appealing to consciousness in the L2 classroom. In J. H. Hulstijn & R. Schmidt (Eds.), *Consciousness in second language learning, AILA Review, 11*, 57–68.

Hartley, J., Bartlett, S., & Branthwaite, J. A. (1980). Underlining can make a difference — sometimes. *Journal of Educational Research, 73*, 218–224.

Hayes, J. R., & Flower, L. S. (1980). Identifying the organization of writing processes. In L. W. Gregg & E. R. Steinberg (Eds.), *Cognitive processes in writing* (pp. 3–30). Hillsdale, NJ: Lawrence Erlbaum.

Hosenfeld, C. (1976). Learning about learning: Discovering our students' strategies. *Foreign Language Annals*, 9, 117–129.

Hulstijn, J. (1989). Implicit and incidental second language learning: Experiments in the processing of natural and partly artificial input. In H. W. Dechert & M. Raupach (Eds.), *Interlingual processes* (pp. 49–73). Tübingen: Gunter Narr Verlag.

Kowal, M., & Swain, M. (1994). From semantic to syntactic processing: How can we promote it in the immersion classroom? Unpublished manuscript, Modern Language Center, Ontario Institute for Studies in Education.

Krashen, S. (1985). *The input hypothesis: Issues and implications.* London: Longman.

Lightbown, P. (1985). Input and interaction for second language learners in and out of classrooms. *Applied Linguistics*, 6, 263–273.

Lightbown, P., & Spada, N. (1990). Focus on form and corrective feedback in communicative language teaching: Effects on second language learning. *Studies in Second Language Acquisition*, *12*, 429–448.

Long, M. (1991) Focus on form: A design feature in language teaching methodology. In K. de Bot, R. Ginsberg, & C. Kramsch (Eds.), *Foreign language research in cross-cultural perspective* (pp. 39–52). Amsterdam: John Benjamins.

Lorch, R. F. (1989). Text-signaling devices and their effects on reading and memory processes. *Educational Psychology Review*, *1*, 209–234.

Ozete, O. (1988). Focusing on the preterit and imperfect. *Hispania*, *71*, 687–691.

Pavesi, M. (1986). Markedness, discoursal modes, and relative clause formation in a formal and informal context. *Studies in Second Language Acquisition*, 8, 38–55.

Raimes, A. (1987). Language proficiency, writing ability, and composing strategies: A study of ESL college student writers. *Language Learning*, *37*, 439–468.

Reckart, D. A. (1978). Teaching the Spanish past tense: Theory and practice. *Bulletin-CILA, 28*, 33–49.

Rutherford, W., & Sharwood Smith, M. (1985). Consciousness raising and universal grammar. *Applied Linguistics*, 6, 274–282.

Schmidt, R. (1983). Interaction, acculturation, and the acquisition of communicative competence. In N. Wolfson & J. Manes (Eds.), *Sociolinguistics and second language acquisition* (pp. 137–174). Rowley, MA: Newbury House.

Schmidt, R. (1990). The role of consciousness in second language learning. *Applied Linguistics, 11*, 17–46.

Schmidt, R. (1993). Awareness and second language acquisition. *Annual Review of Applied Linguistics, 13*, 206–226.

Schmidt, R. (1994). Deconstructing consciousness in search of useful definitions for applied linguistics. *AILA Review, 11*, 11–26.

Sharwood Smith, M. (1981). Consciousness raising and the second language learner. *Applied Linguistics*, 2, 159–168.

Sharwood Smith, M. (1991). Speaking to many minds: On the relevance of different types of language information for the L2 learner. *Second Language Research*, 7, 118–132.

Sharwood Smith, M. (1993). Input enhancement in instructed SLA: Theoretical bases. *Studies in Second Language Acquisition, 15*, 2, 165–179.

Shook, D. J. (1990). *L2 reading and grammar acquisition: An input-processing perspective*. Unpublished manuscript.

Smagorinsky, P. (1994). Think-aloud protocol analysis: Beyond the black box. In P. Smagorinsky (Ed.), *Speaking about writing: Reflections on research methodology* (pp. 3–19). London: Sage Publications.

Stokes, J. (1985). Effects of student monitoring of verb inflection in Spanish. *Modern Language Journal*, 69, 377–384.

Stratman, J. F., & Hamp-Lyons, L. (1994). Reactivity in concurrent think-aloud protocols: Issues for research. In P. Smagorinsky (Ed.), *Speaking about writing: Reflections on research methodology* (pp. 20–54). London: Sage Publications.

Swain, M. (1985). Communicative competence: Some roles for comprehensible input and comprehensible output in its development. In S. Gass & C. Madden, (Eds.), *Input in second language acquisition* (pp. 235–253). Rowley, MA: Newbury House.

Swain, M. (1991). French immersion and its offshoots: Getting two for one. In B. F. Freed (Ed.), *Foreign language research and the classroom* (pp. 91–103). Lexington, MA: D. C. Heath.

Swain M., & Lapkin, S. (1989). Canadian immersion and adult second language teaching: What is the connection? *Modern Language Journal, 73*, 150–159.

Swain, M., & Lapkin, S. (1994). *Problems in output and the cognitive processes they generate: A step towards second language learning.* Unpublished manuscript, Modern Language Center, Ontario Institute for Studies in Education.

Swarts, H., Flower, L. S., & Hayes, J. R. (1984). Designing protocol studies of the writing process: An introduction. In R. Beach & L. Bridwell (Eds.), *New directions in composition research* (pp. 53–71). New York: Guilford Press.

Tomlin, R., & Villa, V. (1994). Attention in cognitive science and second language acquisition. *Studies in Second Language Acquisition, 16*, 183–203.

Vann, R., & Abraham, R. (1990). Strategies of unsuccessful language learners. *TESOL Quarterly, 24*, 177–197.

White, J. (1994, March). *Input enhancement: Some evidence from children.* Paper presented at the 28th Annual Convention of TESOL International, Baltimore, MD.

White, L. (1991). Adverb placement in second language acquisition: Some effects of positive and negative evidence in the classroom. *Second Language Research, 7*, 133–161.

APPENDIX A: EXPERIMENTAL MATERIALS USED

UNENHANCED VERSION

Había una vez una chica que vivía en el bosque. Caperucita Roja, ese era su nombre porque siempre llevaba una capa roja, visitaba a su abuela los fines de semana. Un día la madre le dijo: "Caperucita, anda visita a la abuela, que está enferma, y llévale esta canasta de comida."

En el camino, Caperucita se encontró con el lobo y le dijo: "Hola chica ¿a dónde vas?" "Voy a la casa de mi abuela que está enferma," respondió Caperucita y siguió en camino.

El lobo quería comerse a Caperucita así que se adelantó a la casa de la abuela y se la comió a ella primero. El lobo se puso la ropa de la abuela y se metió a la cama.

Cuando Caperucita llegó, el lobo imitó la voz de la abuela. Caperucita preguntó al lobo por qué tenía esos ojos y esas orejas tan grandes. El lobo respondió que para verla y oirla mejor. En seguida, Caperucita preguntó por qué tenía la boca tan grande. El lobo respondió, "¡Para comerte mejor!"

Un cazador que pasaba cerca escuchó los gritos de Caperucita. El cazador disparó al lobo y salvó a la niña y a la abuela que seguía viva en el estómago del lobo.

el bosque	woods	*el lobo*	wolf	*el cazador*	hunter
la canasta	basket	*adelantarse*	to go on ahead	*disparar*	to shoot

NOW PLEASE BEGIN THINKING ALOUD...REMEMBER TO SAY EVERYTHING THAT YOU'RE THINKING, WHETHER YOU THINK IT'S IMPORTANT OR NOT.

Narrate the sequence of pictures that you have been given, describing what happened to María and José last Christmas:

Era diciembre del año pasado…

<u>Había</u> una vez una chica que <u>vivía</u> en el bosque. Caperucita Roja, ese <u>era</u> su nombre porque siempre <u>llevaba</u> una capa roja, <u>visitaba</u> a su abuela los fines de semana. Un día la madre le <u>dijo</u>: "Caperucita, anda visita a la abuela, que está enferma, y llévale esta canasta de comida."

En el camino, Caperucita se <u>encontró</u> con el lobo y le <u>dijo</u>: "Hola chica ¿a dónde vas?" "Voy a la casa de mi abuela que está enferma," <u>respondió</u> Caperucita y <u>siguió</u> a camino.

El lobo **<u>quería</u>** comerse a Caperucita así que <u>se adelantó</u> a la casa de la abuela y <u>se</u> la <u>comió</u> a ella primero. El lobo <u>se puso</u> la ropa de la abuela y <u>se metió</u> en la cama.

Cuando Caperucita <u>llegó</u>, el lobo <u>imitó</u> la voz de la abuela. Caperucita <u>preguntó</u> al lobo por qué **<u>tenía</u>** esos ojos y esas orejas tan grandes. El lobo <u>respondió</u> que para verla y oirla mejor. En seguida, Caperucita <u>preguntó</u> por qué tenía la boca tan grande. El lobo <u>respondió</u>, "¡Para comerte mejor!"

Un cazador que <u>pasaba</u> cerca <u>escuchó</u> los gritos de Caperucita. El cazador <u>disparó</u> al lobo y <u>salvó</u> a la niña y a la abuela que **<u>seguía</u>** viva en el estómago del lobo.

el bosque	woods	*el lobo*	wolf	*el cazador*	hunter
la canasta	basket	*adelantarse*	to go on ahead	*disparar*	to shoot

NOW PLEASE BEGIN THINKING ALOUD...REMEMBER TO SAY EVERYTHING THAT YOU'RE THINKING, WHETHER YOU THINK IT'S IMPORTANT OR NOT.

Narrate the sequence of pictures that you have been given, describing what happened to María and José last Christmas:

Era diciembre del año pasado…

¡ojo!
ir de compras to shop
el ladrón theif
los paquetes packages
caer to fall
escapar to escape
la estatua statue
chocar (qu) to collide

Jennifer Leeman, Igone Arteagoitia,
Boris Fridman, & Catherine Doughty
Georgetown University

INTEGRATING ATTENTION TO FORM WITH MEANING: FOCUS ON FORM IN CONTENT-BASED SPANISH INSTRUCTION

ABSTRACT

This study examined the effects of *focus on form* instruction (Long 1991) compared with purely communicative instruction in an attempt to determine whether input enhancement techniques could increase learner's accuracy and/or suppliance of L2 forms, all the while maintaining a focus on meaning. This research question is of great interest as there is little agreement over the relative importance of accuracy and communication in classrooms (Whitley 1993), and many recent studies have suggested that L2 learners in purely communicative settings never acquire completely native-like proficiency in the target language (e.g., Harley and Swain 1985, Swain and Lapkin 1989). Results show that only participants in the Focus on Form group demonstrated significantly improved accuracy and suppliance of the target forms, thus suggesting that it is possible to increase accuracy within a content-based instructional setting.

INTRODUCTION

In recent decades there has been great debate about whether or not grammar should be included in foreign language classes and, if so, how it could be incorporated. The traditional rule-based explanations and manipulation of target forms, widespread before the introduction of the communicative approaches, are almost universally rejected by applied linguists and practicing foreign language teachers, as research has shown that the ability to accurately manipulate target forms on

Leeman, Jennifer, Arteagoitia, Igone, Fridman, Boris, & Doughty, Catherine (1995). Integrating attention to form with meaning: Focus on form in content-based Spanish instruction. In Richard Schmidt (Ed.), *Attention and awareness in foreign language learning* (Technical Report #9) (pp. 217–258). Honolulu, Hawai'i: University of Hawai'i, Second Language Teaching & Curriculum Center.

discrete item tests does not correlate with accuracy in semi-spontaneous speech. For example, in a study of the acquisition of the subjunctive in Spanish, Terrell, Baycroft, and Perrone (1987) found that although explicit instruction resulted in improvement on controlled, form-oriented written tasks, learners were largely inaccurate in less controlled, oral production. While such "focus on forms" has been shown to be ineffective for L2 acquisition (Long 1991), there is also evidence from immersion classrooms that a purely communicative "focus on meaning" is not sufficient (Harley 1993). For example, Harley and Swain (1985) found that even after years of content-based instruction in French immersion classes, students' language was still plagued by error and, with certain types of verb morphology (e.g., the conditional tense), their performance was less than 50% accurate. Similarly, Swain and Lapkin (1989) found that native-like accuracy was not achieved even after more than 5,000 hours of meaning-based instruction.

The inadequacy of purely content-based instructional design may be partially due to the fact that the input that learners receive is often deficient in that it does not include the full range of functional uses of certain forms (e.g., the use of French *vous* as a formal singular pronoun — see Swain 1992). This absence of use in the input is likely to be reflected in the learners' interlanguage. Additionally, Swain cites an immersion history course in which students frequently used the present tense to discuss past events without correction by the teacher. Thus, a focus only on meaning provides insufficient input of certain forms and no means by which to encourage practice of others. Since these forms are necessary for native-like communication outside of the classroom, special steps may be necessary in order to provide more practice of neglected features.

Recently, many applied linguists have advocated complementing communicative instruction with a component designed to improve formal accuracy. The recommended techniques can all be considered to be different types of input enhancement (Sharwood Smith 1993). While the techniques themselves are varied, the theoretical underpinnings are, in most cases, quite similar. In general, there is a rejection of the notion that all that is necessary for L2 acquisition is exposure to comprehensible input (Krashen 1977), accompanied by the belief that learners must attend to formal aspects of the target language input if they are to make the necessary adjustments to their own output (Sharwood Smith 1990, 1993; Schmidt 1993; VanPatten 1989). There is still no consensus on what causes certain forms to be more noticed[1] than others, though a number of explanations have been proposed. Such proposals discuss (a) limits on processing capacity (Van Patten 1989, 1995), (b) communicative value of the forms (VanPatten 1989, 1995; Bransdorfer 1989)/importance for accessing meaning (Terrell, Baycroft, and Perrone 1987; Hulstijn 1989; Schmidt and Frota 1986), (c) perceptual saliency (Doughty 1991, VanPatten 1989), or (d) the learner's developmental 'readiness' (Pienemann 1985; Sharwood Smith 1991).

Regardless of differences in factors suggested to determine attention to formal aspects of the target language, there is a consensus that increased noticing of some kind is beneficial to the learner. It follows then, that if the input can be manipulated or enhanced in some way so as to draw learners' attention to specific forms, or to form in general, this will be expected to facilitate learning. Clearly, there are many possible ways to manipulate and enhance the input. However, as Sharwood Smith (1991, 1993) cautions, it is inappropriate to assume that external manipulation of the input is the mechanism that will actually increase the learners' attention. For this reason he rejected his own term "consciousness-raising" and coined the more cautious "input enhancement." In addition, he stressed that artificially-induced noticing might not result in the target forms being incorporated into the developing interlanguage. In other words, forms may be noticed perceptually, but not linguistically: "although learners may notice the signals, the input may nevertheless be nonsalient to their learning mechanisms" (1991:121). Accordingly, the determination of effective means of focus on form is an important research aim.

Of particular interest to the design of the present study were prior empirical attempts to increase perceptual saliency through the manipulation of typographical conventions as discussed by Sharwood

---

1 Throughout this paper the term *noticing* is not meant to imply explicit knowledge or awareness. Instead, it is roughly equivalent to *detection* as described by Tomlin and Villa (1994:192) "the process that selects, or engages, a particular and specific bit of information."

Smith (1991). Shook (1990) used boldfacing and capitalization to increase noticing of Spanish verb morphology, but found no increased noticing of the target morphology (i.e., the auxiliary verb *haber* in the present perfect construction) in either experimental condition. Shook's results should be interpreted with caution, however, as the multiple choice translation and sentence-completion tasks he used to measure participants' noticing were extremely limited. Furthermore, the apparent lack of increased noticing as a result of text manipulation may also have been due to the relatively low saliency of the specific enhancements used.

Perhaps more salient text manipulations would have been more effective in increasing noticing of target structures. Two contrasting enhancements used for two contrasting forms or tenses might better emphasize the difference between the structures. For example, typeface of different colors was used by Doughty (1991) to compare the effects of explicit rule instruction, meaning-oriented instruction, and exposure alone on the acquisition of English relative clauses. Doughty found that rule-oriented and meaning-oriented instruction were equally beneficial for participants' performance on form-oriented tasks but that the latter group (as well as the exposure only group) outperformed the former on comprehension tasks. No one is likely to claim that the beneficial effects observed were the result of the colored typeface on its own. Rather, it is likely that this kind of test manipulation combined with other enhancement techniques (such as juxtaposition and rephrasing) to produce the influence on the learners.

Also of interest for the current study was research showing the effectiveness of providing learners with corrective feedback, a technique classified as "negative input enhancement" by Sharwood Smith (1993:177). For example, Tomasello and Herron (1989) compared two groups of L2 French learners who received different types of input combined with explicit grammar instruction of a variety of structures. One group received positive input, or modeling, of exceptions to rules, while participants in the other group were encouraged to overgeneralize. These latter participants received feedback on the errors they had been led to commit, and they demonstrated superior performance on a subsequent sentence translation task. Carroll, Roberge, and Swain (1992) also found positive effects for feedback in their experimental study of two rules of French suffixation, though participants were unable to generalize their new knowledge to novel items. In a similar study on the acquisition of the English dative alternation, Carroll and Swain (1993) found that participants in four different feedback conditions were able to generalize to novel items. It is likely that the effectiveness of feedback is a result of drawing the learner's attention not only to the relevant aspects of the input, but also to the specific problems of his/her own output.

The studies discussed above have demonstrated the usefulness of various types of input enhancement, though they are unable to shed light on the relative value of the different techniques. Thus there is no clear empirical support in favor of any specific enhancement over another. Nonetheless, there are means by which to classify and choose among types of enhancement. While a number of different classification criteria have been proposed — such as explicitness and elaboration (Sharwood Smith 1991) and timing (Lightbown 1994) — it may ultimately be most worthwhile to classify and evaluate various focus on form techniques based on whether they integrate attention to form with attention to meaning, rather than isolating attention to form as a separate component. Because humans have a limited attentional capacity, performance on an attention-demanding task usually declines when participants are simultaneously required to perform a second task (VanPatten 1989, Tomlin and Villa 1994). However, performance on the first task is not adversely affected when the two tasks are "somehow compatible" (Tomlin and Villa 1994:189). Thus, it seems that tasks or enhancements designed to integrate attention to form with attention to meaning would require less diversion of learners' attentional resources. Moreover, if SLA generally consists of acquiring new form-meaning mappings, it follows that the most efficient type of attention to form would take place in a meaningful context, rather than as an isolated grammar component.

This emphasis on integration, rather than on whether or not techniques are implicit or explicit, is in line with Long's proposal for a focus on form. Long (1991:44–46) does not specifically rule out explicit techniques when he suggests that learners' attention be drawn to linguistic features in any way "appropriate to the students' age, proficiency level, etc." Perhaps more importantly, he recommends syllabi which "overtly draw students' attention to linguistic elements as they arise incidentally in lessons whose overriding focus is on meaning, or communication." Long stresses that the communicative interaction should remain the priority at all times and should be interrupted only briefly, if at all. Although many metalinguistic enhancement techniques naturally lead to long interruptions (e.g., a discussion of a given tense), what makes them undesirable is not the fact that they are explicit, but rather, that they serve to separate form from meaning rather than to integrate the focus on form within the focus on meaning.

There are a number of studies in which researchers have experimentally attempted to increase attention to form within an overall focus on meaning. One such study was conducted by Hulstijn (1989), who compared the effects of exposing participants to target sentences and assigning them tasks designed to require focus either on meaning or on formal properties of the input. Hulstijn then administered cued recalls and repetition tasks to all participants. Like Doughty (1991), Hulstijn found that not only did the meaning group score better than the form group on the recalls, but they also showed no disadvantage on at least some of the form-oriented tasks. Similarly, in their 1993 study, Spada and Lightbown also found that meaning-based instruction was improved by focus on form consisting of various techniques, including corrective feedback. Although Spada and Lightbown (1993:218) originally set out to compare a purely communicative control group with one that was communicative but with added focus on forms, they suggest that it was the unplanned "context-embedded focus on form" which occurred unexpectedly in their control group that caused it to outperform the experimental group. Their findings exemplify how a combination of enhancement techniques, all integrated within a overall focus on meaning, can be beneficial.

In summary, it is clear that there is a consensus among SLA researchers that noticing a form is a prerequisite for its acquisition. While there are varied accounts of what causes learners to attend to formal aspects of the input they receive, there is general agreement that drawing attention to the target forms will facilitate acquisition. Results from studies suggest that a number of enhancement techniques are beneficial: classroom instruction which integrates attention to form with attention to meaning will be beneficial for learners' acquisition.

AIMS

The current study investigated the effects of integrating a *focus on form* into content-based foreign language instruction. *Focus on form* was operationalized to include a number of input enhancement techniques which varied in degrees of explicitness and elaboration (Sharwood Smith 1991) but which nonetheless all took place during instruction where meaning remained the primary focus in all activities. Unlike much previous research, metalinguistic discussion was excluded from this study in order to avoid jeopardizing this form-meaning integration. The study is unique in that it attempted to compare two types of content-based instruction — a purely communicative focus on meaning versus integrated focus on form — within an intact, adult foreign language classroom setting, rather than in an experimental or immersion setting. In the Focus on Form group, an attempt was made to draw students' attention to the target usage of the preterit and imperfect tenses in Spanish during the content-based instruction in order to improve accuracy and increase use. The comparison of this group to the Purely Communicative group, which received no input enhancements, aims to determine whether it is possible to increase accuracy and use while still maintaining a focus on meaning.

HYPOTHESES

Following Schmidt (1990, 1993, 1994) and others (cf. Long 1991, VanPatten 1995), we assumed that attention is necessary for learning and generally expected, therefore, that techniques designed to draw students' attention to formal aspects of the target language during communication would be beneficial. Like Long (1991), we believe that the most effective type of attention to form occurs in a communicative meaning-based context. This belief motivated the specific hypotheses of this study which were as follows:

1. Instruction with focus on form would improve participants' accuracy in the use of preterit and imperfect tenses in

comparison with content-based instruction which had a pure focus on meaning.

2. Instruction with focus on form would increase participants' frequency in the use of preterit and imperfect tenses in comparison with content-based instruction which had a pure focus on meaning.

OPERATIONALIZATION OF CONSTRUCTS

Content-Based Instruction was considered, in this study, to be instruction in which specific topics (e.g., history, literature, etc.) are discussed in the target language, and information and ideas exchanged are central to the lesson. Content-based instruction is often purely communicative, but it can contain focus on form.

Purely Communicative Instruction is instruction in which there is no attempt to draw students' attention to formal aspects of language. Error correction is of incorrect information rather than of inaccurate language.

Focus on Form is that instruction where meaning is still central to the lesson, and there is also an attempt to draw students' attention to specific formal aspects of the target language. A variety of techniques are employed and attention to form is always integrated with attention to meaning.

TARGET STRUCTURE

The distinction between the preterit and the imperfect in Spanish is notoriously difficult for L2 learners, probably due to the often subtle differences in meaning between the two. Though there is still no consensus as to the exact semantic differences between the two forms (cf. Whitley 1986), there is agreement that the contrast is essentially aspectual. In general, the preterit is used to express perfective actions in the past while the imperfect expresses iterative and durative, as well as imperfective, meanings. In some cases only one of the two forms is acceptable in an isolated sentence, as in the following examples:

- Only the preterit is acceptable:

La Guerra Civil Española ***durabal/duró*** *de 1936 a 1939*

'The Spanish Civil War **lasted** from 1936 to 1939'

- Only the imperfect is acceptable:

Franco ***estaba/*estuvo*** *en el poder cuando Juan Carlos llegó a España.*

'Franco **was** in power when Juan Carlos arrived in Spain.'

Nonetheless, there are also instances in which either form would be acceptable in a given sentence, with contrastive meanings:

- Either preterit or imperfect is acceptable:

Los republicanos ***huían/huyeron*** *cuando los nacionalistas entraron en Madrid.*

'The Republicans **were fleeing/fled** when the Nationalists entered Madrid.'

It is not at all surprising, then, that even advanced L2 learners of Spanish are still working out the preterit-imperfect distinction in their interlanguage.

METHOD

PARTICIPANTS

The participants for this study were L2 Spanish learners enrolled in two university Advanced Spanish II classes which were taught by the same instructor (a native speaker of Spanish).[2] The regular course curriculum combines content-based lessons on Spanish history and culture with explicit grammar instruction. However, for the duration of the study reported here, there were no metalinguistic explanations or exercises. In this course, classes meet three times per week for 50 minutes with approximately 45 class meetings during the semester. Advanced Spanish II is designed as a sixth semester course, and all participants took Advanced Spanish I during the previous semester. Participants' background prior to that course was somewhat varied, as was determined by a questionnaire given to all participants. Some began their study of Spanish at the university and completed four semesters before entering Advanced I, while others were admitted directly based on their performance on a placement test administered by the Spanish Department. All 30 students in both classes (with one exception)[3] agreed to participate in this study. Only those participants whose L1 was English and who were present for the entire treatment period were included in the final analyses (n = 22).

The decision to use these particular participants was based on a number of factors. One of the researchers was coordinator of this course, and thus was familiar with the curriculum and able to work closely with the instructor in carrying out the experimental procedures. In addition, the fact that this level of the language sequence was already designed to be principally content-based made it

---

2 We are very grateful to José del Valle for allowing us to use his classes in this study, and for carrying out the instructional treatments with such care. We are also grateful to all the students who participated.

3 The one student who chose not to be included in the study took part in all class activities during the treatment period. She also participated in the pre and posttest semi-spontaneous production tasks, but these were not assessed. None of the subjects were informed as to who had or had not agreed to participate.

possible to carry out the study with minimum disruption to the regular curriculum. Moreover, the nature of the content itself, Spanish history, lent itself to the use of the target structures, and an examination of the regular course materials showed them to be rich in both preterit and imperfect forms.

PROCEDURES AND MATERIALS

The effects of focus on form vs. purely communicative instruction on the acquisition of the preterit-imperfect distinction in Spanish were investigated quasi-experimentally using a pretest/posttest design. Of the two intact classes utilized in this study, one was randomly chosen to receive focus on form instruction while the other received purely communicative instruction. The number of participants ultimately included was 10 in the Focus on Form group and 12 in the communicative group.

Pre- and posttests consisted of four tasks: an in-class communicative task (debate), an in-class essay, an appropriateness judgment task, and a modified cloze paragraph. The design of these tasks was motivated by pedagogical considerations and prior empirical findings on instructed second language acquisition. Because the widely-accepted goal of foreign language instruction is to help learners' develop communicative abilities in the target language, and because much SLA research has found instruction to be beneficial only for improving ability on forms in manipulation drills, two of the tasks were designed to elicit naturalistic language. Because the debate and the essay tasks required semi-spontaneous production, the items varied naturally from the pre- to the posttest. In contrast, the other two tasks were identical for both the pre- and posttests, and they were included in order to provide a more highly controlled instrument by which to compare the participants.

THE DEBATES

The debates dealt with various aspects of Spanish history (e.g., *Was the fall of the Spanish Empire unavoidable?*), In advance of the debates, which took place during the regular class meetings, participants were given specific topics related to readings and class discussions, were asked to prepare arguments defending all possible positions and were expected to be prepared to provide examples to support their claims (see Appendix A). In class, participants were randomly assigned to teams of 2 or 3 participants each and told which position to defend. They were not allowed to use any written materials or notes during the debates, nor did either experimental group receive any feedback during these debates. The pretest debate took place two weeks before the experimental period began, and the posttest debate occurred one week after the treatment ended. Both debates were video-taped for later analysis.

THE ESSAYS

As part of the regular in-class exams, participants wrote short essays about Spanish history, art and culture. For both the pre- and posttests, participants were given a choice of several related topics which required the use of the past tense reference. For example, on the pretest many participants wrote about the romanization of the Iberian Peninsula. Since participants were not allowed to use any books or notes while writing, and because they did not know the questions in advance, these essays were considered semi-spontaneous writing samples. Essays written one week before the treatment began were used as the pretest, while those used for the posttest were written five days after the last class meeting of the treatment period.

THE APPROPRIATENESS JUDGMENT TASK

Three days before the experimental instruction period began, participants were asked to complete an appropriateness judgment task. Each item in this task consisted of a sentence accompanied by a picture. The sentences contained two clauses, the second of which was underlined. Participants were instructed to mark whether or not the second clause completed the sentence such that it corresponded to the picture. They were also required to circle and correct any mistakes in the underlined clause. All the sentences included were grammatical, therefore only the appropriateness for the corresponding picture was in question. In all cases, the inappropriateness of a sentence was a result of the tense or aspect of the second verb. A first version of the task contained 32 target and distracter items, though 12 of these were eliminated after a pilot test was conducted with 20 native speakers of Spanish, due to the inconsistency of answers. Only the 15 items (12 target items and 3 distracters) for which there was 100% agreement among the native speakers were included in the version administered to the L2 participants. They completed the same task 3 days after the last class meeting of the experimental period.

THE MODIFIED CLOZE PARAGRAPH

Immediately after both administrations of the appropriateness judgment task, participants were next asked to complete a modified cloze paragraph. This task was different from a traditional cloze exercise in that all verbs appeared in the infinitive form. Participants were asked to supply the appropriate form of the verb for 16 items (12 target items and 4 distracters). This paragraph was also completed by a group of 16 native speakers of Spanish (from 4 different countries). Due to the variation found in their responses, only items for which there was at least 80% agreement (12 out of 16) were included in the analysis.

The experimental instructional treatment included two consecutive regularly scheduled class meetings. While the bulk of the treatment took place in the classroom, some of the materials and activities were designed to be completed as homework. The materials created by the researchers for the purely communicative and for the focus on form instructional treatments were consistent with the course curriculum. In general, these materials were quite similar for both groups and were designed to require attention to meaning, and during these two class periods, both groups received positive and negative feedback related to informational content.

The principal difference between the materials in the two treatments was that those for the Focus on Form group contained enhancements intended to draw participants' attention to the target structure. Furthermore, only in the Focus on Form group did the instructor provide feedback related to the use of the target structure. Such correction procedures were varied and included recasting of the entire utterance with added emphasis on the correct verb form, facial gestures signaling inaccuracy, and providing the correct preterit or imperfect form. We turn now to the details of the instructional materials used during the treatment.

Before the first class meeting, all participants received a reading passage on twentieth century Spanish history with a high number of occurrences of the target structure. The Focus on Form group received an enhanced version in which all verbs in the preterit and imperfect were underlined and highlighted (a different color was used for each) to make them highly salient. Participants in the Focus on Form group were also instructed to pay special attention to how temporal relationships were expressed in Spanish.

All participants also received questions based on the passage (e.g., *What were the various groups that participated in the Spanish Civil War?*) and were asked to be prepared to discuss their answers. These questions contained both preterit and imperfect forms and were designed to elicit the use of these structures. The Focus on Form group received the same questions as the Purely Communicative group, however, once again, all preterit and imperfect verbs were underlined and color-coded and were prefaced by explicit instructions for students to pay attention to how temporal relationships were expressed, and also to use care in their own expression (see Appendix B and Appendix C).

In the first class meeting, participants in both groups discussed the readings and questions for which they had prepared. In the Focus on Form group, participants were verbally instructed to be careful about how they expressed time relations, and the teacher provided feedback as described above. At the end of the class period, all participants were provided with the topics of the debate to take place the following class period. Much like the debates included in the pre- and posttests, all participants were asked to be prepared to defend opposing views on historical events (e.g., *Who was responsible for the Spanish Civil War: the left or the right?*). As was the case with other written materials, the instructions given to the Focus on Form group were enhanced with highlighting and underlining while the Purely Communicative group received an unenhanced version (see Appendix D).

The debate itself took place during the second class meeting of the treatment. As was the case in the other debates, participants were randomly assigned to teams (2 or 3 participants each) and told to defend a specific position. While two opposing sides debated, the rest of the class listened. Participants in the Focus on Form group were instructed to be especially careful expressing temporal relations and they received feedback during the debates. The participants in the Purely Communicative group received no instructions regarding form, nor did they receive feedback on anything other than content (it should be recalled that focus on form and Purely Communicative groups were in different Spanish classes).

These debates were also video-taped, and the tapes formed the basis of a homework assignment. Participants in both groups viewed the video filmed in their own class and evaluated their classmates' performance, as well as their own. They were asked to note content errors, to outline the arguments on both sides of all topics and to write 1–2 paragraphs stating which team they thought had won each debate and why. Participants in the Purely Communicative group were instructed to use content as the evaluation criterion, while participants in the Focus on Form group were instructed to additionally consider how well the arguments were expressed.

CODING AND SCORING PROCEDURES

Before beginning the actual coding, the two native speaker raters, one from Mexico and the other from Spain, were socialized to the procedure. The first rater coded all of the data from the pre- and posttest debates. Next a random sample representing approximately 11% of the total (55 out of 486 tokens) was coded by the second rater. Some differences between the raters occurred in instances where the first rater had coded a response as non-target-like. Thus, in order to increase reliability, all the data coded as non-target-like by the first rater was also coded by the second rater (approximately 31% of all verbs with past reference). In the case of remaining differences, the two raters discussed the item until they reached an agreement. If no such agreement could be reached, that item was excluded from analysis. The essay task was coded by the second rater after the extensive socialization on coding the debates.

The coding socialization resulted in the following framework for analyzing the spoken and written data. Only verbs with a past reference (simple tenses only)[4] were coded, and these were scored based only on the tense-aspect paradigm. In other words, only tense and aspectual information was considered while errors of person and number were ignored. In total, seven coding categories were created to account for both the appropriate native-like usage and the actual form utilized: (1) preterit instead of imperfect, (2) imperfect instead of preterit, (3) present instead of preterit, (4) present instead of imperfect, (5) historical present, (6) imperfect, and (7) preterit. This type of coding system was employed in order to capture various potential influences of instruction on the participants' interlanguage. Categories were subsequently conflated to provide an overall accuracy score which reflects use of the appropriate tense in obligatory contexts (categories (1)–(4) are non-target-like; and (5)–(7) are target-like). Suppliance scores, on the other hand, were obtained by calculating how often participants used a verb marked for the past (regardless of accuracy) when either the preterit or the imperfect was required. Thus a subject who consistently used the preterit in contexts requiring the imperfect, and vice-versa, would have a very low accuracy score but a very high suppliance score.

Participants' responses on the cloze paragraph were coded in the same way, using native speaker responses to determine the target usage. The appropriateness judgment task, on the other hand, involved production of past tense reference verbs only when participants rejected the sentence provided, and thus there was no need for the coding categories mentioned above. Instead, scores were calculated by awarding one point each time a subject's response matched the native speakers' consensus judgment. Prior to administering this task, the researchers decided to exclude from analysis any item on which a subject circled a word other than the underlined verb, as this would suggest that the subject was basing his/her decision on some criterion other than the preterit/imperfect distinction. In fact, this occurred frequently, forcing the exclusion of a large number of items which had been judged as inappropriate. It became clear that there was no satisfactory means by which to determine whether or not participants

4 From here on, the term 'past reference' will be used to refer to simple tenses only.

had used the preterit/imperfect distinction to judge those sentences which they did accept. Participants' lack of prior experience with this type of task, in contrast with the other three tasks which at various points had been used during the regular course curriculum, may have affected the results. For these reasons, the data obtained for the judgment task had to be excluded from the final analyses. Finally, because the number of tokens elicited varied across tasks, participants' accuracy and suppliance scores for each task were calculated proportionally.

RESULTS

HYPOTHESIS 1: ACCURACY

Pre- and posttest accuracy scores for spoken and written tasks are given in Table 1.[5]

Table 1: Accuracy scores by task and group

Debates: Purely Communicative group

	Pretest	Posttest	Change	%Change
median	80.91	75.00	**–5.91**	–7.3%
mean	76.79	79.17	**2.38**	3.1%
tokens	3–22	5–28	n=10*	

Debates: Focus on Form group

	Pretest	Posttest	Change	%Change
median	66.67	85.71	**19.04**	28.6%
mean	65.98	85.12	**19.14**	29.0%
tokens	9–41	6–31	n=5*	

Essays: Purely Communicative group

	Pretest	Posttest	Change	%Change
median	63.57	68.34	**4.77**	7.5%
mean	68.19	69.42	**1.23**	1.8%
tokens	8–19	7–17	n=10*	

5 Accuracy scores on the debate task are reported by intended meaning (preterit or imperfect) on Tables 2 and 3.

Essays: Focus on Form group

	Pretest	Posttest	Change	%Change
median	82.58	83.98	**1.40**	1.7%
mean	77.87	82.46	**4.60**	5.6%
tokens	2–14	12–17	n=10*	

Cloze Paragraph: Purely Communicative group

	Pretest	Posttest	Change	%Change
median	83.33	66.67	**–16.67**	–20.0%
mean	71.97	69.15	**–2.82**	–4.1%
tokens	9–12	11–12	n=10*	

Cloze Paragraph: Focus on Form group

	Pretest	Posttest	Change	%Change
median	66.67	75.00	**8.33**	12.5%
mean	73.99	72.44	**–1.55**	–2.1%
tokens	11–12	10–12	n=9*	

In order to ensure that the purely communicative and the Focus on Form groups started the treatment with equivalent interlanguage knowledge of the preterit and imperfect, their pretest accuracy scores on all tasks were compared. Since the two groups in the study were intact groups, and given the small size of the samples, a non-parametric statistical analysis was employed. The results of the Wilcoxon rank sums test show no significant difference between the groups' accuracy scores at the outset of the study (cloze paragraph: $z = 0.304$, $p=.761$; debates: $z = 1.04$, $p=.298$; and essays: $z = 1.134$, $p=.256$).

To investigate the validity of our first hypothesis, i.e., whether focus on form instruction improved accuracy of the target structures in comparison with purely communicative instruction, pretest and posttest scores on all tasks for each group were compared. A comparison of the median scores of the pre- and posttests shows an improvement for the Focus on Form group on all three tasks (see Figure 1).

Figure 1: Median accuracy scores (all tasks)
Focus on Form group

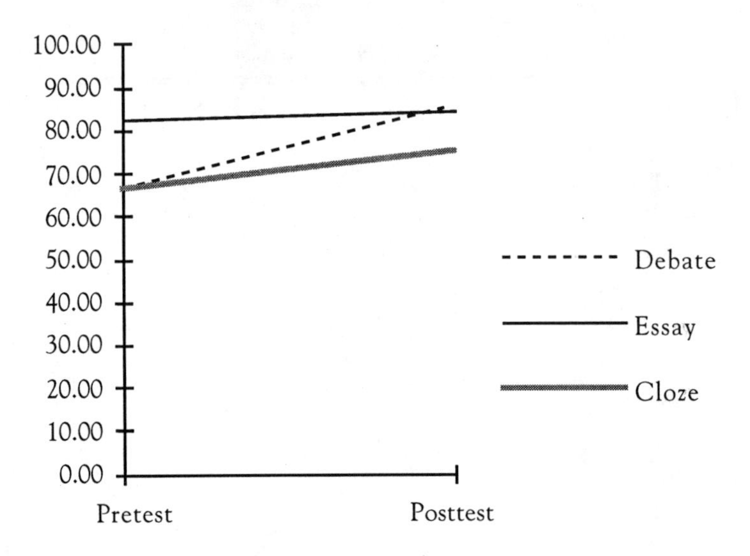

On the other hand, the Purely Communicative group's scores increased for the essays, but actually decreased for the other two tasks (see Figure 2).

**Figure 2: Median accuracy scores (all tasks)
Purely Communicative group**

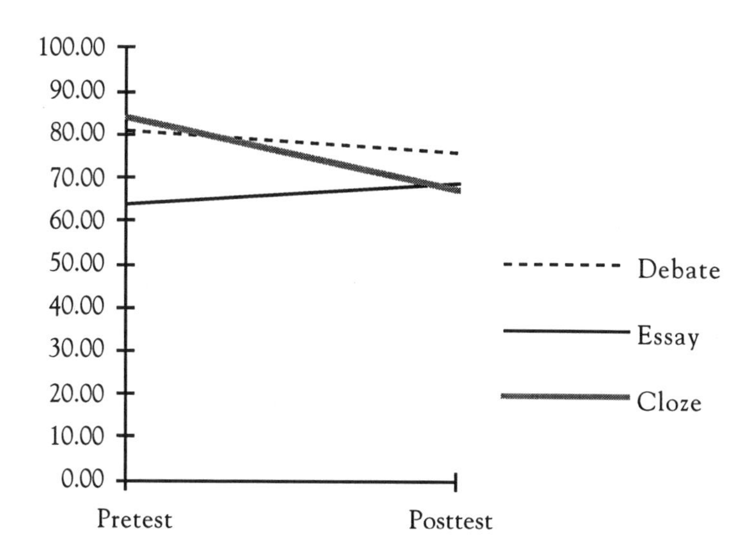

The significance of the pretest to posttest change in each group for each task was assessed using a Wilcoxon matched-pairs signed-ranks test. On the debates, the 5 participants in the Focus on Form group who were present for both debates had a median score of 66.7 on the pretest and 85.7 on the posttest, which represents a gain of 19 (percentage gain = 28.6%). The Purely Communicative group median pretest score was 80.9 and the posttest median was 75, representing a change of –5.9 (percentage change = –7.3%). For the Focus on Form group, the improvement was found to be statistically significant ($z=2.023$, $p=.043$). In contrast, the changes in the scores of the Purely Communicative group were not significant ($z=-.059$, $p=.953$). A careful look at each individual subject's performance on the two debates shows that in the Focus on Form group, there was consistent improvement among all participants while there was no such result in the Purely Communicative group (see Figures 3 and 4 below).

Figure 3: Individual debate accuracy scores
Focus on Form group

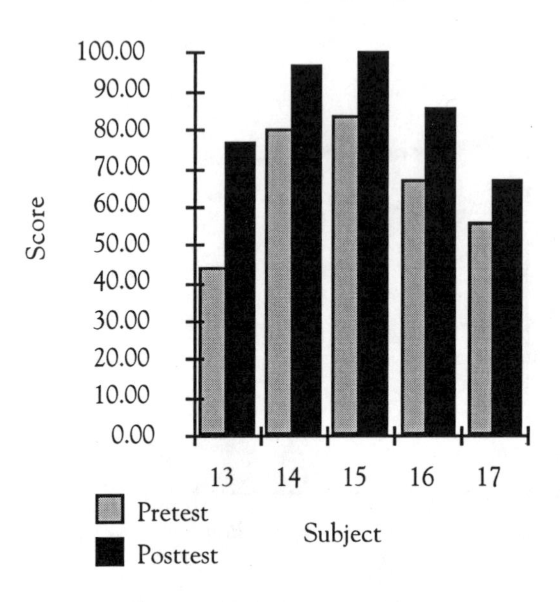

Figure 4: Individual debate accuracy scores
Purely Communicative group

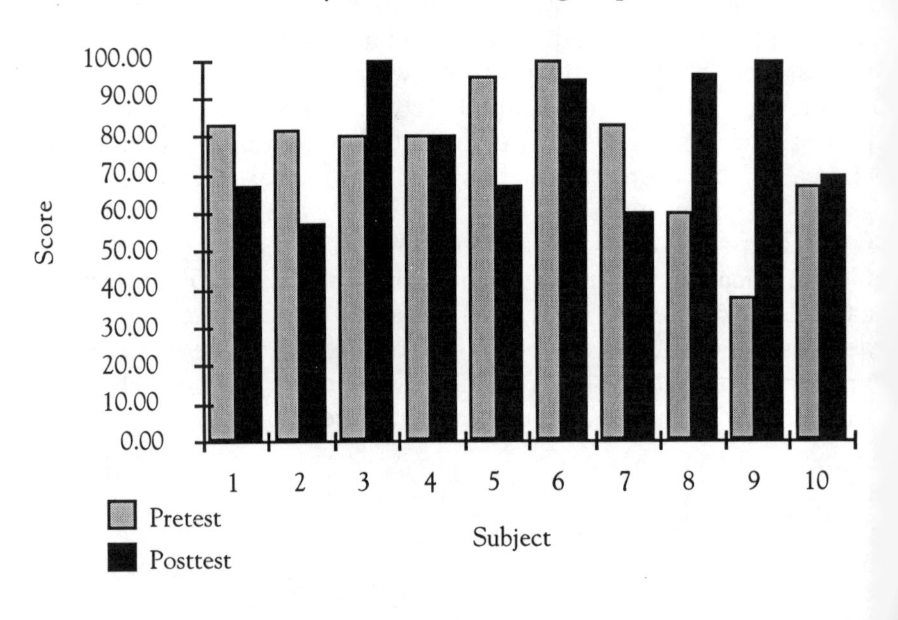

As for the essays, the Focus on Form group had a median score of 82.6 on the pretest and 84 on the posttest, a gain of 1.4 (1.7%). The Purely Communicative group obtained median scores of 63.6 and 68.3, for a gain of 4.8 (7.5%). Neither groups' gains reached significance (Focus on Form group, z=–.533, p=.594; Purely Communicative group, z=–.255, p=.799).

On the cloze paragraph the median scores were 66.7 on the pretest and 75 on the posttest for the Focus on Form group (gain = 8.33, 12.5%), and 83.3 on the pretest and 66.7 on the posttest for the Purely Communicative group (change = –16.67, –20%). These changes were not found to be significant for either group (focus on form, z=–.533, p=.594; communicative, z=–.978, p=.3281).

HYPOTHESIS 2: SUPPLIANCE

On all tasks, whenever participants produced an inappropriate form in place of either the preterit or the imperfect, this form was in the present tense. In addition, there were no instances where participants overgeneralized either the preterit or imperfect to other contexts. That is, while the preterit and imperfect were often substituted for each other, or replaced by the present, they never appeared in contexts requiring any other form.

On both the pretest and the posttest all participants obtained suppliance scores which were greater than 98% on the cloze paragraph and essay task, and thus the only task which can provide insight as to our second hypothesis, i.e., that focus on form instruction would increase participants' use of the target forms, is the debate.

There were no significant differences in suppliance scores between these groups at the outset of the study (z=–.245, p=.807). Each group's pretest was compared to its posttest in order to determine whether any change had taken place. For the Focus on Form group, the median suppliance scores were 86.7 on the pretest and 100 on the posttest, which represents a gain of 13.3 (15.3%). The Purely Communicative group had median scores of 82.6 and 94, respectively. This group's median gain was 5 (6.3%).

The pretest and posttest suppliance scores for each group were submitted to a Wilcoxon matched-pairs signed-ranks test in order to determine the significance of the gains. The improvement was found to be significant for the Focus on Form group ($z=-.2023$, $p=.043$), but not for the Purely Communicative group ($z=-.415$, $p=.678$). In other words, only the Focus on Form group demonstrated a significant increase in their use of the preterit and imperfect in required contexts. As was the case for accuracy, the Focus on Form group showed consistent improvement from the pretest to the posttest, while the Purely Communicative group exhibited no such pattern (see Figures 5 and 6).

Figure 5: Individual suppliance scores
Focus on Form group (Debate)

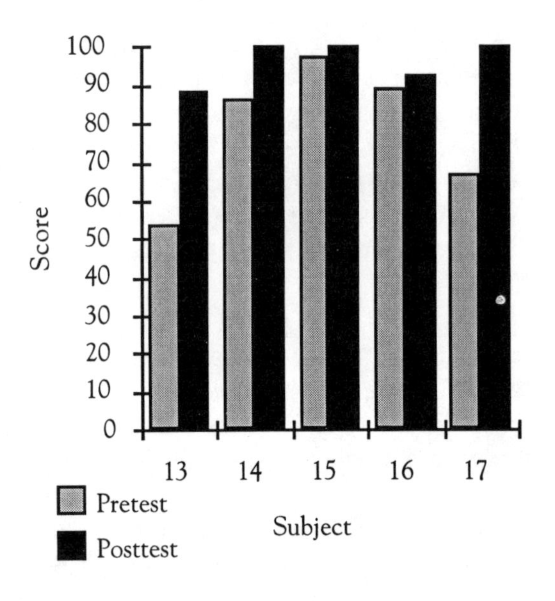

Figure 6: Individual suppliance scores Purely Communicative group (Debate)

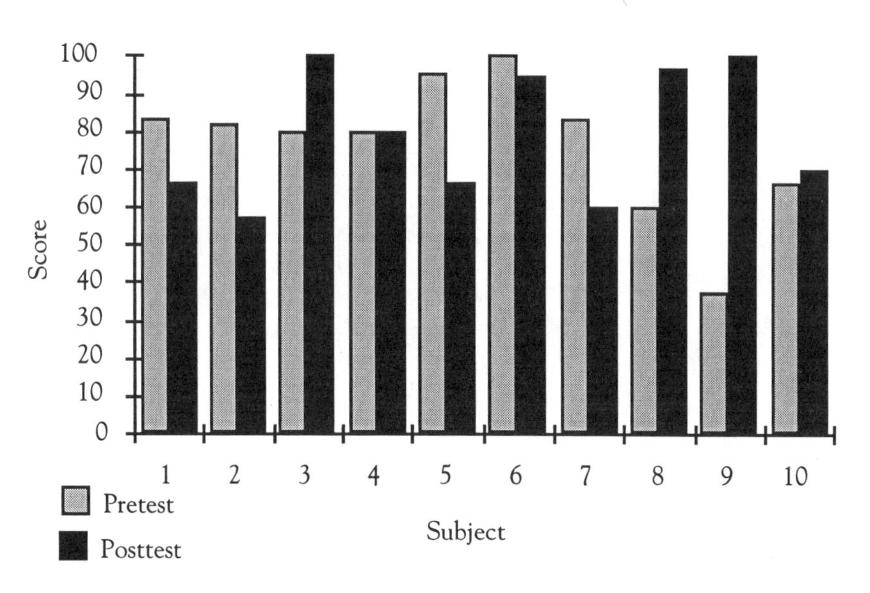

In order to better understand participants' interlanguage production, the data were further analyzed according to the intended meaning. All past reference verbs were divided into two groups: those where native-like usage of a past reference verb would require preterit, and those where native-like usage would require the imperfect.[6] For each intended *meaning* (preterit or imperfect), the number of tokens of each *form* (preterit, imperfect, and present) was then tallied (as shown in Tables 2 and 3).

6 In some cases the *historical present* would also be native-like. In these instances, intended meaning was based on which past tense form would be appropriate.

Table 2: Production, accuracy, and suppliance with intended imperfect meaning

PURELY COMMUNICATIVE GROUP

	Tokens		Imperfect form (=accuracy)			Preterit form			Imperfect or preterit (=suppliance)			Present form		
subject	Pre	Post	Pre	Post	Chng	Pre	Post	Chng	Pre	Post	Chng	Pre	Post	Chng
1	4	12	75	66.7	–8.3	25	8.3	–16.7	100	75.0	–25.0	0	25	25
2	13	4	92.3	50	–42.3	0	25	25	92	75	–17	7.7	25	17.3
3	4	4	75	100	25	0	0	0	75	100	25	25	0	–25
4	6	3	66.7	66.7	0	0	0	0	67	67	0	33.3	33.3	0
5	14	6	100	83.3	–16.7	0	0.0	0.0	100	83.3	–16.7	0.0	16.7	16.7
6	3	4	100	100	0	0	0	0	100	100	0	0	0	0
7	1	1	100	100	0	0	0	0	100	100	0	0	0	0
8	6	13	50	92.3	42.3	16.7	0.0	–16.7	66.7	92.3	25.6	33.3	7.7	–25.6
9	5	4	20	100	80	20	0	–20	40	100	60	60	0	–60
10	1	1	0	100	100	0	0	0	0	100	100	100	0	–100
median			75	96.2	–21.2	0	0	0	83.7	96.2	–12.5	16.3	3.8	–12.5
mean			67.9	85.9	–18	6.2	3.3	–2.8	74.1	89.2	15.2	25.9	10.8	–15.2

FOCUS ON FORM GROUP

subject	Tokens		Imperfect form (=accuracy)			Preterit form			Imperfect or preterit (=suppliance)			Present form		
	Pre	Post	Pre	Post	Chng	Pre	Post	Chng	Pre	Post	Chng	Pre	Post	Chng
13	18	7	16.7	71.4	54.7	22.2	14.3	−7.9	38.9	85.7	46.8	61.1	14.3	−46.8
14	15	24	80	100	20	6.7	0	−6.7	86.7	100	13.3	13.3	0	−13.3
15	19	9	68.4	100	31.6	26.3	0	−26.3	94.7	100	5.3	5.3	0	−5.3
16	8	11	62.5	90.9	28.4	25	0	−25	88	91	3	12.5	9.1	−3.4
17	6	4	50	100	50	0	0	0	50	100	50	50	0	−50
median			62.5	100	37.5	22.2	0	−22.9	86.7	100	13.3	13.3	0	−13.3
mean			55.5	92.5	36.9	16.0	2.9	−13.2	71.6	95.3	23.8	28.4	4.7	−23.8

Table 3: Production, accuracy, and suppliance with intended preterit meaning

PURELY COMMUNICATIVE GROUP

	Tokens		Preterit form (=accuracy)			Imperfect form			Imperfect or preterit (=suppliance)			Present form		
subject	Pre	Post	Pre	Post	Chng	Pre	Post	Chng	Pre	Post	Chng	Pre	Post	Chng
1	2	0	100	—	—	0	—	—	100	—	—	0	—	—
2	9	3	66.7	66.7	0	0	0	0	67	67	0	33.3	33.3	0
3	1	3	100	100	0	0	0	0	100	100	0	0	0	0
4	4	7	100	85.7	–14.3	0	14.3	14.3	100	100	0.0	0	0	0
5	7	6	85.7	50	–35.7	14.3	50	35.7	100	100	0.0	0	0	0
6	0	15	—	93.3	—	—	6.7	—	—	100	—	—	0	—
7	5	4	80	50	–30	0	0	0	80	50	–30	20	50	30
8	4	15	75	100	25	25	0	–25	100	100	0	0	0	0
9	3	2	66.7	100	33.3	0	0	0	67	100	33	33.3	0	–33.3
10	5	9	80	66.7	–13.3	20	33.3	13.3	100	100	0.0	0	0	0
median			80	85.7	–5.7	0	0	0	100	100	0	0	0	0
mean			83.8	79.2	4.6	6.6	11.6	–5.0	90.4	90.7	–0.4	9.6	9.3	0.4

FOCUS ON FORM GROUP

	Tokens		Preterit form (=accuracy)			Imperfect form			Imperfect or preterit (=suppliance)			Present form		
subject	Pre	Post	Pre	Post	Chng	Pre	Post	Chng	Pre	Post	Chng	Pre	Post	Chng
13	23	10	65.2	80	14.8	0	10	10	65.2	90	24.8	34.8	10	–24.8
14	0	7	—	85.7	—	—	14.3	—	—	100	—	—	0	—
15	18	22	100	100	0	0	0	0	100	100	0	0	0	0
16	1	3	100	66.7	–33.3	0	33.3	33.3	100	100	0	0	0	0
17	3	2	66.7	0	–66.7	33.3	100	66.7	100	100	0	0	0	0
median			83.3	80	3.3	0	14.3	–14.3	100	100	0	0	0	0
mean			83.0	66.5	16.5	8.3	31.5	–23.2	91.3	98	–6.7	8.7	2	6.7

Because participants varied in the number of times they expressed each meaning, the use of each form for each meaning is presented as a ratio. As is apparent in Tables 2 and 3, on the pretest, participants in both groups had higher accuracy and suppliance scores when the intended meaning was preterit than when it was imperfect. They not only used the preterit when the meaning was imperfect more than vice-versa, but they also used the present more often with imperfect meaning. In fact, at the time the pretest data was collected, there was almost no use of the present with preterit meaning.

Interestingly, while both groups show increased accuracy and suppliance scores overall and with imperfect meaning, the Focus on Form group actually shows decreased accuracy with preterit meaning, due to an increase of the imperfect form in these contexts. In other words, on the posttest, the Focus on Form group appears to have overgeneralized the imperfect form, thus producing it consistently in obligatory contexts, and often in contexts requiring the preterit.

DISCUSSION

The results outlined in the previous section at least partially support our first hypothesis, i.e., that the Focus on Form group would show superior improvement when compared to the Purely Communicative group. The Focus on Form group increased or maintained accuracy on all tasks, while the Purely Communicative group improved slightly on only one and worsened on the other two. There are several possible reasons for why the results from the debate offered the strongest support for our two hypotheses. First, this task was the one which required the most naturalistic production. The Focus on Form group's superior performance is understandable if we consider that of the four tasks, the semi-spontaneous speech is the one that most closely represents true acquisition of the target forms. In addition, the debate was very similar to the one which took place in the experimental period, thus it is not surprising that the most impressive effects of instruction were found here.[7]

In regard to the second hypothesis, there is evidence that focus on form instruction led to increased use of the target forms, as indicated by the statistically significant increase in the suppliance score. This was not the case for the Purely Communicative group, which demonstrated no such significant change. This finding is especially important in that it shows that focus on form instruction did not cause a decrease in use of the targeted forms. In other words, focus on form instruction, including corrective feedback, did not cause participants to utilize an avoidance strategy. Instead, these results suggest that learners' use of specific forms can effectively be increased within a communicative context.

The tense by tense analysis of accuracy and suppliance showed that, in the pretest debate, participants almost never substituted the present (or any other form) for the preterit. The fact that there was initially less use of the imperfect, on the other hand, might indicate that this

[7] The fact that debates were used in both treatment and measurement is not problematic for our claims about the superiority of focus on form instruction as this was the case for both groups.

tense may have been more difficult for these participants. This finding is consistent with Kaplan's (1987) finding that L2 learners of French made more errors with the French imperfect than with the *passé composé* (which is semantically equivalent to the Spanish preterit). The greater interlanguage use of the present when the intended meaning was imperfect may also reflect priority given to aspect rather than tense. It may also be a result of L1 influence if learner's have associated the English past with the preterit, as Larsen-Freeman has suggested (personal communication).

The positive effects of focus on form instruction seem to be the result of increased learner attention to the target form. While it is still not possible to monitor participants' cognitive activity (but see Jourdenais et al., this volume), there was some non-quantifiable external evidence that at least some of them noticed the enhancements in the input they received. For example, one student, upon receiving the homework text, asked "Are these words highlighted for a reason?" (the instructor's response was "What do you think?"). At least some participants also seemed aware of the feedback they received and one person in the Focus on Form group clearly used feedback as a way to evaluate his own performance in a debate. When asked to comment on how well he had expressed himself during the debate, he said that his oral expression had been good and offered as evidence the fact that the instructor had corrected him only once.

Nonetheless, it also seems that not all of the enhancements were noticed by all the participants. For example, many participants in the Focus on Form group, when instructed to evaluate the (experimental period) debates based both on the strength of the arguments and on how well these arguments were expressed, made absolutely no reference to the latter. While no quantitative claims can be made, it does suggest that at least some learners prioritize meaning over form, despite the emphatic instructions they received to consider both. Another possibility is that the instructions to evaluate expression were misinterpreted by some to mean organization, rather than linguistic form. On the other hand, a number of participants did comment specifically on the target structure, which seems to indicate that instruction did increase their attention to these forms. For example, one subject wrote "I understand my mistakes with temporal relations." Another wrote "my temporal relations were not very good. I forgot to express things in the past." This is particularly interesting because the instructions for the viewing and evaluating the debate referred only to how well the students had expressed themselves in general, and made no reference to the target structure or temporal relations.

It could be argued that the improvements in the Focus on Form group were a result of increased monitoring, rather than acquisition of the target forms, especially if we take into account that all participants had prior metalinguistic training in the use of the target forms. However, if the observed gains were the result only of increased monitoring, we would not expect the greatest improvements to be on precisely the type of task that has been shown to lack such monitoring: semi-spontaneous speech. While participants' gains may be partially a result of extra effort to speak accurately, this in no way weakens the claim the focus on form instruction is beneficial. If Terrell, Baycroft and Perrone (1987) are correct in maintaining that L2 speakers in purely communicative environments do not improve their accuracy when there is no communicative pressure to do so, focus on form instruction may be effective due to increased pressure on the learner. In the case of focus on form instruction, this pressure is exerted through feedback, which serves the same role as miscommunication might in a natural setting: the learner is confronted with the unacceptability of his/her utterance and is encouraged to modify it in order to continue the communicative interaction. The other enhancements of focus on form instruction serve to make the target form more salient, as well as to attract the learners' attention.

CONCLUSION

This study has shown that integrated focus on form instruction can result in increased accuracy and use of specific target forms. We must keep in mind that the number of participants was small, and of course replications of our results must be obtained before making any strong claims. It is also necessary to investigate the effects of focus on form instruction with learners at different proficiency levels and with differing degrees of metalinguistic knowledge in the use of the target forms. In addition, it will be interesting to compare the effects of focus on form instruction on forms of differing communicative value. These will be the aims of future studies.

REFERENCES

Bransdorfer, R. (1989). Processing function words in the input: Does meaning make a difference? Paper presented at the annual meeting of the American Association of Teachers of Spanish and Portuguese, San Antonio, Texas.

Carroll, S., & Swain, M. (1993). Explicit and implicit negative feedback: An empirical study of the learning of linguistic generalizations. *Studies in Second Language Acquisition, 15* , 357–386.

Carroll, S., Roberge, Y, & Swain, M. (1992). The role of feedback in second language acquisition: Error correction and morphological generalization *Applied Linguistics*, *13*, 173–198.

Doughty, C. (1991). Second language instruction does make a difference. *Studies in Second Language Acquisition*, *13*, 431–469.

Harley, B. (1993). Instructional strategies and SLA in early French immersion. *Studies in Second Language Acquisition*, *15*, 245–259.

Harley, B., & Swain, M. (1985). The interlanguage of immersion students and its implications for second language teaching. In A. Davies, C. Criper, & A. P. R. Howatt (Eds.), *Interlanguage* (pp. 291–311). Edinburgh: Edinburgh University Press.

Hulstijn, J. (1989). Implicit and incidental second language learning: Experiments in the processing of natural and partially artificial input. In H. W. Dechert & M. Raupach (Eds.), *Interlingual processes* (pp. 49–73). Tübingen: Narr.

Kaplan, M. A. (1987). Developmental patterns of past tense acquisition among foreign language learners of French. In B. VanPatten & James Lee (Eds.), *Foreign language learning: A research perspective* (pp. 52–60). Rowley, MA: Newbury House.

Krashen, S. (1977). The monitor model for adult second language performance. In M. Burt, H. Dulay, & M Finocchiaro (Eds.), *Viewpoints on English as a second language* (pp. 152–161). New York: Regents.

Lightbown, P. M. (1994). The importance of timing in focus on form. Paper presented at the Second Language Research Forum, Concordia & McGill Universities, Montreal.

Long, M. H. (1991). Focus on form: A design feature in language teaching methodology. In K. de Bot, D. Coste, C. Kramsch, & R. Ginsburg (Eds.), *Foreign language research in a cross-cultural perspective* (pp. 39–52).

Pienemann, M. (1985). Learnability and syllabus construction. In K. Hyltenstam & M. Pienemann (Eds.), *Modeling and assessing second language acquisition* (pp. 23–75). Clevedon: Multilingual Matters.

Schmidt, R. (1990). The role of consciousness in second language learning. *Applied Linguistics, 11*, 129–158.

Schmidt, R. (1993). Awareness and second language acquisition. *Annual Review of Applied Linguistics, 13* , 206–226.

Schmidt, R. (1994). Deconstructing consciousness in search of useful definitions for applied linguistics. *AILA Review, 11*, 11–26.

Schmidt, R., & Frota, S. (1986). Developing basic conversational ability in a second language: a case study of an adult learner of Portuguese. In R. Day (Ed.), *Talking to learn: Conversation in second language acquisition* (pp. 237–326). Rowley, Mass. : Newbury House.

Sharwood Smith, M. (1991). Speaking to many minds: On the relevance of different types of language information for the L2 learner. *Second Language Research, 7*, 118–132.

Sharwood Smith, M. (1993). Input enhancement in instructed SLA: Theoretical bases. *Studies in Second Language Acquisition, 15* , 165–179.

Shook, D. (1990). L2 reading and grammar acquisition: An input-processing perspective. Unpublished manuscript.

Spada, N., & Lightbown, P. M. (1993). Instruction and the development of questions in L2 classrooms. *Studies in Second Language Acquisition, 15*, 205–224.

Swain, M. (1992). Manipulating and complementing content teaching to maximize learning. In E. Kellerman, R. Phillipson, L. Selinker, M. Sharwood Smith, & M. Swain (Eds.), *Foreign/second language pedagogy research* (pp. 234–250). Clevedon: Multilingual Matters.

Swain, M., & Lapkin, S. (1989). Canadian immersion and adult second language teaching: What's the connection? *Modern Language Journal, 73*, 150–159.

Terrell, T., Baycroft, B., & Perrone, C. (1987). The subjunctive in Spanish interlanguage: Accuracy and comprehensibility. In T. R. Dvorak, J. F. Lee, & B. VanPatten (Eds.), *Foreign language learning: A research perspective* (pp. 33–51). New York: Newbury House.

Tomasello, M., & Herron, C. (1989). Feedback for language transfer errors. *Studies in Second Language Acquisition*, *11*, 384–395.

Tomlin, R. S., & Villa, V. (1994). Attention in cognitive science and second language acquisition. *Studies in Second Language Acquisition*, *16*, 183–203.

VanPatten, B. (1989). Can learners attend to form and content while processing input? *Hispania*, *72* , 409–417.

VanPatten, B. (1995). Cognitive aspects of input processing in second language acquisition. In P. Hashemipour, R. Maldonado, & M. van Naerssen (Eds.), *Studies in language learning and Spanish linguistics in honor of Tracy D. Terrell* (pp. 170–183). New York: McGraw Hill.

Whitley, M. S. (1986). *Spanish/English contrasts*. Washington DC: Georgetown University Press.

Whitley, M. S. (1993). Communicative language teaching: An incomplete revolution. *Foreign Language Annals*, *26*, 137–154.

APPENDIX A: POSTTEST DEBATE INSTRUCTIONS

Discusión: El desastre y la Generación del '98

1. ¿Qué fue "el desastre"?
2. ¿El Desastre realmente fue algo que ocurrió en un sólo año (1898)?
3. ¿Cuál era la importancia del desastre para la Generación del '98?
4. ¿Cuál era la visión de la religión de los miembros de la Generación del '98?

Temas de debate:

Prepare argumentos para defender cada una de las siguientes posiciones:

1. El Desastre del '98:
   - A. Fue la culminación inevitable de años de decadencia
   - B. Fue el resultado de factores específicos de ese momento histórico
2. La Iglesia Católica hasta la Guerra Civil:
   - A. Era una fuerza reaccionaria que había contribuído a los desastres y las crisis.
   - B. Era una fuerza positiva que intentaba preservar los valores espirituales y nacionales.

APPENDIX B: READING QUESTIONS — PURELY COMMUNICATIVE GROUP

El siglo XX: Desde Alfonso XIII hasta Francisco Franco

Lea las fotocopias y conteste las siguientes preguntas.

1. Describa las circunstancias del conflicto en Marruecos. ¿Cuál fue la reacción a la guerra en España?
2. ¿Cuál fue la posición de España en la Primera Guerra Mundial? ¿Cuáles fueron las consecuencias de esta posición?
3. ¿Qué eran la UGT y la CNT? ¿Qué querían?
4. ¿Quién fue Primo de Ribera? ¿Cómo llegó al poder? ¿Cómo perdió el poder?
5. ¿Cuáles fueron algunas de las reformas que se llevaron a cabo durante la Segunda República?
6. ¿Cómo era la situación política y social en los últimos años de la Segunda República?
7. ¿Cuándo empezó la Guerra Civil? ¿Cuáles eran los dos bandos? ¿Cómo empezó?
8. ¿Cúal fue la reacción internacional a la Guerra Civil? ¿Cuál era la situación en Europa en ese momento?
9. ¿Cómo terminó la Guerra Civil? ¿Qué sistema político se estableció?

Términos claves:

república (vs. democracia)
monarquía
dictadura
anarquía
fascismo
gobierno vs. sistema político

constitución
promulgar una ley; promulgar una constitución
sindicato
huelga
sublevarse/sublevación

APPENDIX C: READING QUESTIONS — FOCUS ON FORM GROUP

NOTE: Past reference verbs were also highlighted in contrasting colors

---

El siglo XX: Desde Alfonso XIII hasta Francisco Franco

Lea las fotocopias y conteste las siguientes preguntas. *Presente especial atención a cómo se expresan las relaciones temporales.*

1. Describa las circunstancias del conflicto en Marruecos. ¿Cuál **fue** la reacción a la guerra en España?
2. ¿Cuál **fue** la posición de España en la Primera Guerra Mundial? ¿Cuáles **fueron** las consecuencias de esta posición?
3. ¿Qué **eran** la UGT y la CNT? ¿Qué **querían**?
4. ¿Quién **fue** Primo de Ribera? ¿Cómo **llegó** al poder? ¿Cómo **perdió** el poder?
5. ¿Cuáles **fueron** algunas de las reformas que **se llevaron** a cabo durante la Segunda República?
6. ¿Cómo **era** la situación política y social en los últimos años de la Segunda República?
7. ¿Cuándo **empezó** la Guerra Civil? ¿Cuáles **eran** los dos bandos? ¿Cómo **empezó**?
8. ¿Cúal **fue** la reacción internacional a la Guerra Civil? ¿Cuál **era** la situación en Europa en ese momento?
9. ¿Cómo **terminó** la Guerra Civil? ¿Qué sistema político **se estableció**?

Términos claves:

república (vs. democracia)
monarquía
dictadura
anarquía
fascismo
gobierno vs. sistema político
constitución
promulgar una ley; promulgar una constitución
sindicato
huelga
sublevarse/sublevación

APPENDIX D: DEBATE TOPICS — FOCUS ON FORM GROUP

NOTE: Past reference verbs were highlighted in contrasting colors

---

Discusión: la Segunda República y la Guerra Civil

1. ¿Cómo **eran** diferentes y qué **tenían** en común la dictadura de Franco y la dictadura de Primo de Ribera?
2. ¿ **Se justificaba** la sublevación del ejército?
3. ¿Los gobiernos republicanos **podían** haber hecho algo para evitar la sublevación de los militares?
4. ¿Cuáles **eran** las raíces históricas del conflicto?

Temas de debate

Prepare argumentos para defender cada una de las siguientes posiciones. *Tenga cuidado especial al expresar las relaciones temporales:*

1. Los grupos participantes en la Guerra Civil
   - A. **Había** dos bandos que se **oponían**
   - B. **Había** muchos grupos diversos que no **tenían** mucho en común
2. Los grupos responsables de la Guerra Civil
   - A. Los gobiernos republicanos y la izquierda **tenían** la culpa
   - B. Los militares y la derecha **tenían** la culpa
3. La posición de los "países democráticos"
   - A. **Tenían** la obligación de apoyar la Segunda República
   - B. **Hicieron** bien en no intervenir en la Guerra Civil

Riikka Alanen
University of Jyväskylä

INPUT ENHANCEMENT AND RULE PRESENTATION IN SECOND LANGUAGE ACQUISITION

ABSTRACT

This study investigated how rule presentation and visual input enhancement affected the acquisition of structural language elements by L1 English beginning learners of semi-artificial Finnish. Learning targets, locative suffixes *–ssa* ('in'), *–ssa* ('on') and *–lla* ('on') and four types of consonant alternation, were embedded in two reading comprehension tasks. Participants (N=36), who were students at the University of Hawai'i, Mānoa, were divided into a control group and three treatment groups. The input the participants in the treatment groups were exposed to was manipulated in the following ways: the visual enhancement of the learning targets by the use of italics (Enhance); explicit rule presentation (Rule); and a combination of both (Rule & Enhance). Learners were also asked to think aloud during the study phase. The following order of achievement was predicted: Control < Enhance < Rule < Rule & Enhance. While the results partially supported this, the effect of visual enhancement was not immediately obvious. However, the learners' productions revealed that visual enhancement seemed to have a facilitating effect on the learners' recall and use of the targets, especially those of locative suffixes. It also appeared that omission and over-generalization frequently occurred in the productions of the groups that had received no explicit form-focused instruction, while L1 transfer characterized the performance of the rule-based groups. Think-alouds revealed that learning outcomes were greatly influenced by the learners' focus of attention. Those learners who had paid attention to the targets during the study phase also appeared to have acquired at least some aspects of them, regardless of the treatment they had received.

Alanen, Riikka (1995). Input enhancement and rule presentation in second language acquisition. In Richard Schmidt (Ed.), *Attention and awareness in foreign language learning* (Technical Report #9) (pp. 259–302). Honolulu, Hawai'i: University of Hawai'i, Second Language Teaching & Curriculum Center.

INTRODUCTION

The role of input enhancement and explicit instruction in second language acquisition has been heavily debated in recent years (Sharwood Smith, 1993; VanPatten and Cadierno, 1993). This question is closely related to such basic issues in second language research as the fundamental nature of L2 learning and teaching and the exact relationship between input and intake. What is the significance of explicit, implicit and incidental knowledge and learning, and the role of attention and consciousness in this process? The present study attempts to show how certain features of linguistic input and the attention paid to them during the learning process are related to the learning outcomes.

How do we learn what we learn? The key to our understanding how second language learning takes place is to understand how the input the learner is exposed to becomes intake. In any language learning situation, as we all know, there is always input, that is, the target language material the learner is exposed to during the process of language learning. Intake refers to that part of the input the learner has actually incorporated into his or her developing knowledge system, that part of the input the learner has perceived and processed, i.e., has learned (Chaudron, 1985; VanPatten, 1989). How input becomes intake is a complex process we do not quite understand yet; however, we know that certain factors play an important role in this process (Chaudron, 1985; Sharwood Smith, 1993; VanPatten and Cadierno, 1993). The role of attention and consciousness, in particular, has attracted a great deal of interest in recent years. Must learners consciously attend to features in the input in order to learn them, or, do learners need to be aware of what they are learning in order for learning to take place (VanPatten, 1989; Schmidt, 1990, 1992)?

Schmidt (1990) distinguishes among three key issues that are related to the role of consciousness in input processing: (1) subliminal learning, by which Schmidt refers to the question of whether conscious awareness at the level of noticing is necessary for language learning; (2) incidental learning, which refers to the question of whether it is necessary deliberately to pay attention in order to learn; and (3) implicit learning, which Schmidt uses to refer to the question of whether learner hypotheses based on input are the result of conscious insight and understanding or an unconscious process of abstraction. Schmidt comes to the conclusion that incidental learning is both possible and effective, when the task demands serve to focus learners' attention on what is to be learned, but that even so, deliberately paying attention may have a facilitative effect, and may be necessary for the acquisition of redundant grammatical features by adult learners. Implicit learning remains a controversial issue.

As used by Schmidt, noticing refers to what is also known as focal awareness. According to Schmidt, noticing is a necessary step in the acquisition process. The nature and role of noticing has later been further refined. According to Schmidt (1992), noticing is the subjective manifestation of attention, and, further, that attention is the necessary and sufficient condition for storage in memory. Above all, noticing is a private experience. However, it can be operationally defined as availability for verbal report, which has important implications for research. There are certain reservations in the use of verbal report as evidence of noticing, though. First, the lack of a verbal report cannot be taken as evidence of failure to notice unless the report is gathered either concurrently or immediately following the experience. Even then, it has to be remembered that there are conscious experiences that are inherently difficult to describe. If these reservations are kept in mind, verbal reports can be used to verify, or falsify, claims concerning the role of noticing in language learning (for an example, see Schmidt and Frota, 1986).

EXPLICIT INSTRUCTION AND VISUAL INPUT ENHANCEMENT

What features in linguistic input does the learner attend to? The noticeability of linguistic elements seems to play a role in this process. According to Schmidt (1990; cf. Hulstijn, 1989), the noticeability of linguistic elements depends on several factors, including, among others, perceptual salience, frequency, task demands and prior knowledge and expectations created in part by, for example, instruction.

The concept of perceptual salience requires further clarification. Perceptual salience usually refers to the effect caused by quite concrete physical attributes of the target structure. However, salience can also be a psychological construct that is a function of both the learner and the linguistic input (Ellis, 1993). The use of the term salience in this sense comes very close to Schmidt's notion of noticeability. Individual factors that in this case might influence salience include the learners' stage of cognitive development and their knowledge of other foreign languages, whereas features of input that determine salience might include complexity and similarity/dissimilarity between the learner's L1 and L2. Frequency of occurrence probably also plays a role.

The nature of implicit learning has been heavily debated. Reber's (1976, 1989) position has been that learners are able to implicitly acquire abstract rule systems, i.e., grammars. Dulany, Carlson and Dewey (1984), on the other hand, after studying the effects of implicit and explicit learning instructions on the acquisition of complex rule systems, came to the conclusion that learners' grammaticality judgments can be attributed more to the existence of conscious rules within informal grammars, and not to unconscious representations of a formal grammar. Reber, Kassin, Lewis and Cantor (1980) investigated what combination of explicit and implicit learning modes would be most effective in learning new and complex grammars. They came to the conclusion that the best results were obtained when participants were presented with explicit information about the structure of the grammar in the initial stages and then were given examples generated by it. It appears that when the number of variables in the learning materials is limited and their critical features are salient, learners benefit from instruction that direct them to learn explicitly. It is to be noted, as Ellis (1993) points out, that explicit learning does not necessarily mean that learners are given sets of explicit grammatical rules; rather, explicit learning is a more conscious operation of creating and testing hypotheses about the nature of structures present in the input.

Ellis (1993) studied the interaction of explicit and implicit knowledge on the acquisition of soft mutation in Welsh in three experimental conditions: "Random" learners were exposed to randomly ordered instances of Welsh soft mutation; "Rule" learners first learned the rules; and "Rule & Instance" learners were given the rules and also saw them applied to instances. After the results of over 71,000 trials were analyzed, it turned out that Rule & Instance learners were the slowest to learn, but they were the only ones to develop an abstract schema for the application of soft mutations. Moreover, when they were exposed to new examples they were able to generalize correctly. They were also able to explicitly formulate the new rules and succeed on well-formedness judgments. Ellis' findings lend support to the notion that the presentation of explicit knowledge has a beneficial effect on second language acquisition if combined with appropriate linguistic input.

There has been some research into the role of attention and consciousness in the acquisition of formal properties as opposed to the acquisition of lexical elements, that is, content, of a language. Hulstijn (1989) investigated the implicit and incidental (i.e., unintentional) acquisition of formal properties of a language to find an answer to the question of whether it is sufficient for learners to pay attention to the meaning of the linguistic materials they hear or read, or whether it is necessary for learners to pay attention to their form as well. In two experiments, he studied the acquisition of genuine and semi-artificial structural language elements in Dutch by L2 learners and native speakers of Dutch. The findings seemed to provide support for the claim that, for implicit and incidental learning of structural language elements to take place, attention to form at input encoding was a sufficient condition. On the other hand, he found no conclusive evidence to support the claim that exclusive attention to meaning inhibits the acquisition of structural language elements.

VanPatten (1989) studied the effect of attention to form as opposed to attention to meaning on L2 Spanish listening comprehension. The results indicated that learners may have difficulty in comprehending content if they are at the same time performing a task that involves conscious attention to non-communicative grammatico-morphological forms (VanPatten, 1989: 413).

Doughty (1991) investigated the effect of instruction on the acquisition of English relative clauses by nonnative speakers of English. In her study, the participants were divided into three groups. One group received no instruction other than exposure to the same linguistic input (a text containing relative clauses) that the other participants were using. Two experimental groups received different types of instruction: a meaning-oriented group was taught by using a comprehension-based approach to language teaching, while the other group received more traditional rule-based instruction on the formation and use of relative clauses. In both experimental groups, visual, or non-linguistic, perceptual cues served to focus participants' attention on the major components of relative clauses. Her findings showed that instruction had at least a short-term positive effect on the outcome of the learning process. Moreover, the meaning-based group showed improvement both in the target of instruction and reading comprehension. As both experimental groups improved to an equivalent degree, and significantly more than the control group did, it seemed that this success could not be attributed to the use of metalinguistic rules. Rather, as Doughty (1991: 463) suggests, perceptual salience may have been instrumental in the success of the instructional treatment.

Long (1991) has discussed the effect of a *focus on form* (as opposed to *focus on forms*) in second language acquisition. It may be that instruction that specifically draws learners' attention to linguistic form in context in some meaningful way (as opposed to teaching of linguistic structures in isolation) has a positive effect on the rate of acquisition, and perhaps on the ultimate level of attainment in second language proficiency as well. Doughty's (1991) findings seem to support this hypothesis. Pedagogical rules often help learners to focus their attention on critical attributes of the target of acquisition (Long, 1991; Schmidt, 1990).

METHOD

The general aim of the study was to investigate the role of input enhancement in second language acquisition. The two ways the input in this experiment was manipulated were the visual enhancement of the target structures and explicit rule presentation. In particular, the aim of the experiment was to study the role of explicit rule-based, form-focused instruction vs. implicit meaning-based instruction in the acquisition of structural language elements in semi-artificial Finnish. How would the performance of beginning language learners depend on the treatment they received?

The specific conditions the effect of which on the acquisition process this study investigated were the presentation of explicit metalinguistic rules on the use of the target structures before the learning phase, and the visual highlighting of the targets through italics in linguistic input. Both were seen as a means of focusing the learners' attention on linguistic form. The overt task of the learners, however, was not the acquisition of structural language elements. Instead, in the learning phase, they were given short passages in Finnish to read for meaning. This focus on content was further reinforced by telling the students that they would later be asked questions in English about the content the passages. In this sense, the experiment focused on the incidental acquisition of structural language elements. Since the meanings of all linguistic forms were given to the students in the glossary, their formal analysis was not needed to carry out the task properly.

All learners attended two learning sessions. Both times they read a short passage in Finnish. Embedded in the input were the learning targets, certain locative suffixes and four types of consonant alternation. The learners were asked to think aloud during the study phase. These verbal reports were tape recorded to find out whether the treatment the learners received affected their focus of attention. At the end of the last session, the students were asked to complete a set of Finnish sentences by using the correct locative form of a noun. How well the students carried out this task was assumed to depend on the extent to which the students had paid attention to formal aspects of language. Thus, a situation was created in which the learner had to be able to supply a linguistic form after a task during which they had been asked to concentrate on meaning.

PARTICIPANTS

Thirty six students at the University of Hawai'i at Mānoa volunteered for the study. None knew any Finnish. The participants were between 18 and 45 years of age, the average age being 23.8 years. As the participants' degree of verbal expertise (defined as the amount and degree of formal instruction received in a foreign language) was likely to be a factor, an attempt was made to control it (McLaughlin and Nayak, 1989). Consequently, only students who had either taken or were currently taking a foreign language course were asked to participate in the study. An attempt was made to place a roughly equal number of more experienced students such as language majors, as well as male and female students in each group. It is to be noted that several factors that may have affected the results of this experiment were not controlled for, including the level of proficiency achieved in the languages studied, naturalistic language learning experience, and language aptitude.

LEARNING MATERIALS AND TARGET STRUCTURES

The input chosen for the study was semi-artificial Finnish. There were several reasons for selecting Finnish as the target language. First, the researcher was familiar with it, as it is her native language. More importantly, the knowledge of Finnish is very rare outside Finland. In other words, it was a language one could assume that the prospective learners in this study had no previous knowledge of. Thus, the role of prior knowledge and exposure to the target language outside the classroom could be controlled for. Even more importantly, Finnish is typologically very different from English, Spanish, Japanese, Chinese, Hawaiian or other languages the learners in this experiment knew. Finnish is an agglutinative language in which grammatical relations are expressed by a complex system of inflectional endings (cases) rather than function words. For example, *auto* ('car')+ *–ssa* ('in') > *autossa* ('in a/the car'). One area of interest in the experiment was to see how the learners would process linguistic input so different from the languages they already knew. Another aspect of Finnish worth pointing out is that there are no articles or linguistic gender, and that there are double consonants and vowels everywhere. This is no orthographic whim; there is almost a one-to-one correspondence between the phonological and orthographic levels in Finnish. To indicate a long phoneme, Finnish simply doubles the grapheme. In the following discussion, the terms *vowel* and *consonant* are used to indicate units at the orthographic level of language.

Finnish input was modified and simplified to make the learning task easier for the learners; hence the term "semi-artificial." For example, the vowels *a* and *o* were used instead of umlaut vowels *ä* and *ö* and certain vocabulary items were replaced with shorter or more familiar looking words (in other words, false cognates were created). For example, *kulho* 'bowl' became *bouli* and *kärpänen* 'fly' became *lyy*. Word order was also fixed (in Finnish it is free). The purpose in doing this was to reduce the processing load for the learners and thus avoid the scattering of their resources. This, of course, affects the ecological validity of the experiment; such modifications were deemed necessary mainly because of the short duration of the experiment. The grammatical system as such was that of Finnish.

The materials consisted of two short descriptive passages in Finnish (Lesson 1 and Lesson 2) with a picture and Finnish-English glossary of all words and word forms contained in the passage. The length of the passages was 87 words in Lesson 1 and 98 words in Lesson 2. The bulk of the text consisted of various place expressions such as follows:

Greippi ja banaani on boulissa.	'A grapefruit and a banana are in the bowl'
Poyta on matolla.	'The table is on the mat'
Vati ja kuppi on myos poydalla.	'A plate and a cup are also on the table'
Meloni on vadilla.	'A melon is on the plate'

No locative form occurred without a base form, which was always present in the immediate linguistic environment, most often in the preceding sentence. The number and relative frequency of the learning targets in the input are shown in Table 1.

Table 1: Number and relative frequency of learning targets in the input

Target	Lesson 1		Lesson 2		Lessons 1 & 2	
Locative suffixes						
-lla ('on')	6	37.5%	7	31.8%	13	34.2%
-ssa ('in')	5	31.3%	7	31.8%	12	31.6%
-ssa ('on')	5	31.3%	8	36.4%	13	34.2%
Consonant changes						
kk → *k*	4	36.4%	4	33.3%	8	34.8%
pp → *p*	3	27.3%	2	16.7%	5	21.7%
tt → *t*	2	18.2%	3	25.0%	5	21.7%
t → *d*	2	18.2%	3	25.0%	5	21.7%

Two types of learning targets from two different levels of language were involved in the study. The first type of targets involved the use of certain Finnish locative suffixes: *–lla* ('on'), *–ssa* ('in') and *–ssa* ('on'). These are elements of the morphosyntactic level of language which in Finnish perform roughly the same function as prepositions do in English. The function of *–lla* roughly corresponds to that of the English preposition *on* or *at* or phrase *on top of* (something). For example, *Tuoli on matolla* can be translated as 'the chair is on the mat.' The locative suffix *–ssa* has several functions in Finnish, of which two were used in the experiment. First, the suffix *–ssa* corresponds to the English preposition *in* in the sense of containment or static position inside an object; secondly, *–ssa* is also used in Finnish to express close contact or attachment, for which English uses the preposition *on*. For example:

Kukka on kupissa 'The flower is in the cup'

but also:

Ampiainen on ruusussa 'The bee is on the rose'

Sormus on sormessa 'The ring is on the finger'

Since the learners were all native speakers of English, certain learning difficulties were predicted on the basis of this cross-linguistic difference. It is known that the learning of prepositions with closely related meanings can be quite difficult (Ijaz, 1986). Moreover, in this case a single form in L1 (such as the preposition *on*) manifests itself as two in L2 (the Finnish suffixes *–ssa* and *–lla)*, which again could cause some problems (Stockwell, Bowen and Martin, 1965). L1 transfer in one form or another was thus expected to play a role.

The second set of learning targets consisted of examples of word-internal morphophonological variation known as consonant gradation. Consonant gradation is a linguistically conditioned phenomenon in Finnish that is triggered by the presence of a suffix such as these locative suffixes (Karlsson, 1982; Branch, 1989). The consonants in question change from double into single consonants (*kk*→*k*, *pp*→*p*, and *tt*→*t)* or change their quality *(t*→*d*). To put it simply, the alternation is triggered by the change in the quality of syllables from open ([C] V [V]) into closed ([C] V [V] C) ones (e.g., *kup* + *pi* ('cup') + *–ssa* ('in') > **kup* + *pis* + *sa* > *ku* + *pis* + *sa* = *kupissa* ('in the cup').

Thus, two types of structural language elements were included in the study, one with a more or less clearly definable semantic content, the other which was semantically empty (Hulstijn, 1989). Would learners' performance differ according to the nature of the learning target, that is, would it be easier for them to learn structural elements with a relatively clear form-function relationship and semantic content?

TREATMENTS

Participants (N=36) were divided into a control group and three treatment groups. The treatments differed as follows: (1) the Control group (N=9) received the text as such only; (2) the Enhance group (N=9) were given the same text except that the learning targets embedded in the input were made perceptually salient by printing them in italics; (3) the Rule group (N=9) were first given a one-page explicit description of the grammatical rules governing the use of the learning targets (see Appendix 1); and (4) the Rule & Enhance group (N=9) were given both the rules and the version of the text that contained the italicized learning targets. Consequently, the Control and Enhance groups received no explicit rule-based form-focused instruction on the use of the target structures. These groups were expected to concentrate exclusively on meaning; in the following, they will be referred to as meaning-based groups while Rule and Rule & Enhance will be referred to as rule-based groups.

PROCEDURE

All learners individually attended two sessions of Finnish instruction. All lessons took place at the language study center of the University of Hawai'i. The interval between the sessions was on the average 7 days for Control, 7.67 days for Enhance, 8.44 days for Rules, and 6.22 days for Rule & Enhance. The learners were not told that the input had been modified to a certain extent. At the beginning of each lesson, the students received test instructions in which they were asked to read the following passage and try to understand its meaning. They were also told that they would be asked questions about the content of the passage after each lesson, but not that they would also be given a word translation task after each session, or a sentence completion test after they had finished the "course." The participants were also asked to describe their thoughts on tape during the study phase. As it was not possible to train the learners to do so, the study instructions also included a short example of what such thinking aloud might look like.

Each subject had 15 minutes to study the materials. Those learners who received the rule descriptions were given an additional 5 minutes to study the rules. These one-page descriptions were then taken away so the learners were unable to refer to them during the reading comprehension task. After both lessons, the participants were given a short reading comprehension test and a 12-item word translation task. Both these tasks served the purpose of focusing the learners' attention on content rather than on form. After the second and final session, the students were given a sentence completion test in which they were asked to complete a Finnish sentence with a locative construction (see Appendix 2). This was, of course, the real task. The word the learners were to use in this task together with its meaning was given in brackets as well as the meaning of other lexical items in the sentence. This was done to ensure that all learners would understand the basic meaning of the Finnish sentence they were supposed to produce. To carry out this task correctly, the learners had to be able to form locative expressions in Finnish and apply their knowledge about the changes the Finnish consonants undergo in such circumstances. Finally, the students were also asked to judge the grammaticality of a number of Finnish sentences containing locative expressions, give a short explanation or otherwise indicate why they thought a sentence was ungrammatical, and to restate or give the rules that in their opinion governed the use of linguistic forms in the passages.

INSTRUMENTS, SCORING AND TYPES OF DATA

The following instruments and sources of data were used to measure the learners' performance at various stages of the experiment.

Sentence completion test. A 33-item sentence completion test was designed to measure the learners' acquisition of learning targets. The students were asked to complete a set of Finnish sentences by using the correct locative form of a noun. How well the students' carried out this task depended on how well they had acquired the targeted language elements. The participants were given separate scores for the correct form of the locative suffix and consonant alternation. The maximum score was 33 for locative suffixes and 23 for consonant alternation (in ten cases there was no consonant changed involved). Nine of the items were created to test the students' production of *–ssa* ('in') and *–lla* ('on') each, while 15 items tested the learners' ability to produce the correct form of *–ssa* ('on'). Several instances of the four types of consonant alternation were included in the test, as well. The learners were also given separate scores for each of these subsets. Sixteen of the locative items and 11 of the consonant changes in the sentence completion test contained a structure the students had already been exposed to in the reading passages. 17 of the locative items and 12 of the consonant changes were in structures that were completely new. The learners' productions were later classified and the number and relative frequency of different forms analyzed and compared across the learner groups.

Comprehension test. To measure the students' comprehension, two short tests containing ten true-false statements in English about the content of each passage were created.

Word translation test. Two short tests of 12 items each in which the students had to translate Finnish words into English were also administered. No statistically significant differences were found between the learner groups as regards their success in the reading comprehension and word translation tasks and, consequently, the results of these two tests will be excluded from the following discussion (for a more detailed discussion, see Alanen, 1992).

Grammaticality judgment test. The students were also given a test in which they were asked to judge the grammaticality of 20 Finnish sentences with both the correct and incorrect versions of the learning targets embedded, and to give reasons for their judgments by indicating or describing the potential error. The purpose of this task was not so much to measure the participants' acquisition of the learning targets but to obtain information about the learners' awareness of the target structures and the explicit linguistic knowledge they had formed on the basis of input. However, the students were also given scores for each correct judgment if the reason they gave was also correct.

Rule statements. The students were given a questionnaire in which they were asked to state (in the case of Control and Enhance) or restate (in the case of Rule and Rule & Enhance) the rules they thought governed the use of linguistic forms in the input. Those learners who had received visually enhanced input were also asked whether they had noticed the highlighting, and if they had whether they had considered any reason for it. The aim was, again to gather data about the learners' awareness of the target structures and their knowledge of explicit linguistic rules.

Think-aloud protocols. To gain insight into what the learners were doing during the study phase, especially what features of the input they attended to, the learners were asked to describe their thoughts, to think aloud during the learning period. These study sessions were recorded. The tapes were then analyzed primarily to find out whether the students had noticed the target structures. The use of this method was based on an assumption that noticing is available to verbal report. It is to be noted, however, that the learners in this experiment were not trained to "think aloud." Even when prompted, some participants may not have been as forthcoming in their verbal reports as others. This has to be taken into account in analyzing the reliability of the learners' verbal reports. An attempt was also made to gauge the learners' ideas about the structural elements in the input by using grammaticality judgments supplemented with explanations and rule statements as other sources of data.

HYPOTHESES

The following hypotheses were made about the acquisition of the learning targets:

1. The order of learning outcomes in the sentence completion test for both locative suffixes and consonant gradation was hypothesized to be: Control < Enhance < Rule <Rule & Enhance. It was hypothesized that those learner groups that received rule-based instruction on the learning targets would perform better than those with no such instruction. This hypothesis was based on the assumption that explicit knowledge would direct some of the learners' attention to linguistic form (Schmidt, 1990). It was also hypothesized that Enhance who received enhanced input would outperform Control because of the greater perceptual salience of the targets (Doughty, 1991). The group that was hypothesized to outperform all others was the one that received both explicit rule-based instruction and enhanced input, since they would benefit both from the rules and the greater salience of the target structures

(Reber et al. 1980; Ellis, 1993). The salient structures would perhaps also serve as additional examples of rules they had already been presented with.

The purely formal grammatical phenomenon of consonant gradation was included in the study to see how the acquisition of this purely formal and (in this input) redundant linguistic phenomenon might differ from the acquisition of the locative suffixes which have a clear meaning. An assumption was made that to notice the change in consonants, the learners' attention would have to be focused on it, and the more explicitly the better. Subsequently, it was hypothesized that the groups that received explicit instruction would show greater learning effects than the groups with no such instruction. As to the visual cues, an assumption was made that they would facilitate the learning, enough for Enhance to perform slightly better than Control, and Rule & Enhance to outperform Rule, but not by much. The predicted order for the acquisition of consonant gradation was thus the same as for the acquisition of locative suffixes.

2. It was hypothesized that the explicit, rule-based groups would perform better than the meaning-based groups on the grammaticality judgments task and rule statements, with Rule & Enhance performing the best.

DATA ANALYSIS

Raw scores were obtained for the locative suffixes and consonant alternation from the sentence completion test. The participants' scores on the comprehension and word translation and grammaticality judgment tests were also analyzed. One-way ANOVAs and *post hoc* Scheffé procedures were carried out, as well as Pearson product-moment correlations between various test scores. The participants' grammaticality judgments, rule statements and think-alouds were also analyzed. Notes were taken about the learners' comments on the learning targets and vocabulary items.

RESULTS

TEST SCORES

ANOVAs were conducted on the scores for locative suffixes and consonant changes in the sentence completion test. The ANOVAs revealed a significant effect for treatment in the case of all locative suffixes ($df=3$, $F=4.72$, $p=.01$) and consonant changes ($df=3$, $F=9.98$, $p=.00$). A *post hoc* Scheffé test carried out on the raw scores on locative suffixes, however, could not show which of the group means differed from each other significantly at the .05 level. When the scores were transformed into percentages, the Scheffé test indicated that both Rule and Rule & Enhance differed significantly from Control with Rule also differing significantly from Enhance. The Scheffé test carried out on the raw scores on consonant changes revealed that Rule and Rule & Enhance were significantly different from both Control and Enhance but not from each other. The means and standard deviations of each group's scores are displayed in Table 2.

Table 2: Mean raw scores and standard deviations for all locative suffixes and consonant changes

Target	Control	Enhance	Rule	Rule & Enhance
Suffixes (n=33)				
Mean	10.44	9.33	20.44	20.44
SD	10.70	8.30	8.03	6.09
Consonant changes (n=23)				
Mean	3.44	2.56	14.22	14.22
SD	5.55	4.85	6.48	7.46

Note: In all learner groups, N= 9.

To gain a better understanding of the learners' performance on different locative suffixes and consonant changes, the ANOVAS were also conducted on the learners' scores on each subset of the sentence completion test. The ANOVAs revealed a significant effect for treatment on the *–ssa* ('in') and *–lla* ('on') subsets of locative suffixes and on the *kk→k*, *tt→t* and *pp→p* subsets of consonant changes. Eta squared revealed that 50% of the variance in the scores of the *–lla* ('on') subset could be accounted for by the treatment. The Scheffé test revealed that, by and large, the effect for treatment was due to the contrast between the rule-based and meaning-based groups. For the *–ssa* ('on') and *t→d* subsets, the Scheffé test was unable to show significant contrasts. There are several possible explanations for this for the *–ssa* ('on') and *t→d* subsets. First, in the further analysis of data, it appeared that if the learners in Control and Enhance had acquired a suffix, it was always *–ssa*, which they then tended to apply in all cases. This, of course, resulted in the correct productions on the *–ssa* ('on') subset. On the other hand, the learners in Rule and Rule & Enhance were somewhat prone to use *–lla* in cases where *–ssa* would have been correct, which, again, had the effect of lowering their scores. The *t→d* sound change was not acquired very well by any of the groups, perhaps due to the relative infrequency of the form in the input. The means and standard deviations are displayed in Table 3 and the results of the ANOVAs in Table 4.

The results of the grammaticality judgment test also showed that some differences existed between the groups. The ANOVA revealed no significant effect for treatment in whole test itself (df=3, F=2.70, p= .06) but when the ANOVA was carried out on the learners' scores on the items targeting locative suffixes, a significant effect for treatment was revealed (df=3, F=1.41, p=.01). The lowest mean on these items was for the Rule & Enhance group. In reexamining the data, it appeared that some participants in this group had a tendency to judge the correct uses of *–ssa* ('on') as incorrect, indicating that they had expected *–lla* ('on') to be used instead. The means and standard deviations of the grammaticality judgment test are displayed in Table 5.

Table 3: Mean raw scores and standard deviations for all types of locative suffixes and consonant changes

Target	Control	Enhance	Rule	Rule & Enhance
Locative suffixes				
-ssa ('in') (n=9)				
Mean	4.00	2.78	7.00	7.11
SD	10.70	8.30	8.03	6.09
-ssa ('on') (n=15)				
Mean	6.00	5.67	8.89	7.78
SD	6.87	5.56	4.70	4.84
-lla ('on') (n=9)				
Mean	.22	.33	4.56	5.56
SD	.44	1.00	3.32	3.75
Consonant changes				
kk → *k* (n=7)				
Mean	1.22	1.00	5.11	5.22
SD	2.22	2.29	2.09	2.05
pp → *p* (n=6)				
Mean	1.22	.44	4.44	3.78
SD	1.99	1.33	2.35	2.11
tt → *t* (n=6)				
Mean	.56	.78	4.33	3.67
SD	1.33	1.30	2.44	2.24
t → *d* (n=4)				
Mean	.44	.33	.44	1.56
SD	.88	1.00	1.01	1.67

Table 4: Results of ANOVA for all types of locative suffixes and consonant changes

Target	*df*	MSB	F	*p*	*eta squared*
Locative suffixes					
-ssa ('in')	3	42.59	5.27	.01	.33
-ssa ('on')	3	17.58	.57	.64	.05
-lla ('on')	3	70.00	10.67	.00	.50
Consonant changes					
kk → *k*	3	49.44	10.55	.00	.50
pp → *p*	3	33.81	8.62	.00	.45
tt → *t*	3	32.77	9.09	.00	.46
t → *d*	3	2.99	2.14	.11	.17

Table 5: Mean raw scores and standard deviations of the grammaticality judgment task

Target	Control	Enhance	Rule	Rule & Enhance
Whole test (n=20)				
Mean	9.56	11.22	13.38	10.13
SD	2.35	1.20	4.17	3.44
Suffixes (n=8)				
Mean	4.22	4.67	5.13	3.00
SD	1.39	.87	1.36	1.07
Consonants (n=10)				
Mean	3.63	4.11	5.5	4.88
SD	1.19	1.54	3.15	2.90

The results of the learners' rule statements are shown in Table 6. The learners were given one point for each rule that correctly described the distribution of a target structure. Vague descriptions such as "there were endings that affect meaning, but that's all" were not accepted. There was very little difference between the two meaning-based groups as to the number of correct rules they were able to formulate. There was a difference, though, in what kind of information the learners provided as the rules given by Enhance tended to be more detailed than the rules given by Control.

Table 6: Average number of correct rule statements

Target	Control	Enhance	Rule	Rule & Enhance
Suffix rules (n=3)				
Mean	.38	.44	2.78	2.13
SD	.52	.53	.44	1.13
Consonant rules (n=4)				
Mean	.25	.22	1.44	1.00
SD	.46	.44	1.59	1.60

LEARNERS' PRODUCTIONS

In examining the findings, it became apparent that the statistical analysis of the test scores alone could not adequately describe the learning outcomes. For the full description of data, it was necessary to classify and analyze the students' productions. The expected relative frequency of each type of locative suffix in the sentence completion test was: 27.3% for *–lla* ('on'), and 72.7% for *–ssa*. The relative frequencies of these forms in the learner groups' productions are displayed in Table 7. Their distribution was not taken into account; only their occurrences were counted. The ANOVAs revealed a significant effect for treatment on the occurrence of zero-form (i.e., no ending) (df=3, F=5.15, p=.01) and the suffix *–lla* ('on') (df=3, F=13.38, p=.00). Eta squared also revealed that as much as 56% of the variability in the occurrence of *–lla* ('on') could be accounted for by the treatment. A Scheffé test showed that the effect for treatment in the occurrence of *–lla* ('on') was due to the contrast between the rule-based and meaning-based instruction. The Scheffé procedure also revealed that the effect for treatment in the occurrence of zero-form was due to the contrast between no treatment (Control) and treatment, regardless of whether it consisted of the visual enhancement of the target structures, rule presentation or combination of both.

Table 7: Relative frequencies of zero-form, *–ssa* and *–lla* in learner productions

Suffix	Control	Enhance	Rule	Rule & Enhance
zero-form	37.4%	2.4%	0%	0.7%
-ssa	39.1%	34.3%	54.9%	52.9%
-lla	2.0%	1.0%	26.3%	36.4%
	(78.5%)	(37.7%)	(81.2%)	(90.0%)

Note: In addition to zero-form, *–ssa*, and *–lla*, the learners produced several other non-target like forms.

The occurrence of zero-forms in the productions of Control is all the more remarkable because an attempt was made during the experiment to ensure that all participants had indeed understood the instructions correctly. For example, one subject, when asked to translate the sentence *Banaani on bouli* she had just produced, which literally means *The banana is the bowl*, answered, 'The banana is in the bowl.' The low relative frequency of *–ssa* and *–lla* forms in the productions of the learners in Enhance is due to the great variety of non-target like suffixes they used such as *–assa*, *–sa*, *–esa*, *–sse*, *–ous*, etc.

To further analyze the learners' production of various suffixes, their occurrence in various subsets of the test was also calculated. The occurrence of *–lla* ('on') in the subsets targeting *–ssa* ('in'), *–ssa* ('on') and *–lla* ('on') is displayed in Table 8. The occurrences were analyzed by giving the participants a score for each use. The ANOVA revealed a significant effect for treatment both in the subset targeting *–ssa* ('on') (*df* = 3, F=6.85, *p*=.00) and in the subset targeting *–lla* ('on') (*df*=3, F=9.49, *p*=.00). The Scheffé test revealed that the effect for instruction in the subset targeting *–ssa* ('on') was due to the contrast in the use of *–lla* ('on') by Rule & Enhance on one hand and both meaning-based groups on the other hand. It is to be noted that in this subset the use of *–lla* ('on') was not considered target-like. In the subset targeting *–lla* ('on'), the Scheffé procedure revealed that the significant effect for treatment was due to the difference between the rule-based and meaning-based groups.

Table 8: Occurrence of *–lla* in the learner productions for the subsets targeting *–ssa* ('in'), *–ssa* ('on') and *–lla* ('on')

Target	Control	Enhance	Rule	Rule & Enhance
-ssa ('in') (n=9)				
Mean	.00	.00	.67	1.00
SD	.00	.00	1.32	1.22
Percent	0%	0%	7.4%	11.1%
-ssa ('on') (n=15)				
Mean	.33	.00	3.33	5.67
SD	.71	.00	2.92	5.36
Percent	2.2%	0%	22.2%	37.8%
-lla ('on') (n=9)				
Mean	.22	.33	4.56	5.56
SD	.44	1.00	3.32	3.75
Percent	2.5%	3.7%	50.6%	61.7%

There was relatively little variation in target consonants as the consonants were either changed or not. Some participants' productions seemed to indicate that they were over-generalizing. For example, *hylylla* (or *hylulla*) was used for *hyllylla* ('on the shelf') in the productions of a number of rule-based learners. The production of *hylylla* seemed to indicate that some learners were extending the rule about the change of double consonants into corresponding single ones to cover not just the voiceless stops but the consonant *l* as well.

NOTICING, RULE AWARENESS AND THE ACQUISITION OF THE LEARNING TARGETS

Three sources of data were used in this study to investigate the extent to which the learners seemed to be aware of structural elements in the input and what the learners seemed to have consciously attended to during the experiment. First, the think-aloud protocols revealed interesting aspects about the learners' approach to the task and their explicit comments on the suffixes and/or consonant changes. Secondly, grammaticality judgments and especially the explanations they gave for their judgments were quite revealing. Thirdly, the students' rule formulations and restatements were also used as indicators of their awareness of structural language elements (the validity of this measure suffered, though, because it was administered after the grammaticality judgment task). Figures 1, 2, 3 and 4 display the number of explicit comments made by the learners in think-alouds, rule statements and grammaticality judgment tasks, and their scores on the locative suffixes in the sentence completion test. In all these tasks, if the learner had made any explicit mention of any of the target structures, in general or particular, it was recorded. The points thus obtained were added up and then used as the learner's score. Only clear, explicit instances were used; any probables inferred by the researcher were left out. Incomplete rules were also excluded. The measure is thus rather conservative.

Figure 1: Number of explicit comments and locative suffix score by Control

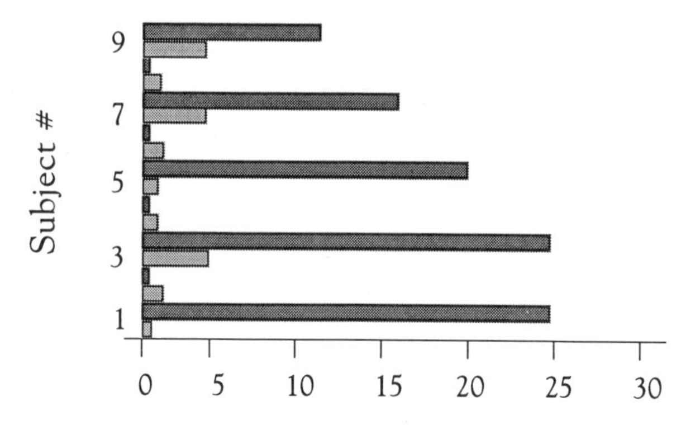

Figure 2: Number of explicit comments and locative suffix score by Enhance

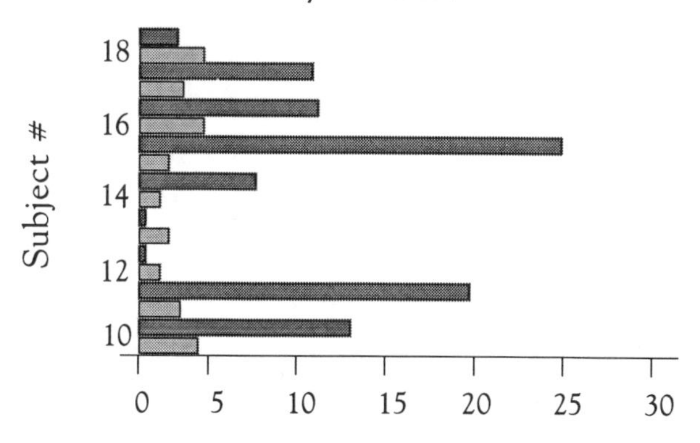

Figure 3: Number of explicit comments and locative suffix score by Rule

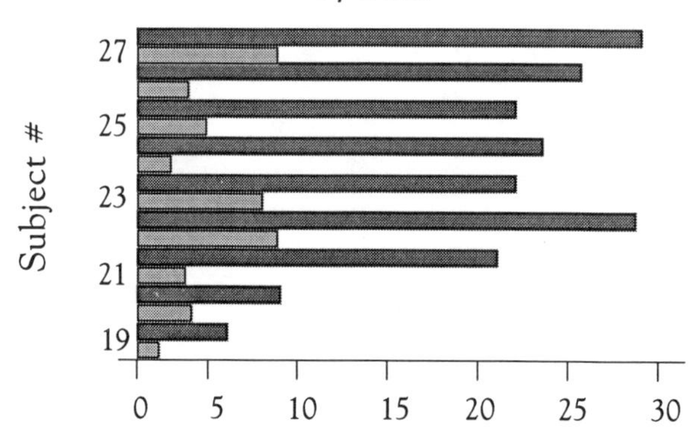

Figure 4: Number of explicit comments and locative suffix score by Rule & Enhance

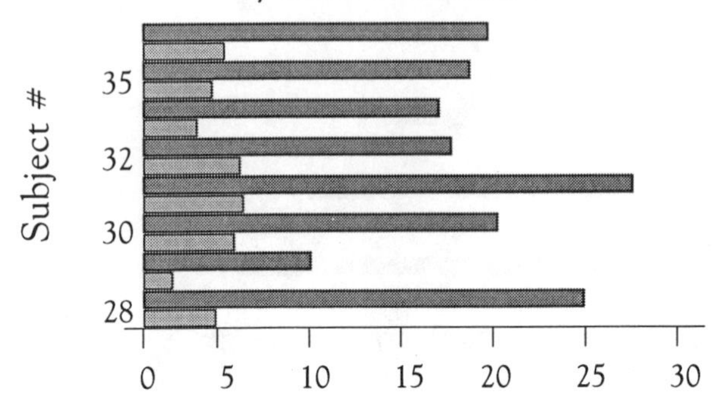

Table 9: Statistical significance of correlation coefficients between the number of explicit comments on target structures and the learners' test scores.

Target	Control	Enhance	Rule	Rule & Enhance
Locative suffixes				
-ssa ('in')	n.s.	n.s.	n.s.	n.s.
-ssa ('on')	n.s.	n.s.	n.s.	n.s.
-lla ('on')	.89 **	.71 *	n.s.	n.s.
All suffixes	n.s.	n.s.	.69 *	.85 **
Consonant changes				
$kk \rightarrow k$	.84 **	.76 *	n.s.	n.s.
$pp \rightarrow p$	n.s.	.68 *	n.s.	.71 *
$tt \rightarrow t$	n.s.	n.s.	n.s.	n.s.
$t \rightarrow d$	.89 **	n.s.	n.s.	.77 **
All consonants	.79 *	.80 **	n.s.	n.s.

*p<.05; **p<.01

Pearson product-moment correlations between this measure of rule awareness and the learners' scores on locative suffixes and consonant alternation were also calculated. The statistical significance of the correlation coefficients is displayed in Table 9.

The performance of individual language learners in the various learner groups was quite revealing. Subject 3 in Control mentioned in her rule statement that *–illa* was used to indicate "something that was in something," whereas *–ssa* was used to indicate "something that was on something." Subject 5 also said that *–ssa* meant the same as the English preposition *on*. This is perfectly understandable when one remembers the nature of the input. Participants 2 and 8 produced no forms and were unable to give any rules although they mentioned suffixes in general in their rule statements. They also made no explicit comments on the learning targets in their think-alouds. Only three participants, 3, 7 and 9, and possibly 5 and 6, in this group commented on them. On the other hand, Subject 1 performed quite well in the test although he made no comments on the locative suffixes in his think aloud. Although he mentioned them in the grammaticality judgment task; his rule statements are unfortunately missing.

The learners in Enhance made more comments, but their productions varied. For example, Participants 10, 11, 13, 16, 17, and 18 all mentioned the suffixes in their think-alouds. Subject 16 serves as a good example of the finding obtained in earlier research that the explicit rules that the participants give (or are given) are not necessarily the same as the ones they seem to follow in actual performance during the test. Subject 16 noted that 'if there is something 'in' or 'on' an object, you have to use *–ussa* or *–ulla* type of ending with the noun.' Her productions reveal a much more complicated pattern, though. It appears as if the form of the ending depends on the last vowel of the noun. For example, she added *–ssi* to words ending with *–i*, *–sso* to words ending with *–o*, *–ssu* to words ending with *–u* etc. although she was by no means consistent in this.

The learners in the rule-based groups were generally able to restate the rules. There were some inaccuracies that this time were quite consistent with the participants' productions. Subject 19, for example, stated that *–lla* is used to express 'on' or 'attached to.' Five of the participants in this group made explicit comments on the target suffixes in their think alouds (Participants 22, 23, 24, 25, and 27) and all of them possibly referred to them. Subject 23 was unable to remember *–lla* when asked to restate the rule, but used it during the test. Subject 29 was the only subject in Rule & Enhance who made no mention of the suffixes in her think aloud. Her performance was also quite interesting as she used the variant *–llya* for *–lla*, a possible indication of some sort of phonological encoding taking place during the learning phase. Participants 35 and 36 were most inaccurate in their rule statements as they omitted the function of *–ssa* to express 'on' altogether. Instead, they used *–lla* in this function throughout the sentence completion test. This was quite interesting as the input contained numerous examples of *–ssa* used in the sense of 'on.'

DISCUSSION

The following questions, from general to more specific, were asked in this paper about the role of consciousness and attention in input processing:

- What is the significance of explicit, implicit and incidental knowledge and learning, and the role of attention and consciousness in second language acquisition process?

- Must learners consciously attend to features in the input in order to learn them?

- What features in the linguistic input does the learner attend to?

- How does the performance of beginning language learners in this experiment depend on the presentation of explicit rule knowledge and the visual enhancement of the target structures?

- Would the treatment the learners received affect their focus of attention?

- Would the learners' performance differ according to the nature of the learning targets, i.e., would it be easier for them the learn structural elements with a relatively clear-cut form-function relationship and semantic content?

Various hypotheses were made in the beginning of the experiment about the influence of rule presentation and visual input enhancement on the nature and direction of learning outcomes. It was hypothesized that the groups that received explicit rule-based instruction on the target structures would outperform the two groups that received no such instruction. This hypothesis was largely supported by the results.

However, no clear-cut differences between Control and Enhance on one hand, and Rule and Rule & Enhance on the other hand, emerged. Visual input enhancement appeared not have had an effect on learners' performance. There could be several explanations for this. First, individual and between-groups differences could have affected the students' performance. An attempt was made to balance the groups, but it turned out that the learners in Rule & Enhance were generally slightly younger (their average age was 21.3 years) than those in other groups. Furthermore, the greater average success of the learners in Control seemed to have been largely due to a few good language learners. Secondly, the method of highlighting may not have been perceptually salient enough, although most of the students in both Enhance and Rule & Enhance reported having noticed the use of italics. Not all of them had considered a reason for their use. Had they noticed the targets but not understood them or formed conscious hypotheses about their use? In other words, although they had become aware of the targets, had they failed to acquire them since they had generally not consciously formed hypotheses about their use? The performance of Enhance is crucial in this respect. Since they had no rules or hypotheses available, visual highlighting was their only method of input enhancement.

The analysis of the learners' productions, in particular of their errors, revealed certain differences between groups that received highlighted and non-highlighted versions of the reading materials. Control participants produced zero-forms on the items targeting locative suffixes significantly more than other groups, including Enhance, as the *post hoc* Scheffé procedure revealed. The lower scores of Enhance in the sentence completion test, in which only target-like expressions were accepted, are partly explained by the great variety of forms they produced. It appeared, though, that since the participants were generally able to recall an ending with /s/ visual enhancement of the suffixes may have caused the learners to pay more attention to the suffixes than would have been normal within the context of the learning task. The inability of Enhance to recall the exact form of the suffixes may have been due to insufficient attention or too shallow processing (Hulstijn, 1989, 1992). According to Logan (1988), attention is a necessary and sufficient condition for encoding a stimulus into long-term memory (Schmidt 1990), but its efficient retrieval depends on both the quantity and the quality of attention at the time of encoding. Thus, although the learners paid attention to the target structures, this may not have lasted long enough or was too superficial for efficient retrieval to take place later during the sentence completion task.

Visual enhancement appeared to have affected the production of the less frequent *–lla* form, as well. Rule & Enhance produced more *–lla* forms than Rule. This was the only instance where Rule & Enhance performed clearly better than Rule and thus followed the predicted learning order. Also, there was less variance by learners in Rule & Enhance as to their productions (almost 90% of their forms were either *–ssa* or *–lla* in contrast to 81.2% in Rule), which may have been caused by extra attention brought on by highlighting.

In general, the learners' productions revealed interesting differences between the rule-based and meaning-based groups. If the participants in Control and Enhance showed evidence of having acquired a locative suffix, it was nearly always *–ssa*, which they then went on to use as a generic place marker in the sentence completion test. The greater frequency of *–ssa* structures in the input may have played a role: the ratio of *–ssa* to *–lla* forms in the input was 2:1. The semantic-conceptual overlap in the input between *–lla* ('on') and *–ssa* ('on') may have been a contributing factor as well.

The productions of the students in the rule-based groups appeared to be of different types than those made by the meaning-based groups. While over-generalization of the more frequent form *–ssa* was most common in Control and Enhance, the learners in Rule and Rule & Enhance in particular showed a tendency to use *–lla* ('on') in cases where *–ssa* ('on') was expected. Thus, although explicit instruction on the structural language elements had an overall beneficial effect on the acquisition process, it also appeared to give rise to a particular type of error as it may have induced an over reliance on L1 routines among learners. These errors could have been caused by instruction itself (Selinker, 1972). However, the apparent translation equivalence of *–lla* ('on') and the preposition 'on' was never explicitly stated in the metalinguistic description given to the students but a longer phrase that generally described the meaning of the suffix such as static position on top of an object was used instead. The learners were given an example of the use of *–lla* which was translated into English as *on*, however, which might have influenced the learners to some extent as did the other examples in the passages that were translated in the glossary.

Similar results have been reported, for example, by Pica (1983), who studied the acquisition of grammatical morphemes such English plural *–s* in the speech of adult ESL speakers in three learning contexts (naturalistic, instructed and mixed). Very interesting was her finding that instruction affected the learners' production in the target language by triggering over suppliance of grammatical morphology in linguistic context in which it was not needed. In contrast, those learners who had acquired the morphemes under naturalistic learning conditions showed a tendency to omit plural *–s* in linguistically redundant environments. She suggested that different learning conditions appeared to affect learners' hypotheses about the target morphology and their strategies for using it. However, as Pica pointed out, since the effect of the learners' exposure to English outside the classroom before and during the experiment was not controlled for, no claims could be made about the rate of acquisition or ultimate level of attainment in different learning contexts. The results of this experiment provide further support for Pica's findings, especially since in the present experiment, the starting level and exposure to the target language was known and controlled for.

As regards the acquisition of consonant gradation, a similar pattern emerged as in case of the locative suffixes. There was a clear difference between the rule-based groups and meaning-based groups, but the expected differences in the performance of the two rule-based and meaning-based groups never became obvious, most likely for the same reasons as discussed above. The only instances where Rule & Enhance was significantly better than any of the other three groups, including Rule, were the items targeting *t*→*d*. This change was generally not well learned. The change itself occurred eight times (34.8%) in the input, more than any other single consonant alternation. However, the relative frequency of all double-to-single consonant alternations was clearly higher (65.1%). These changes were also reported more often. The fact that the participants in Rule & Enhance learned this less frequent sound change slightly better may thus have been due to highlighting.

It was also hypothesized that the rule-based groups would perform better in the grammaticality judgment task than the meaning-based groups, especially since the learners were expected to give a short explanation. Moreover, Rule & Enhance was expected to perform best. However, the performance of Rule & Enhance was, on the whole, surprisingly poor, especially on the endings. This may have been due to the fact that many grammatically incorrect items in the test involved structures for which English would use preposition *on*. Among Rule & Enhance, there were several participants, Ss 35 and 36 in particular, who appeared to have a "rule" in their interlanguage that assumed translation equivalency between *–lla* and the preposition *on* (this was reflected in their rule statements, as well). In this respect, their judgments were quite consistent.

The relatively good performance of Enhance in the grammaticality judgment test was rather surprising, considering their performance in the sentence completion task. Since both the suffix and the consonant were highlighted simultaneously, it may have been easier for the participants in Enhance to notice the connection between consonant alternation and the presence of a suffix, and, above all, use it as a simple criterion in a receptive task. As a matter of fact, the order of achievement predicted for the sentence completion test was partly realized in the grammaticality judgment task (apart from the performance of Rule & Enhance) as the order of achievement was Control < Enhance < Rule.

As predicted, there was apparently a clear effect for treatment on the language learners' ability to formulate explicit rules. There appeared to be two tendencies that were especially important. First, the tendency of the rule-based groups to be at least fairly accurate in restating the rule, but failing to fully apply it in the actual language production, became rather clear. For example, although they were aware that the Finnish suffix *–ssa* is sometimes used in the same function as the English preposition *on*, there was a tendency among the learners in these groups to extend the use of *–lla* ('on') to *–ssa* ('on') structures, as we have seen. It is almost as if the learners, once made aware of the connection between *on* and *–lla*, were content to store the suffix in their long-term memory as a lexical variant of the English preposition. Secondly, there appeared a tendency among the meaning-based groups to form rules about the linguistic input that were based on incorrect assumptions. The learners often seemed to pay attention to the quality of the last vowel. Some were even looking for grammatical gender as the explanation of the endings. Most participants in Enhance were able explicitly to produce some linguistic forms in their rule statements, while the participants in Control were very vague. Those participants in Control who were able to make explicit comments about the suffixes or consonants were also the ones who performed best in the sentence completion task. This is quite consistent with the earlier research on the relationship between explicit knowledge and task performance (Dulany et al., 1984). It also reveals how the learners' prior knowledge and expectancies influenced their focus of attention and hypothesis formulation, as Schmidt (1990) has suggested.

An attempt was made in this study to determine the effect of noticing and awareness of rules on the acquisition process. An assumption was made in the study that in order to become aware of a rule, or form a hypothesis, one first had to notice the linguistic elements involved (Schmidt, 1990). To study the effect of awareness of target structures, a statistical measure was developed that used the number of explicit comments on the target structures in the think-alouds, rule statements and grammaticality judgments to form a single variable of awareness of target structures. There was statistically significant positive correlation between the learning outcomes and the extent to which the learners commented on the target structures, especially among Control and Enhance. This may be a reflection of underlying individual differences in carrying out the learning task. Learners who seemed to actively form hypotheses about the nature of structural language elements embedded in the input even when the task demands did not force them to do so, may also have been inclined to point them out or speculate about them.

The fact that also some of the participants in Control were able to acquire some of these forms revealed the importance of individual differences in second language acquisition. No such huge differences emerged among the three treatment groups. It could be that even a small amount of help in focusing the learners' attention of learning targets may help to level some of the differences among individual language learners. It may be that input enhancement also influenced learners' approach to the task without their being aware of it, and caused them pay more attention to structural language elements, which becomes evident in their think-aloud protocols.

CONCLUSION

The results of the experiment seem to provide support for the claim that, at least for incidental learning of structural language elements to take place, attention to form at input encoding is a sufficient condition (cf. Hulstijn, 1989). The fact that all learners in Enhance actually had acquired a suffix, regardless of its form, in contrast to those learners in Control who had not, suggests that input enhancement had some effect on the learning process. The purpose of the enhancement was to focus the learners' attention on the learning targets, i.e., to make them notice the structures, which appears to have been sufficient for at least some learning to take place. The findings of Doughty (1991) were thus supported. These findings appear also to be in accordance with Long's (1991) suggestion of focus on form as the factor underlying the effect of instruction.

The connection between noticing, or paying attention, and learning became clear especially in the performance of the two meaning-based groups. Those learners in Control and Enhance who showed some evidence of having acquired the target structures were usually the ones who had noticed them and subsequently mentioned them in their think-alouds. The present study found little evidence to support a claim that there can be learning without noticing. All learners who appeared to have acquired the learning targets made at least some comment on the learning targets either in their think-alouds, rule statements or grammaticality judgment task. Some evidence for incidental learning of structural language elements was obtained. It is to be noted that if by incidental we mean unintentional learning of elements, we have to clarify what we mean by intention (not an easy task). If we take it to refer to the acquisition of targets not mentioned in the task demands, then most of the progress showed by learners in this experiment falls under the category of incidental learning. If, on the other hand, we mean by incidental learning effortless acquisition, only the performance of Enhance could be called as evidence of incidental learning. The notion of depth of processing, or mental effort expended by the learner seem to be quite crucial in this context (Hulstijn, 1989, 1992). No evidence was found for implicit learning of the use of suffixes and consonant gradation, although the short duration of the experiment and relatively limited input makes it difficult to draw any hard and fast conclusions. Also, there was some indication that the explicit knowledge the learners had developed and had access to, for example, in their rule statements, did not always match their performance. The learners' responses often seemed to be constructed on the basis of different rules than the ones mentioned by them.

The overall effect of explicit rule-based instruction on the acquisition of a morphosyntactic phenomenon such as Finnish locative suffixes was clearly beneficial. It also appeared that perceptual salience of the input alone affected the learning process by speeding up hypothesis formation within the group, even if the experimental results were not entirely successful. This in itself is quite interesting as it indicates that perceptual saliency acted as a spur for learners' cognitive processes, which apparently stored at least parts of the knowledge so that it could be later used even though the immediate task demands did not require them to do so. The findings of this study seem to support Schmidt's (1990) prediction that focusing learners' attention on form might have a beneficial effect on the acquisition of such features of a target language that are (or are felt to be by the learners) redundant or less salient.

To sum up, it appears that the treatments the learner groups received in this experiment affected their performance in basically two ways. First, it speeded up their acquisition of linguistic forms on the syntactic and phonological/orthographic level. Secondly, it affected the acquisition process so that all learners in the treatment groups showed some evidence of having acquired at least some of the forms. This effect was apparently due to the fact that all learners thus treated focused their attention on the learning targets at some point or another during the learning phase, whereas the performance of the untreated group was more depended on the characteristics and background factors of the individual learners.

The differences among learners in their approach to the overt task were very clear. The approach they had adopted had significant consequences for their performance on the sentence completion task that required good recall of structural language elements. It turned out that the participants who were expected to concentrate exclusively on meaning did not always do so, and this affected the results. Thus, the intended learning conditions, i.e., the treatments given to various learner groups, did not necessarily match the actual learning conditions, what the learners actually did during the learning task. Thus, it might be more appropriate to talk about the effect of different teaching conditions on the acquisition of the learning targets. In addition to overt, external task, i.e., reading the passages for meaning, some learners seemed to have, perhaps partly influenced by their own interests and motivation, another agenda, an inner task on which they voluntarily spent some effort and quite conscious attention. It would be perhaps more appropriate to talk about the effect of teaching conditions on the acquisition process, for what participants' paid attention to during the learning phase apart from the over learning task was still to a certain extent determined by the learners themselves. In allowing this freedom to the students, the experimental conditions were closer to actual classroom conditions.

Finally, there is an important methodological note to be made. In this experiment, it became evident that underlying a learner's response to a single task may be a whole network of inner hypotheses and assumptions that are very difficult for the researcher to gain access to unless such hypotheses are given a chance to manifest themselves on another type of task. It may be that the process of second language acquisition is so complex that research that aims at gaining an understanding of even the smallest part of it should be carried out by using various methods and instruments to measure the learners' progress.

ACKNOWLEDGMENTS

This paper is based on research carried out at the University of Hawai'i at Mānoa for the author's master's thesis in ESL in 1992. A version of the paper was presented at the XXI Linguistics Colloquium in Oulu, Finland, in May 1994 and at the 29th annual TESOL convention in Long Beach, California, in March 1995. I would like to thank my teachers and fellow students in the Department of ESL, whose assistance and advice with various aspects of this project were invaluable. I am extremely grateful to all the participants who participated in the study. I would also like to thank my teachers and colleagues at the University of Jyväskylä for their support. Finally, I would like to thank the ASLA/Fulbright Foundation for their financial support, which made my stay in Hawai'i possible.

REFERENCES

Alanen, R. (1992). *Input enhancement and rule presentation in second language acquisition*. Unpublished MA thesis, University of Hawai'i at Mānoa, Honolulu.

Branch, M. (1989). Finnish. In B. Comrie (Ed.), *The world's major languages* (pp. 593–617). New York: Oxford University Press.

Chaudron, C. (1985). Intake: On models and methods for discovering learners' processing of input. *Studies in Second Language Acquisition*, *7*, 1–14.

Doughty, C. (1991). Second language acquisition does make a difference: Evidence from an empirical study of SL relativization. *Studies in Second Language Acquisition*, *13*, 431–469.

Dulany, D. E., Carlson, R. A., & Dewey, G. I. (1984). A case of syntactical learning and judgment: How conscious and how abstract? *Journal of Experimental Psychology: General*, *113*, 541–555.

Ellis, N. (1993). Rules and instances in foreign language learning: Interactions of explicit and implicit knowledge. *European Journal of Cognitive Psychology*, *5*, 289–318.

Hulstijn, J. H. (1989). Implicit and incidental second language learning: Experiments in the processing of natural and partly artificial input. In H. W. Dechert & M. Raupach (Eds.), *Interlingual processes* (pp. 49–73). Tübingen: Gunter Narr Verlag.

Hulstijn, J. H. (1992). Retention of inferred and given word meanings: experiments in incidental vocabulary learning. In P. Arnaud & H. Béjoint (Eds.), *Vocabulary and applied linguistics* (pp. 113–125). London: MacMillan.

Ijaz, I. H. (1986). Linguistic and cognitive determinants of lexical acquisition in a second language. *Language Learning*, *36*, 401–451.

Karlsson, F. (1982). *Finnish grammar*. Juva: WSOY.

Logan, G. D. (1988). Toward an instance theory of automatization. *Psychological Review*, *95*, 492–527.

Long, M. H. (1991). Focus on form: A design feature in language teaching methodology. In K. de Bot, R. Ginsberg, & C. Kramsch

(Eds.), *Foreign language research in cross-cultural perspective* (pp. 39–52). Amsterdam: John Benjamins.

McLaughlin, B. & Nayak, N. (1989). Processing a new language: Does knowing other languages make a difference? In H. W. Dechert & M. Raupach (Eds.), *Interlingual processes* (pp. 5–16). Tübingen: Gunter Narr Verlag.

Pica, T. (1983). Adult acquisition of English as a second language under different conditions of exposure. *Language Learning, 33*, 465–497.

Reber, A. (1976). Implicit learning of synthetic languages: The role of instructional set. *Journal of Experimental Psychology: Human Learning and Memory, 2*, 88–94.

Reber, A. (1989). Implicit learning and tacit knowledge. *Journal of Experimental Psychology: General, 118*, 219–235.

Reber, A., Kassin, S. M., Lewis, S., & Cantor, G. (1980). On the relationship between implicit and explicit modes in the learning of a complex rule structure. *Journal of Experimental Psychology: Human Learning and Memory, 6*, 492–502.

Schmidt, R. (1990). The role of consciousness in second language learning. *Applied Linguistics, 11*, 129–158.

Schmidt, R. (1992). Psychological mechanisms underlying second language fluency. *Studies in Second Language Acquisition, 14*, 357–385.

Schmidt, R. & Frota, S. (1986). Developing basic conversational ability in a second language: A case study of an adult learner of Portuguese. In R. Day (Ed.), *Talking to learn: Conversation in second language acquisition* (pp. 237–236). Rowley, MA: Newbury House.

Selinker, L. (1972). Interlanguage. *International Review of Applied Linguistics, 10*, 209–231.

Sharwood Smith, M. (1993). Input enhancement in instructed SLA: Theoretical bases. *Studies in Second Language Acquisition, 15*, 165–179.

Stockwell, R., Bowen, J., & Martin, J. (1965). *The grammatical structures of English and Spanish.* Chicago: University of Chicago Press.

VanPatten, B. (1989). Can learners attend to form and content while processing input? *Hispania, 72*, 409–417.

VanPatten, B. & Cadierno, T. (1993). Explicit instruction and input processing. *Studies in Second Language Acquisition*, *15*, 225–243.

APPENDIX 1: RULE DESCRIPTION GIVEN TO RULE AND RULE & ENHANCE

<u>The ending *–ssa*</u> is used to refer to (1) static position inside the object to which it has been added, i.e., that something is inside or contained by the noun that carries this ending. For example, *talossa* means 'in the house' (*talo* 'house' + *–ssa* 'in'). This notion of containment is closely related to the idea of close or attachment or direct contact between two objects: thus, *–ssa* is also used to refer to (2) close contact and/or attachment of an object to another object or surface to which the ending has been added. For example, pieces of clothing or jewelry, even bandages are seen to be closely attached rather than being on the surface of their respective body parts. Because of the fact that *–ssa* has two meanings, sentences sometimes have two meanings as well. For example, the sentence *Kuva on kuoressa* (*kuva* = 'picture', *on* = 'is', *kuore* = 'envelope') can mean either that there is a picture inside the envelope, or that there is a picture attached to or printed on the envelope.

<u>The ending *–lla*</u> is used to refer to static position on top of an object. For example, *matolla* (*matto* = 'mat' + *–lla* 'on') can be roughly translated as 'on the mat'.

These case endings are very regular. They are always added to the base form of the noun. However, there are certain systematic sound changes that take place inside some words when the endings *–ssa* and *–lla* are added to them (these sound changes are then reflected in the spelling of the nouns): (1) whenever there is a double consonant *pp*, *tt* and *kk* near the end of the base form, it changes into the corresponding single consonant *p*, *t* and *k* when a suffix is added, e.g., *tippa, tipassa* = 'in the drop'; (2) whenever the single consonant *t* occurs near the end of the base form, it changes into *d* when a suffix is added, e.g., *lato*, *ladossa* = 'in the barn'. These changes do not apply when *pp*, *tt* and *kk*, or *t* are not near the end of the word.

APPENDIX 2: SENTENCE COMPLETION TASK

Use the last word in brackets to form *meaningful* Finnish sentences so that all sentences contain a place expression (for example, in English, "The man is in the car"). To help you in your task, the meanings of the Finnish words are given in quotation marks. The verb *on* 'is, are' has already been given.

1.	*Banaani on* ___________	(*banaani* 'banana', *bouli* 'bowl')
2.	*Greippi on* ___________	(*greippi* 'grapefruit', *lata* 'box')
3.	*Pinni on* ___________	(*pinni* 'pin', *hattu* 'hat')
4.	*Perhonen on* ___________	(*perhonen* 'butterfly', *lilja* 'lily')
5.	*Raita on* ___________	(*raita* 'stripe', *mekko* 'dress')
6.	*Reppu on* ___________	(*reppu* 'backpack', *jakka* 'stool')
7.	*Liisa on* ___________	(*Liisa, huone* 'room')
8.	*Maito on* ___________	(*maito* 'milk', *lasi* 'glass')
9.	*Nimi on* ___________	(*nimi* 'name', *koppa* 'basket')
10.	*Ruusu on* ___________	(*ruusu* 'rose', *tapetti* 'wallpaper')
11.	*Kukka on* ___________	(*kukka* 'flower', *kuppi* 'cup')
12	*Tuli on* ___________	(*tuli* 'fire', *takka* 'fireplace')
13.	*Naarmu on* ___________	(*naarmu* 'scratch', *penkki* 'bench')
14.	*Laukku on* ___________	(*laukku* 'bag', *tuoli* 'chair')
15.	*Ketju on* ___________	(*ketju* 'anklet', *nilkka* 'ankle')
16.	*Teksti 'Yves Saint Laurent' on* ___________	(*teksti* 'label', *laukku* 'bag')
17.	*Mies on* ___________	(*mies* 'man', *rata* 'railroad track')
18.	*Kuppi on* ___________	(*kuppi* 'cup', *poyta* 'table)
19.	*Poyta on* ___________	(*poyta* 'table', *matto* 'mat')
20.	*Nappi on* ___________	(*nappi* 'button', *takki* 'coat')

21. *Tahra on* ____________ (*tahra* 'stain', *peitto* 'bed cover')

22. *Teksti on* ____________ (*teksti* 'label', *reppu* 'backpack')

23. *Grilli on* ____________ (*grilli* 'grill', *nurme* 'lawn')

24. *Lyy on* ____________ (*lyy* 'fly', *greippi*' grapefruit')

25. *Piippu on* ____________ (*piippu* 'chimney', *katto* 'roof')

26. *Takki on* ____________ (*takki* 'coat', *kaappi* 'closet')

27. *A-vitamiini on* ____________ (*A-vitamiini* 'vitamin A', *maito* 'milk

28 *Tahti on* ____________ (*tahti* 'star', *lippu* 'flag')

29. *Potti on* ____________ (*potti* 'pot', *hylly* 'shelf)

30. *Vesi on* ____________ (*vesi* 'water', *kaivo* 'well')

31. *Kaiverrus on* ____________ (*kaiverrus* 'inscription', *laatta* 'tablet'

32. *Vita on* ____________ (*vita* 'chain', *kaula* 'neck')

33. *Sohva on* ____________ (*sohva* 'sofa', *kuisti* 'porch')

Peter Robinson
University of Queensland

APTITUDE, AWARENESS, AND THE FUNDAMENTAL SIMILARITY OF IMPLICIT AND EXPLICIT SECOND LANGUAGE LEARNING

ABSTRACT

This study examines evidence for the claims of Krashen and Reber that nonconscious learning under implicit and incidental conditions is insensitive to measures of individual differences in cognitive abilities, in contrast to learning under conscious rule-search and instructed conditions. Participants were 104 learners of English as a second language. Individual differences were assessed using two subtests of the Modern Language Aptitude Test. Following training on easy and hard second language rules, learning was assessed through a grammaticality judgment test. Rule awareness was assessed on the basis of responses to a debriefing questionnaire. The relationships between aptitude, rule learning, and rule awareness for participants trained in each condition are described. Results suggest that aptitude is related to both learning and awareness in the implicit, instructed and rule-search conditions, though not in the incidental condition. Awareness defined as noticing did not lead to a higher level of learning for participants in any condition, though at the level of looking for rules it led to superior learning for implicit learners, and at the level of verbalizability to superior learning for both implicit and rule-search learners.

INTRODUCTION

Recent experimental second language research has contrasted the effects of learning under conditions that instruct participants to consciously focus on form with learning under conditions that require meaning-based or memory-based processing with no conscious focus

Robinson, Peter (1995). Aptitude, awareness, and the fundamental similarity of implicit and explicit second language learning. In Richard Schmidt (Ed.), *Attention and awareness in foreign language learning* (Technical Report #9 (pp. 303–357). Honolulu, Hawai'i: University of Hawai'i, Second Language Teaching & Curriculum Center.

on form (N. Ellis, 1993; de Graaff, 1995; DeKeyser, 1994; Doughty, 1991; Hulstijn, 1990; Hulstijn and de Graaff, 1994; Robinson, 1994b). This research has been prompted by rival claims regarding the facilitative effects of conscious awareness of the form of input during second language acquisition (SLA). Schmidt (1990, 1993; Schmidt and Frota, 1986) has argued that conscious awareness of form at the level of *noticing* is necessary to subsequent second language development and that consciousness at the level of rule awareness is strongly facilitative of subsequent learning. In contrast, Krashen (1981, 1982, 1985, 1992) has argued that second language development is largely the result of unconscious acquisition processes that are facilitated by a focus on meaning alone. Conscious attempts to look for grammatical rules, or to understand pedagogically presented rules, lead only to *learning* and to the development of a peripheral system that is independent of the *acquired* system developed by unconscious processes. Krashen has also claimed that measures of individual differences in cognitive abilities, such as those operationalized in aptitude batteries like the Modern Language Aptitude Test (MLAT) (Carroll and Sapon, 1959), draw on abilities under conscious control. These therefore predict only the development of the learned system. There has, however, to date been no experimental SLA research that has examined the effects of aptitude on learning under conditions that require a conscious focus on form versus conditions that do not.

Dual-system explanations of human learning, like those proposed for second language development by Krashen, are the subject of much recent debate in the general field of cognitive psychology. The present paper first reviews recent research in this area and relates the debate over the interpretation of its findings to Krashen's acquisition/learning distinction. The findings of an experimental study of second language learning are then reported (Robinson, 1994b). This study examined the acquisition of simple and complex pedagogic rules of English grammar by second language learners following exposure under four training conditions. Two conditions simulated the exposure to second language input that Krashen (1981, 1982) has argued leads to acquisition: an incidental, meaning-focused condition, and to learning, an instructed, form-focused condition. These conditions were matched by parallel conditions familiar from the experimental work of Reber (1989, 1993): an implicit, instructed-to-remember condition and an explicit, conscious rule-search condition. The relationship of learning under each condition to two measures of language learning aptitude is examined in light of the claim that implicit learning and unconscious acquisition are uninfluenced by individual differences. The relationship of the measures of aptitude to three measures of the extent of awareness during training under all conditions is also examined with a view to determining the extent to which individual differences in aptitude can trigger awareness of rules during training under each condition.

DUAL-SYSTEM EXPLANATIONS OF HUMAN LEARNING

A number of current theories of human learning propose that learning proceeds by means of two functionally separate systems which access separate forms of memory and which are differentially regulated by consciousness. For example, Anderson (1983), Squire (1992), and Willingham, Nissen and Bullemer (1989) have all claimed that two systems are responsible for declarative (factual) knowledge of the world and procedural knowledge of how to apply factual knowledge during skilled performance. These proposals differ over the issue of the interface between these forms of knowledge. Anderson (1983) argues for an interface position and specifies mechanisms that are responsible for converting declarative knowledge into procedural knowledge, whereas Squire (1992) and Willingham *et al.* (1989) maintain that the two knowledge bases are qualitatively different and non-interfaced. Reber (1989, 1993) has also argued that human learning takes place by means of two functionally separate systems. *Implicit* learning takes place in the absence of conscious efforts to learn the structure of a complex stimulus domain, in contrast to *explicit* learning, which takes place when learners are consciously searching for or applying rules to the stimulus domain. Unlike Anderson, Reber does not specify theoretical mechanisms for interfacing the two forms of knowledge, and unlike Squire he does not refer to neurophysiological evidence of the structure of memory to support a non-interface position. Reber's claims are based solely on behavioral evidence of learning under conditions that manipulate differences in participants' awareness of what is to be learned (Robinson, 1994b, 1995; Schmidt, 1994).

SLA researchers have also proposed distinctions between forms of knowledge arising during second language development and have debated the issue of whether they are interfaced (Bialystok, 1979, 1981; R. Ellis, 1990, 1993; Odlin, 1986; Robinson, 1993, 1994a). In particular, the views of Krashen have been influential in this debate. Like Squire and Reber, Krashen has proposed a dual-system explanation of second language development in which an unconsciously acquired knowledge base develops independently of a consciously learned knowledge base. Second language development, Krashen claims, is largely the result of the cognitive processes that underlie acquisition, since conscious learning is restricted to a relatively small number of easy rules, such as the rule for use of the plural morpheme, which requires a simple additive process and which is semantically transparent. Hard second language rules, such as the rule for Wh-question formation, which involves extensive permutation of word order and which is semantically opaque, can only be acquired (Ellis, 1990, p. 167; Krashen, 1982, pp. 97–98; Robinson, 1994b, chapter 2). Additionally, the conditions that must be met for the learned system to operate are stringent: the learner must know the rule, be focused on form, and have time to access the rule. Consequently, the contribution of the learned system to language production is limited, serving only to monitor or edit the output initiated by the acquired system. Further, Krashen claims that individual differences in language learning aptitude will only affect learning, whereas acquisition will be relatively unaffected by such differences (Krashen, 1981). Despite extensive criticisms of Krashen's acquisition/learning distinction (Gregg, 1984; McLaughlin, 1978) and of his claims that second language development is largely the result of unconscious processes (Schmidt, 1990, 1993), the dual-system explanation for second language development he proposed has continued to be influential in second language research and has recently been invoked by Schwartz (1986, 1993) and by Zobl (1992). Schwartz invokes Krashen's distinction in support of the claim that the properties of human grammar falling within the scope of Universal Grammar (Chomsky, 1986; White, 1989) can only be unconsciously acquired, whereas properties falling outside the scope of UG can be consciously learned. Zobl argues that the results of learning on post-tests of grammatical knowledge following meaning-focused instruction without an explicit, conscious focus on form display smaller standard deviations and population variances (and therefore fewer individual differences) than the results of learning following form-focused instruction.

Krashen's dual-system hypothesis and Schmidt's counter proposal that conscious awareness of the form of input at the level of noticing is necessary to subsequent second language development do not specify in detail the relationship of acquisition and learning processes, or the act of noticing, to key cognitive constructs such as memory or attention. Although the role of attentional processes during SLA has recently been discussed in some detail (Tomlin and Villa, 1994), there has to date been little extended discussion of the role of memory (though see Robinson, 1995; Robinson and Ha, 1993). However, an extensive experimental literature exists in the field of cognitive psychology that details the methodology and results of empirical studies of learning and memory task performance under conditions that manipulate the degree of conscious awareness of what is learned and remembered. Some findings from this research regarding the role of memory and awareness in learning are briefly reported below.

MEMORY RESEARCH AND DUAL-SYSTEM EXPLANATIONS OF LEARNING

Some support for dual-system explanations of learning has come from recent studies of human memory. Squire and Cohen (1984), Nissen, Knopman and Schacter (1987), and Squire and Zola-Morgan (1991) argue that claims for non-interfaced forms of knowledge are supported by neurophysiological evidence for distinct procedural and declarative systems of memory. Studies of preserved learning in amnesics with brain impairments have revealed that lesions to the hippocampus and neocortex surrounding the amygdala produce memory impairments, while lesions to the amygdala do not. Consequently, Squire and Zola-Morgan (1991) suggest that the amygdala is responsible, in part, for the memories and abilities that are preserved in amnesics, including abilities to make associative links between stimuli and sensory modalities and other functions important to skill development and procedural learning (see also Thompson, 1986, and Gluck and Granger, 1993, for reviews of the neurophysiological evidence for separate memory systems).

Arguments for a functional distinction between two forms of memory have also been proposed on the basis of evidence of behavioral differences in performance on direct and indirect memory tests. In these studies, stimuli, usually word lists, are presented during a study phase. In direct tests of memory, participants are explicitly instructed to recall the earlier presented stimuli, or to identify which of a series of words had been previously presented. Such cued recall and recognition tests require conscious attempts to retrieve the stimuli presented during the study phase. In contrast, indirect tests do not make the need to retrieve earlier experiences explicit in the task instructions. In such tasks (e.g., word fragment completion tasks) a list of partially completed letter strings is presented, and participants are asked to complete them. Participants are not directly instructed to recall the words, but the facilitative effects of memory for them is inferred from the faster response time and increased accuracy in completing word fragments based on earlier presented words. Claims have been made that performance on direct memory tests draws on consciously accessed explicit memory, whereas performance on indirect tests draws on unconsciously accessed implicit memory. Claims for the dissociation of these forms of memory are based on the fact that performance on indirect tests (and therefore implicit memory) is robust in the face of aging and clinical disorders such as amnesia, whereas performance on direct tests (and explicit memory) is not. These claims are currently the subject of much debate, since many attribute the results of differences in memory test performance reported in these studies not to different memory systems but to transfer of processing strategies encouraged by the different task instructions during direct and indirect memory tests (Richardson-Klavehn and Bjork, 1988; Robinson, 1994b, 1995; Schacter, 1987).

AWARENESS AND DUAL-SYSTEM EXPLANATIONS OF LEARNING

There has been a considerable amount of recent research into the proposal that the two systems in dual-system explanations of learning involve two different states of awareness (Brody, 1989; Dulany Carlson and Dewey, 1985; Green and Shanks, 1993; Hayes and Broadbent, 1988; Lewicki, 1985; Lewicki, Hill and Bizot, 1988 Perruchet and Pacteau, 1990; Reber, 1989, 1990, 1993). Reber, fo example, has used two different types of ordered stimulus display to study the relationship between awareness and learning, the most common of which has been artificial grammar experiments (Carr and Curran, 1994; McLaughlin, 1980; Robinson, 1995; Schmidt, 1994). In these experiments, participants are exposed to strings of letters generated by an artificial finite state grammar. Implicit learning has been claimed to occur following instructions simply to memorize examples of letter strings conforming to an abstract finite state grammar, whereas explicit learning has been claimed to occur following attempts to consciously search for the rules underlying the strings, or to apply previously taught rules to the strings. Importantly, the rules regulating the artificial grammars used in these experiments have been claimed to be complex, since Reber claims that the complexity of the stimulus domain is a condition that must be met if implicit learning processes are to be displayed. If the rules to be learned are too simple, or if critical aspects of the stimulus display are made salient to learners, they will adopt a conscious hypothesis testing mode and attempt to learn in the manner of participants in the explicit conditions. In transfer tests which require participants to discriminate between letter strings conforming to the artificial grammar and strings which violate it, participants in the implicit condition have been consistently observed to perform at above chance accuracy and in the majority of studies performed by Reber have been found to perform better than participants in the explicit conditions.

The delivery of these conditions has been assessed in post-experimental verbal report sessions in which participants are asked about the rules underlying the stimulus display. Participants in the implicit memorization conditions have been found to be unable to verbalize the knowledge they gained during training. Based on this evidence Reber has claimed (i) that the product of implicit learning is abstract knowledge of the rules of the grammar and (ii) that the process whereby this knowledge is accumulated is inaccessible to conscious awareness. There is considerable dispute over the interpretation of results offered in support of these two claims. Critics have argued that the knowledge acquired during implicit learning is not abstract but is based on fragmentary knowledge of co-occurring bigrams or trigrams (Perruchet and Pacteau, 1990; Vokey and Brooks, 1992). Others have criticized the claim that the knowledge acquired during implicit learning is unavailable for verbal report (Brody, 1989;

Perruchet and Amorim, 1992; Shanks and St. John, 1994), arguing that the verbal report measures used are insensitive measures of awareness.

INDIVIDUAL DIFFERENCES AND DUAL-SYSTEM EXPLANATIONS OF LEARNING

Much of the research reviewed above has aimed at providing evidence of functional dissociations between implicit and explicit processes and establishing neurophysiological evidence for the dual-system hypothesis account of human learning. Compared with performance by normal participants, for example, performance by amnesics with bilateral hippocampal lesions is impaired on direct memory tasks requiring conscious recall, as well as on rule-search and instructed learning tasks requiring explicit learning. In contrast, performance is unimpaired on indirect memory tests and implicit learning tasks. Summarizing the evidence for dissociations Reber concludes that "there seems to be no question about the robustness of implicit processing systems when compared with explicit processing systems. Unconscious processes clearly show greater resistance to insult and injury than do conscious processes" (Reber, Walkenfield and Hernstadt, 1991: 889). Reber *et al.* note, however, that there has been little research directed to the related claim that implicit learning and memory are relatively unaffected by population variance in standard measures of cognitive ability such as intelligence. In the field of SLA Krashen (1981, 1982) has made similar claims regarding the sensitivity of measures of language learning aptitude, such as the MLAT (Carroll and Sapon, 1959), to language development. Such measures, Krashen claims, predict variance in conscious learning but do not predict variance in unconscious acquisition processes. This is because the components of aptitude batteries like the MLAT measure abilities, such as the paired associates test of memory (a direct memory test), and the words in sentences test of grammatical sensitivity (which is an unspeeded task, focused on form, and invoking consciously learned rule knowledge) create the conditions for access to the learned, but not the acquired system. As in the field of general cognitive theory, however, there has been little SLA research into this implication of the dual-system hypothesis of learning.

RESEARCH QUESTIONS FOR THE PRESENT STUDY

The preceding discussion motivates five research questions.

RQ1: Do differences in the extent of conscious focus on form manipulated by the training conditions differentially affect the learning of easy and hard second language rules?

Both Krashen (1981, 1982) and Reber (1989, 1993) have claimed that learning that results from conscious awareness of the form of input is inferior to the implicit learning or acquisition that occurs in the absence of such awareness. They claim this is particularly evident where the stimulus domain is complex. Where the rules to be learned are easy, then Krashen claims instruction can be effective. Reber argues that where the stimulus domain is simple and the relevant structural attributes of rules are salient to the learner then implicit learning will not be displayed, since the simplicity and salience of the rules regulating the stimulus domain will cause learners to adopt a conscious rule-search strategy. However, where the rules to be learned are complex, learners in the nonconscious implicit and incidental learning conditions should out-perform those in the instructed and rule-search conditions.

RQ2: Does aptitude affect learning in all conditions?

Both Reber and Krashen have also argued that differences in measures of cognitive attributes such as aptitude should only be related to conscious learning. Learning in the nonconscious implicit and incidental conditions should be insensitive to aptitude differences.

RQ3: Do the implicit, incidental, rule-search and instructed conditions differentially affect the extent of rule awareness that develops during training?

Reber has argued that despite performing at above chance accuracy on the grammaticality judgment tests of well and badly formed strings of letters generated by the artificial grammars used in his studies, learners in the implicit condition of his studies are unaware of the rule-governed nature of the stimulus domain. Krashen also assumes that learners who are acquiring knowledge incidentally do so without consciously noticing or looking for rules. Consequently both implicit and incidental learners should perform poorly on these measures of awareness relative to learners in the rule-search and instructed conditions.

RQ4: Does the level of awareness developed during training affect the extent of learning equally in all conditions?

Schmidt (1990, 1993) has claimed that conscious *noticing* is necessary to subsequent learning, and therefore learners in all conditions who claim to have noticed rules should outperform those who do not. Similarly, the level of awareness indicated by the fact that participants were looking for or could verbalize rules should also be positively related to learning in all conditions, relative to participants who were not looking for or able to verbalize rules. However, if Krashen and Reber's claims about the negative influence of conscious learning processes are correct, then participants in the unconscious implicit and incidental conditions who do claim to have been aware during training should perform poorly in learning complex rules relative to learners who do not claim to have been aware.

RQ5: Is aptitude positively related to the level of awareness developed during training in all conditions?

The final research question addresses the relationship between awareness and aptitude. It seems likely that both those participants who become aware in the implicit and incidental conditions and those who demonstrate superior levels of awareness in the instructed and rule-search conditions, will be those with higher scores on the aptitude measures. However, two component measures of aptitude were used in the present study, a memory measure and a grammatical sensitivity measure. Since different learning conditions may bias participants to rely more on memory (e.g., the implicit condition) or on grammatical sensitivity (e.g., the rule-search condition) it may be that awareness is triggered by different components of aptitude in learning under each condition. This could be used as evidence for a transfer-appropriate processing account of the results of learning under each condition (Blaxton, 1989; Robinson, 1995), rather than as support for a dual-system explanation.

METHOD

DESIGN

The following factors were included in the present study:

- Learning condition, with four levels: (i) implicit condition, (ii) incidental condition, (iii) explicit rule-search condition, and (iv) explicit instructed condition, a between participants factor.

- Rules to be learned, with two levels of difficulty: simple versus complex, a within-subject factor.

- Two measures of language learning aptitude: paired-associate learning (measure of memory) and grammatical sensitivity (inductive learning).

- Three measures of awareness; did participants *notice* any rules, were they *looking for* rules, and could they *verbalize* rules?

The dependent measure was accuracy of response to a transfer grammaticality judgment task following training. (Speed of response on the transfer grammaticality judgment test was also recorded. See Robinson, 1994b for analyses of this data).

PARTICIPANTS

Participants for the study were ninety four Japanese native speakers, five Korean and five Mandarin Chinese native speakers, aged between 19–34 years. They were enrolled in language programs in Hawai'i and had been placed into intermediate level language programs, as determined by scores on placement tests within their host institutions. Participants were offered $10 in return for their participation in the study and were selected on the basis of the results of a pretest showing them to be unfamiliar with the rules used in the study.

IDENTIFICATION OF EASY AND HARD RULES

To identify the pedagogic rules used for the study, a grammaticality judgment test of twenty five structures that ranged in degree of structural complexity and likely familiarity was given to a group of participants who were comparable in age, proficiency level, language background and length of exposure to English to the participants used in the experimental study. The eight sentences most consistently and incorrectly rated ungrammatical were selected as the basis for pedagogic rules, which were written by the researcher by analyzing and explaining key elements of the constructions. These pedagogic rule formats were then given to fifteen experienced ESL teachers to rate for complexity using a seven point rating scale. A week later, the same teachers were asked to rate the structures described by the rules for their complexity using a Q-sort with cards illustrating the eight structures.

Two of the rules were consistently rated by teachers as distinct in complexity. This difference in complexity was confirmed by the results of the Q-sort of the relevant structures. These rules were a rule for describing how to form pseudo clefts of location, e.g., "Where Mary and John live is in Chicago not in New York" (the hard rule), and a rule describing the fact that subject verb inversion is allowed in sentences where adverbials of movement/location are fronted, e.g., "Into the house John ran/ran John" (the easy rule). The rules are illustrated in Appendix A. Participants for the experimental study completed the same grammaticality judgment test used to identify the sentences upon which rules were based, and if they rated the easy and hard rule sentences as ungrammatical on the pretest they were selected for the study (see Robinson 1994b for a fuller explanation of this procedure).

TRAINING CONDITIONS

Reber's conditions (instructed-to-remember vs. rule-search) and Krashen's conditions (focus on meaning vs. instruction) were operationalized as training sessions on a Macintosh computer using MindLab software (Meike, 1988). Each subject was randomly assigned to one of these conditions, making a total of twenty six participants per condition. Participants performed two training sessions during which they viewed forty sentences, twenty based on the easy rule of English and twenty based on the hard rule of English identified following the procedures described above. Sentences were presented for the same length of time, ten seconds per sentence, and in the same random order for participants in all conditions. Participants in all conditions took part in a task familiarization activity during which the demands of the training task and the procedures for answering questions using keys on the keyboard were described.

In the implicit condition, participants were informed that the task they were about to perform was a memory task. After the timed ten second presentation of each sentence during training, they were asked questions about the location of words in the sentence of the form "Were the words _____ and _____ next to each other in the sentence?" Participants answered yes or no using designated keys on the keyboard. Feedback ("correct" or "incorrect") was displayed on screen until they pressed a key to signal they were ready to continue, whereupon the next stimulus sentence was presented.

In the incidental condition participants, were informed that the task they were to perform was a comprehension activity during which they were to read sentences in order to answer yes/no comprehension questions. As in all other conditions, sentences were presented for ten seconds, followed by a comprehension question on the content of the stimulus sentence. After responding yes or no to this question, participants were given feedback before they proceeded to view the next sentence.

In the rule-search condition, participants were first informed that they were to try and find the rules exemplified by the sentences they would see. After presentation of each stimulus sentence, they were asked questions such as, "Have you found the rules yet?" or "Are you still looking for the rule,?" to which participants responded yes or no. No feedback was given in this condition, since the nature of their answers could not be anticipated. After answering the follow up question they proceeded directly to viewing the next sentence.

In the instructed condition, participants first viewed explanations of the easy and hard rules. They were instructed to apply these rules to the sentences they were to see and were shown how to do this. During training, participants saw each sentence for ten seconds, followed by a question about the metalinguistic form of the sentence, such as, "Did the subject of the sentence come before the verb?" Participants responded yes or no to this question and were given feedback. After pressing a key to continue, they then viewed the next sentence.

THE TRANSFER TASK

After training, participants in all conditions completed a grammaticality judgment task (see Appendix C). Accuracy of responses to novel sentences conforming to the easy and hard rules was recorded. Twenty easy rule sentences and twenty hard rule sentences were presented in the same fixed random order for each subject. These were made up of ten grammatical examples and ten ungrammatical examples of the same easy and hard rule types presented during training. (See Robinson 1994b for fuller discussion of the design of the transfer set sentences).

APTITUDE MEASURES

Scores on the Words in Sentences subtest of the MLAT (Carroll and Sapon, 1959) were obtained based on a forty five item multiple choice test of grammatical knowledge. This test requires participants to identify analogies between the grammatical function of items in pairs of sentences and were used as a measure of participants' grammatical sensitivity. Scores on the Paired Associates subtest of the MLAT were also used. This test requires participants to view a list of twenty four paired associates (English and Kurdish words) for three minutes. Participants then selected the correct paired Kurdish associate from a choice of five given for each English word. A combined score for performance on these two tests was also calculated and used as an overall measure of aptitude. One way ANOVAs of performance on each of the subtests and the combined score showed no significant differences in aptitude for participants assigned to the four experimental conditions. The aptitude data for participants in each condition was also examined for significant kurtosis and skewedness and was found to be normally distributed.

The MLAT was chosen as the source of the aptitude data because it is the most widely accepted measure of aptitude available for participants of the age of those used in the present study. Scores on the MLAT have been shown to consistently predict differences in foreign language learning success (Stansfield, 1990; Carroll, 1993). There are, however, no currently available versions of the MLAT in the languages of the participants used for this study. Since the aptitude tests used in the present study were in English, and not the native language of the participants, it is possible that differences in scores on the aptitude test might simply reflect differences in the proficiency of participants. No separate measure of proficiency was obtained from participants in the present study which could be used to directly address this issue. However, there are three indirect pieces of evidence to support the independence of the aptitude scores and participants' level of proficiency. Firstly, scores by a group of Japanese native speakers equivalent to the ninety four Japanese participants taking part in the present study in terms of age, previous educational experience, and extent of exposure to English instruction were obtained on the aptitude subtests and on the Michigan English Placement Test (MEPT). There were low correlations between scores on the aptitude tests and the MEPT, and no correlations in the high .80s that would be necessary to support the claim that the proficiency and aptitude tests were measuring the same abilities. Secondly, there were no significant correlations between memory and grammatical sensitivity scores for the participants in any of the conditions of the present study, indicating that the subtests measured separate components of aptitude and were not homogeneously affected by proficiency level. Finally, the results reported below, show no consistent pattern of correlations between aptitude scores and performance on easy and hard rules across conditions. However, this would likely have been the case if the aptitude measures reflected no more than proficiency differences, since proficiency would have been expected to affect learning performance in each condition equally (for fuller discussion of the independence of aptitude and proficiency in the present study see Robinson, 1994b).

AWARENESS MEASURES

Following completion of the transfer test, all participants completed a written questionnaire. The questions were first briefly explained by the researcher before participants completed the questionnaire in their native language. Answers to three questions on the questionnaire were used to determine participants' level of awareness during training. They were coded yes or no as having noticed rules during training based on responses to the question, "Did you notice any rules of English underlying the sentences you saw in the training sessions?" They were coded yes or no as having looked for rules based on answers to the question, "Were you looking for rules of English grammar when you saw the sentences during training?" They were coded yes or no as able verbalize rules on the basis of their response to the question, "Can you describe what the rules were that were illustrated by the sentences you saw during training?" Participants were coded as able to describe the easy rule, the hard rule, or both based on any attempt at a metalinguistic description of these rules, or the presentation and comment on a relevant exemplar of the rules.

ANALYSES PERFORMED

To address Research Question 1, a repeated measure ANOVA of accuracy of responses to the twenty easy rule sentences and the twenty hard rule sentences in the transfer grammaticality judgment test was performed using SuperANOVA statistical software. Planned comparisons of performance by all possible pairs of conditions on easy and hard rule sentences were also performed.

To address Research Question 2, correlations of accuracy of performance on easy and hard rule sentences with scores on the two aptitude subtests and the combined aptitude score were performed for participants in each condition. Pearson's r was reported together with the significance level for each correlation.

To address Research Question 3, a two way chi-square of responses to the three awareness questions was performed for participants in each condition.

To address Research Question 4, repeated measure ANOVAs of accuracy of performance on easy and hard rules were performed for participants in each condition, grouped as +/– noticed rules, +/– looking for rules and +/– able to verbalize rules.

To address Research Question 5, the repeated measure ANOVAs were performed for the same groups with aptitude scores on the memory and grammatical sensitivity tests as the dependent variables. The alpha level was set at $p<.05$ for all analyses.

RESULTS

RQ1: Do differences in the extent of conscious focus on form manipulated by the training conditions differentially affect the learning of easy and hard second language rules?

The results of the repeated measure ANOVA on responses to all sentences in the transfer set show a significant main effect for the factor Condition ($F(3,100)=6.799$, $p=.0003$) and for the factor Rule ($F(3,100)=70.566$, $p=.0001$), with no significant interaction between Rule and Condition. Post-hoc Scheffé comparisons show the instructed condition to be significantly superior to the implicit, incidental and rule-search conditions ($p<.05$). Results of separate ANOVAs on responses to easy and hard rule sentences show a significant main effect for Condition in response to hard rule sentences ($F(1,100)=3.255$, $p=.02$), and to easy rule sentences ($F(3,100)=7.494$, $p=.0001$). Results of Scheffé post-hoc comparisons show a significant difference at the $p<.05$ level between instructed and rule-search learners in performance on hard rule sentences, and a significant difference between instructed learners and those in the implicit, incidental and rule-search conditions in performance on easy rule sentences. These relationships are graphically illustrated in Figure 1.

Figure 1: Accuracy of response to easy and hard rule transfer set sentences by subjects in all conditions.

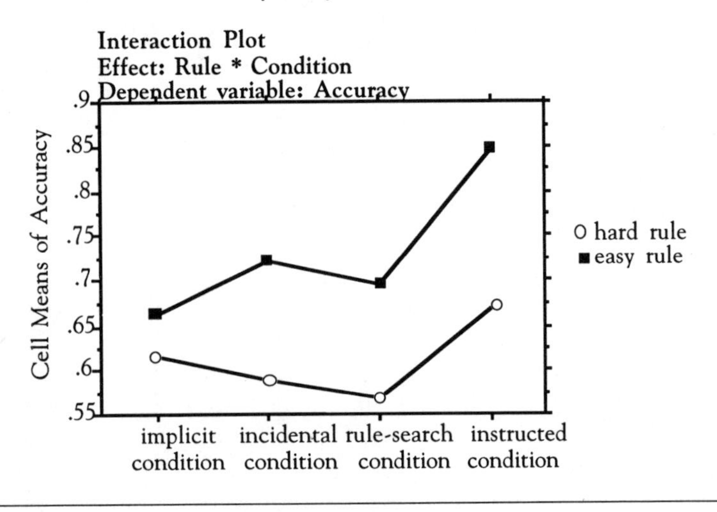

RQ2: Does aptitude affect learning in all conditions?

The results of the correlations of performance on the aptitude subtests, and the combined score for aptitude, with accuracy of response to easy and hard rule transfer set sentences are presented in Table 1. There are significant correlations at p<.05 level between performance on easy and hard rule sentences and Grammatical Sensitivity for those in the implicit condition. There are no significant correlations of aptitude and accuracy on either rule for participants in the incidental condition. Grammatical Sensitivity is significantly correlated with rule-search performance on easy rule sentences, and Memory is significantly correlated with rule-search performance on hard rule sentences. There are also significant correlations of Grammatical Sensitivity with performance on both easy and hard rules for instructed learners, and of Memory with performance on easy and hard rules.

Table 1: Summary of the correlations of aptitude subtests and accuracy on easy and hard rules under each condition

Condition/Rule	Grammatical sensitivity subtest	Memory subtest	Combined aptitude scores
Implicit			
easy	.693*	.299	.521*
hard	.746*	.250	.520*
Incidental			
easy	.353	.309	.389
hard	.285	.136	.234
Rule-search			
easy	.604*	.419	.556*
hard	.374	.511*	.504*
Instructed			
easy	.540*	.489*	.626*
hard	.563*	.461*	.620*

*=p<.05

RQ3: Do the implicit, incidental, rule-search and instructed conditions differentially affect the extent of rule awareness that develops during training?

The cell frequencies of the two-way chi-square of responses to the debriefing questionnaire are presented in Table 2. These show large numbers of participants in all conditions claim to have noticed rules in the sentences they viewed during training, though these rules may not, of course, have been those that motivated the presentation of sentences. There is no significant difference between conditions with respect to the extent of noticing, but a significant difference with respect to the extent to which participants claimed to be looking for rules during training. Post-hoc cell contributions show this effect to be attributable to the differences between those in the explicit instructed and rule-search conditions, and those in the implicit condition. There are no significant differences between conditions with respect to the ability to verbalize rules, though twice as many participants verbalized rules after training in the instructed condition compared to participants trained in other conditions.

Table 2: Summary of cell frequencies for noticing, searching and verbalizing in each condition

	implicit	incidental	rule-search	instructed
noticed	11	17	16	19
looked* for rules	9	15	20	20
able to verbalize	6	7	7	14

* = significant difference using chi-square, $p<.05$

RQ4: Does the level of awareness developed during training affect the extent of learning equally in all conditions?

The results of the ANOVAs of the accuracy of responses to easy and hard rule sentences in the transfer set by participants in each condition, grouped as aware or unaware at the levels of noticing, looking for rules, and able to verbalize rules, are given below.

Awareness at the level of noticing doesn't increase accuracy on either rule in any condition. Results of the ANOVA for accuracy of response on the hard rule sentences shows no significant main effect for the factor Noticing ($F(1,96)=.796$, $p=.37$), no significant main effect for Condition ($F(3,96)=2.44$, $p=.068$), and no significant interaction of Noticing and Condition. Results of the ANOVA for accuracy on the easy rule similarly shows no main effect for Noticing ($F(1,96)=.021$, $p=.88$). There is a significant main effect for Condition ($F(3,96)=5.658$, $p=.001$) but no significant interaction of Noticing and Condition. Means and standard deviations of accuracy of participants in each condition on hard rule and easy rule sentences, divided by awareness at the level of noticing, are given in Figures 2 and 3. Planned a priori means comparisons of aware and unaware participants in each condition also reveal no significant differences in accuracy on either rule in any condition.

Figure 2: Accuracy on the hard rule and awareness at the level of noticing.

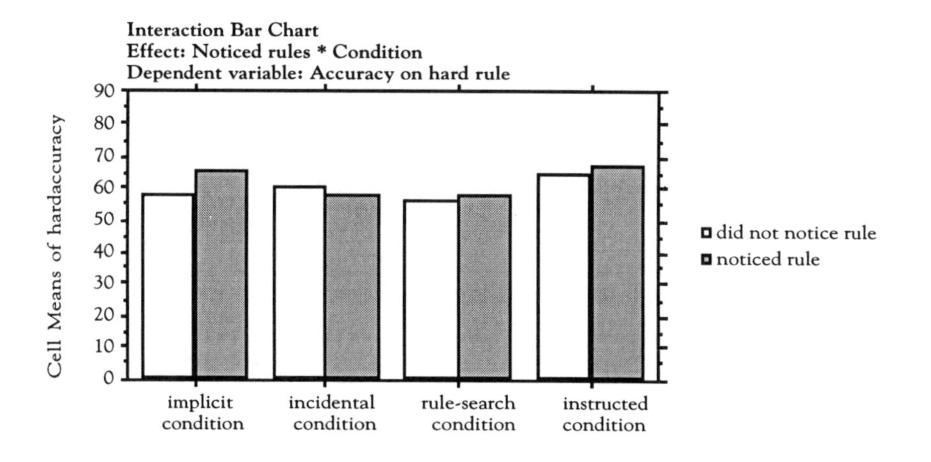

Figure 3: Accuracy on the easy rule and awareness at the level of noticing.

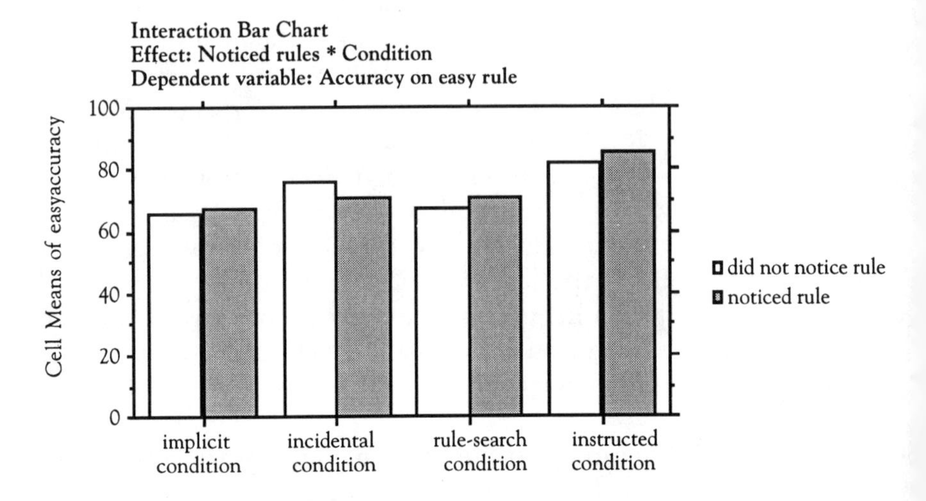

Results of the ANOVA for accuracy of response on the hard rule sentences shows no significant main effect for the factor Looking For Rules (F(1,96)=.138, p=.711), a significant main effect for Condition (F(3,96)=2.88,p=.039), but no significant interaction of Looking for Rules and Condition. Similarly there is a nonsignificant main effect for Looking For Rules (F(1,96)=.456, p=.501) on easy rule accuracy, a significant main effect for Condition (F(3,96)=6.197, p=.001) but no significant interaction of Looking For Rules and Condition. Means and standard deviations of accuracy of participants in each condition on hard rule and easy rule sentences, divided by awareness at the level of looking for rules, are given in Figures 4 and 5. Planned a priori means comparisons of performance by aware and unaware participants in each condition, however, do reveal significant differences on the easy rule (p=.031) and the hard rule (p=.024) for participants in the implicit condition. In both cases, participants in the implicit condition who reported they were looking for rules are significantly more accurate than those who were not.

Figure 4: Accuracy on the hard rule and awareness at the level of looking for rules.

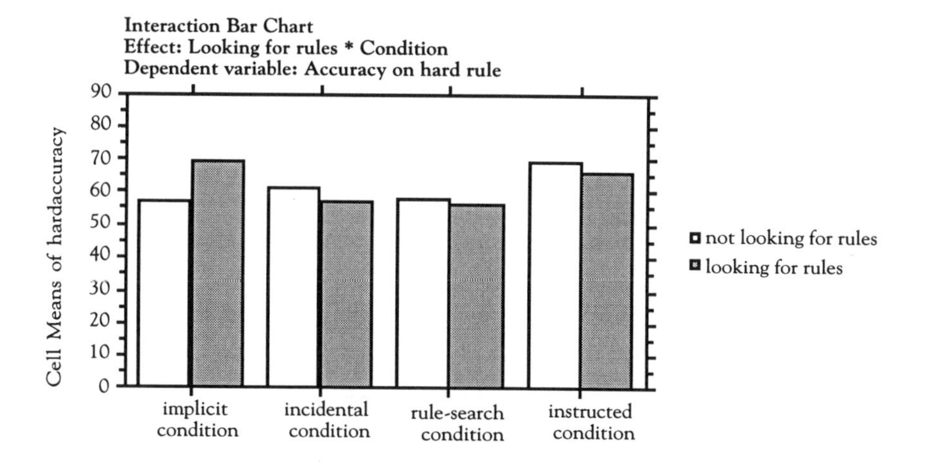

Figure 5: Accuracy on the easy rule and awareness at the level of looking for rules.

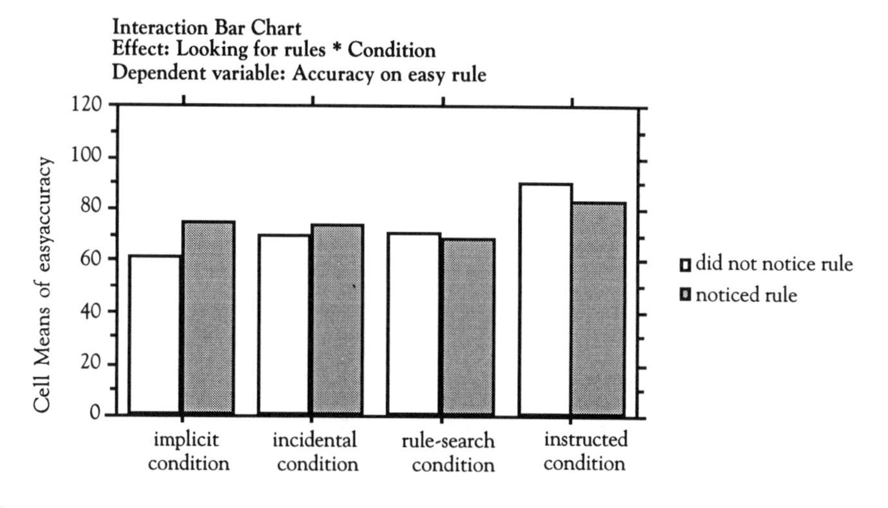

The ANOVA for accuracy of response on the hard rule sentences shows a significant main effect for the factor Able To Verbalize (F(1,96)=14.583, p=.0001). There is no significant main effect for Condition and no significant interaction of Able To Verbalize and

Condition. Similarly, there is a main effect for the factor Able To Verbalize on easy rule accuracy (F(1,96)=7.219, p=.008) There is a significant main effect for Condition (F(3,96)=4.499, p=.005), but no significant interaction of Able To Verbalize and Condition. Means and standard deviations of accuracy of participants in each condition on hard rule and easy rule sentences, divided by awareness at the level of able to verbalize, are given in Figures 6 and 7.

Figure 6: Accuracy on the hard rule and awareness at the level of ability to verbalize.

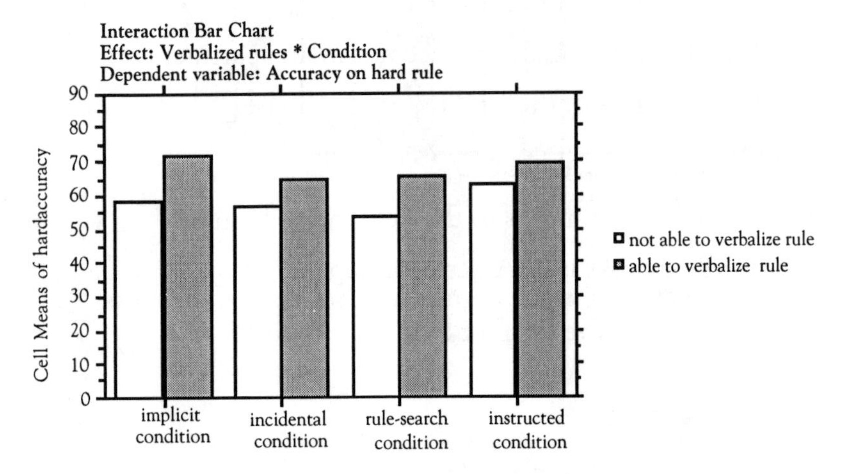

Figure 7: Accuracy on the easy rule and awareness at the level of ability to verbalize.

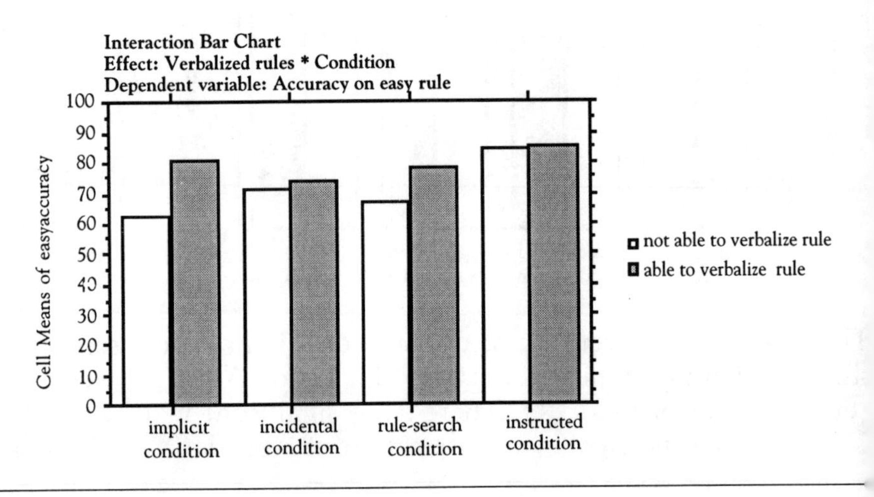

Planned a priori comparisons of performance by aware and unaware participants in each condition reveal significant differences in accuracy on the easy rule (p=. 005) and the hard rule (p=. 015) for participants in the implicit condition, and a significant difference in accuracy on the hard rule (p=.022) for participants trained in the rule-search condition. In each case, participants able to verbalize rules are more accurate than those who cannot.

SUMMARY OF THE RELATIONSHIP BETWEEN AWARENESS AND ACCURACY

The analyses presented above show no significant main effect for awareness at the level of noticing or of looking for rules on accuracy on either easy or hard rule sentences during the transfer task. However, there are significant main effects for awareness at the level of able to verbalize on both easy and hard rule accuracy. Planned comparisons showed significant differences in the accuracy of aware and unaware participants in the implicit condition at the levels of looking for rules and ability to verbalize. Awareness at these levels positively affected implicit learners accuracy on both easy and hard rules. Planned comparisons also revealed a significant difference in accuracy of performance on easy rules for those rule-search participants who were able to verbalize rules. Level of awareness did not affect accuracy of performance on either rule for incidental or instructed participants. These results are summarized in Table 3.

RQ5: Is aptitude positively related to the level of awareness developed during training in all conditions?

To address this question, scores on the Grammatical Sensitivity and Memory subtests were used as dependent variables for ANOVAs, with level of awareness during training and training condition as grouping factors. As in the previous analyses, a priori planned comparisons of scores on the aptitude subtests for aware and unaware participants in each condition were made.

Table 3: Summary of the planned comparisons of the accuracy of aware and unaware participants in each condition

	LEVEL OF AWARENESS		
Condition/Rule	Noticed rules	Looked for rules	Verbalized rules
Implicit			
easy	n.s.	p=.03	p=.01
hard	n.s.	p=.02	p=.005
Incidental			
easy	n.s.	n.s.	n.s.
hard	n.s.	n.s.	n.s.
Rule-search			
easy	n.s.	n.s.	n.s.
hard	n.s.	n.s.	p=.02
Instructed			
easy	n.s.	n.s.	n.s.
hard	n.s.	n.s.	n.s.

APTITUDE AND NOTICING

With respect to scores on the Grammatical Sensitivity subtest there is no significant main effect for the factor Noticing ($F(1,96)=2.542$, $p=.114$), though there is a significant main effect for Condition, ($F(3,96)=2.707$, $p=.049$) and a significant interaction of Noticing and Condition ($F(3,96)=4.242$, $p=.007$). A priori planned comparisons show that there are significant differences in the Grammatical Sensitivity of participants who claimed to have noticed rules only for those in the rule-search condition ($p=.002$), with those rule-search participants who claimed to have noticed rules having higher Grammatical Sensitivity scores than those who didn't. With respect to scores on the Memory subtest there is an almost significant main effect for Noticing (F(1,96)=3.595, p=.061), but no significant main effect for Condition, and no significant interaction of Condition and Noticing. Planned a priori comparisons show that only for participants trained in the instructed condition are there significant differences in the Memory scores of participants who noticed and participants who didn't (p=.017), with those participants who noticed rules having higher Memory scores than those who didn't.

Figure 8: Grammatical sensitivity scores for awareness at the level of noticing.

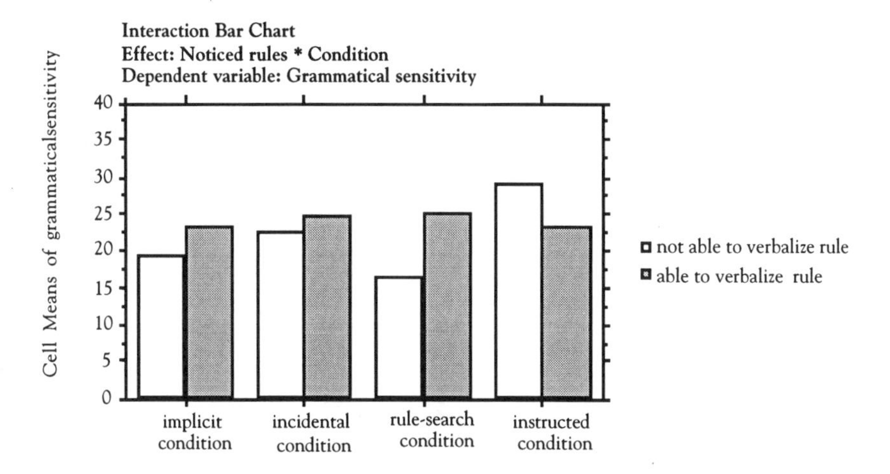

Figure 9: Memory scores for awareness at the level of noticing.

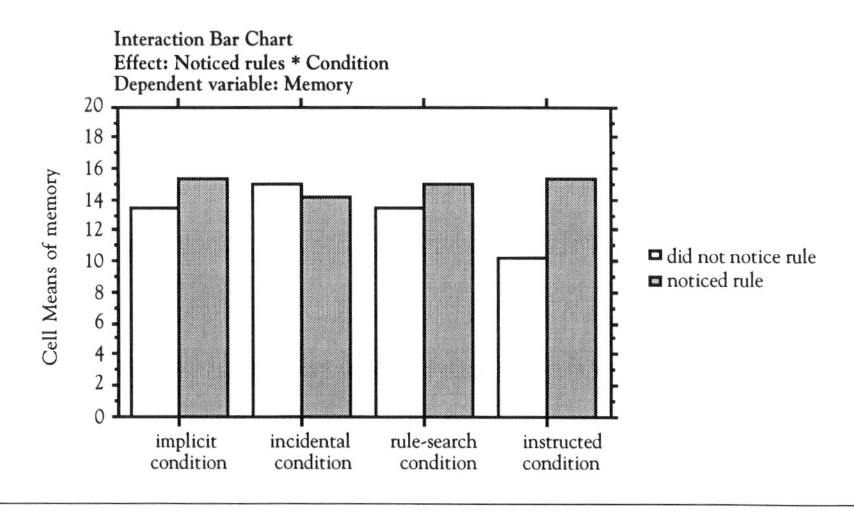

APTITUDE AND LOOKING FOR RULES

With respect to scores on both the Grammatical Sensitivity and Memory subtests there are no significant main effects for awareness at the level of Looking For Rules, and no main effects for Condition. Planned comparisons show a significant difference only for the Grammatical Sensitivity scores of aware and unaware participants at this level in the in the implicit condition (p=.016), with those participants who claimed to be looking for rules in this condition scoring higher on the test of Grammatical Sensitivity.

Figure 10: Grammatical sensitivity scores for awareness at the level of looking for rules.

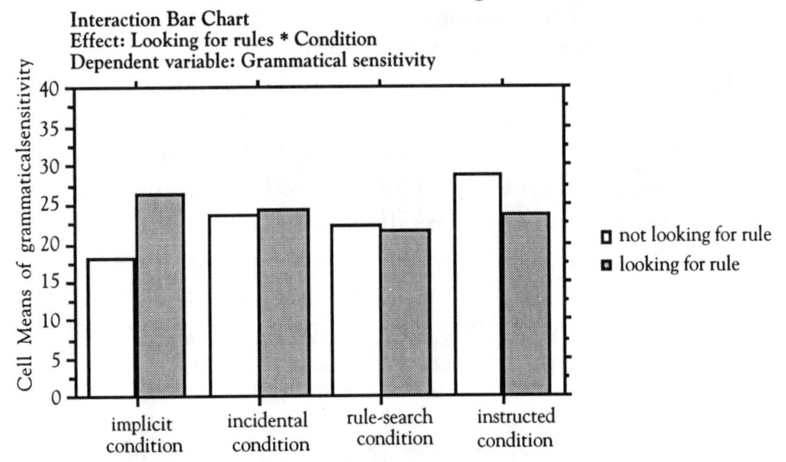

Figure 11: Memory scores for awareness at the level of looking for rules.

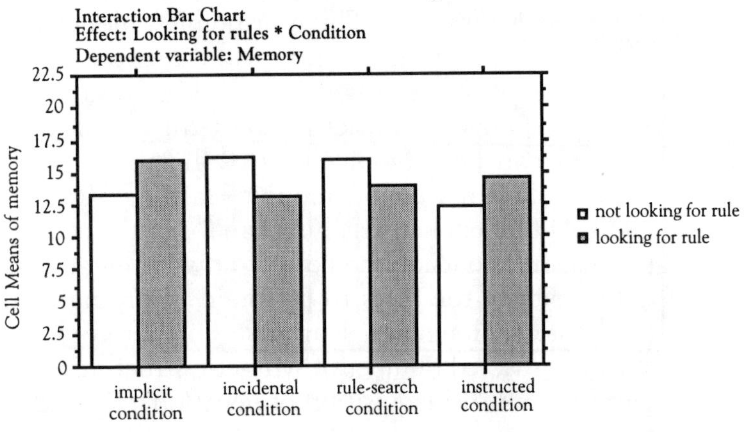

Finally, there are significant main effects for the factor Able To Verbalize with respect to Grammatical Sensitivity scores (F(1,96)=5.089, p=.02) and Memory scores (F(1,96)=4.198, p=.043) with no significant main effects for Condition. Planned comparisons show significant differences only for the Grammatical Sensitivity of aware and unaware participants at this level in the implicit condition, with higher Grammatical Sensitivity for those able to verbalize rules than for those who are not (p=.002) (see Figures 12 and 13).

Figure 12: Grammatical sensitivity for awareness at the level of ability to verbalize.

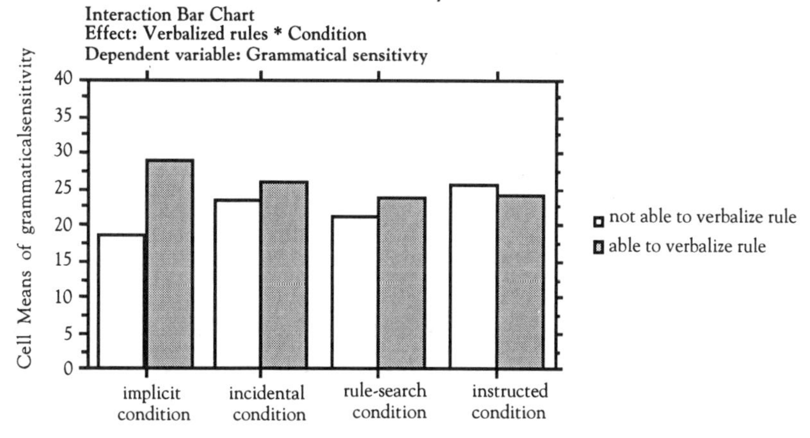

Figure 13: Memory scores for awareness at the level of ability to verbalize.

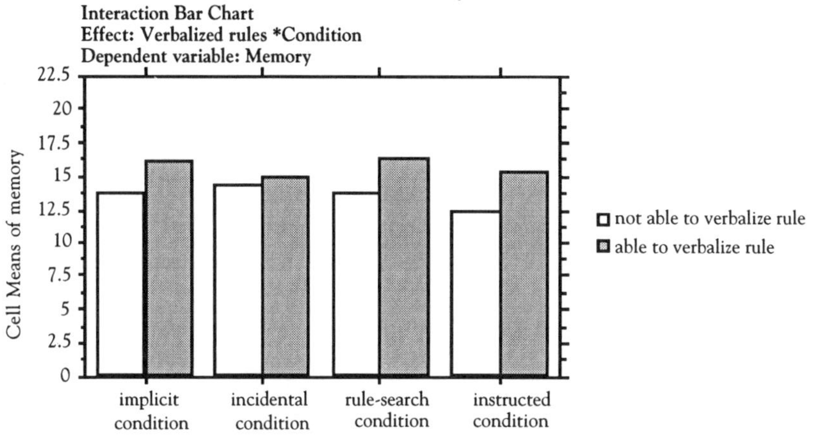

SUMMARY OF THE RELATIONSHIP BETWEEN APTITUDE AND AWARENESS

The analyses presented above show no significant differences in aptitude, as measured by the Grammatical Sensitivity and Memory subtests, for participants who claimed to have Noticed rules versus those who did not, or for participants who claimed to have been Looking For Rules versus those who did not. There was, however, a significant difference between aptitude scores as measured by both subtests for participants who were Able To Verbalize Rules versus those who were not. In all cases, with the exception of the Grammatical Sensitivity scores of instructed participants, this is a positive relationship, with participants in each condition who are able to verbalize having higher aptitude scores. Planned comparisons

Table 4: Summary of the planned comparisons of aptitude for aware and unaware participants in each condition

LEVEL OF AWARENESS			
Condition/Aptitude measure	Noticed rules	Looked for rules	Verbalized rules
Implicit			
Grammatical sensitivity subtest	n.s.	p=.007	p=.002
Memory subtest	n.s.	p=.02	p=.005
Incidental			
Grammatical sensitivity subtest	n.s.	n.s.	n.s.
Memory subtest	n.s.	n.s.	n.s.
Rule-search			
Grammatical sensitivity subtest	p=.002	n.s.	n.s.
Memory subtest	n.s.	n.s.	p=.02
Instructed			
Grammatical sensitivity subtest	n.s.	n.s.	n.s.
Memory subtest	p=.017	n.s.	n.s.

showed significant differences between the Grammatical Sensitivity scores of participants in the rule-search condition who claim to have noticed rules, and between the Memory scores of instructed participants who claimed to have noticed rules. There were significant differences in the Grammatical Sensitivity scores of aware and unaware participants in the implicit condition at the level of looking for rules and able to verbalize. These relationships are summarized in Table 4.

DISCUSSION

In the sections below evidence from this study is used to address each of the research questions posed in the introduction. These findings are then summarized in support of the claim that learning under each of the conditions operationalized in the present study is fundamentally similar, to the extent that it results from the transfer of those conscious processing strategies facilitated by training task demands, to the context of the transfer grammaticality judgment task.

CONSCIOUSNESS AND RULE COMPLEXITY

Reber's and Krashen's claims that nonconscious learning conditions produce superior learning when the stimulus domain is complex is not supported by this study. Training in the implicit and incidental conditions did not lead to superior learning of the complex rule relative to training in the conscious conditions. The instructed condition had a higher mean accuracy on the complex rule compared to performance by participants trained in other conditions, and instructed participants were significantly more accurate on this rule than rule-search participants. In addition, instructed participants were significantly more accurate in performance on easy rule sentences in the transfer test compared to participants trained in other conditions. These results, then, lend support to Schmidt's claim that consciousness at the level of rule awareness is facilitative of learning, at least with respect to simple rules, and run counter to the claim that complex rules are most effectively learned nonconsciously.

APTITUDE AND LEARNING

As Table 1 shows, there are significant positive correlations of Grammatical Sensitivity scores and performance on easy and hard rules for participants trained in the implicit condition. This is possibly to be expected for implicit participants' performance on easy rules, given Reber's argument that a complex stimulus domain is a prerequisite for the operation of implicit processes. However, significant positive correlations with the measure of Grammatical

Sensitivity are not predicted by Reber with respect to implicit learners' performance on complex rules. One interpretation of these results is that some participants in the implicit condition, given their extensive background in learning English, and the formal nature of their previous ESL instruction began to consciously analyze, search for and find the rules underlying the presented sentences. Interestingly, the component of aptitude that predicts accuracy of performance on both rules in this condition is Grammatical Sensitivity, not Memory. This is despite the fact that in the implicit condition task instructions predisposed participants to rely on memory, and despite the claims that knowledge that is gained during implicit conditions in Reber's experiments is the result of memory for co-occurring bigrams and trigrams (Perruchet and Pacteau, 1990; Vokey and Brooks, 1992). If such piecemeal knowledge had been resulting from exposure in the implicit condition and successfully guiding grammaticality judgments, then a stronger correlation with Memory scores would have been expected.

While the result for implicit learners runs counter to Reber's claims, the result for incidental learners supports Krashen's claim that acquisition processes, stimulated by a focus on meaning, are uninfluenced by individual differences assessed by aptitude tests. As Table 1 shows, there are no significant correlations of accuracy of performance on easy or hard rules with the scores obtained on the aptitude subtests. As predicted by Krashen, there are significant correlations of performance on easy and hard rules with both Grammatical Sensitivity and Memory scores for participants in the instructed condition. The results of aptitude/accuracy correlations for those in the rule-search condition are also in line with Reber's predictions. Grammatical Sensitivity scores correlate significantly with rule-search performance on the easy rule, suggesting that, as Reber has claimed, looking for rules will help if the rules are easy. Additionally, these data suggest that in the domain of second language learning, looking for rules that are easy will be effective if the learner is sufficiently sensitive to the grammatical regularities of the structures to be learned. There is also a significant correlation of accuracy on hard rules with Memory scores, suggesting that where the stimulus domain is complex then memory-based processing strategies are most effectively deployed during rule-search.

LEARNING CONDITION AND AWARENESS

The present study classified participants as aware or unaware at the levels of noticing rules, looking for rules and ability to verbalize rules. The results of the analyses presented in Table 2, show evidence of widescale awareness at each of these levels during training under all conditions.

Schmidt (1990, 1993) has argued that noticing the form of input, i.e., attentional allocation leading to detection and rehearsal in short-term memory (Robinson, 1995), is a necessary stage in second language learning. Of course, consciousness at the level of noticing is not *sufficient* for learning to occur, and what is noticed may be rehearsed in short-term memory only temporarily, then subsequently lost. In addition, with regard to the measure of noticing obtained here, it is not clear from participants' responses to this question whether the rules they noticed were those that the training sessions were intended to present. It seems likely, in fact, that participants claiming to have noticed rules may have noticed the occurrence of morphemes and structures in the sentences regulated by sub-rules or rules other than the target of instruction. As the results presented in Table 2 above show, large numbers of participants in all conditions did claim that they had noticed rules during training. However, the analysis of the relationship of noticing to learning shows it is not significant for participants in any condition. Participants who claimed to have noticed rules learned no more than those who did not.

Of the three measures of awareness only the level of looking for rules distinguishes participants in all three conditions. Despite this, there are still large numbers of participants in the implicit and incidental conditions who report that they were looking for rules, casting doubt on the claim that learning under these conditions proceeds nonconsciously. Many of those reporting that they were looking for rules in the instructed condition probably interpreted the question to mean applying the rules they had been taught to sentences during training. It is unclear why six participants in the rule-search condition did not report that they were looking for rules. Of course this could have meant that they gave up after a certain point due to lack of success or fatigue, or due to the fact that they thought they had successfully found the rules and no longer needed to look.

The third measure of awareness used, the ability to verbalize rules, was interpreted liberally to mean the ability to produce a relevant structural comment or description of component parts of the rules. Although the result of the chi-square of the data reported in Table 2 shows no significant differences between the conditions on this measure of awareness, twice as many instructed participants were able to verbalize rules. This is not surprising, given the fact that these participants were taught the rules during training. Nonetheless a large number of instructed participants did not attempt to verbalize the rules they had been taught, either due to poor memory for them, or to fatigue. Following Schmidt's claim that consciousness at the level of rule awareness is strongly facilitative of later learning, one would expect that the ability to verbalize rules would be more strongly predictive of success in learning in all conditions than the report that rules had been noticed or looked for. As Figures 6 and 7 show, this is so, but only for participants in the implicit and rule search conditions. Given the fact that instructed learners had been made aware of rules during training, it is perhaps not surprising that measures of awareness obtained using the questionnaire do not predict success in learning, since awareness was experimentally induced. The ability to apply the knowledge of which they were aware was likely more critical for instructed learners.

AWARENESS AND SUCCESS IN LEARNING

As the results summarized in Table 3 show, different levels of awareness are related to success in learning easy and hard rules for participants trained in implicit and rule-search conditions, though there is no relationship between awareness and learning for participants trained in incidental and instructed conditions and no difference in the learning performance of aware and unaware participants in any condition at the level of noticing. Awareness at the level of looking for rules, however, is positively related to learning for participants in the implicit condition (see Figures 4 and 5). Possibly this is due to the fact that participants in this condition, with high Grammatical Sensitivity, actively searched for and found rules despite the task instructions. The results reported in Figure 10 support this interpretation, since participants who were looking for rules in this condition had higher Grammatical Sensitivity scores than those who weren't. Looking for rules, however, did not contribute to successful learning for participants in the rule-search condition, who had all been told to search for rules, or for participants in the instructed condition who had been taught the rules. In fact, as Figures 7 and 8 show, those participants in the instructed condition who reported themselves to have been looking for rules performed worse than those who did not, possibly due to the fact that these participants had difficulty remembering the rules they had been taught. Awareness at the highest level of ability to verbalize rules also relates positively to the learning performance of participants in the implicit condition (see Figures 6 and 7), again supporting the interpretation that some participants in this condition became aware of, searched for and found rules consciously, despite the task instructions simply to remember the presented sentences. Ability to verbalize rules also relates positively to the learning performance of rule-search participants on easy rules, but not hard rules, confirming that task instructions to look for rules are more likely to lead to effective conscious learning only where the stimulus domain is simple, as is claimed by Reber. Once again, all participants in the instructed condition had been taught the rules, and therefore verbalizing rules fails to distinguish more from less successful learners in this condition. Success in this condition is likely to be related to a complex of abilities drawn on in applying the rules successfully, rather than the ability to remember them alone. As Figure 7 shows, there is no mean difference in the learning performance of instructed learners who verbalized and did not verbalize the easy rule, suggesting that those who did not describe it in answering the questionnaire had remembered and applied it as successfully as those who did. However, as Figure 6 shows, this is not true of performance on the hard rule for instructed learners who did not verbalize the rule, suggesting this rule was indeed harder to maintain and apply during training.

Finally, two comments should be made on the comparability of learning in the implicit and incidental conditions with respect to the awareness data. First, implicit and incidental learners differ in thi respect: implicit learners are positively affected by increases in awareness and aptitude, whereas incidental learners are not. Second, i Krashen's and Reber's claims about the negative influence o conscious learning processes are correct, then aware participants in the implicit and incidental conditions should have performed poorl in learning complex rules relative to learners who were not aware. This was not so. As the summary of results for the relationship between awareness and learning shows (see Table 3) awareness at the levels of looking for rules and ability to verbalize rules positively affected performance by implicit learners on easy and hard rules alike (see Figures 4, 5, 6 and 7) and did not negatively affect performance on hard rules for incidental learners (see Figures 4 and 6). Awareness at the level of noticing did not negatively affect performance on hard rules for participants in either condition (see Figure 2). In summary, the positive effects of awareness on learning for implicit learners, and the lack of negative effects of awareness on learning hard rules for implicit and incidental learners are both findings that cast doubt on Reber's and Krashen's claims about the superiority of nonconscious learning processes in complex stimulus domains.

APTITUDE AND AWARENESS

The results of this study support the claim that awareness is triggered by different components of aptitude in the implicit, rule-search and instructed conditions. There is no evidence that aptitude negatively affects the extent of awareness in any condition. The positive relationship between aptitude and awareness differs across conditions, suggesting that different conditions predispose participants to draw differentially on memory and grammatical sensitivity. Memory is positively related to awareness at the level of noticing for instructed participants (see Figure 9), while Grammatical Sensitivity is positively related to noticing for participants in the rule-search condition (see Figure 8). This is to be expected given the nature of the task demands in each of these conditions. Instructed participants are led to notice rules in the training set sentences as a consequence of applying the rules they had been learned. It is likely, therefore, that for instructed learners differences in the ability to remember these rules would contribute to the extent of awareness. For participants in the rule-search condition, on the other hand, Grammatical Sensitivity is positively related to the extent to which rules are noticed, since these participants have to search for and identify underlying grammatical regularities, rather than simply remember previously taught rules. Grammatical Sensitivity also positively affects awareness at the level of looking for rules (see Figure 10), and ability to verbalize rules (see

Figure 12) for implicit learners, suggesting that the variety of conscious awareness facilitated by this task condition is not memory-based, but rather is based on more analytic capacities. Once again, as with the results reported above for the relationship between aptitude and learning (see Table 1), participants in the incidental condition differ from those in other conditions to the extent that aptitude differences do not predict differences in awareness at any of the three levels examined in the present study.

SUMMARY AND CONCLUSION

The results of the present study support the interpretation that learning in each condition was fundamentally similar to the extent that it occurred as a consequence of the variety of conscious processing induced by the nature of the particular task demands imposed during training. To this extent, task demands also determined the role individual differences in memory and grammatical sensitivity played in learning under different conditions. A broad summary of the aptitude, awareness and learning condition interactions revealed in this study would be that the tasks presented to learners in the implicit, incidental, rule-search and instructed conditions differed in the demands they made on learner resources like memory and grammatical sensitivity, and that where the demands of the task performed in any condition were matched by an individual learner's strength in those resources, then aptitude often led to awareness, which often was associated with superior levels of learning. This interpretation is oppositional to the claim that learning under implicit versus rule-search, or incidental versus instructed conditions reflect the processing operations of distinct nonconsciously and consciously accessed systems. A similar transfer appropriate processing interpretation of the results of implicit learning and memory studies has been made elsewhere (Blaxton, 1989; Graf and Ryan, 1990; Hamann, 1990; Roediger, Challis and Weldon, 1989; Whittlesea and Dorken, 1993), and is favored here for two reasons.

First, the present study provides no evidence that learning in the implicit and incidental conditions is superior to instructed or rule-search learning on the hard rule, as predicted by Reber and Krashen. Second, the questionnaire data provide no support for the claim that the learning that does occur following training in the implicit and incidental conditions is the result of nonconscious processes. Large numbers of participants in all conditions claimed to have noticed rules during training. What was noticed is likely to have differed across conditions as a consequence of differences in task demands, which directed attention at different aspects of the stimulus sentences during training. While awareness at the level of noticing did not lead to successful learning for participants in any condition, awareness at the level of looking for rules and ability to verbalize rules predicted superior learning of both rules for participants in the implicit condition. Successful learning in this condition was therefore facilitated by conscious awareness. Successful learning of easy rules was also associated with awareness at the level of verbalizability for rule-search learners, though successful learning of hard rules was not, suggesting, as Reber has claimed, that rule-search is likely to be a less successful strategy where the stimulus domain is complex.

An interesting question is why task instructions to search for rules did not facilitate performance on the hard rule for participants in the rule-search condition, when the self-reported act of searching for rules by participants in the implicit condition *did* facilitate learning of the hard rule. One possible answer to this is that a small number of participants with high aptitude in the implicit condition became aware of the rule-governed nature of the sentences during training and began to actively search for rules. This would account for the high correlations of Grammatical Sensitivity and learning reported for implicit learners. Given their high aptitude, this small group of participants would be more likely to find the rules they were searching for than the larger group of rule-search learners, with lower average Grammatical Sensitivity scores.

While the success of participants in the implicit condition is likely to be attributable to individual differences in aptitude which trigger a switch to conscious rule search, successful learning in the incidental condition shows no significant correlation with the measures of aptitude taken, and successful learning for this group alone is independent of the levels of awareness reported. This appears to support Krashen's claims for the aptitude independence of acquisition processes facilitated by the nature of the meaning-based processing encouraged in this condition. However, large numbers of participants did claim to have noticed and looked for rules in this condition, so conscious processes were clearly implicated in whatever incidental learning occurred. The fact that awareness did not lead to superior incidental learning is probably a consequence of the fact that such awareness was of semantic and lexical aspects of the sentences, and this was therefore ineffective in directing attention to the salient structural properties of the stimulus sentences that led to successful learning for participants in other conditions.

The conclusions regarding the interaction of aptitude, awareness and learning drawn above can only be provisional, given the lack of findings from comparable studies to support them and the nature of the conditions operationalized in this study. It is possible, for example, that the advantages identified for instructed learners over all others on easy rules are only short-lived and that learning resulting from exposure in other conditions, though far less extensive, is more permanent. Studies of the durability of the learning that occurred under the conditions operationalized in the present study are needed to address this issue. It is also possible that increasing the amount of exposure to sentences by extending the period of training would have led to stronger evidence of learning in the incidental condition, particularly given N. Ellis' characterization of the results of implicit learning in his own recent experimental study as "laboriously slow" (1993: 309) and Krashen's claim that acquisition is a gradual process requiring massive exposure to comprehensible input. Similarly, providing richer semantic contexts for the sentences may have aided incidental learners by encouraging greater engagement with the meaning, and greater depth of processing. More challenging questions than the simple yes/no questions posed to incidental learners in this study may also have had the same effect (cf. Prabhu's argument that second language tasks must pose a reasonable challenge if they are to facilitate incidental learning [Prabhu, 1987: 56] and Hulstijn's claim that problematicity of meaning is needed to elicit the level of learner attention necessary for incidental learning to occur [Hulstijn, 1990: 50]). These modifications to learning conditions, however, will also need to be accompanied by a the use of a variety of measures of relevant individual differences in cognitive abilities, such as those measures of aptitude and working memory used by Sasaki (1993) and Geva and Ryan (1993), as well as by sensitive measures of the extent of conscious awareness during learning, if the full complexity of the interaction between aptitude, awareness and second language learning is to be revealed by future experimental studies. The present study has suggested that such complexity can be expected, and that second language learning processes unmediated by awareness and insensitive to aptitude differences may be too simple to be true.

REFERENCES

Anderson, J. (1983). *The architecture of cognition*. Cambridge, MA: Harvard University Press.

Bialystok, E. (1979). Explicit and implicit judgments of L2 grammaticality. *Language Learning*, *29*, 81–103.

Bialystok, E. (1981). The role of linguistic knowledge in second language use. *Studies in Second Language Acquisition*, *4*, 31–45.

Blaxton, T. A. (1989). Investigating dissociations among memory measures: Support for a transfer appropriate processing framework. *Journal of Experimental Psychology: Learning, Memory and Cognition*, *15*, 657–688.

Brody, N. (1989). Unconscious learning of rules: Comment on Reber's analysis of implicit learning. *Journal of Experimental Psychology: General*, *118*, 236–238.

Carr, T., & Curran, T. (1994). Cognitive factors in learning about structured sequences. *Studies in Second Language Acquisition*, *16*, 205–223.

Carroll, J. B. (1993). *Human cognitive abilities: A survey of factor-analytic studies*. New York: Cambridge University Press.

Carroll, J. B., & Sapon, S. M. (1959). *The modern language aptitude test*. New York: The Psychological Corporation.

Chomsky, N. (1986). *Knowledge of language: Its nature, origin and use*. New York: Praeger.

de Graaff, R. (1995). Implicit and explicit learning of artificial language. Unpublished manuscript, Free University, Amsterdam.

DeKeyser, R. (1994). Implicit and explicit learning of L2 grammar: A pilot study. *TESOL Quarterly*, *28*, 188–194.

Doughty, C. (1991). Second language instruction does make a difference: Evidence from an empirical study of SL relativization. *Studies in Second Language Acquisition*, *13*, 431–470.

Dulany, D., Carlson, R., & Dewey, G. (1985). On consciousness in syntactic learning and judgment: A reply to Reber, Allen and Regan. *Journal of Experimental Psychology: General*, *114*, 25–32.

Ellis, N. (1993). Rules and instances in foreign language learning: Interactions of explicit and implicit knowledge. *European Journal of Cognitive Psychology*, 5, 289–318.

Ellis, R. (1990). *Instructed second language development*. Oxford: Blackwell.

Ellis, R. (1993). The structural syllabus and second language acquisition. TESOL *Quarterly*, *27*, 91–113.

Geva, E., & Ryan, E. B. (1993). Linguistic and cognitive correlates of academic skills in first and second languages. *Language Learning*, *43*, 5–42

Gluck, M., & Granger, R. (1993). Computational models of the neural bases of learning and memory. *Annual Review of Neuroscience*, 16, 667–706.

Graf, P., & Ryan, L. (1990). Transfer-appropriate processing for implicit and explicit memory. *Journal of Experimental Psychology: Learning, Memory and Cognition*, 16, 978–992.

Green, R. E. A., & Shanks, D. R. (1993). On the existence of independent explicit and implicit systems: An examination of some evidence. *Memory and Cognition*, *21*, 304–317.

Gregg, K. (1984). Krashen's Monitor and Occam's razor. *Applied Linguistics*, 5, 79–100.

Hamann, S. B. (1990). Levels-of-processing effects in conceptually driven implicit tasks. *Journal of Experimental Psychology: Learning, Memory and Cognition*, 16, 970–977.

Hayes, N., & Broadbent, D. (1988). Two modes of learning for interactive tasks. *Cognition*, *28*, 249–276.

Hulstijn, J. (1990). Implicit and incidental second language learning: Experiments in the processing of natural and partly artificial input. In H. W. Deceit & M. Raupach (Eds.), *Interlingual processing*, (pp. 50–73). Tubingen: Gunter Narr.

Hulstijn, J., & de Graaff, R. (1994). Under what conditions does explicit knowledge facilitate the acquisition of implicit knowledge? A research proposal. *AILA Review*, *11*, 97–112.

Krashen, S. (1981). *Second language acquisition and second language learning*. Oxford: Oxford University Press.

Krashen, S. (1982). *Principles and practice in second language learning*. Oxford, New York: Pergamon.

Krashen, S. (1985). *The input hypothesis: Issues and implications*. Oxford, New York: Pergamon.

Krashen, S. (1992). Formal grammar instruction: Another educator comments. *TESOL Quarterly*, *26*, 409–411.

Lewicki, P. (1985). Nonconscious biasing effects of single instances on subsequent judgments. *Journal of Personality and Social Psychology*, *48*, 563–574.

Lewicki, P., Hill, T., & Bizot, E. (1988). Acquisition of procedural skill about a pattern of stimuli that cannot be articulated. *Cognitive Psychology*, *20*, 24–37.

McLaughlin, B. (1978). The Monitor Model: Some methodological considerations. *Language Learning*, *28*, 309–332.

McLaughlin, B. (1980). On the use of miniature artificial languages in second language research. *Applied Psycholinguistics*, *1*, 357–369.

Nissen, M. J., Knopman, D. S., & Schacter, D. (1987). Neurochemical dissociation of memory systems. *Neurology*, *37*, 789–794.

Meike, B. (1988). *MindLab 2.1*. Dartmouth College: Software Development Department.

Odlin, T. (1986). On the nature and use of explicit knowledge. *IRAL*, *24*, 123–144.

Perruchet, P., & Amorim, M.A. (1992). Conscious knowledge and changes in performance in sequence learning: Evidence against dissociation. *Journal of Experimental Psychology: Learning, Memory and Cognition*, *18*, 785–800.

Perruchet, P., & Pacteau, C. (1990). Synthetic grammar learning: Implicit rule abstraction or fragmentary knowledge? *Journal of Experimental Psychology: General*, *119*, 264–275.

Prabhu, N.S. (1987). *Second language pedagogy*. Oxford: Oxford University Press.

Reber, A. S. (1989). Implicit learning and tacit knowledge. *Journal of Experimental Psychology: General*, *118*, 219–235.

Reber, A. S. (1990). On the primacy of the implicit: Comment on Perruchet and Pacteau. *Journal of Experimental Psychology: General*, *119*, 340–342.

Reber, A. S. (1993). *Implicit learning and tacit knowledge*. Oxford: Clarendon Press.

Reber, A. S., Walkenfield, F. F. , & Hernstadt, R. (1991). Implicit and explicit learning: Individual differences and IQ. *Journal of Experimental Psychology: Learning, Memory and Cognition, 17*, 888–896.

Richardson-Klavehn, A., & Bjork, R. (1988). Measures of memory. *Annual Review of Psychology, 39*, 475–543.

Robinson, P. (1993). Problems of knowledge and the implicit/explicit distinction in SLA theory. *University of Hawai'i Working Papers in ESL, 12*, 90–138.

Robinson, P. (1994a). Implicit knowledge, second language learning and syllabus construction. *TESOL Quarterly, 28*, 160–166.

Robinson, P. (1994b). Learning simple and complex second language rules under implicit, incidental, rule-search and instructed conditions. Unpublished Ph.D. dissertation, University of Hawai'i at Mānoa.

Robinson, P. (1995). Attention, memory and the 'noticing' hypothesis. *Language Learning, 45*,

Robinson, P., & Ha, M. (1993). Instance theory and second language rule learning under explicit conditions. *Studies in Second Language Acquisition, 15*, 413–438.

Roediger, H. L., Weldon, M. S., & Challis, B. H. (1989). Explaining dissociations between implicit and explicit measures of retention: A processing account. In H. L. Roediger, & F. I. Craik (Eds.), *Varieties of memory and consciousness*, (pp. 3–41). Hillsdale, NJ: Lawrence Erlbaum.

Sasaki, M. (1993). Relationships among second language proficiency, foreign language aptitude and intelligence: A structural equation modeling approach. *Language Learning, 43*, 313–344.

Schacter, D. L. (1987). Implicit memory: History and current status. *Journal of Experimental Psychology: Learning, Memory and Cognition, 13*, 501–518.

Schmidt, R. (1990). The role of consciousness in second language learning. *Applied Linguistics, 11*, 129–158.

Schmidt, R. (1993). Awareness and second language acquisition. *Annual Review of Applied Linguistics (1993), 13*, 206–226.

Schmidt, R. (1994). Implicit learning and the cognitive unconscious: Of artificial grammars and SLA. In N. Ellis (Ed.), *Implicit and explicit learning of languages*, (pp. 165–209). London: Academic Press.

Schmidt, R., & Frota, S. (1986). Developing basic conversational ability in a second language: A case study of an adult learner of Portuguese. In R. Day (Ed.), *Talking to learn: Conversation in second language learning* (pp. 237–326). Rowley, Mass: Newbury House.

Schwartz, B. D. (1986). The epistemological status of second language acquisition. *Second Language Research, 2*, 120–159.

Schwartz, B. D. (1993). On explicit and negative data effecting and affecting competence and linguistic behavior. *Studies in Second Language Acquisition, 15*, 147–163.

Shanks, D. R. , & St. John, M. F. (1994). Characteristics of dissociable human systems. *Behavioral and Brain Sciences, 17*, 367–447.

Squire, L. (1992). Declarative and non declarative memory: Multiple brain systems supporting learning and memory. *Journal of Cognitive Neuroscience, 4*, 232–243.

Squire, L., & Cohen, N. (1984). Human memory and amnesia. In J. McGaugh, G. Lynch, & N. Weinberger (Eds.), *Proceedings of the conference on the neurobiology of learning and memory* (pp. 3–64). New York: Guildford Press.

Squire, L., & Zola-Morgan, S. (1991). The medial temporal lobe memory system. *Science, 253*, 1380–1386.

Stansfield, C. (Ed.) (1990). *Language aptitude reconsidered.* Washington: Center for Applied Linguistics.

Thompson, R. F. (1986). The neurobiology of learning and memory. *Science 233*, 941–947.

Tomlin, R., & Villa, V. (1994). Attention in cognitive science and SLA. *Studies in Second Language Acquisition, 16*, 183–204.

Vokey, J., & Brooks, L. (1992). Salience of item knowledge in learning artificial grammars. *Journal of Experimental Psychology: Learning, Memory and Cognition, 18*, 328–344.

White, L. (1989). *Universal grammar and L2 acquisition.* Amsterdam John Benjamins.

Whittlesea, B. W. A., & Dorken, M. D. (1993). Incidentally, things in general are particularly determined: An episodic-processing account of implicit learning. *Journal of Experimental Psychology, General, 122*, 227–248.

Willingham, D. B., Nissen, M. J., & Bullemer, P. (1989). On the development of procedural knowledge. *Journal of Experimental Psychology: Learning, Memory and Cognition, 15*, 1047–1060.

Zobl, H. (1992). Sources of linguistic knowledge and uniformity of nonnative performance. *Studies in Second Language Acquisition, 14*, 387–403.

APPENDIX A: THE EASY AND HARD PEDAGOGIC RULE FORMATS

THE EASY RULE

Some sentences contain a subject, a verb, and a location phrase or a time phrase. Here are some examples:

Joan (subject) *crashed* (verb) *into the wall.* (location phrase)

John (subject) *slept* (verb) *in the morning.* (time phrase)

Location and time phrases can be moved to the front of the sentence:

Into the wall Joan crashed.

On Tuesday morning John slept.

The verb can also come before the subject, but only when location phrases are at the front of the sentence.

Into the wall (location phrase) *crashed* (verb) *Joan.* (subject)

* *On Tuesday morning* (time phrase) *slept* (verb) *John.*

The * means this sentence is ungrammatical.

THE HARD RULE

Some sentences tell about the locations of two things, e.g.,

Alice stands on the right and Judy stands on the left.

We can change this sentence to focus on one of the locations, e.g.,

Where Alice stands is on the right.

To make sentences like these, first, choose the subject whose location you want to emphasize, 'Alice', then place 'where' in front of it.

Where Alice

Next, follow the subject with the verb, 'stands'.

Where Alice (subject) *stands* (verb)

Note that the verb cannot come before the subject:

* *Where stands* (verb) *Alice* (subject)

The * means this sentence is ungrammatical.

Next add a singular form of the verb 'be' which agrees in tense followed by the phrase describing the location of the subject:

Where Alice stands is on the right.

Where Alice stood was on the right.

If the verb does not agree in tense, the sentence is ungrammatical:

* *Where Alice stands was on the right.*

The second location can also be contrasted with the focus location by joining them using 'not'. This 'not' is required. Without it the sentence is ungrammatical.

Where Alice stands is on the right not on the left.

* *Where Alice stands is on the right the left.*

APPENDIX B: THE TRAINING SET SENTENCES BASED ON THE EASY AND HARD PEDAGOGIC RULE FORMATS

EASY RULE SENTENCES

Easy grammatical type 1

Paul drove across the city.

Mary sank under the sea.

Jill walked over the bridge.

John ran into the house.

Easy grammatical type 2

Up the road came Eric.

Off the horse fell Amy.

Down the hill slid Jack.

Onto the boat jumped Sue.

Easy grammatical type 3

Round the track Bill raced.

Through the forest Jane went.

Past the river Helen rode.

Out of the shop Jim rushed.

Easy grammatical type 4

Lori ate at five o'clock.

Ron left on Thursday night.

Roland returned at midnight.

Peggy slept on Tuesday morning.

Easy grammatical type 5

In the afternoon Elaine arrived.

At the weekend Randy exercised.

On Christmas day Lily phoned.

In the morning Claire jogged.

HARD RULE SENTENCES

Hard grammatical type 1

The girl plays in the park and the boy plays in the yard.

The letter is in the bag and the book is on the chair.

John works in the shop and Mary works in the hospital.

The milk is in the glass and the coffee is in the jar.

Hard grammatical type 2

Where Helen is is in New York.

Where the phone is is in the bedroom.

Where Sue is is in the car not in the boat.

Where the cheese is is on the plate not in the basket.

Hard grammatical type 3

Where the children are is on the beach.

Where Eric and Jill are is at home.

Where Jim and Amy are is in the kitchen not in the garden.

Where the people are is in the park not in the church.

Hard grammatical type 4

Where the cat sleeps is on the floor.

Where Bill eats is at the table.

Where the President lives is in Washington not in Boston.

Where Jane sits is on the sofa not on the stool.

Hard grammatical type 5

Where the birds nest is in the tree.

Where Paul and Jack surf is at Waikiki.

Where Steve and Mark swim is in the pool not in the ocean.

Where the students meet is in the library not in the restaurant.

APPENDIX C: THE TRANSFER SET SENTENCES

EASY RULE SENTENCES

Easy grammatical type 1

Craig walked into the room.

Lisa fell onto the grass.

Easy grammatical type 2

Across the street raced Tom.

Out of the door ran Kate.

Easy grammatical type 3

Through the window Maria stared.

Over the town Lucy flew.

Easy grammatical type 4

Peter woke at eight o'clock.

Wendy started on Monday morning.

Easy grammatical type 5

On her birthday Gabi sang.

In the evening Dick studied.

Easy ungrammatical type 1

On Saturday night danced Charley.

At nine thirty left Robert.

In the afternoon spoke Ian.

On Sunday painted Graham.

At night ate Judy.

Easy ungrammatical type 2

Golfed Debbie in the morning.

Died Stan on Friday night.

Departed Fred at nine thirty.

Crawled Mick through the tunnel.

Slipped Maggy off the roof.

HARD RULE SENTENCES

Hard grammatical type 1

The pen is in the box and the pencil is in the drawer.

Lisa reads in the bedroom and Mick reads in the study.

Hard grammatical type 2

Where L.A. is is in California.

Where the car is is in the driveway not in the road.

Hard grammatical type 3

Where the apples are is in the bowl.

Where Ann and Ian are is at the movies not at the zoo.

Hard grammatical type 4

Where Judy teaches is at the university.

Where Peter waits is by the stairs not in the cafe.

Hard grammatical type 5

Where my parents vacation is in Europe.

Where Maria and Joe relax is by the pool not on the beach.

Hard ungrammatical type 1

Where is Bill is in the country not in the city.

Where cooks Jim is in the kitchen not in the bathroom.

Hard ungrammatical type 2

Where Carl writes are at a desk not on the floor.

Where the soldiers fight are in Europe not in Hawaii.

Hard ungrammatical type 3

Where the bird is was in the sky not in the sea.

Where the plane lands was in the airport not at the dock.

Hard ungrammatical type 4

What the King lives is in a palace not in an apartment.

What the dog is is in the yard not in the house.

Hard ungrammatical type 5

Where the horse stands is in the field in the barn.

Where Mark works is in America in Japan.

Jan H. Hulstijn
Free University Amsterdam

NOT ALL GRAMMAR RULES ARE EQUAL: GIVING GRAMMAR INSTRUCTION ITS PROPER PLACE IN FOREIGN LANGUAGE TEACHING

ABSTRACT

This chapter is based on the so-called "weak interface" assumption, according to which explicit instruction of grammatical regularities facilitates the acquisition of a foreign or second language. The issue of grammar teaching should, however, not be approached in an all-or-none fashion. Explicit teaching and practising makes more sense with some rules than with others. The main aim of this chapter is to sensitize foreign language teachers and course designers to the differential nature of grammar rules and to provide them with some criteria with which they can weigh their relative priority. The criteria are illustrated with examples from four non-agglutinative Indo-European languages: Spanish, French, German and English.

INTRODUCTION

Bethania is a 28-year-old Portuguese woman who has been living in the Netherlands for more than two and a half years. She participates in a study on the acquisition of Dutch as a second language (Hulstijn, 1982). "In the beginning," she says, "I felt shy, but now I feel confident enough to talk to people in Dutch and I learn a lot from such conversations." In a language test eliciting the oral production of various sentence structures, she produces correct structures of subject-verb inversion in main clauses and verb-final constructions in embedded clauses. After the test, the researcher has an interview with

Hulstijn, Jan H. (1995). Not all grammar rules are equal: Giving grammar instruction its proper place in foreign language teaching. In Richard Schmidt (Ed.), *Attention and awareness in foreign language learning* (Technical Report #9) (pp. 359–386). Honolulu, Hawai'i: University of Hawai'i, Second Language Teaching & Curriculum Center.

her in order to assess whether she has any explicit, verbalizable, knowledge of these two word order rules. She does not know them; she can not formulate them; and when the researcher finally formulates them for her, she does not show any sign of recognition.

Isabelle also participates in the study. This 24-year-old woman from Spain has lived in the Netherlands for three years. In the oral production test, she often (but not always) forgets to produce the subject-verb inversion in main clauses and incorrectly uses main clause word order in embedded clauses. Afterwards, in the interview, it becomes clear that she knows both rules. She can formulate them explicitly. "But," she says, "when I speak I don't think of the rules."

All over the world, in virtually every foreign language course for adult learners, whatever the language being taught, there are learners like Bethania and Isabelle. Some learners don't know the explicit rules, but apply them correctly; others do know the rules, but that does not seem to prevent them from making grammatical errors. One may well ask then whether grammar teaching should be abandoned altogether. Some experts in foreign language pedagogy did and do indeed take this standpoint. The *direct method*, introduced at the end of the nineteenth century, the behaviouristic *audiolingual method*, most influential during the sixties of the twentieth century, and the *natural approach* of the early eighties (Krashen, 1982, 1992, 1993) all play down the role of explicit grammar teaching, albeit for partly different reasons (for a well-balanced historical overview see Stern, 1992, chapter 12). Adherents of these methods claim that the development of competence in a foreign language has its own course, and that it can hardly be affected by grammar teaching. Although learners often do ask for rules, rules will not help them a great deal. Rules only offer a pseudo grip on the matter, creating a false stronghold. This position has come to be known as the "non-interface position" (see Hulstijn and de Graaff, 1994, for a theoretical account of the non-interface, strong interface, and weak interface positions).

Most foreign-language teachers, on the other hand, especially those who teach a language which is not their mother tongue, strongly believe in the usefulness of grammar teaching, indeed in its necessity. This belief may have been created during their school years, if they learned foreign languages according to the *grammar-translation* method. Also this belief may have been created or reinforced during their studies at a teacher training college. Memorization of foreign-language grammar rules, foreign-language grammar exercises, and various other tasks requiring the application of explicit grammar rules often form an important part of that study. Consequently, many teachers spend much class time on grammar, often at the detriment of practising listening, reading, speaking and writing skills and without critically asking themselves what the return may be of explicitly teaching and practising even the most detailed of grammar rules.

This chapter takes a middle position. The question of whether time should be devoted to grammar teaching in foreign language courses for adults cannot be answered with a straightforward "yes" or "no." It appears that a majority of experts in the fields of language pedagogy and second-language acquisition research are converging on a heavily qualified "yes," represented in the so-called "weak interface position" (e.g., Bley-Vroman, 1988; Celce-Murcia, 1991, 1992; Doughty, 1991; Ellis, 1990; Hulstijn and de Graaff, 1994; Larsen-Freeman, 1991; Larsen-Freeman and Long, 1991; Lightbown and Spada, 1993; Rutherford, 1987; Rutherford and Sharwood Smith, 1985; Schmidt, 1993, 1994; Sharwood Smith, 1993; Stern, 1992; Terrell, 1991; VanPatten and Cadierno, 1993a, 1993b).

During the eighties, linguists proposed plausible claims that some fundamental principles of language (such as the principles of binding, subjacency, and structure-dependency) need not be learnt by foreign-language learners because they have already been (implicitly) acquired during first-language acquisition. These principles, along with some "parameters" (such as the pro-drop and head-direction parameters), belong to the core of what linguists call Universal Grammar. Currently, it is an open question whether the setting of parameters for a foreign language can be influenced by explicit rule teaching or whether this is solely a matter of implicit learning (Cook, 1994). However, it is likely that explicit teaching can foster the acquisition of the many grammar rules outside the core of universal grammar. They make up the majority of the rules to be found in ordinary grammar books used by foreign-language learners. Furthermore, research suggests that for a restricted number of syntactic structures (e.g., basic word order patterns and the acquisition of negation), there appears to be a natural order of development which instruction can not alter, although the acquisition of such principles may be boosted by instruction. While theoretical and empirical research is being conducted on these issues, the wisest thing for teachers and course designers to do in the meantime is to adopt the middle position.[1]

In the remainder of this chapter, I will first try to provide a further rationale for this middle position and will then try to specify this position in practical terms. I will deal with two preliminary factors concerning grammar teaching, course objectives and learners' educational background. I will then present and discuss some factors which teachers and course designers should take into account when weighing the relative importance of various types of grammar rules. The concluding section provides a summary of these factors and draws conclusions.

---

1 A full discussion of the accessibility of universal grammar during foreign-language learning and of the (im)permeability of the so-called developmental sequences is beyond the scope of this paper. For a recent, thorough, critical, but fair assessment see Cook (1993), especially chapters 5 and 9, and Cook (1994).

A RATIONALE FOR A QUALIFIED "YES" TO GRAMMAR TEACHING

Before discussing the values of explicit grammar teaching, it is useful to realise that the notion of "difficulty" or "complexity" can be given different meanings. (In the context of the present discussion, it is not necessary to make a principled distinction *between* complexity and difficulty, and I will therefore use these labels interchangeably.) There are numerous notions of difficulty, some of which approach difficulty from the perspective of the foreign-language learner and some take a linguistic/pedagogic perspective.[2] These perspectives do not necessarily exclude each other, since, in the end, all meanings of difficulty boil down to claims concerning "difficulty for the learner." Here are some of these meanings of difficulty:

- Difficulty in terms of prior metalinguistic knowledge. Explicit grammar rules will be less difficult for learners familiar with linguistic notions such as subject, direct object, transitive verb, preposition, auxiliary, indefinite, particle, participle etc., than for learners with little linguistic schooling who may be unfamiliar with such notions.

- Difficulty in terms of contrasts between foreign and first language. Explicit foreign-language grammar rules will be less difficult for learners when they do not differ fundamentally from corresponding first-language rules than when they do.

- Difficulty in terms of duration of acquisition. Some rules can be acquired quickly while the acquisition of other rules stretches over a long period of time. One could call the latter rules more difficult than the former ones, but that, of course, would be a totally different meaning of "difficulty" than in the other cases mentioned.

---

2 Similarly, there are various meanings of the term "rule": cognitive, linguistic, pedagogic. See Westney, 1994, for a good treatment of the status of rules in pedagogic grammar.

- Difficulty in terms of reliability. Reliable rules, i.e., rules with few or no exceptions, could be said to be less difficult than unreliable rules (rules with many exceptions).

- Difficulty in terms of purely formal vs. formal-semantic distinctions. When a form distinction corresponds with a meaning distinction (e.g., plural –*s*: *door/doors*), it may be more salient and therefore less difficult to detect and acquire than when there is no corresponding semantic distinction (e.g., third person singular –*s*: *you run/he runs*).

Bearing in mind that the term difficulty can be interpreted in various ways, let us consider the stances towards explicit grammar teaching of two prototypical language teachers, called A and B. Teacher A expresses the following view: "I only present and explain the grammar topics with which my students experience difficulty. Many grammatical phenomena are easy enough to be picked up from the language to which my students are exposed. I therefore restrict my teaching to the explanation of the really hard phenomena, the ones students can't figure out on their own." Teacher B, however, expresses an oppositional view: "I don't give an explicit treatment of complex grammatical issues. I limit my explicit teaching to simple issues, expressible by means of rules of thumb which can be easily comprehended by my students."

The different views of teachers A and B illustrate what I call the "contradiction of grammar teaching." On the one hand, with teacher B, we might be tempted to limit ourselves to the explicit teaching of only those rules which have few or no exceptions, can be formulated clearly, do not contain grammatical jargon, and can be easily comprehended by students. On the other hand, with teacher A we are inclined to argue that such rules may well be redundant because of their reliability, simplicity and comprehensibility. Students might acquire the grammatical forms involved easily, without explicit instruction. It is precisely the form-regularities that are *not* so salient, obvious, exceptionless and clear-cut that need to be presented and explained explicitly, because without such explicit treatment, students may not be able to discover and acquire them. With teacher B however, we could rebut this claim with the counterclaim that the effectiveness of reliable, comprehensible rules of thumb is that they accelerate and smooth the course of language development, albeit that they may not be necessary. Furthermore, with teacher B, we might raise general pedagogic objections against rules which cannot be formulated succinctly and comprehensibly.

Is there a solution to this contradiction? As an answer to this question I have three considerations to offer:

- A final answer to this issue cannot yet be given on the basis of empirical evidence. There is some evidence that teaching is more effective when explicit grammar is provided than when it is not, but it is highly unlikely that this statement can be generalised without limitations (Ellis, 1990 chapter 6; Larsen-Freeman and Long, 1991, chapter 8; Cook, 1994). It is far more likely that explicit grammar instruction is beneficial in some cases and non-beneficial or even detrimental in other cases, as will be illustrated in the next section.

- Since the issue cannot yet be settled in a clear-cut way on the basis of empirical evidence, it is of great importance that teachers attain an awareness of the existence of this contradiction. Teachers familiar with these different points of view are likely to adopt a differentiated view on the matter; they are less likely to answer the question concerning explicit grammar instruction with an unqualified "yes, always" or "no, never."

- While waiting for more evidence from empirical research, we would be well advised to follow teacher B's rather than A's view. It would therefore be better to refrain from providing our students with vague and incomprehensible rules pertaining to phenomena which seldom occur in normal language use.

COURSE OBJECTIVES AND EDUCATIONAL BACKGROUND OF LEARNERS

The first two things one must take into account, when considering grammar teaching, are (i) What are the course objectives?, and (ii) What is the educational background of the learners? In a fifty hour course to teach travelers some survival command of the language, it is likely that its linguistic content must be restricted to the learning of the most frequent speech acts and the most useful vocabulary. In such a course, teachers may abandon grammar altogether, referring rule-minded learners to some elementary rules in the written course materials. They will emphasize, however, that the little class time available will be spent on listening, speaking and some reading rather than on grammar.

A second case in which grammar teaching may not make much sense is when a language course is to be taught to adults with little or no prior education. Illiterate learners or literate learners who have only been to elementary school, may not profit from explicit grammar rules. They may only be confused and frustrated by such rules, wrongly believing that they are too stupid to learn another language.

Thus, there are at least two situations in which the teaching of explicit grammar rules does not make sense. That, however, does not mean that no attention should be paid to the grammatical correctness of learners' spoken (or written) productions altogether. There is more to grammar teaching than the presentation and explanation of explicit rules. The teacher can perfectly well focus learners' attention on how to say something correctly, at some moments during the course. For instance, after learners have made themselves roughly familiar with the meaning and communicative function of an expression (e.g., for asking whether a table is free in a cafeteria), the teacher may focus their attention on the pronunciation of a word in that expression, on the inflectional form of a word in the expression, on the presence of a function word which must not be omitted, on the order of words, etc.

FACTORS DETERMINING EXPLICIT GRAMMAR TEACHING

In this section, I will leave aside foreign-language courses with very elementary objectives and courses for learners with little educational background. I will assume that the teacher or course designer is dealing with language courses of considerable length, with course objectives at the Threshold Level (Van Ek, 1980) or beyond, and with learners who have completed education at the secondary level (high school). There are five factors which course designers and teachers must take into account in answering, for each grammatical phenomenon again, the question if and how the phenomenon should be taught. These factors (scope, reliability, frequency, mode of command, and comprehensibility of explanation) will be dealt with in the remainder of this section. Examples of the factors of scope, reliability and frequency will first be given in relation to lexical rules and then in relation to non-lexical rules. A final preliminary remark to be made here is that, in this section, the term "rule" will be used to refer to pedagogical rules as found in ordinary textbooks, not to mental representations or abstract principles of grammar.

RULES OF LEXICAL MORPHOPHONOLOGY ("LEXICAL RULES")

To begin with, it is helpful to distinguish between rules which do and rules which do not pertain to morphophonological features of lexical items (including pronunciation and orthography of these features). For ease of reference, I will drop the label "morphophonological" from the nomenclature and will henceforth call them lexical and non-lexical rules respectively[3]. Here are some examples of lexical rules:

[3] Indo-European languages are characterized by flection on their main lexical categories, nouns (N), verbs (V), and adjectives and adverbs (A). A distinction can be made between contextual and inherent flection (Booij, 1993). A common example of contextual flection, i.e., flection determined by factors outside the lexical item itself, is agreement: e.g., an adjective in French, German and Spanish takes on a suffix contingent on the gender, number or case of the noun

- rules specifying grammatical gender (German, Spanish, French);
- rules specifying plural formation of nouns (German, Spanish, French, English);
- rules specifying the formation of comparative and superlative derivations of adjectives;
- rules specifying past tense and past participle formation of verbs;
- rules specifying whether verbs will take the equivalent of 'to be' or 'to have' as an auxiliary in the perfect tense (German, French);
- rules specifying which syllable of a multisyllabic word will bear word stress.

To determine whether lexical rules should be explicitly taught or not, teacher and course designer should first of all consider their scope, their reliability, and the frequency of occurrence of the relevant lexical items.

---

to which it belongs; and the finite verb takes an ending which agrees in person o number with the grammatical subject. However, the form of a flectiona morpheme (e.g., a suffix or prefix) can also be determined by features inherent t the lexical item. For instance, nouns and verbs in most Indo-European language can be classified according to declension (N) and conjugation (V) categorie Each category usually has its own flection, i.e., its own bound morphemes adde as suffixes or prefixes to the stem or the root of the lexical item. Thus, the forr of a lexical suffix can be lexically determined although its presence may b contextually driven. For example, a German noun functioning as the direc object of a transitive verb is provided with an accusative case suffix (contextu flection), but the form of this suffix differs according to the grammatical gend of the noun (inherent flection). Inherent flection, then, belongs to the realm what I call "lexical rules," but contextual flection does not.

Scope

For the teaching of lexical rules, one has to consider how many lexical items they cover. This will be called "scope." For instance, in Spanish, which distinguishes masculine and feminine nouns, there are some (formal) gender rules, covering large numbers of nouns. Most words ending in the vowel *–o* are masculine, whereas words ending in the vowel *–a* are feminine. Some (semantic or etymological) gender rules, however, pertain to small numbers of lexical items. For instance, nouns referring to mountains, rivers, and to the points of the compass, and words ending in *–a* but of Greek origin are masculine. According to the scope principle, then, teachers and course designers should give more priority to the former than to the latter rules. Small scope rules might be withheld altogether or given only to advanced learners.

Most Indo-European languages distinguish various verb classes according to the way they are conjugated. In Spanish and French, for instance, there is a small number of regular classes (three and four classes respectively), each covering large numbers of verbs. However, in languages such as German and English, there is only one large class of regular ("weak") verbs as well as some two to three hundred "strong" verbs, divided into subclasses differing in size from a handful to approximately thirty verbs. The scope of the regular classes in French and Spanish is much larger than the scope of even the largest strong class in German and English. It therefore makes more sense to present learners of Spanish and French with the conjugation rules of the main verb classes than to present learners of German and English with the conjugation rules of even the largest strong verb classes. It should be noticed, however, that such a decision need not exclusively be based on the scope of the rules but also on their "reliability," a notion that I will now turn to.

Reliability

Many lexical rules do not apply in an absolute sense but only probabilistically. Such rules, or "probabilistic tendencies" can be said to differ in reliability, i.e., in the extent to which they hold true (Bates and MacWhinney, 1989). Consider the following examples concerning noun gender in German (masculine, feminine and neuter), as specified by Mills (1986:33):

1. Of the approximately 15.000 singular nouns ending in *–e* about 13,500 (90%) are feminine.

2. Of the 15 monosyllabic nouns beginning with *Kn-*, 14 are masculine (93%).

3. Of the 107 monosyllabic nouns ending in a consonant cluster containing a nasal (e.g., *–nd, –mp*), 75 are masculine (70%).

4. Of the 45 nouns ending in *–ier*, 27 are neuter (60%).

According to the scope principle, rules 1 and 3 have more priority than 2 and 4. According to the reliability principle, rules 1 and 2 have more priority than 3 and 4. A combined application of the principles of scope and reliability gives rule 1 highest priority, rule 4 lowest priority, and rules 2 and 3 a priority in between.

Frequency

Scope and reliability are not the only criteria to consider. Frequency must sometimes be taken into consideration as well. The more frequently individual flectional forms (of verbs, nouns and other lexical categories) occur in normal language use, the better candidates they are for the alternative route of vocabulary learning without rules. There is growing evidence from the psycholinguistic literature that native speakers produce frequently occurring flectional forms automatically, as they appear to be readily available and accessible in their mental lexicon. For instance, the use of a frequent regular past tense form such as *worked* may not consist of the retrieval of the uninflected base form *work* followed by a suffixation process (adding the suffix *–ed*), but rather of the retrieval of the ready-made form *worked* (Stemberger and MacWhinney, 1988; for a somewhat different view, see Pinker and Prince, 1992).

Let us look at another illustration of the role played by the frequency criterion in the domain of the lexicon. In German, the masculine noun *Arzt* 'doctor' has a regular plural *Ärzte* (with umlaut, or vowel shift), but the masculine noun *Arm* 'arm' has the irregular plural *Arm* (without vowel shift). Both plural forms belong to language users everyday vocabulary. It is highly plausible therefore that not only the irregular *Arme* but also the regular *Ärzte* are readily available in the mental lexicon of the adult native speaker, i.e., that the production of even the regular *Ärzte* does not have to be composed (via the retrieval of the root form and the subsequent application of umlaut plus suffixation). If this is a plausible account of the lexical production process in adult native speakers,[4] then foreign language instructors should seriously consider stressing neither the regularity of *Ärzte* (by giving the rule) nor the irregularity of *Arme* (by explicitly incorporating it in a list of exceptions to the rule). They should rather follow the alternative vocabulary learning route (to be explained in the next section) by telling their learners to note down and commit to memory, for each noun, both the singular and the plural form.[5]

Finally, let us look at an example of using the frequency criterion in order to decide that the exception to a rule could well be explicitly mentioned by the teacher because the exception does occur very often in normal language use. As we have seen, the general rule in Spanish is that nouns ending in *–a* are feminine. There are, however, some exceptions to this rule and some of these exceptions, such as the masculine noun *día* 'day', occur very frequently. Other exceptions do not occur frequently, such as the noun *Mosa* (the name of a river). Thus, it would be quite conceivable that frequent exceptions will be explicitly taught whereas non-frequent exceptions will not.

In summary, in the case of lexical rules, teachers and course designers need to take into account the factors of scope, reliability and frequency in a combined fashion so as to assess their relative usefulness. Each of these three factors is quantitative in nature but their importance cannot be simply read off the figures. The examples

---

4 Again, it must be emphasized that the empirical evidence from psycholinguistic research is only suggestive, not beyond dispute.

5 Of course, encouraging learners to follow the vocabulary route need not imply withholding rules from them. Denying learners access to information does not appear to be a wise policy. Now that the field of second and foreign language teaching and learning is entering an age of learner autonomy (Brown, 1994: 80), learners must not be denied access to information from which some might benefit. However, teachers may warn learners that such rules may turn out to be of limited value to them.

given in this section purport to show that the weighing of these factors can be a fairly subtle affair, far from a blind application of straightforward numerical criteria.

The route of vocabulary learning

For lexical rules, regardless of their scope, there is, in principle, an alternative to teaching them explicitly. This alternative is simply that learners are told to learn the lexical, morphological forms separately. Thus, teachers of Spanish need not tell the rules and subrules for noun gender; they may only instruct their learners to write down in their notebooks the gender of each noun they have to learn (expressed by the definite article, *el* for masculine and *la* for feminine) and memorise the nouns together with their definite article. Similarly, teachers of German and English need not give their learners the rules of forming the simple past and the past participle of "weak" verbs. In principle, they may instead instruct their learners to write down in their notebooks for each verb, strong or weak, the form of the simple past and of the past participle (e.g., *work/worked/worked*, and *bear/bore/borne*), since there are no reliable rules determining whether a verb is weak or strong in the first place. Thus, even for the large class of regular (weak) verbs, the learner has to learn that these verbs are regular (weak), a feature which in itself cannot be predicted on the basis of a reliable rule.[6]

Generality must prevail over completeness

If the teacher and/or course designer have decided, in spite of the above argument, to provide students with all the information, they should heed the simple pedagogic advice that generality must prevail over completeness (in a beginners' course), and that not all rules should be presented in the same lesson. For instance, if the designer of a Spanish course for beginners has decided that learners be given all

6 The alternative route of vocabulary or rote learning might also be applicable in cases of formulaic expressions beyond the lexical level, i.e., in cases of fixed grammatical multi-word constructions. For example, in a French course for beginners, the teacher might postpone a grammatical analysis of the expression "asseyez-vous" (sit down) by presenting this expression as if it were one unanalyzable word.

rules of noun gender (despite the fact that some of these rules have a small scope and pertain to nouns which seldom occur), it would not be wise to provide learners with all these rules and have them practice these rules in a single lesson. It would be much wiser to give some general rules (larger scope and higher reliability) first and the remaining rules (smaller scope and lower reliability) in later lessons.

NON-LEXICAL RULES

In the case of non-lexical rules (i.e., rules which do not pertain to morphophonological features of lexical items), teachers and course designers can try to determine the relative importance of explicit rule presentation by also considering the factors of frequency, reliability and, if applicable, scope. Again, I will give some examples of each factor, in the order mentioned.

Frequency

Frequently occurring grammatical phenomena must be given greater priority in language instruction than grammar rules whose instances do not occur so often. Let us look at two examples.

German has two important word order rules specifying the place of the finite verb in declarative main clauses (second position) and in embedded clauses (final position).[7] Another word order rule pertains to the order of phrases expressing time and place: "time precedes place," unless place is expressed by means of a pronominal form ("pronominal place precedes time").

Which rules should have priority in a language course? The two rules specifying the place of the finite verb or the rules specifying the order of phrases of time and place? In both oral and written language, sentences with finite verb forms by far outnumber sentences containing both temporal and local phrases. Thus, according to the frequency criterion, the finite verb rules should have more priority than the time-place rules.

---

[7] There are exceptions to this rule as well as to most rules to be mentioned in the remainder of this chapter, but these exceptions are irrelevant in the present context and are therefore left aside.

Let us consider another example. In German, French and Spanish, verbs can be inflected both in the indicative and in the subjunctive mood. It seems that the subjunctive is seldom used in colloquial German but much more often in Spanish, with French holding a position in between. Using the frequency of use criterion then, the designer of a German course is likely to postpone the introduction of the subjunctive much longer than the designer of a Spanish course (or even leave it out altogether and introduce some frequent subjunctive forms, such as *möchte*, *könnte*, and *sei*, simply as individual lexical items). This example also shows that the frequency of a grammatical phenomenon (and hence its pedagogic weight) may vary across languages.

Reliability

Highly reliable rules (i.e., rules with few or no exceptions) may have precedence over rules with low reliability. For instance, the English SVO word order rule (subject + verb + object) has an extremely high reliability. Exceptions, such as "The red one I want" (OSV) or "Likes apple pie, John" (VOS), are stylistically marked, rare and infrequent. The explicit presentation of the SVO rule may therefore have a high priority in ESL courses, especially in ESL courses for speakers with non-SVO mother tongues.

Notoriously problematic is the formulation of reliable rules for the place of negation words, such as *nicht* in German, *no* in Spanish. and *not* in English. For instance, a rule such as "When you want to negate a sentence containing a definite direct object, put *nicht* after it" is not altogether reliable. One of the main reasons for this is that negation is a phenomenon influenced by syntax, morphology, semantics and pragmatics in combination. More generally even, one could say that many semantic and pragmatic rules are known for their conspicuously low reliability. This may be caused by the use of potentially confusing metaphorical labels. Examples of confusing metaphorical labels are "perspective" and "(in)formal)" in the following two rules respectively:

- "In German, use the present perfect when your *perspective* lies in the present time and use the simple past when your *perspective* lies in the past itself."

• "In French, use 'vous' in *formal* and 'tu' in *informal* situations."

Teachers would do well to explicitly warn their students of the low reliability of such rules. They may even choose another label, such as "tendency," to set them apart from rules.

One of the most pressing dilemmas for teachers is the choice between giving simple but not entirely reliable rules on the one hand, and complete, exhaustive information on the other. For instance, teachers of German may provide their students with the simple, but not entirely reliable rule that the finite verb in an embedded sentence takes final position (as in *Sie wissen daß ich das nicht gesehen* ***habe***). If they were to give some subrules also (e.g., the finite verb forms of the auxiliaries *haben* and *werden* precede two infinitives, as in *Sie wissen daß ich das unmöglich* ***habe*** *sehen können*), their information would become more complete, but at the price of greater difficulty (in one sense, as discussed above). Often such a dilemma can be solved by heeding the following sound pedagogic principle: give general, but not entirely reliable, rules in an earlier stage (e.g., in a beginners' course) and provide subrules later (e.g., in a course for advanced learners). Thus, as was said in the section on lexical rules, generality must prevail over completeness, at least in a beginners' course.[8]

Scope

Sometimes scope must be taken into account too. This is the case when a rule applies only to a limited (large or small, but finite) number of members of a grammatical (sub)category. For instance, one

---

8 Teachers often ask whether students must discover the rule themselves or whether the teacher should formulate the rule. I prefer the following answer, based on pedagogical principles. First, never formulate a rule without providing illustrative examples. The examples (if well chosen) will probably be more effective than the rule. Second, only ask students to discover the rule themselves if you are almost certain they will successfully derive the correct rule from the examples. If they derive an incorrect rule, not receiving immediate feedback on their incorrect inference, it may cost much effort to replace the incorrect by the correct one. Third, variation in teaching and learning procedures can be stimulating. Thus, there is no principled objection to providing the rule in some cases and having students to discover the rule in other cases.

of the adverb placement rules of English applies to a limited number of adverbs, namely the rule that frequency adverbs such as *never*, *always*, and *sometimes* have a preferred preverbal position (e.g., *I always forget my keys* vs. **I forget my keys always*). Teachers have to weigh, on the one hand, providing their students with this generalization, using the category label "frequency adverbs," against, on the other hand, stating, for each frequency adverb individually, that it takes preverbal position. In this decision, the scope of the generalization, i.e., the number of adverbs falling into the category of frequency adverbs, should be taken into account.[9]

Mode of command: Receptive versus productive

For some grammar phenomena, it may be sufficient that learners acquire only a receptive knowledge, at least in the beginning and intermediate stages of acquisition. This, in turn, may have implications for the degree of explicitness with which the corresponding rules be presented and explained. For instance, Spanish has several suffixal allomorphs with which nouns can be altered into diminutives. These allomorphs differ slightly according to the

---

9 One might call this placement rule of frequency adverbs a lexical rule and therefore argue that it need not be mentioned in this section, since the scope of lexical rules has already been dealt with in the previous section. However, the lexical rules in the previous section pertained to morphophonological phenomena only. Thus the frequency-adverb rule is not a lexical rule in that sense.
It should be noted that one can only speak of the scope of a rule, not of the scope of a set of individual items. Understandably, it is sometimes hard to distinguish between scope and reliability. In English, for instance, some verbs have "dative alternation," i.e., they can appear in both a double object construction ("I told her the story") and in a prepositional construction ("I told the story to her"), whereas other verbs can only appear in the prepositional construction ("I reported the story to her," but not *"I reported her the story"). If either subcategory could be labeled, that is, if a generalization could be formulated for either subcategory (see Carroll and Swain, 1993, for examples), we would be dealing with a case of scope. However, if no generalization could be made, we would only have a set of individual items (verbs, in this case) behaving identically in a certain respect (e.g., forbidding or allowing the double object construction). These individual items could be seen as exceptions to a rule; we would then be dealing with the reliability of that rule.

morphological and phonological make-up of the nouns to which they are added. Thus, suffixation depends on whether nouns consist of one or more syllables and on whether they end in *-n* and *-r* or in other letters (phonemes). There are three allomorphs for feminine nouns (*-cita*, *-ecita*, and *-ita*) and three allomorphs for masculine nouns (*-cito*, *-ecito*, and *-ito*). In order to recognize a form as a diminutive during reading or listening, however, the language learner need not know the particularities of these six alternative allomorphs. A simple statement that diminutives can be recognized by the endings *-ita* and *-ito* will do for reading and listening. Of course, this rule is unreliable for speaking and writing. But, in the case of such a purely formal, non-semantic rule, whose violations (**pueblito* and **florita* rather than correct *pueblecito* and *floretica*) can hardly result in a misunderstanding of the utterance's meaning, teacher and course designer may be satisfied with an unreliable rule, at least in a beginners' course.

Comprehensibility of rule explanation

A further question which teachers have to ask themselves, for every single rule, is whether it can be explained in a comprehensible way.. Comprehensibility can be affected:

- by the use of grammatical jargon with which learners are not familiar;
- by the fact that the rule to be explained pertains to semantic distinctions absent in any language known to the learners (first language or other foreign languages) and therefore uncommon to them;
- by a combination of these two learner-related factors.

First of all, let us consider grammatical jargon. Is it possible to avoid grammatical jargon? Which jargon can't be avoided? Rules couched in incomprehensible jargon will confuse and demotivate rather than elucidate learners. For instance, as noted above, negation is a complex phenomenon. Again, let us take German negation as an example. There are two common negators, *kein* ('no') and *nicht* ('not').

Teachers of German to learners with a non-Germanic first language have to explain:

- when to use either form (*kein* is associated with indefinite noun phrases, whereas definite noun phrases are associated with *nicht*);

- what the place of *nicht* in the sentence is relative to other constituents (e.g., before prepositional phrases, before adjectives and adverbs, after definite direct objects, after finite intransitive verbs, after adverbs, before any phrase in case of phrase negation in contrast to clause negation, etc.).

In fact, even these rules are not fully adequate from a linguistic point of view. An adequate description would require that the teacher explain the potential extensions of negative quantifiers on a fairly abstract level. Perhaps then, teachers should abandon explicit explanations of this sort and use many well-chosen and well-organized examples in their grammar lessons instead. Thus, they may provide a list of sentences or phrases, laid out in two columns, positive sentences and phrases at the left side and their corresponding negative counterparts on the right side, listed in groups, such that each negation type is represented with a handful of examples.[10]

Another threat to the comprehensibility of grammar explanations may originate from subtle, non-obvious differences in meaning between forms. For instance, how should teachers explain to learners whose mother tongue does not have different determiners for definite and indefinite noun phrases when to say "The teacher has a red car" (with an indefinite article) and when to say "The teacher's car is red" (with a definite article)? Of course, teachers can make use of labels such as "definite article" and "indefinite article" in order to refer to differences

---

10 Here again, it should be understood that I am not advocating the actual withholding of abstract rules, couched in grammatical jargon, from learners who request grammatical information. My point is that such rules will help only few learners, and that learners may benefit more from well-organized examples. Teachers can satisfy the curiosity of the few grammar-minded learners in their classes by briefly mentioning the abstract rules or by referring them to a grammar book.

in *form*, visible at the surface structure. But what terminology will they use to explain the difference in *meaning* between these forms? Should they use terminology of set mathematics? Should they use jargon such as "generic use," "specific," and "unique reference"? Should they go into matters of shared and non-shared information between speaker and hearer as assumed by the speaker? Should they use sophisticated linguistic terminology?[11] Can this be done in lesson one of a beginners' course introducing definite and indefinite articles?

Other notorious difficulties lie in the explanation of the semantic differences between two or more alternative forms non-existent in students' first languages, such as

- between indicative and subjunctive mood (e.g., in Spanish),
- between simple past and present perfect (in German and English),
- between *presente perfecto*, *pretérito definido*, and *pretérito imperfecto* (in Spanish),
- between the active and passive voice (in English, German, French, Spanish; cf. Tomlin, 1994).

For such differences no clear-cut, highly reliable rules can be formulated. They must be couched in vague terms using soft metaphors such as perspective of the speaker/hearer, or perspective from the present or from the past. The difficulties are especially grave when the language to be taught is the same as the language of instruction (i.e., in second language courses as opposed to foreign language courses). Teachers of second language courses may therefore refrain from trying to convey subtle semantic differences in the second language. Instead they might provide their learners with a number of well-chosen and well-organized examples, pointing out the critical formal differences, perhaps mentioning a few semantic keywords,

[11] Master (1994) showed that explicit teaching of the English article system to adult ESL university students improved their performance in comparison to control groups not receiving explicit instruction.

while telling learners that clear rules can't be given and that they must simply try to develop a feeling for the meaning of the formal differences in question.

SUMMARY AND CONCLUSIONS

Let me summarize the factors that teachers and course designers have to take into account when considering whether a grammar rule will be explicitly taught and, if so, how it will be taught. This summary will be formulated as a list of recommendations.

1. First preliminary consideration: If you are to teach a very short course aimed at reaching survival knowledge only, spend the little time there is on vocabulary rather than on grammar, and do listening, reading and speaking activities rather than grammar exercises.

2. Second preliminary consideration: If your learners have a low educational background (not more than a few years of secondary school), do not present explicit grammar rules (at least not in courses at beginning or intermediate proficiency levels).

3. If you are to teach a language course to learners with a high educational background (more than a few years of secondary school), and if the course has higher objectives than some survival skills only, and if you are inclined to teaching the foreign language grammar rules that differ from corresponding rules in your learners' first language, then take into account the following points:

   - Estimate the *frequency* of occurrences of the linguistic phenomena falling under a rule.

   - Establish the *reliability* of the rule (the extent to which it holds).

   - If appropriate, determine the *scope* of the rule, i.e., the number of items to which the rule applies.

- Take into account whether students need only have a *receptive* command of the rule (for reading and listening), or whether they also need to have a *productive* command of the rule (in speaking, writing).

- Estimate the possibility of explaining the rule *in a comprehensible way* (without much jargon).

4. Then make the following evaluations:

- Estimate what the "return" might be of giving learners the rule. For instance, a rule large in scope and/or high in reliability may give a higher return than a rule small in scope and/or low in reliability and should therefore be given more priority.

- Consider the possibility of providing "simple", general, but not entirely reliable rules in earlier lessons and more complete information later on.

- In the case of lexical phenomena, consider whether you will abandon the rule altogether and show your learners the alternative route of vocabulary learning (rote learning, formulaic learning) instead. The vocabulary route seems especially appropriate when the relevant form of the lexical item occurs frequently in normal language use, regardless of whether that form can be considered a "regular" formation (resulting from a rule large in scope and/or high in reliability) or an "irregular" one.

- If it is hardly possible to explain the rule in a comprehensible way (without much jargon), seriously reconsider the matter. If you can expect that the rule in question will create confusion rather than enlightenment, you should show restraint in providing such a rule while giving a display of well-chosen examples instead. It is better to give no rule at all than an incomprehensible rule. If necessary, satisfy the curiosity of the grammar-minded learners in your class by briefly mentioning the abstract rule or by referring them to a grammar book.

Whatever the decisions taken by course designer and teacher concerning the question whether to teach explicit grammar rules or not, it is important to bear two facts in mind, as the examples of Bethania and Isabelle at the beginning of this chapter illustrate. First, it is perfectly well possible to focus learners' attention on grammatical correctness without explicitly teaching grammar, and second, grammar teaching has its limits.

The effect of grammar teaching may not be visible immediately in an improvement of the grammaticality of learners' written or spoken output. As has recently been suggested by Schmidt (1994), VanPatten (1994), Hulstijn and de Graaff (1994) and others, the main effect and function of grammar teaching is perhaps that:

- it helps the learner to bring order in the input.
- it facilitates the understanding of the (written or spoken) input;
- it therefore may boost or support the "natural" acquisition process (i.e., the development of implicit knowledge).

With the criteria provided in this chapter, embedded in this modest view on the facilitative role of explicit pedagogical rules, course designers and teachers should be able to give grammar its proper place in the foreign and second language curriculum. They will then adopt a differentiated approach to grammar teaching, since "Not all grammar rules are equal!"

ACKNOWLEDGMENTS

I would like to thank Geert Booij, Rick de Graaff, and Richard Schmidt for their critical but highly valuable comments on an earlier version of this paper.

REFERENCES

Bates, E., & MacWhinney, B. (1989). Functionalism and the competition model. In B. MacWhinney & E. Bates (Eds.), *The crosslinguistic study of sentence processing* (pp. 3–73). Cambridge: Cambridge University Press.

Bley-Vroman, R. (1988). The fundamental character of foreign language learning. In W. Rutherford & M. Sharwood Smith (Eds.), *Grammar and second language teaching* (pp. 19–30). New York: Newbury House/Harper & Row.

Booij, G. E. (1993). Against split morphology. In G. Booij & J. van Marle (Eds.), *Yearbook of Morphology 1993* (pp. 27–49). Dordrecht, the Netherlands: Kluwer.

Brown, H. D. (1994). *Teaching by principles: An interactive approach to language pedagogy*. Englewood Cliffs, NJ: Prentice Hall.

Carroll, S., & Swain, M. (1993). Explicit and implicit negative feedback: An empirical study of the learning of linguistic generalizations. *Studies in Second Language Acquisition*, *15*, 357–386.

Celce-Murcia, M. (1991). Second language grammar: Learning and teaching. *TESOL Quarterly*, *25*, 459–480.

Celce-Murcia, M. (1992). Formal grammar instruction. *TESOL Quarterly*, *26*, 406–409.

Cook, V. (1993). *Linguistics and second language acquisition*. London: Macmillan

Cook, V. (1994). The metaphor of access to universal grammar in L2 learning. In: N. C. Ellis (Ed.), *Implicit and explicit learning of languages* (pp. 477–502). London: Academic Press.

Doughty, C. (1991). Second language instruction does make a difference: Evidence from an empirical study of SL relativization. *Studies in Second Language Acquisition*, *13*, 431–469.

Ellis, R. (1990). *Instructed second language acquisition*. Oxford: Basil Blackwell.

Hulstijn, J. H. (1982). *Monitor use by adult second language learners*. Unpublished doctoral dissertation, University of Amsterdam.

Hulstijn, J. H., & de Graaff, R. (1994). Under what conditions does explicit knowledge of a second language facilitate the acquisition of implicit knowledge? A research proposal. *AILA Review, 11*, 97–112.

Krashen, S. (1982). *Principles and practice in second language acquisition.* New York: Pergamon Press.

Krashen, S. D. (1992). Formal grammar instruction. *TESOL Quarterly, 26*, 409–411.

Krashen, S. D. (1993). The effect of formal grammar teaching: Still peripheral. *TESOL Quarterly, 27*, 722–725.

Larsen-Freeman, D. (1991). Consensus and divergence on the content, role, and process of teaching grammar. In J. E. Alatis (Ed.), *Georgetown University Round Table on Language and Linguistics* (pp. 260–272). Washington, D.C.: Georgetown University Press.

Larsen-Freeman, D., & Long, M. H. (1991). *An introduction to second language acquisition research.* London: Longman.

Lightbown, P.M., & Spada, N. (1993). *How languages are learned.* Oxford: Oxford University Press.

Master, P. (1994). The effect of systematic instruction on learning the English article system. In T. Odlin (Ed.), *Perspectives on pedagogical grammar* (pp. 229–252). Cambridge, UK: Cambridge University Press.

Mills, A. E. (1986). *The acquisition of gender: A study of English and German.* Berlin: Springer.

Pinker, S., & Prince, A. (1992). Regular and irregular morphology and the psychological status of rules of grammar. *Proceedings of the 1991 Meeting of the Berkeley Linguistics Society.* Berkeley, CA.: Berkeley Linguistics Society.

Rutherford, W. E. (1987). *Second language grammar: Learning and teaching.* London: Longman.

Rutherford, W., & Sharwood Smith, M. (1985). Consciousness raising and universal grammar. *Applied Linguistics, 6*, 274–282.

Schmidt, R. (1993). Consciousness, learning and interlanguage pragmatics. In G. Kasper & S. Blum-Kulka (Eds.), *Interlanguage pragmatics* (pp. 21–42). Oxford: Oxford University Press.

Schmidt, R. (1994). Deconstructing consciousness in search of useful definitions for applied linguistics. *AILA Review, 11*, 11–26.

Sharwood Smith, M. (1993). Input enhancement in instructed SLA: theoretical bases. *Studies in Second Language Acquisition, 15*, 165–179.

Stemberger, J. P., & MacWhinney, B. (1988). Are inflected forms stored in the lexicon? In M. Hammond & M. Noonan (Eds.), *Theoretical Morphology: Approaches in Modern Linguistics* (pp. 101–116). San Diego, CA: Academic Press.

Stern, H. H. (1992). *Issues and options in language teaching.* Edited by P. Allen & B. Harley. Oxford: Oxford University Press.

Terrell, T. (1991). The role of grammar instruction in a communicative approach. *The Modern Language Journal, 75*, 52–63.

Tomlin, R. S. (1994). Functional grammars, pedagogical grammars, and communicative language teaching. In T. Odlin (Ed.), *Perspectives on pedagogical grammar* (pp. 140–178). Cambridge, UK: Cambridge University Press.

Van Ek, J. A. (1980). *Threshold level English in an European unit/credit system for modern language learning by adults.* Oxford: Pergamon Press.

VanPatten, B. (1994). Evaluating the role of consciousness in second language acquisition: Terms, linguistic features and research methodology. *AILA Review, 11*, 27–36.

VanPatten, B., & Cadierno, T. (1993a). Explicit instruction and input processing. *Studies in Second Language Acquisition, 15*, 225–243.

VanPatten, B., & Cadierno, T. (1993b). Input processing and second language acquisition: A role for instruction. *Modern Language Journal, 77*, 45–57.

Westney, P. (1994). Rules and pedagogical grammar. In T. Odlin (Ed.), *Perspectives on pedagogical grammar* (pp. 72–96). Cambridge, UK: Cambridge University Press.

ABOUT THE AUTHORS

THE EDITOR

Richard Schmidt is professor of English as a second language and director of the National Foreign Language Resource Center at the University of Hawai'i at Mānoa. He has been at one time or another a teacher, university professor, or teacher trainer in Egypt, Lebanon, Brazil, Thailand, Spain, Japan, and Hungary. He has a strong interest in the teaching of Arabic and Portuguese, in addition to English as a second and foreign language. He has been at the University of Hawai'i for the past twenty years, where he teaches in the MA program in ESL and the doctoral program in second language acquisition. His major research efforts in recent years have dealt with the cognitive aspects of second and foreign language learning and motivation for language learning.

THE AUTHORS

Riikka Aulikki Alanen is a teacher and researcher in the English Department at the University of Jyväskylä, Finland, where she received a master's degree in English philology in 1987 and licentiate of philosophy degree in 1991. She received an MA in English as a second language from the University of Hawai'i at Mānoa in 1992. She is currently a doctoral candidate at the University of Jyväskylä. Her interests include the relationship between learners' language proficiency and judgments on grammaticality judgment tasks and the role of attention and focus on form in second language learning and processing.

Igone Arteagoitia is a doctoral student in Spanish linguistics at Georgetown University with a concentration in applied linguistics. Her research areas of interest include second language acquisition (Spanish and Basque), computer aided language learning and multimedia, corpus linguistics, and discourse analysis. She has taught Spanish, Basque and English as a foreign language, both in the U.S. and in the Basque Country (in Spain). She is currently designing a multimedia software program for teaching and learning Basque.

Beverly Boyson is a Ph.D. student in applied linguistics at Georgetown University. Her research and interests include second language acquisition, language assessment, and teacher education. She has worked at the Center for Applied Linguistics in Washington, DC in the area of foreign language educational testing.

Catherine Doughty is an assistant professor of linguistics at Georgetown University, where she teaches courses in language acquisition, language testing, and computer-assisted language learning. Her research interests include focus on form in classroom SLA, the development of the L2 in content-based programs, and the interface between language acquisition research methodology and language testing.

Boris Fridman is a professor in the Department of Linguistics at the Escuela Nacional de Antropología e Historia (Mexico). He earned a masters degree from Gallaudet University (1990–1992), with Fulbright and Ford-MacArthur scholarships. He is currently in the linguistics Ph.D. program at Georgetown University, with a scholarship from the Consejo Nacional de Ciencia y Tecnología.

Jan H. Hulstijn is associate professor in applied linguistics and, since 1983, head of the Dutch as a Second Language Department of the Free University in Amsterdam. He has been involved in language teaching (Dutch L2), teacher training, materials development (including computer courseware), curriculum development, program evaluation, and the introduction of national Dutch L2 exams in the Netherlands. His research has been devoted to cognitive aspects of L2 grammar and vocabulary learning.

Diane Huot is professor in the Department of Languages and Linguistics at Laval University, where she works in the areas of French as a second language and language teacher training. She has experience in the teaching of French as a second language to learners of various ages and backgrounds. She recently participated in a study sponsored by CONFEMEN (Conference of Francophone Ministers of Education) concerning the language needs and areas of interests of primary school children in francophone Africa. She is presently pursuing a longitudinal study of attention in L2 acquisition.

Renée Jourdenais is a Ph.D. candidate in applied linguistics at Georgetown University. Her research interests involve the cognitive processes of second language acquisition.

Hae-Young Kim, previously trained in English in her home country Korea and then in Applied Linguistics in New Zealand, is seeking a Ph.D. degree in Second Language Acquisition at the University of Hawai'i at Mānoa. While her primary interests are in second language pedagogy and teacher education, she has recently been working on phonological issues involved in L2 listening comprehension and discourse of L2 speech production.

Jennifer Leeman is currently working on a doctorate in applied linguistics in the Department of Spanish at Georgetown University. Her research interests include focus on form in L2 classrooms, computer-assisted language learning, and the acquisition of L2 phonology. She has taught both ESL and Spanish as a foreign language.

Mitsuhiko Ota is a doctoral candidate in applied linguistics at Georgetown University. His interests center on the cognitive mechanisms of language acquisition.

W. Kahuhu Palmeira is a doctoral student in the program in second language acquisition at the University of Hawai'i at Mānoa. Her primary interests concern revitalization of the Hawaiian language, especially through Hawaiian language immersion education. She has served as a member of the 'Aha Kauleo, an advisory council to the State of Hawai'i Department and Board of Education and is the parent of a child enrolled in immersion from its start in 1987.

Michael A. Roberts is a senior lecturer in the Department of East Asian Studies at the University of Waikato in Hamilton, New

Zealand. He is concurrently enrolled as a doctoral candidate in the Department of East Asian Languages and Literatures at the University of Hawai'i at Mānoa. He is currently conducting research into the relationship between typological markedness and the effectiveness of foreign language instruction.

Peter Robinson is a graduate of the Ph.D. program in second language acquisition at the University of Hawai'i at Mānoa. He has taught courses in second language teaching and learning at the universities of Pittsburgh, Hawai'i, Queensland, and Singapore and has published widely on a number of topics, both theoretical and applied.

Stephanie J. Stauffer is a Ph.D. candidate and fellow in applied linguistics at Georgetown University. Her research interests include uses of the Internet and computer-mediated communication for L2 teaching and task construction and feedback in computer-assisted language learning software. She has authored papers appearing in the *Proceedings of the Georgetown University Round Table on Languages and Linguistics* (1994 and 1995) and in the *Working Papers of the International University of Japan* (1994).

PRAGMATICS OF JAPANESE AS NATIVE AND TARGET LANGUAGE

GABRIELE KASPER
(Editor)

This technical report includes three contributions to the study of the pragmatics of Japanese:

- A bibliography on speech act performance, discourse management, and other pragmatic and sociolinguistic features of Japanese;
- A study on introspective methods in examining Japanese learners' performance of refusals;
- A longitudinal investigation of the acquisition of the particle *ne* by non-native speakers of Japanese.

125 pp.

(SLTCC Technical Report #3) ISBN 0–8248–1462–2 $10.

A BIBLIOGRAPHY OF PEDAGOGY & RESEARCH IN INTERPRETATION & TRANSLATION

ETILVIA ARJONA

This technical report includes four types of bibliographic information on translation and interpretation studies:

- Research efforts across disciplinary boundaries: cognitive psychology, neurolinguistics, psycho-linguistics, sociolinguistics, computational linguistics, measurement, aptitude testing, language policy, decision-making, theses, dissertations;
- Training information covering: program design, curriculum studies, instruction, school administration;
- Instruction information detailing: course syllabi, methodology, models, available textbooks;
- Testing information about aptitude, selection, diagnostic tests.

115 pp.

(SLTCC Technical Report #4) ISBN 0–8248–1572–6 $10.

PRAGMATICS OF CHINESE AS NATIVE AND TARGET LANGUAGE

GABRIELE KASPER
(Editor)

This technical report includes six contributions to the study of the pragmatics of Mandarin Chinese:

- A report of an interview study conducted with nonnative speakers of Chinese;
- Five data-based studies on the performance of different speech acts by native speakers of Mandarin: requesting, refusing complaining, giving bad news, disagreeing, and complimenting.

312 pp.

(SLTCC Technical Report #5) ISBN 0–8248–1733–8 $15

THE ROLE OF PHONOLOGICAL CODING IN READING *KANJI*

SACHIKO MATSUNAGA

In this technical report the author reports the results of study which she conducted on phonological coding in readin *kanji* using an eye-movement monitor and draws som pedagogical implications. In addition, she reviews curren literature on the different schools of thought regardin instruction in reading *kanji* and its role in the teaching non-alphabetic written languages like Japanese. 64 pp.

(SLTCC Technical Report #6) ISBN 0–8248–1734–6 $1

DEVELOPING PROTOTYPIC MEASURES OF CROSS-CULTURAL PRAGMATICS

THOM HUDSON
EMILY DETMER
J. D. BROWN

Although the study of cross-cultural pragmatics has gained importance in applied linguistics, there are no standard forms of assessment that might make research comparable across studies and languages. The present volume describes the process through which six forms of cross-cultural assessment were developed for second language learners of English. The models may be used for second language learners of other languages. The six forms of assessment involve two forms each of indirect discourse completion tests, oral language production, and self assessment. The procedures involve the assessment of requests, apologies, and refusals.

(SLTCC Technical Report #7) ISBN 0–8248–1763–X $15.

VIRTUAL CONNECTIONS: ONLINE ACTIVITIES & PROJECTS FOR NETWORKING LANGUAGE LEARNERS

MARK WARSCHAUER
(Editor)

Computer networking has created dramatic new possibilities for connecting language learners in a single classroom or across the globe. This collection of activities and projects makes use of email, the World Wide Web, computer conferencing, and other forms of computer-mediated communication for the foreign and second language classroom at any level of instruction. Teachers from around the world submitted the activities compiled in this volume — activities that they have used successfully in their own classrooms.

AVAILABLE SPRING 1996
(SLTCC Technical Report #8) $30.

ATTENTION & AWARENESS IN FOREIGN LANGUAGE LEARNING

RICHARD SCHMIDT
(Editor)

Issues related to the role of attention and awareness in learning lie at the heart of many theoretical and practical controversies in the foreign language field. This collection of papers presents research into the learning of Spanish, Japanese, Finnish, Hawaiian, and English as a second language (with additional comments and examples from French, German, and miniature artificial languages) that bear on these crucial questions for foreign language pedagogy.

(SLTCC Technical Report #9) ISBN 0–8248–1794–X $20.